Make it!
Bring it! Eat it!

Tres Leches Cake,
page 365

Getting together with friends and family has never been so easy. Whether it's a casual potluck or a holiday sit-down dinner, if you divide up the menu, no one has to do all the work. And everyone has a good time!

Easy and Italian

To keep the Eggplant Parmesan (top) warm, cover it with towels, and uncover just before serving. Marinated olives (right) make for a simple starter and pretty hostess gift.

Everyone loves Italian night. Begin this easy yet elegant get-together with marinated olives made in advance and toted in a pretty jar. The Eggplant Parmesan is not only memorable, it feeds a crowd and is a snap to prepare. A classic Caesar salad partners well with the eggplant. Carry the components separately and assemble the salad when you get to where you're going. Dessert is a delightful and impromptu medley of grilled figs dabbed with mascarpone cheese, crumbled blue cheese, honey, and toasted walnuts.

Mindy's Grilled Figs with Honey, Walnuts, and Crumbled Stilton is a quick dessert to assemble, if the ingredients are brought ready to go.

ITALIAN NIGHT WITH FRIENDS

* * *

ZESTY MARINATED OLIVES,
page 464

*

EGGPLANT PARMESAN WITH
FRESH BASIL, *page 272*

*

THE BEST CAESAR SALAD, *page 92*

*

BRAISED WHITE BEANS
WITH ROSEMARY, *page 320*

*

MINDY'S GRILLED FIGS
WITH HONEY, WALNUTS, AND
CRUMBLED STILTON, *page 436*

A GRADUATION PARTY

* * *

TURKEY BURGERS ON THE GRILL
WITH PESTO MAYONNAISE,
page 232

*

FRESH TOMATO PIE, *page 296*

*

BIG GREEN SALAD WITH
ORANGE, AVOCADO, AND RED
WINE VINAIGRETTE, *page 94*

*

PEACH AND BLUEBERRY CRISP,
page 430

Feeding a Crowd

The beauty of "What can I bring?" is that many hands make the task seem lighter. This is especially true when feeding crowds. Delegate the jobs, hand out the recipes, and you can pull this menu together with no trouble at all. One person makes the turkey burger patties and has them ready to grill. Another brings the condiments and buns; someone else makes a big green salad; another the tomato pies, and then for dessert, the luckiest of all makes an outstanding salute to summertime—a Peach and Blueberry Crisp. Don't forget the vanilla ice cream!

When it's hot outside, let lemonade (top) quench that summer thirst. Tomato pies (center), made with ripe summer tomatoes, are irresistible. Spoon the Peach and Blueberry Crisp (bottom), warm or room-temperature, into bowls, and top with scoops of ice cream.

Warm and Cozy Buffet

Come indoors for a winter get-together with friends. Roast pork tenderloins in your oven and ask a friend to bring the braised red cabbage cooked with apples. Have the bakers in the group prepare the South Carolina–style corn bread made with chopped broccoli and the apricots with a crumble topping flavored with butter and spices. Light the fire, pour the wine, and settle in for an easy evening with no worries.

Braised red cabbage (top), baked apricots (center), and Broccoli Corn Bread (bottom) are perfect sides for the baked pork tenderloin.

A HEARTY FALL BUFFET

* * *

ANITA'S OVEN-BAKED PORK
TENDERLOIN, *page 234*

*

BROCCOLI CORN BREAD,
page 262

*

BRAISED RED CABBAGE WITH
APPLES AND WINE, *page 264*

*

SWEET AND SAVORY
BAKED APRICOTS, *page 312*

SUMMER IN THE BACKYARD

* * *

JULIA'S CHILLED ZUCCHINI SOUP,
page 72

*

CUCUMBER AND TOMATO SALAD
WITH SWEET DILL VINAIGRETTE,
page 112

*

EIGHTEEN-MINUTE SALMON
WITH A FRESH GINGER GLAZE,
page 218

*

TRES LECHES CAKE PILED WITH
STRAWBERRIES, *page 365*

Cool Dishes for Warm Days

When the warm weather rolls around, think cool, preparing ahead of time a feast for the eyes and the palate. Begin with a refreshing zucchini soup, a great do-ahead, served from the refrigerator or thermos. Follow with a gorgeous tomato and cucumber salad arranged artfully on a pretty plate. Use the ripest, best tomatoes you can find. Bake a fillet of salmon in a tangy ginger and garlic glaze in advance, then chill and serve cold. For dessert, slice into a Tres Leches Cake frosted with whipped cream and topped with fresh strawberries.

A Party for the Kids

Planning a kids' party brings out the child in all of us. It's time to be visual and whimsical. Think nautical for this get-together. Fill up an inflatable pool with water or turn on the sprinklers and let the children get wet. But first feed them a fun, finger-food meal of homemade chicken tenders dipped in honey-mustard sauce with plenty of carrot and celery sticks and individual watermelon boats. Pour lemonade or a flavored water, and have milk on hand to wash down the peanut butter cookies. Whether it's for a birthday, an end-of-the-school-year celebration, or to welcome a new child to the neighborhood, this is a party anyone will enjoy.

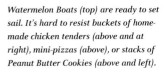

Watermelon Boats (top) are ready to set sail. It's hard to resist buckets of home-made chicken tenders (above and at right), mini-pizzas (above), or stacks of Peanut Butter Cookies (above and left).

INTRODUCTION

I remember wanting to cook it all. There was something athletic about inviting friends for dinner and beginning a three-day marathon of cleaning, cooking, and more cleaning. I returned from cooking school in Paris full of vigor, able to bake my own croissants, clean my own fish, make my own sauces. It was also a time when there was little takeout available in the South, so if you wanted ratatouille in the heat of summer, you made your own. If you craved cassoulet when it was cold, you pulled out your Le Creuset pan. In essence, if you invited friends to dinner, you cooked it all.

Then came family life and the real world. Mine is a two-career and five-person household; I lead a busy and overscheduled life—possibly a lot like yours. Saturdays are spent watching my children's tennis matches or in the garden or at the computer on deadline or cleaning out the garage. Don't get me wrong, I wouldn't trade this for the world, but entertaining could easily have become a thing of the past had I not remembered that familiar question my circle of cousins and aunts and uncles posed when someone was hosting a picnic or a luncheon or a birthday dinner—"What can I bring?" Here was the key to the success of our family get-togethers. Everyone brought a favorite dish. It was potluck but with a plan.

And so the question became the answer—getting together with friends is so much more relaxing when the meal is communal. Offering to bring a warm casserole or a big green salad or a chocolate cake makes the dinner party and the picnic and the office lunch—and all those other reasons we gather together and share a meal—possible for busy people today. It allows us to savor impromptu dinner parties, neighborhood covered-dish suppers, girls' night out parties, Super Bowl, Thanksgiving, tailgating, and Sunday lunch without headaches. All is made possible because everyone helps out.

When *Atlanta Journal-Constitution* food editor and friend Susan Puckett shared this book idea with me several years ago, she urged me to write a book about this unique way of entertaining, one that so many people take for granted.

I have thoroughly enjoyed this process but have to say that the seemingly simple question "What can I bring?" is wonderfully complex. There is no one answer. The right recipe varies with the event, time of year, time of day, region of the country, and individual tastes. One thing is certain, however—bringing food is a good thing. When you prepare a favorite recipe to share with others, you nurture them. It is a gift from your heart. And divvying up the menu enables a great feast to take place with the burden on no one person.

Plus, sharing food lets everyone taste the cooking of others, something I consider the greatest benefit of all. I know that on Easter Sunday I will yearn for my Aunt Elizabeth's banana pudding, and that if it's Thanksgiving and our family is in Chattanooga visiting relatives, one of my husband's cousins will bring the Broccoli Brag Casserole. I know that before Christmas I'll bite into Mindy's pound cake or that if an investment club meeting rolls around at Currey's home, we might savor her top-notch King Ranch Chicken casserole. You see, I may like my own cooking, but I love the food prepared by family and friends!

My mission has always been to share ways to cook simple and joyous food. I tackled the cake-baking predicament about eight years ago when I wrote *The Cake Mix Doctor*. Now, I'm taking on potluck. This book is filled with more than 200 recipes that I am pleased to share with you. With just about every recipe I include "tote notes"—creative and practical ways to transport the dish to a gathering—as well as tips on how to save time by planning ahead. And because I want you to use this cookbook over and over, recipes are accompanied by a handy place to record when you made the recipe, things you want to remember for the next time around, and any special touches you added. Throughout the book I share menus so you can visualize how these recipes come together into a meal, and you'll also find "grab and go" ideas for when you just have no time to cook.

I hope you'll agree that these dishes taste great, look dazzling, and when it's all over, offer the greatest compliment of all—an empty bowl.

Enjoy!

HAPPY BIRTHDAY PARTY

* * *

HOME-FRIED CHICKEN
TENDERS, *page 226*

*

R. B.'s GRILLED PIZZA,
page 63

*

WATERMELON BOATS WITH
SUMMER FRUITS,
page 160

*

CLASSIC PEANUT BUTTER
COOKIES, *page 384*

A HOLIDAY CELEBRATION PARTY

* * *

ROASTED BEET SALAD WITH
WALNUTS AND BLUE CHEESE
DRESSING, *page 96*

*

GRILLED LEG OF LAMB WITH
GREEK CHIMICHURRI SAUCE,
page 248

*

BOURSIN POTATO GRATIN,
page 284

*

CRANBERRY TART, *page 423*

Something Special

The house is dressed for the holidays, so prepare a menu to showcase your holiday home and to entertain friends and family. Roast or grill a leg of lamb studded with garlic cloves. Divide up the scalloped potatoes packed with creamy Boursin cheese; the wonderful roasted beet and romaine salad crowned with oranges, toasted walnuts, and blue cheese; and the festive fresh and bright cranberry tart topped with a sugary and buttery crunch. Serve warm with a spoonful of vanilla ice cream or whipped cream. After all, the holidays are quite special.

Tote the makings for the beet salad (above) in a basket. Keep the Boursin Potato Gratin (bottom left) warm in the oven before serving. The Cranberry Tart (below), delicious warm or cold, makes the perfect ending.

Something Sweet

Pull out the linens, light the candles, pour good Champagne and coffee. This menu is all about sweet things— a layer cake soaked in orange marmalade, a dramatic Chocolate Zuccotto, a lemon cheesecake with a gingersnap crust, and chewy coconut macaroons dipped in chocolate. It might be a bridal shower, a post-theater gathering, or a party to celebrate a new house, a job promotion, a friend moving back to town. Here's to a sweet occasion, made even sweeter with these recipes.

Tote the Orange Marmalade Cake (top) in a handy cake saver. Chill the Chocolate Zuccotto (bottom right) before slicing. The Lemon Icebox Cheesecake (lower left) is dazzling, decorated with fresh raspberries and currants, and a mint sprig.

YOU'RE ENGAGED!

* * *

ORANGE MARMALADE CAKE, *page 353*

*

CHOCOLATE ZUCCOTTO CAKE, *page 372*

*

LEMON ICEBOX CHEESECAKE WITH A
GINGERSNAP CRUST, *page 370*

*

COCONUT ALMOND MACAROONS, *page 390*

PERFECT PAPER ▶
Cute decorative
Chinese take-out
boxes hold cookies,
spiced nuts, and
other homemade
hostess gifts.

◀ KEEPSAKE JARS
Pack marinated
tomatoes, chutney,
jams, and dessert
sauces in pretty
canning jars.

It's a Wrap!

Six Great Ways to Take It to the Party in Style

▲ BOX IT Hang on to clean shirt
boxes with lids, line them with
parchment paper, and tuck tea
sandwiches inside.

▲ DISPOSABLES Salad-a-go-go
is now so easy thanks to handy
disposable plastic containers.

◀ COOK AND SERVE
Casseroles, cobblers, and
sides go from the oven to
the table when you've got
a sturdy basket lined with
pretty towels or napkins.

KEEP IT WARM ▶
Chili stays warm in a
thermos, and the garnishes
keep fresh and ready to
sprinkle on when they're
packed in glass containers
with handy snap-on lids.

What Can I Bring? Cookbook

What Can I Bring? Cookbook

by ANNE BYRN

Photographs by Susan Goldman

WORKMAN PUBLISHING, NEW YORK

For Bebe, again.
She always knew what to bring.

Library of Congress Cataloging-in-Publication Data is available.
ISBN-13: 978-0-7611-4392-5 (pb)
ISBN-13: 978-0-7611-4640-7 (hc)

Cover design: Paul Hanson
Book design: Barbara Balch
Color insert design: Lisa Hollander
Photography: Susan Goldman
Food stylist: Roscoe Betsill with Robert Hessler
Prop stylist: Sara Abalan

Workman books are available at special discounts when purchased in bulk
for premiums and sales promotions as well as for fund-raising or educational
use. Special editions or book excerpts also can be created to specification.
For details, contact the Special Sales Director at the address below.

Workman Publishing Company, Inc.
225 Varick Street
New York, NY 10014-4381
www.workman.com
www.cakemixdoctor.com

Printed in the United States of America

First printing October 2007
10 9 8 7 6 5 4 3 2 1

Acknowledgments

Many of you have asked how I write cookbooks while being a busy mother of three active children. Do I have a fancy test kitchen? A staff of cooks? Round-the-clock nannies? My answer to the first question is that I have a wonderful kitchen in my home where I test recipes. As for the second question, I rely on the help of my sister and friends. Thanks goes to Martha Bowden, Mindy Merrell, R. B. Quinn, and my sister Susan Anderson for their diligence, humor, and creativity in helping me test and create recipes for this book. And as for the nanny, it's me, with the help of Diane Hooper, who makes everything run smoother.

To all my friends in Nashville and beyond, thank you for generously sharing your recipes. A special thanks to Beth, Jan, Currey, Libby and David, Sally, Ann, Margaret, Missy, Lou Ann, Fleurie, Katy, Corabel and Martin, Mary Eleanor, Wyeth, Bette, Jess, Barb, Judy, and Marie. Thanks to my sister Ginger, my cousin Joe, my sister-in-law Flowerree, and my good friend Becky for their ongoing support. Thanks also to John's mom, Flowerree, and his Aunt Janet, who are so expert in party planning that I'd love to call them the original party girls, but better not.

To my agent Nancy Crossman, who loved this book idea from the get-go, a big thank you. And to my publisher Peter Workman, editor Suzanne Rafer, and her assistant Helen Rosner, thank you for another great book. Thanks also to Paul Hanson, Lisa Hollander, Barbara Balch, Irene Demchyshyn, Jenny Mandel, Pat Upton, and Ron Longe at Workman for their creativity and dedication in getting this book onto the shelves. A special thanks to Barbara Mateer for her expert copy editing. And thanks to Amy Lewis, Justin Nisbet, and Jen Johnson who manage my website and keep me in the twenty-first century.

To my friend Susan Puckett at *The Atlanta Journal-Constitution,* thank you for mentioning this book idea. I could not get it out of my head.

To my understanding family— John, Kathleen, Litton, and John—who have once again persevered through the drama a new book brings. Thank you for your endless humor and love when the kitchen was in chaos or when I had to retreat upstairs to my office once again to type recipes.

And lastly, thanks to the readers of my books. I value your feedback and appreciate the recipes you share. Your ongoing enthusiasm makes my job a real pleasure.

Anne Byrn
Nashville, Tennessee

CONTENTS

Introduction ix

WHAT CAN I BRING? 101
. . . .
PAGE XI

Some things to keep in mind when putting together a meal prepared by more than one cook: choosing the right dish, supplies to have on hand or bring with you, tips on traveling with food, and a few thoughts on kitchen etiquette.

APPETIZERS AND SOUPS
. . . .
PAGE 1

So many to choose from . . . and so easy to make. Whether you bring the Olive Cheese Puffs or the Caramelized Onion Spread, the Asian Chicken Lettuce Wraps or Little Crisp Crab Cakes, the Summertime Gazpacho or Tuscan White Bean Soup, you'll be getting the party off to a great start.

THE BEST SALADS
. . . .
PAGE 89

Both main dish salads and side salads are welcome at any picnic or potluck. With the right containers, it's easy to tote The Best Caesar Salad, Theresa's Romaine and Apricot Salad, a Fresh Green Been Salad with Crumbled Feta Vinaigrette, and a Sliced Tomato Salad with Basil and Buttermilk Dressing. For mains, pack up a Chicken and Basmati Rice Salad or a Chilled Shrimp Rémoulade or one of my other favorite choices.

CROWD-PLEASING MAIN DISHES
. . . .
PAGE 169

Main dishes to tote and main dishes to make when you're the host. Easy-to-carry mains include Susan's Chicken Potpie, January Lamb Stew, and a savory Mushroom and Gruyère Cheesecake. Dishes best made when there's no travel involved include lemony Cuban Chicken Legs, Braised Pork Loin with Prunes and Almonds, and Grilled Dry-Rub Flank Steaks.

SENSATIONAL SIDES

PAGE 251

Sides like to steal the spotlight and these are sure to, no matter what the entrée is. Curried Corn and Bell Peppers, Green Beans with a Spicy Tomato Sauce, Sweet Potato Casserole with Pecan Crunch, and Sweet and Savory Baked Apricots are just some of the winners in this chapter.

DAZZLING DESSERTS

PAGE 335

Who doesn't like to be in charge of the grand finale? Whether you decide to tote a rich German Chocolate Cake, a Fresh Apple Cake with Caramel Glaze, a plate of Butter Pecan Sugar Cookies, or a Deep Dish Cherry Cobbler— the choice seems endless—everyone will be clambering for your share of the meal.

IT'S A GIFT

PAGE 441

When you want to bring a little something to the host who's doing it all, think beyond a bottle of wine. Zucchini Walnut Bread, Sour Cream Cinnamon Streusel Loaves, a ceramic jar filled with Homemade Pesto, or Refrigerator Peach Preserves all make delicious and thoughtful gifts.

Conversion Tables 483

Bibliography 484

Twelve "Mini Indexes" 485

Index 490

What Can I Bring? 101

You would think, by now, I'd know what to bring. And, pretty much, I do. But I used to tremble after I asked that question. You see, where I live it's not unusual to have some event that calls for food every weekend—whether it's dinner at a friend's house, a school picnic, a church fund-raiser, or a tennis team potluck. Although I have a classic Caesar salad, a tried-and-true baked beans, a creamy Southern potato salad, and garlic bread that has everyone coming back for seconds in my repertoire, I found myself stuck in a recipe rut.

So I set off in search of new recipes that I could turn to the next time I opened my mouth and asked the question. I'm delighted to report that I found all sorts of new and inventive dishes I had never dreamed of—everything from easy-to-tote appetizers through desserts, plus some food that makes good gifts. Now I also have a sweet potato cake scented with nutmeg, grilled vegetables with a pesto dip, a colorful salad of papaya and arugula, and the most delicious salmon that you smoke in your own backyard. And that's just a small sampling.

So, what can you bring? Fear no more. Come with me and find out.

How to Pick the Right Recipe

Just like great dishes that you plan on serving at home, ones that travel well should reflect the season of the year, the time of day that the event is being held, and the crowd who'll be enjoying the dishes. As a really general rule, warm appetizers, soups, and desserts are best in the fall and winter, whereas cold soups and desserts are nirvana in the heat of summer.

Salads are wonderfully seasonal. Serve Waldorf salad in the fall, when apples are at their best, and whip up a fresh green salad with berries strewn on top in the spring or summer. Some dishes are tied to an occasion—who can imagine the Super Bowl without chili? Or Thanksgiving without a sweet potato casserole or a pumpkin pie?

Obviously, great recipes that travel well don't slip and slide in transit. They stay hot if they are supposed to be, or cold if they're best eaten chilled. They are quick to assemble when you're on-site—or require no work at all. And if they have only a handful of ingredients, that's even better.

The right recipe also fits the guests. Is it a group of young, adventurous eaters or an older group, who may prefer less spicy, less exotic fare? Are children included? Will there be vegetarians coming or any people with food allergies? It's smart to ask the host about who will be attending the gathering and then select your recipe accordingly.

Chances are that recipes well liked by you and your family will also be well received at a potluck. But there is something else to consider: The best dishes not only taste delicious, they look appetizing on a platter or in a bowl. When some friends from our wine-tasting group gathered outdoors by Marie's backyard pool one spring evening, we became intent on spreading Marie's wonderful dip onto French bread rounds. It was a simple recipe she had gotten from her sister—canned white beans, good olive oil, and fresh basil pureed together. But, piled into a deep white bowl and garnished with shiny black kalamata olives and a scattering of basil slivers, it was stunning. Even the simplest food—sliced tomatoes, sliced melon, sliced ham, a few good cheeses—looks extraordinary on a pretty platter. It is how you present food that garners those first "oohs" and "aahs." So, dig around for a few attractive serving pieces.

To Plan or Just Take Potluck?

One of my favorite toting stories involves my husband's cousin Ann Mills, a resident of Charlottesville, Virginia, who should have earned a medal of honor for the food she toted to Chattanooga one summer. Her mother, my husband's Aunt Janet, was celebrating a significant birthday, and her children and their families, scattered across the country, were convening in Chattanooga to host a festive dinner party in Aunt Janet's honor. Ann baked Virginia hams and smoked fillets of salmon, then packed them on ice, placed them in the back of her station wagon, and drove through the cool of the night so that the food would be at its best. The melon-hued slabs of smoked fish, laid out on long white platters, were drizzled with olive oil and garnished with green and black olives and thin lemon slices. Forked onto a cracker, this salmon was unlike any food I had tasted.

Janet's birthday menu was well planned by her children, and if you are feeding a crowd there is peace of mind in knowing what everyone will bring. My family does this at Thanksgiving and on the Fourth of July, making sure all the necessary sides we look forward to are covered by someone.

But what if in the true spirit of potluck you just let everyone bring what they want? Office potluck lunches and block parties are great occasions to sit back and watch the food roll in. Often one person will provide the main course and another the drinks. Everyone else will bring the appetizers, sides, and desserts. If you wind up with five potato salads, chances are no two will be the same.

If this scenario has you Type A's feeling anxious, put a little order in things by finding a functional but fun way to organize the meal. Suggest that the women bring salads, the men desserts. Or, divide recipes up by the alphabet—make those with names beginning with the letters closest to "A" responsible for bringing an appetizer, ask the middle of the alphabet to bring the sides, and the end of the alphabet to supply the desserts. You can have order and a well-balanced meal and still share in the spirit of potluck.

Trouble-Free Toting

Okay, you know what you're bringing: Now, how do you get the food to where you're going without

SEALED WITH A KISS:
I LOVE THESE CONTAINERS

To me, the containers listed here are indispensable. They fit into my life and my kitchen space, and when I need to travel with food, I open the drawer or the pantry and they are there, ready to go.

✳ Quart-size glass jars (recycled from mayonnaise or pasta sauce) for toting soup for four.

✳ Glass jars of assorted sizes—perfect for storing vinaigrette, sauces, toasted nuts, confectioners' sugar, you name it. Make sure they have lids that fit.

✳ Glass or stainless steel bowls of all sizes that come with snap-on plastic lids; these transport anything.

✳ A 13 by 9–inch metal baking pan with a plastic lid, good for transporting bars, brownies, cakes, cookies, and tea sandwiches.

✳ A round plastic cake saver, or two. Tupperware cake carriers are not only durable but their lids lock in place; go to www.tupperware.com to see them.

✳ A large, sturdy rectangular woven wooden basket in which you can carry a hot glass or ceramic baking dish.

✳ A second sturdy woven basket that's more square in shape and has a handle and possibly a divider inside allowing you to carry two pies at once. Peterboro Baskets of New Hampshire makes these; go to www.peterborobasket.com.

✳ An attractive woven reed shopping basket with handles; use it to tote a bottle of wine, a bouquet of flowers, a jar of soup, and the makings for salad. Look for one at www.medinabaskets.com. Or, opt for a classic canvas tote from L.L. Bean (www.llbean.com).

✳ A fun collapsible, insulated canvas tote that looks like a shopping basket and keeps food hot or cold; check out www.picnictime.com for this.

✳ A pretty laquered tray with handles— use it to carry an appetizer from the car to the table. Pottery Barn has these (www.potterybarn.com).

✳ Insulated casserole carriers that hold your favorite baking dishes.

✳ Gallon-size resealable plastic bags to hold salad greens for eight.

✳ Small, cup-size resealable plastic bags for a handful of garnish.

✳ Disposable plastic containers of all sizes—one cup, one quart, and one and a half quarts—for sliced tomatoes, fresh fruit, or leftovers.

spilling it in your car or onto your clothes, and keep it looking like it was just prepared? Start with the right container.

Have a look in your cupboards and your pantry because the best containers for toting food are often right there—glass dishes with snap-on plastic lids, plastic containers with lids, glass and ceramic casseroles, pretty trays, baskets, quart-size glass jars, and a slow cooker. I also have a ready stash of disposable plastic and aluminum foil containers, because if I am bringing food to a large gathering when I might need to leave early, or if I am dropping off food and don't want the recipients to have to wash and return dishes, disposables make the handiest carriers.

At the supermarket, look for plastic containers of all sizes. They are perfect for toting salads, desserts, and soups, and you can just leave the container behind. Aluminum foil casserole pans with plastic lids that lock in place are great for side dishes, main dishes,

and most anything that needs to be reheated or baked on-site. Save clean cardboard shirt boxes, then line them with parchment paper or waxed paper to fill with brownies, lemon bars, even tea sandwiches. For storing pasta and rice salads, try large resealable plastic bags. Shake up the salad well in the bag before transferring it to a serving bowl.

One of the simplest ways to transport food is to place it on a serving platter or in a serving bowl, then cover the dish with plastic wrap. Choose plastic wrap that sticks to the sides of the platter securely. Aluminum foil also makes a good cover, but be sure that the food is not tomato-based or chocolate or another highly acidic food that might cause the foil to pit and discolor. If in doubt, cover the food with waxed paper and then wrap that with foil.

If you're toting food on a platter, make sure to write your name with a permanent marker on a piece of tape and stick it on the bottom of the platter. Do keep your heirloom platters at home, opting for inexpensive ones made from nonbreakable plastic or wood or lightweight pottery. I'll never forget taking a rice and shrimp salad, a rather labor-intensive dish, to an office potluck lunch many years ago.

On the way into the office, I dropped it, ruining the salad and breaking the platter I had purchased at a craft fair. You may be better off wrapping each of the components of a dish separately in aluminum foil, or placing them in plastic containers, and assembling the platter when you get to your destination.

For longer trips Bundt cakes survive the most mileage. They arrive in one piece, no matter your mode of transport. Desserts of all types—cakes, pies, and bars—are especially easy to tote in a handy cake carrier with a handle. These are not inexpensive but will last you a long time—as long as you put your name on the carrier and keep track of it.

If it's not unusual for you to tote entire meals to and fro, consider investing in a large, woven wood pie basket with handles, a lid, and an inside shelf, which will easily accommodate two or three dishes. Other accessories to keep on hand are an insulated casserole cover with handles, if you tend to take casseroles, and a large, round, sturdy plastic container with a snap-on lid for carrying pies and anything else that's round. Also good for toting hot food is a large clear plastic box with handles, the sort of thing in which you would store

sweaters. Line it with a clean towel and place it in the back of your car. You can put casseroles or baking dishes filled with hot food right in this bin, making it easy to carry them into a house—then use the bin to tote home the dirty dishes.

Etiquette: Read This, Please

Ah, the many and often prickly questions of potluck protocol: **1.** Should a guest plan on using the host's pantry supplies and kitchenware without notifying the host? **2.** Should a guest waltz in the door with fried chicken, drop the platter in the kitchen, and run for a cold drink? **3.** Should a guest clean up his or her dishes after the party is over? Or, should the host do this? Both the guest and host bear responsibility at a gathering where food is brought and shared, so mind your manners!

LET'S GET THIS PARTY STARTED

Here's a checklist for the host. When the party is at your house, make sure you have all of these on hand.

* Plates

* Bowls, if you are serving soup or ice cream or fruit salad

* Glasses (count on one per person unless you are having a cocktail hour ahead of time, then count on two)

* Hot cups, if you are serving coffee or tea

* Knives, forks, and spoons

* Napkins

* A spare serving dish or platter or two, just in case

* Ice

* Paper towels

* Garbage bags

* Dishwashing soap

* Aluminum foil

* Plastic wrap

* Plastic containers for leftovers

* Resealable plastic bags in a variety of sizes

The answers to those questions?

1. No, bring all the food supplies you need along with as many of the necessary kitchen items as possible.

2. No, when you bring the dish, you need to see it through the evening. Talk with the host as to whether you should replenish the platter, when needed. And make sure you bring a serving spoon or fork if the dish requires one. Should the dish you bring need to be reheated or baked, go ahead and write the name of the recipe on an index card along with the temperature at which it needs to be baked and the length of time it will

take, and place the index card with the dish; that way anyone in the kitchen can help out getting things ready.

3. As for cleaning up your dish, defer to the host. Some may want to wash platters and have them ready for guests to take home. Others might welcome your help. If you are in doubt, rinse the platter, wrap it in a plastic bag, and take it home to wash. Be sure to offer any leftovers to the host.

If you are the host, you have a bit more to consider than the color of the platter and how much plastic wrap to use. You will need to organize your kitchen so there's plenty of room to put the dishes when they arrive and a place where people can do any last-minute assembly. You may also want to clear off a second spot, even the laundry room, where plastic containers, bags, and baskets can be stored until it is time to leave. To make dish identification easier, have freezer tape and permanent markers on hand to label dishes if they are not already marked with their owners' names. And have extra serving trays and utensils on hand because people may not bring their own.

Decide ahead of time where certain dishes will go on the buffet table, and place a note card on the table. This will help you and your guests be better organized. As people arrive they can place their dishes on the table where designated. For dishes that need to be kept warm, have a warming tray, warming drawer, or low oven ready.

City Apartment? How to Entertain a Crowd in Less Space

Fear of crowds is what keeps most people from hosting the big party. Yes, hosts have a few more responsibilities; they also have more control over the gathering and a chance to share their homes with their family and friends. But let's say you live in a small space and that you want to host a potluck meal with more people than you have dining room chairs for. The answer is always simple—the casual buffet, preferred by potluckers everywhere. Here is how my friend Nancy in Chicago and her friends stage such a meal: They unwrap the food and garnish platters in the kitchen and then place the appetizers on the coffee table in the living room for people to help themselves. For beverages, they fill a bar sink, metal tub, or bucket with ice and add bottles of beer, water, and soda, arranging a variety of glasses on the side. The main dishes and sides are served buffet-style from the dining room table, and people sit wherever they like and mix and mingle.

WHAT CAN I DO?
LISTS FOR THE GUEST AND HOST

FOR THE GUEST

1. Do let your host know what recipe you're bringing. And do follow through and prepare the type of dish (appetizer, salad, dessert, and so on) that you said you would.

2. Do select a recipe that needs no on-site assembly or that is easy to put together. Let your host know if you have a slow cooker that needs to be plugged into an outlet or will need a free oven in which to reheat the dish, a warming drawer or tray to keep the food warm, or space in the refrigerator or freezer to keep the food cold.

3. Do ask your host to set aside counter space for food preparation. And do confine yourself to a small area of the host's kitchen or you might be labeled a kitchen hog!

4. Do check to see how many people are coming to the party so you can make enough food to go around.

5. Do bring a serving spoon or fork or a platter, if needed.

6. Do arrive on time if you are bringing the appetizer.

7. Do see your dish through by replenishing it if needed.

8. Do offer leftovers to the host. Rinse your dish or wrap it in a plastic bag before heading home.

FOR THE HOST

1. Do plan a menu so that you have all the courses you desire—for example, an appetizer, salad, main dish, and dessert.

2. Do decide how formal you want the gathering to be—china and glass, or paper and plastic?

3. Do tidy up kitchen counters and free up refrigerator space for the food that will come in the door. If needed, move unnecessary refrigerated items to another refrigerator or cooler.

4. Do set the serving table and decorate it, allowing space for each dish. Place a labeled index card where each dish should go.

5. Do have serving utensils ready in case your guests don't bring their own.

6. Do preset the warming drawer or oven to keep food warm.

7. Do make the trash can accessible, along with paper towels and kitchen towels.

8. Do have the supplies on hand to wrap food to take home.

Same Rules No Matter How Big a Party

At potluck meals you need to plan whether people will stand and eat or sit wherever there's a seat (or available floor space!). If any of the dishes requires a knife, guests will need to be seated at a table or have a lap tray.

It helps to arrange the food for the buffet in a logical sequence—first the main dish, then the sides, salad, and bread. Every dish needs a serving utensil next to it. And the dinner plates need to be large enough to hold the food. Separate the dessert so that it and the dessert plates are displayed on another table, possibly with the coffee.

Always serve beverages in a location away from the food. And have a plan for clearing plates. Provide a place where guests can throw away disposable plates when they have finished eating, or ask several friends to assist you in gathering reusable plates and silverware to rinse in the kitchen. Remember that enlisting the help of friends is crucial to a party's success and to your peace of mind.

POTLUCK

Potluck makes me think of long picnic tables packed with an endless offering of salads, vegetables, casseroles, breads, and desserts. It is a pleasant remembrance. I'd race for the crispiest piece of chicken and the last scoop of banana pudding.

The word *potluck* is said to have been first used in colonial America. If you visited a tavern or home, you were served what was simmering in the pot over the fire, taking "pot luck."

The tradition of potluck has thrived in American rural life as a way of building community. People gathered together to raise barns and build homes, worship, and celebrate. And, to fuel everyone, there was a bounty of regional food.

FYI I designed the recipes in this book with an eye to easy transport. With each recipe you will find instructions for how to wrap the dish for travel. And I have also included tips for making more than one batch in case you are feeding a crowd. Details, details—I hope I have thought of them all so you can relax, fix the food, and have some fun.

APPETIZERS AND SOUPS

When getting together with friends, the season usually gives me a good idea of what to serve for the main course. But often I go blank when it comes to thinking up an appetizer. So was this chapter ever fun to research and write! Now, I can say from experience that nothing is wrong with pulling salted nuts from the pantry if you need to bring a starter to a friend's house, but you can easily create dazzling appetizers or soups by just choosing something to make from the recipes that follow.

The appetizer may be the most welcome food you can tote with you to a party. Offering to make one takes a huge load off the host, and you may find that if you master a recipe well, it might become your signature. And that is a very good thing. My sister Susan, who helped test these dishes, always has wonderful appetizer recipes up her sleeve. She totes layered crab dips to weekend getaways. She keeps spinach balls in her freezer. And Susan is not alone. My friend Jan Ramsey is known for her bruschetta, which is drop-dead fantastic anytime of year. And Marie Masterson's white bean dip is a glorious combination of pureed canned white beans, tomatoes, basil, kalamata olives, and olive oil.

Great appetizers come from good cooks, and they have a few things in common. They are visually appealing. Some, such as the vibrant Cowboy Caviar, come by it naturally. Some need your garnishing help. Take hummus—

resist the urge to plop it on a plate and be done with it. Instead, sprinkle chopped tomatoes or red bell peppers on top, add a leaf of basil, and drizzle on some good olive oil. And consider investing in a few inexpensive chip and dip platters, woven shallow baskets, and bright and colorful trays for serving.

To be memorable, appetizers should also be suited to the season and to the crowd who will devour them. Salsa tastes best and quenches a fatigued summer palate when it is made with fresh ripe tomatoes and chiles. In contrast, the Super Bowl fan will have tortilla chips ready for the wintery hot spinach dip or Twelve-Layer Taco Dip. They're comfy and filling—perfect for nervous nibbling while watching the game with friends.

And here are a few more tidbits of advice, things I have learned along the way. Dips are favorites of guys and teenagers. Place the bowl on a large tray and surround it with an ocean of chips or crackers. Save fussy canapés for predinner party noshing and for girls' parties. Cheese balls are beloved by all during the winter holidays. And tea sandwiches are relished best in summertime. Perhaps it's the nostalgia factor—people often fondly remember eating tomato or cucumber sandwiches when they were young, and children do love these sandwiches.

Soups, too, are a beautiful way to begin the meal or to add to it. A jar of homemade soup brought to a friend is an enormous gesture. It can feed people now or later, and if you pack it in sturdy quart jars with sufficient room for air at the top of the jar, they can be frozen and heated (or simply defrosted) later. Select a soup to fit the weather, such as gazpacho when it is warm outside and white bean when it is cold.

So, there you have it, totable ways to begin the meal. Armed with a great dip, spread, canapé, or soup, you and your recipe will be remembered well.

SUCCESSFUL STARTERS

When recipes aren't easy to pull together I seldom have time for them. I want a quick-fix hors d'oeuvre whether I am sharing it with guests in my home or bringing it to a dinner somewhere else. What I love about the appetizers in this chapter (besides how good they taste) is their simplicity. Either they contain only a few easy-to-buy ingredients or they call for things that are already in your pantry or fridge.

Take Suzanne's Guacamole. Pick up one or two nicely ripened avocados and some fresh cilantro, and the rest of the fixings are likely in your refrigerator. The same goes for Andy's Stolen Salsa. Open up a large can

of tomatoes—a staple in so many kitchens—add seasonings, and it's ready for the tortilla chips.

And that is why Mary's Baked Boursin is a winner—you just need to bake a round of Boursin cheese in a quick sauce of pureed roasted red peppers. Yum—bring out the crackers and dig in. The same with Fleurie's Caramelized Onion Spread—simply sauté some onions and add them to cream cheese with some seasonings.

The Asian Chicken Lettuce Wraps might require a bit more work, but the results are well worth it. Who knew that re-creating a restaurant appetizer could be so easy?
Enjoy!

Veggies with Green Goddess Dipping Sauce

SERVES 8 TO 12 (MAKES ABOUT 2 CUPS DIPPING SAUCE)

PREP: 30 TO 35 MINUTES

TOTE NOTES

If you can arrange the vegetable platter at the party, tote each of the veggies in a separate plastic bag. Bring the dressing in its serving bowl—and remember to bring the platter.

PLAN AHEAD

Here is how to create a vegetable platter ahead of time and still have it looking great a few hours later: Arrange the veggies on the platter around the covered bowl of sauce. Group each vegetable together for a bigger visual pop. Cover the veggies with damp paper towels and then wrap the entire platter in aluminum foil and refrigerate it until you're ready to go.

THANKS TO THE SUPERMARKET PRODUCE AISLE WE can pick up prewashed and trimmed carrots, celery, cauliflower, and broccoli for spur-of-the-moment crudité platters. And yet, it seems this ease has made us lazy, causing us to forget about the seasonal produce that begs to be on that platter and requires very little prep. In the spring and summer add steamed and cooled asparagus spears and thin green beans, slices of tender yellow squash, fresh cucumbers, and yellow and red grape tomatoes. Or think fall and winter with radishes and steamed little potatoes. Pair any or all of these vegetables with this refreshing and vibrant dip and you'll have a veggie platter that people will not be able to leave alone. This dip is a modified Green Goddess dressing, made with a ton of Italian parsley, instead of the traditional tarragon, and a few anchovies. Don't turn up your nose; just try it. You'll find those anchovies add just the right bite and bit of salt, and you'll be spooning this dip over turkey sandwiches—if there is any left.

FOR THE ASSORTED VEGGIES, USE A 6- TO 8-CUP MIX OF ANY OF THE FOLLOWING

Asparagus spears or thin green beans steamed until bright green, then plunged into ice water

Raw broccoli and/or cauliflower florets

Baby carrots

FIND YOUR ARTISTIC SIDE WITH VEGGIE PLATTERS

I attended a lovely holiday party one year where there was the most gorgeous vegetable display I had ever seen. It was presented on a large mirror, and on the mirror were square glass vases of varying heights and widths, as well as lit white votive candles. The dipping sauces were in a few of the shorter vases. Veggies were everywhere, grouped together—clusters of green beans and piles of carrots—so that visually you were hit by their brilliance. And in the taller vases, long slender asparagus and chives with blossoms still attached were loosely arranged like flowers. Obviously someone had taken a lot of care and thought in creating a vegetable masterpiece. You can do this, too.

Cucumbers, peeled, seeded, and sliced into matchsticks

Tiny potatoes boiled until tender, then chilled

Radishes, trimmed and cut in half

Yellow or red cherry or grape tomatoes

Sliced fresh zucchini or yellow squash

FOR THE GREEN GODDESS DIPPING SAUCE

2 medium-size cloves garlic, peeled

1 bunch fresh flat-leaf parsley
   (for about 2 loosely packed cups leaves)

2 scallions, both white and green parts, coarsely chopped

3 to 4 anchovy fillets

1 teaspoon fresh lemon juice, or more to taste

½ teaspoon freshly ground black pepper

½ cup mayonnaise

¼ cup reduced-fat sour cream

RECIPE REMINDERS

Made for

Prep notes

Don't forget

Special touches

Bring again

A WINE FOR
ALL SEASONS

So many wines to choose from, why not let the season be the guide?

Spring: *Uncork an Italian prosecco, a sauvignon blanc from New Zealand, a French Sancerre, or switch to a red and pair a light pinot noir with lamb.*

Summer: *Opt for a light pinot grigio and pinot gris. For a fun wine cooler, mix your house white with a little carbonated Italian fruit juice—mango or grapefruit—or make a white or red sangria. Pick a buttery California chardonnay for grilled fish.*

Fall: *Turn from whites to reds, from Spain, the Rhône Valley, Chile, or Tuscany.*

Winter: *Holidays call for bolder cabernets and zinfandels from California. Splurge on an Oregon pinot noir. Or, pop the cork of a French Champagne.*

1. For the assorted vegetables: Refrigerate the prepared vegetables in separate containers until time to serve.

2. Make the dipping sauce: Using a food processor fitted with a steel blade, with the motor running, drop in the garlic through the feed tube and process until minced, about 5 seconds. Stop the machine. Add the parsley, scallions, anchovies, lemon juice, and pepper and process in short pulses until the parsley, scallions, and anchovies are minced, about 10 seconds.

3. Add the mayonnaise and sour cream and pulse until the dip is smooth, about 15 seconds. Taste for seasoning, adding more lemon juice as desired. Spoon the dip into a glass or ceramic serving bowl and cover with plastic wrap. Refrigerate until serving time.

4. To serve, uncover the dipping sauce and place the bowl on a serving tray. Surround the sauce with the chilled veggies.

BIG BATCH: *This recipe can be expanded as long as you have a large enough serving platter or board. Make double the sauce in the food processor, or you might want to offer a second dipping sauce and just double the amount of veggies.*

TEN GRAB AND GOS

No time to prepare an appetizer? Make a quick stop at the supermarket and you can whip up one of these simple party nibbles in no time.

1. For a crudité platter, buy the veggies ready to go, but make the dip. It's easy—season reduced-fat sour cream with a good pesto sauce. For every cup of sour cream, use 2 tablespoons of pesto.

2. Set out store-bought pimiento cheese in a pretty bowl and surround it with green grapes, green celery spears, Granny Smith apple wedges, and endive spears.

3. Buy a log of goat cheese and garnish it with a spoonful of chutney, coarse black pepper, chopped fresh herbs, or olive tapenade. Serve with crackers.

4. Surround deli hot wings with celery and carrot sticks. Add a bowlful of a good bottled blue cheese dressing for dunking.

5. Pile mini wieners and hard salami slices on a pretty board and arrange little bowls of different mustards and pickles alongside.

6. Make mini sandwiches with deli dinner rolls. Stuff some with turkey, cream cheese, and cranberry relish. Stuff others with ham and mustard blended with orange marmalade.

7. Buy a good deli pâté and drizzle a little good brandy over it before serving it with crackers.

8. Choose an assortment of olives—oil-cured, green, and kalamata—as well as a selection of salted roasted nuts—almonds, walnuts, and pecans. Arrange these in little dishes of all shapes on a pretty platter. To dress up the olives you can add sliced hot peppers or grated orange rind.

9. Buy cucumber slices from the deli salad bar and spread them with a good herbed cream cheese.

10. If you've got a little more time, make a really fast pizza using deli pizza dough. Spread prepared pizza sauce or olive tapenade over the dough, sprinkle mozzarella cheese on top, and garnish it with roasted peppers and fresh herbs. Bake the pizza for about 15 minutes at 400°F, then cut it into small squares.

Suzanne's Guacamole

SERVES 4 TO 8 (MAKES ABOUT 2 CUPS)

PREP: 15 MINUTES

TOTE NOTES

If your host has enough space in the kitchen for you to prepare this at the gathering, bring the avocados and limes uncut. Prechop the scallions, garlic, and cilantro and pack them in separate small plastic bags. And take a small bottle of hot pepper sauce. You'll also need a mixing bowl.

If you make it at home you can tote the guacamole in the serving bowl covered with plastic wrap. Stir it gently before serving.

Either way, don't forget a bag of tortilla chips and something to put them in.

PLAN AHEAD

Guacamole is best eaten within 3 hours of making. Cover the bowl with plastic wrap and refrigerate it.

BEFORE I GOT THIS BOOK IDEA IN MY HEAD, MY EDITOR, Suzanne Rafer, had been telling me about her guacamole. She said it was exceptional, and I love nothing better than good guac. So Suzanne passed along this recipe, and I can tell you that this is the real thing. Suzanne makes a half recipe—enough for two people— but we are into a more quantity style of cooking here in Nashville, so I doubled her recipe, using two avocados. Suzanne says good guacamole starts with good avocados. She uses the nubbly skinned Hass, with its smooth, buttery flesh. And guacamole needs to be tasted along the way; sample this as you make it because avocados vary in size and the amount of seasoning they need. Suzanne also says that if you can't find Hass avocados, you should just offer to bring salsa instead.

2 perfectly ripe Hass avocados (about 1 pound)

3 to 4 tablespoons fresh lime juice (from 2 limes), or more to taste

4 scallions, both white and light green parts, finely chopped

2 medium-size cloves garlic, finely chopped

2 packed tablespoons finely chopped fresh cilantro leaves

½ teaspoon hot pepper sauce, such as Tabasco, or more to taste

Sea salt

Tortilla chips, for serving

1. Cut the avocados in half and remove the pits. Scoop out the flesh and place it in a medium-size nonreactive bowl. Sprinkle 3 tablespoons of the lime juice over the avocados, then mash them to a slightly chunky consistency with a fork, making sure the lime juice gets evenly distributed.

2. Add the scallions, garlic, cilantro, and hot pepper sauce and mix them into the avocados, making sure that they still keep a nice chunky texture. Taste for seasoning, adding salt to taste and more lime juice or hot pepper sauce, if desired. Serve surrounded with lots of fresh tortilla chips.

BIG BATCH: *You can increase—or decrease—this recipe as needed; figure on one avocado feeding two to four people.*

GUAC IN THE BOX

When good avocados are not plentiful, I opt for the ready-made guacamole you find, refrigerated at wholesale clubs and natural food stores. It is top-quality, and I keep a couple of these in the freezer for those times when only guacamole and chips will suffice. But my daughter Litton, who is becoming opinionated about food and likes to add her own touch to recipes, is not satisfied with the guac in the box. She transfers the ready-made to a bowl and adds the juice of a lime half, a handful of chopped fresh tomatoes, and some chopped cilantro leaves. It does taste better.

RECIPE REMINDERS

Made for

Prep notes

Don't forget

Special touches

Bring again

WHAT CAN I DRINK?

When it comes to deciding what to serve to drink at a gathering, much depends on the time of day, the season of the year, the theme, the ages of the guests, and whether alcohol is appropriate. You can always play it safe by serving water. Dress it up by placing it with ice in silver pitchers or serve water from pretty glass carafes with cucumber and lemon slices floating on top.

If the drinks are to be warm and nonalcoholic, think cocoa or cider. If they are to be cold and without alcohol, think lemonade or tea punch.

Kids like punch in little cups, good lemonade, and—especially—smoothies. Set up a smoothie station on the kitchen counter with a blender or two, bowls of fruit, ice, and a variety of fruit yogurts so they can make their own.

If you are serving alcohol, think beer, margaritas, sangria, and mojitos in the summertime. Fix Bloody Marys for fall tailgate parties, eggnog during the winter holidays, and mint juleps or gin and tonics in the spring.

I have learned that it's not so much the beverage but the way it is presented that makes serving drinks fun. Pretty glass goblets make wine taste nicer than plastic cups; glass punch cups are more festive than paper; and iced-down beer in a tub on the patio is more festive than having to grab your own longneck from the kitchen refrigerator.

Since nonalcoholic punch recipes are indispensable, here are a few.

✳

Easy Pink Punch

**SERVES 28 TO 30
(MAKES MORE THAN 1 GALLON)
PREP: 10 MINUTES**

2 quarts cold cranberry juice
   (see Note)
1 can (6 ounces) frozen pink
   lemonade concentrate,
   thawed
1 bottle (2 liters) ginger ale or
   lemon-lime soda, chilled
Ice ring (optional)

1. Place the cranberry juice and thawed lemonade concentrate in a punch bowl and stir to combine.

2. Just before serving, pour in the ginger ale or soda, stir, and serve with the ice ring floating in the punch bowl, if desired.

NOTE: For a pink pineapple punch, use 1 quart of cranberry juice and 1 quart of pineapple juice.

ICE RING To make an ice ring, you'll need a ring mold; pour water into it and freeze it solid. Add slices of strawberry or lemon, raspberries, even cranberries, to the water when it is partially frozen to decorate the ring.

✳

Hot Spiced Apple and Cranberry Cider

SERVES 20 TO 24
(MAKES MORE THAN 3 QUARTS)
PREP: 40 MINUTES

2 quarts apple cider
6 cups (1½ quarts) cranberry juice
¼ packed cup light brown sugar
3 to 4 cinnamon sticks
1 teaspoon whole cloves
1 lemon, sliced

1. Place the apple cider, cranberry juice, brown sugar, cinnamon sticks, cloves, and lemon slices in a large pot and bring to a boil over medium-high heat. Reduce the heat to low and let simmer until the flavor develops, about 10 minutes, then turn off the heat and let steep in the pot for about 30 minutes.

2. Pour the cider through a fine mesh strainer into a clean pot or a slow cooker. Discard the cinnamon sticks, cloves, and lemon.

3. To serve, warm the cider over low heat on the stove or in the slow cooker. The spiced cider can be made a day ahead and refrigerated, covered. Reheat it before serving.

WITCHES' BREW For Halloween parties, serve this—or any apple cider— warm from a cast-iron pot with handles. Or, serve it cold with ice rings decorated with candy corn.

✳

Southern Fruit Tea

SERVES 24 TO 30
(MAKES 1 GALLON)
PREP: 20 MINUTES
CHILL: 3 HOURS

3 quarts hot brewed tea
½ cup sugar
1 quart orange-pineapple juice
1 cup sliced oranges

1. While the tea is still warm, add the sugar to it and stir until it dissolves. Let the tea cool a bit, then stir in the orange-pineapple juice. Refrigerate the tea until chilled, about 3 hours.

2. To serve, pour the fruit tea into pitchers or a punch bowl. Float the orange slices on top.

Andy's Stolen Salsa

SERVES 12 (MAKES ABOUT 3½ CUPS)

PREP: 15 MINUTES

TOTE NOTES

Tote the salsa to the party in a plastic or glass container with a lid.

Bring a serving bowl for the salsa and a platter to set it on, then surround it with tortilla chips, right from the bag.

PLAN AHEAD

You can prepare this salsa up to a week ahead of time. Refrigerate it in a nonreactive container— one made of glass, stainless steel, ceramic, or plastic.

MOST RECIPES HAVE A STORY BEHIND THEM, but this has to be one of the more unique. Andy Young of Greenville, South Carolina, is originally from Houston, Texas. Andy says his brother Allan "stole" this salsa recipe from a longtime Dallas steak house called Del Frisco's, whose chef admitted to stealing it from another restaurateur, Matt Martinez of the Rancho Martinez restaurant. Andy has now stolen the recipe from his brother, but at least he is sharing it with us. Gives new meaning to the phrase "hot" sauce, doesn't it? Andy and his family make and bottle this salsa for Christmas gift giving. I love the hot and sweet contrast of flavors from the jalapeños and balsamic vinegar.

3 medium-size or 2 large cloves garlic, peeled

2 jalapeño peppers (with or without seeds; see Note), chopped

⅓ packed cup fresh cilantro leaves

2 tablespoons balsamic vinegar

½ teaspoon salt

1 tablespoon vegetable oil

1 can (28 ounces) whole tomatoes, undrained

Tortilla chips, for serving

1. Using a food processor fitted with a steel blade or a blender, with the motor running, drop in the garlic through the feed tube and process until minced, about 5 seconds. Stop the machine. Add the jalapeños and cilantro and process in short pulses until minced, about 5 seconds. Stop the machine and scrape down the side of the bowl with a rubber spatula.

2. Add the vinegar, salt, and oil and process in pulses until well combined, 5 to 10 seconds. Add the tomatoes and their juice and pulse briefly until the mixture is still slightly chunky, about 10 seconds. Spoon the salsa into a dish and refrigerate it, covered with plastic wrap, until ready to serve, surrounded by tortilla chips.

NOTE: When you work with the jalapeños be sure not to touch your eyes. For milder palates, remove and discard the seeds and veins. For a hot salsa, remove the stem ends and add the peppers—seeds, veins, and all— to the food processor. I split the difference, adding a jalapeño with its seeds and veins and a second pepper with its seeds and veins removed.

BIG BATCH: *There's plenty of room in a food processor to double the recipe. Should you want more, make separate batches.*

RECIPE REMINDERS

Made for

Prep notes

Don't forget

Special touches

Bring again

Hot Chile, Cheese, and Corn Dip

SERVES 8 TO 10 (MAKES ABOUT 4 CUPS)

PREP: 20 MINUTES ✳ BAKE: ABOUT 30 MINUTES

TOTE NOTES

Tote the dip in an oven-to-table serving bowl that is wrapped in a towel to keep it warm; once you arrive, the dip can be kept on a warming tray. Pop it back in the oven or in the microwave from time to time to reheat it.

Bring the tortilla chips in the bag.

PLAN AHEAD

You can make this dip the day before and refrigerate it covered with plastic wrap. It will take 15 to 20 minutes in a 350°F oven for the dip to reheat.

THE FUN MEXICAN FLAVORS OF THIS RECIPE MAKE it a standout. So does the fact that the dip can be made ahead. It appeals to those who crave south-of-the-border spicy flavors, and by all means adjust the seasonings to suit your taste. Since the flavors are bold and you'll want to eat the dip warm, it's best served in the cooler months, by the fire or in front of a football game on TV. Not only is it supper club perfect, it passed the often picky teenager taste test as well.

1 can (about 15 ounces) yellow corn, drained

1 can (2¼ ounces) sliced black olives, drained

1 can (4 ounces) chopped green chiles, drained

1 jalapeño pepper, seeded, deveined, and chopped

1 jar (2 ounces) chopped pimiento, drained,
     or 2 roasted red peppers, chopped

½ cup (2 ounces) grated Parmesan cheese

1 cup (4 ounces) shredded Monterey Jack
     and Cheddar cheese blend

1 cup mayonnaise

½ teaspoon ground cumin

Tortilla chips, for serving

1. Preheat the oven to 350°F.

2. Place the corn, olives, chiles, jalapeño, pimiento or red peppers, cheeses, mayonnaise, and cumin in a large mixing bowl. Stir to combine well, then spoon the dip into a 4-cup (1-quart) glass or ceramic baking dish.

3. Bake the dip until the top is golden brown, 28 to 32 minutes. Serve the dip warm with tortilla chips. You can place the baking dish on a pretty, heatproof tray and surround it with the tortilla chips or serve the chips in a bowl on the side.

BIG BATCH: *This recipe may be doubled or tripled; you'll need a 2-quart baking dish for a double batch or a 3-quart baking dish for a triple one. Allow for a little extra baking time—up to 45 minutes—for larger batches.*

ANYTIME SURPRISE PARTY

There's always a reason to surprise a good friend or coworker with a party. A Mexican menu is perfect— people love it, it's fun to prepare, and it's easy to take with you.

SUZANNE'S GUACAMOLE, *page 8*

✳

HOT CHILE, CHEESE, AND CORN DIP, *page 14*

✳

TORTILLA CHIPS

✳

CHICKEN ENCHILADAS, *page 178*

✳

PAPAYA AND ARUGULA SALAD, *page 108*

✳

TRES LECHES CAKES PILED WITH STRAWBERRIES, *page 365*

RECIPE REMINDERS

Made for

Prep notes

Don't forget

Special touches

Bring again

Twelve-Layer Taco Dip

SERVES 12 TO 24

PREP: 30 MINUTES ✳ CHILL: 1 HOUR

TOTE NOTES

Tote the dip in the springform pan along with a bag of tortilla chips. You'll need a serving platter, too.

When you arrive, place the springform pan on the serving platter, then unfasten the side and remove the ring. Either scatter the chips around the dip or serve them in a basket on the side.

I'VE TRIED AS MANY VARIATIONS OF THIS POPULAR appetizer as it has layers. How can you miss with the combination of refried beans, sour cream, avocado, lime, cilantro, peppers, and crunchy tortilla chips? While some artistic cooks layer this type of dip free-form on a pretty platter, I love the convenience of a springform (cheesecake) pan. I layer the dip one ingredient at a time and cover the pan with plastic wrap, then chill, tote, and unmold the dip. Just remember to bring home the bottom of your springform pan. Vary the layers as you wish, using black beans instead of refried, salsa instead of fresh tomatoes.

1 can (16 ounces) fat-free refried beans

2 cups (16 ounces) sour cream

2 tablespoons taco seasoning

1½ cups chopped tomatoes (from 2 medium-size tomatoes)

1½ cups chopped ripe avocado, preferably Hass, tossed with the juice of 1 lime (about 2 tablespoons), or 1 generous cup guacamole (see page 8)

4 cups (16 ounces) shredded Cheddar and Monterey Jack cheese blend, or pepper Jack for a spicier dip

1 cup chopped scallions, green parts only

1 can (2¼ ounces; ½ cup) sliced black olives, drained

1 can (4½ ounces) chopped green chiles, drained

2 cups shredded iceberg lettuce

1 loosely packed cup fresh cilantro leaves

Tortilla chips, for serving

1. Spread the refried beans in an even layer in the bottom of a 9-inch springform pan that is at least 2½ inches deep.

2. Combine the sour cream and taco seasoning in a small bowl and spread half of it over the beans. Set aside the remaining cup of sour cream mixture for the ninth layer.

3. Scatter the tomatoes evenly over the sour cream in the springform pan.

4. Scatter the avocado or spread the guacamole evenly over the tomatoes.

5. Sprinkle 2 cups of the cheese on top of the avocado.

6. Scatter the scallions over the cheese.

7. Scatter the black olive slices on top of the scallions.

8. Spoon the chiles on top of the olive slices.

9. Spread the remaining sour cream mixture evenly over the chiles.

10. Scatter the remaining 2 cups of cheese on top of the sour cream.

11. Scatter the lettuce evenly on top of the cheese.

12. Scatter the cilantro leaves on top of the lettuce. Cover the springform pan with plastic wrap and place it in the refrigerator to chill for at least an hour.

13. When ready to serve, uncover and unmold the dip, place it on a serving platter, and serve with the tortilla chips.

BIG BATCH: *This dip feeds an army. If you need to double it for a huge crowd, make a second batch in another springform pan.*

RECIPE REMINDERS

Made for

Prep notes

Don't forget

Special touches

Bring again

Marie's White Bean and Basil Spread

SERVES 10 TO 12 (MAKES ABOUT 2 CUPS)

PREP: 25 MINUTES

**TOTE
NOTES**

*To tote the bean spread,
place it in a pretty
serving bowl and cover
it with plastic wrap. Or,
spoon it into a plastic or
glass storage dish. Don't
garnish the spread yet.*

*Tote the toasted
bread and the tomato,
basil, and goat cheese
garnishes in separate
plastic bags.*

*When you arrive,
garnish the bean spread,
place it on a platter, and
arrange the bread slices
around it.*

PLAN AHEAD

*The bean spread can be
refrigerated for up to
two days. But don't chop
the basil for the garnish
until shortly before you
are ready to leave.*

MARIE MASTERSON OF NASHVILLE IS A GREAT COOK who knows how to keep recipes simple and successful. This recipe has the wonderful flavors of Provence, and Marie served the spread to us one night around the pool, spooned into a pretty bowl and garnished with basil and chopped tomato. Marie likes to pair it with a creamy goat cheese—you spread a little of both on toasted French bread slices. You could just as easily garnish it with crumbled goat cheese. Or eat it without the cheese. Any way you spread it, it is delicious.

1½ cups canned white (great northern) beans
    (from one 15 ounce can), drained

3 plum tomatoes, seeded and chopped (about 1½ cups)

⅓ cup pitted kalamata olives, coarsely chopped
    (about 18 olives)

4 tablespoons extra-virgin olive oil

¼ cup chopped fresh basil, plus 2 tablespoons chopped
    fresh basil, for garnish

1 tablespoon minced garlic

¼ cup (1 to 2 ounces) crumbled goat cheese (optional),
    for garnish

3 to 4 dozen toasted slices of French bread (see box)

1. Place the beans, 1¼ cups of the tomatoes, and the olives, olive oil, ¼ cup of basil, and the garlic in the bowl of a food processor fitted with a steel blade. Process in on and off pulses until the mixture is creamy but not completely smooth.

2. Spoon the spread into a serving bowl and, when ready to serve, garnish with the remaining ¼ cup of tomatoes and 2 tablespoons of basil and the goat cheese, if desired. Surround the serving bowl with slices of French bread.

BIG BATCH: *You can easily double the ingredients to serve twenty to twenty-four people.*

HOW TO MAKE TOASTED FRENCH BREAD SLICES

S lice a loaf of French bread diagonally into slices that are about ¼-inch thick (you will get two to three dozen slices per baguette, depending on the size of the loaf). Place these on a baking sheet and brush the tops with olive oil. Sprinkle the bread with a little kosher salt, if desired. Bake at 400°F until the slices are crisp and nicely browned, 15 to 18 minutes.

You can vary the basic recipe by brushing the bread with olive oil that has been seasoned with minced garlic or dried oregano, salt, and freshly ground black pepper. Or dust the slices of bread with Parmesan cheese before baking, if you like. Stored in resealable plastic bags, the toasted bread will keep for up to three days.

RECIPE REMINDERS

Made for

Prep notes

Don't forget

Special touches

Bring again

Cowboy Caviar

SERVES 10 TO 12 (MAKES ABOUT 4 CUPS)

PREP: 25 MINUTES

TOTE NOTES

For toting, pack the dip in a plastic container with a lid and keep it chilled in a cooler if the weather is hot.

You can tote the tortilla chips right in their bag. Pack a platter or basket to serve them and a serving bowl for the "caviar."

PLAN AHEAD

While you can make this wonderful dip two days in advance, the color of the cilantro and scallion will fade. For best results, make it no more than a day ahead—the flavors will still have time to mingle.

C HANCES ARE YOU'VE TASTED THIS POPULAR RECIPE at a picnic or tailgate party. With black beans, corn, tomatoes, avocado, and Mexican seasoning, it is a favorite for company. My sister Susan Anderson passed along her version of the recipe, and she warned that it is such a crowd-pleaser that people will hover over the serving dish. Susan was right. My family could not budge from the bowl, scooping up each and every morsel. Susan adapted the recipe of her neighbor, Kathy Simcoe, who lives in Atlanta, and Kathy got the recipe from the Woodland Elementary School cookbook. For a special treat, make it with black-eyed peas and serve it on New Year's Eve instead of that other caviar!

2 tablespoons red wine vinegar

½ to 2 teaspoons hot pepper sauce, such as Cholula, Frank's RedHot, or Texas Pete

2 teaspoons olive oil

1 medium-size clove garlic, minced

Dash of freshly ground black pepper

1 can (about 15 ounces) black beans or black-eyed peas, rinsed and drained

1 can (11 ounces) corn, drained

1 ripe avocado, preferably Hass, chopped (1 to 1½ cups)

1 cup chopped tomatoes (from 1 large tomato)

¼ cup sliced scallion, both white and green parts

¼ cup chopped fresh cilantro

Tortilla chips, for serving (Susan likes Tostitos Scoops! for picking up all the tidbits)

1. Place the red wine vinegar, hot sauce, olive oil, garlic, and black pepper in a small mixing bowl and whisk to combine. Set the dressing aside.

2. Place the black beans, corn, avocado, tomatoes, scallion, and cilantro in a large mixing bowl and gently stir to combine. Pour the dressing on top and stir just enough to coat.

3. Spoon the "caviar" into a glass, plastic, or stainless steel serving bowl and refrigerate it, covered, until ready to serve. Then, place the serving bowl on a platter or in a basket and surround it with tortilla chips. Any leftovers are delicious the next day as a salsa for grilled chicken or fish.

BIG BATCH: *Get out your larger cutting board because this recipe doubles well to feed a crowd of twenty to twenty-four, making about 8 cups.*

RECIPE REMINDERS

Made for

Prep notes

Don't forget

Special touches

Bring again

Hummus in a Hurry

SERVES 6 TO 8 (MAKES ABOUT 2 CUPS OF HUMMUS)

PREP: 15 MINUTES * BAKE: ABOUT 6 MINUTES

TOTE NOTES

You can tote the hummus in a plastic container or in a pretty bowl covered with plastic wrap.

Don't forget the pita crisps and a platter to hold everything.

PLAN AHEAD

The baked pita triangles can be stored in a resealable plastic bag for up to a week. Hummus keeps well in the refrigerator for up to three days.

YOU MIGHT WONDER WHY ANYONE WOULD WANT to make their own hummus what with all the hummus in supermarkets ready for sampling. As handy and tempting as that hummus is with its rainbow assortment of flavors, you just cannot beat the fresh flavor of the hummus you can quickly whip up in a food processor or blender at home.

FOR THE PITA TRIANGLES

4 pita rounds (6 inches)
2 tablespoons olive oil
Kosher salt (optional)

FOR THE HUMMUS

3 medium-size or 2 large cloves garlic, peeled
1 can (about 15 ounces) chickpeas (garbanzo beans)
1 teaspoon kosher salt, or more to taste
$\frac{1}{2}$ teaspoon ground cumin, or more to taste
Dash of cayenne pepper, or more to taste
3 tablespoons fresh lemon juice, or more to taste
3 tablespoons olive oil

1. Make the pita triangles: Preheat the oven to 400°F.

2. Brush both sides of the pita rounds with the 2 tablespoons of olive oil. Stack one pita round on top of another and, using a large sharp knife, cut the stack of pitas into 8 wedges or triangles. Repeat with the remaining 2 pitas. Place the pita wedges on baking sheets and sprinkle them with kosher salt, if desired.

MAKING A HUMMUS FLOWER

Want a beautiful way to serve hummus? Spread the hummus on a large, pretty, round serving plate. Beginning at the center, place a pita crisp in the hummus with the point of the triangle pointing up. Arrange the remaining pita crisps in the hummus in the same way so that they form a spiral of triangles resembling the petals of a flower. Arrange basil leaves around the edge of the hummus like the leaves of the flower and place a spoonful of olive tapenade in the middle for the center of the flower.

3. Bake the pitas until lightly browned, 5 to 7 minutes. Let the pita crisps cool before storing them in a resealable plastic bag.

4. Make the hummus: Using a food processor fitted with a steel blade or a blender, with the motor running, drop in the garlic through the feed tube and process until minced, about 5 seconds. Stop the machine.

5. Drain the chickpeas, setting aside the liquid. Add the chickpeas, salt, cumin, and cayenne pepper to the minced garlic. Process in short pulses until the chickpeas are minced, about 5 seconds. Stop the machine and scrape down the side of the bowl with a rubber spatula.

6. Add the lemon juice, 3 tablespoons of olive oil, and 2 tablespoons of the reserved chickpea liquid to the processor bowl. Process until the hummus is smooth, adding 1 to 2 more tablespoons of the chickpea liquid as needed—the hummus should have the consistency of a milkshake. Taste for seasoning, adding more salt, cumin, cayenne pepper, and/or lemon juice, as desired. Spoon the hummus into a serving bowl, cover with plastic wrap, and refrigerate until ready to serve.

BIG BATCH: *I have successfully doubled the hummus recipe to feed twelve to sixteen, but you have to take care to stir down the contents of the food processor to make sure the chickpeas are evenly pureed.*

Can't Eat Just One Spinach Balls

SERVES 12 (MAKES ABOUT 4 DOZEN)

PREP: 15 MINUTES ✳ BAKE: ABOUT 12 MINUTES

TOTE NOTES

It's easy to tote baked spinach balls wrapped in aluminum foil. When you arrive, reheat them right in the foil; they will be heated through after 3 to 5 minutes in a 350°F oven.

Be sure to bring the serving platter.

THIS RECIPE MAKES A WONDERFUL APPETIZER YOU taste at a holiday party and say, "Mmm," after the first spinach ball, then "Mmm, I've got to get that recipe," after popping the fourth one into your mouth. They're made from frozen chopped spinach to which you add butter, stuffing mix, eggs, and Parmesan cheese, then bake. The recipe makes a whole bunch, so you can freeze them—perfect for those of you who like to have make-ahead appetizers tucked away. And the spinach balls bake beautifully straight from the freezer, so you can serve them hot as your supper club arrives.

6 large eggs

12 tablespoons (1½ sticks) butter, melted

1 box (6 ounces) chicken-flavored stuffing mix

2 packages (10 ounces each) frozen chopped spinach, thawed and drained well

1 cup (4 ounces) shredded Parmesan cheese

¼ teaspoon freshly ground black pepper

1. Place the eggs in a large mixing bowl and beat with a whisk until they are lemon colored. Add the melted butter, stuffing mix, drained spinach, Parmesan, and black pepper, and stir to combine. Using your hands, roll the spinach mixture into balls about 1 inch across; you will get from 46 to 48 balls. The spinach mixture will be loose but don't worry, it will firm up in the oven.

2. When ready to bake, preheat the oven to 350°F.

3. Place the spinach balls on baking sheets and bake them until they are browned around the edges, 11 to 13 minutes for unfrozen spinach balls. Transfer the spinach balls to a serving platter and serve warm.

BIG BATCH: *The spinach ball recipe doubles and triples well; you'll need a very large bowl in which to mix the ingredients.*

FREEZE 'EM

The spinach balls can be frozen for up to two months. Arrange unbaked spinach balls on a baking sheet and place them in the freezer until firm, about 1 hour. Transfer the frozen spinach balls to resealable plastic freezer bags and return them to the freezer. They can be baked without thawing and will be done after 13 to 15 minutes in a 350°F oven. (If you tote frozen spinach balls to bake on site and they thaw en route, they'll only take about 12 minutes to bake.)

PLAN AHEAD

Once they have cooled, baked spinach balls can be refrigerated, wrapped in aluminum foil, for up to two days.

RECIPE REMINDERS

Made for

Prep notes

Don't forget

Special touches

Bring again

Deborah's Hot Spinach Dip

SERVES 10 TO 12 (MAKES ABOUT 4 CUPS)

PREP: 15 MINUTES ✳ BAKE: 20 TO 25 MINUTES

TOTE NOTES

This is a highly totable appetizer, and you have three choices—bake it before you leave home, bake it at the gathering, or reheat it once you arrive. If you bake it at home, cover the baking dish with aluminum foil and wrap a clean towel around it to keep it warm.

If you bring the dip ready to bake, then carry the bacon crumbles in a small plastic bag to sprinkle on top once the dip is baked.

An already baked dip can be reheated in a 350°F oven for 15 to 20 minutes or in the microwave on high power for 2 to 3 minutes.

PLAN AHEAD

The unbaked dip can be refrigerated, covered, for one day.

I F YOU'RE LOOKING FOR THAT BIG, RICH, HOT DIP TO serve from fall throughout the winter holidays, this is it. Pile it into a chafing dish or a pretty casserole, offer plenty of tortilla chips for dipping, and wait for the "oohs" and "aahs." The recipe came to me from my friend Currey Thornton in Nashville, and Deborah is her sister-in-law, who passed along the recipe. Currey served it to the ladies in our investment club. We're all old high school classmates, and let's just say we do a lot more eating, talking, and recipe swapping at meetings than we do investing in the stock market!

1 package (10 ounces) frozen chopped spinach, thawed and drained well

1 can (about 14 ounces) plain artichoke hearts, drained and chopped

1 package (5 ounces) herbed cream cheese, such as Boursin

1 cup (4 ounces) grated Parmesan cheese

1 cup (8 ounces) reduced-fat sour cream

½ cup mayonnaise

1 jar (2 ounces) chopped pimiento, drained

6 slices bacon, cooked, drained, and crumbled

Tortilla chips, pita crisps, or bagel chips, for serving

1. Preheat the oven to 400°F.

2. Place the spinach, artichokes, herbed cream cheese, Parmesan, sour cream, mayonnaise, and pimiento in a large mixing bowl and stir to combine well. Spoon the dip mixture into an 11 by 7–inch baking dish.

3. Bake the dip until it is bubbly, 20 to 25 minutes (allow more time for the dip to bake if it has been refrigerated).

4. When ready to serve, scatter the bacon over the warm dip (if you fried the bacon earlier, you may want to run it under the broiler to recrisp it a bit). Serve the dip with tortilla chips, pita crisps, or bagel chips.

WHEN YOU ARRIVE: *If your host has a chafing dish, use it to keep the dip warm (check with your host to be sure there's fuel for the chafing dish on hand). Spoon the hot dip from the baking dish into the warm chafing dish, garnish it with the crumbled bacon, and add some chopped fresh parsley for color, if desired.*

BIG BATCH: *This recipe doubles well for a large gathering. Bake each batch in its own baking dish; you can count on each batch serving twelve. After you've transferred one batch to a chafing dish, it can be replenished with more warm dip as the party progresses.*

RECIPE REMINDERS

Made for

Prep notes

Don't forget

Special touches

Bring again

Mary's Baked Boursin in a Roasted Red Pepper Sauce

SERVES 6

PREP: 10 MINUTES * BAKE: 12 TO 15 MINUTES

TOTE NOTES

The best way to tote this appetizer is to assemble it and cover the baking dish with plastic wrap. Once at the gathering, uncover the dish, and place it in a 350°F oven to bake. It will be warm in 15 minutes or less.

Bring along whatever garnishes you desire in separate containers.

You can tote the bread already sliced or slice it when you arrive.

Don't forget an attractive serving tray.

PLAN AHEAD

If you assemble the dish ahead of time, it can be kept in the refrigerator, covered, for several hours.

M Y CLEVER COUSIN MARY GRISSIM BROUGHT THIS yummy appetizer to a family gathering and we devoured every morsel. Served attractively in a shallow ceramic dish, it is an eye-catching combination of brilliant red peppers and seasoned cream cheese. And it's amazingly easy to assemble—perfect for those last-minute requests to bring an hors d'oeuvre to a small dinner party. For six servings you need two cups of roasted red peppers, a round of Boursin, and a loaf of French bread, plus a few pantry staples. It's ready in no time, so you can bake it on-site and serve it warm.

2 cups roasted red peppers (from a 16-ounce jar)

1 tablespoon extra-virgin olive oil

¼ teaspoon salt

¼ teaspoon freshly ground black pepper

1 package (5 ounces) Boursin cheese or another garlic and herb–flavored cream cheese

Sprinkle of dried Italian seasoning and/or hot pepper flakes

Pesto, pitted kalamata olives, and/or 1 sprig fresh rosemary, for garnish

1 loaf French bread, sliced ¼-inch thick on the diagonal, or toasted French bread rounds (see box, page 19)

1. Preheat the oven to 350°F.

2. Place the peppers, olive oil, salt, and pepper in a food processor and pulse until the peppers are finely chopped but not pureed, 10 to 15 pulses. Pour the pepper sauce in a 1-quart shallow ceramic or pottery baking dish.

3. Unwrap the cheese and place it on top of the sauce in the middle of the baking dish. Scatter the Italian seasoning and/or pepper flakes, if desired, over the cheese and sauce.

4. Bake the cheese until the sauce is warm and the cheese is soft, 12 to 15 minutes. Garnish the cheese with a little pesto, some olives, and/or a rosemary sprig. Place the baking dish on a serving tray and surround it with French bread slices or toasted French bread.

BIG BATCH: *Double the recipe by baking two rounds of cheese in a shallow 2-quart baking dish. You will need to increase the baking time to nearly 20 minutes so the additional sauce has time to heat thoroughly.*

RECIPE REMINDERS

Made for

Prep notes

Don't forget

Special touches

Bring again

Fleurie's Caramelized Onion Spread

SERVES 10 TO 12 (MAKES ABOUT 2½ CUPS)

PREP: 15 MINUTES ✳ COOK: 25 TO 30 MINUTES

TOTE NOTES

You can tote the spread right in its serving bowl, covered with plastic wrap.

Bring along spreaders and bags of bagel chips or pita crisps.

PLAN AHEAD

The spread can be made up to three days in advance.

MY HUSBAND'S COUSIN, FLEURIE SOMMERS, WHO lives in Houston, Texas, is a grand cook and hostess, and when she and her siblings planned an eightieth birthday party for their mother in Chattanooga, Fleurie set out deep bowls of this delicious spread for sampling. What makes the spread so unusual is that the onions are slowly cooked and caramelized in butter or olive oil, and then they are blended with mayonnaise, cream cheese, and sour cream. Yellow onions tend to brown more easily and are sweeter in flavor. Yet red onions give the spread a pretty purple tint, so the choice is yours. Spread it on bagel chips, pita crisps, or most any cracker you've got in the pantry.

2 tablespoons butter or olive oil
4 cups sliced yellow or red onions (3 medium-size onions)
1 package (8 ounces) cream cheese, at room temperature
½ cup mayonnaise
½ cup sour cream
¼ teaspoon cayenne pepper, or more to taste
¼ teaspoon salt, or more to taste
Bagel chips or pita crisps, for serving

1. Place the butter or olive oil in a large frying pan over low heat. Add the onions and cook, stirring with a wooden spoon from time to time, until they caramelize and turn a golden brown, 25 to 30 minutes. Remove the pan from the heat and let the onions cool for about 10 minutes.

2. Place the cream cheese, mayonnaise, sour cream, cayenne pepper, and salt in a food processor fitted with a steel blade and pulse until smooth, 5 to 7 times. Scrape the onions into the processor and, using short pulses, combine the onions with the cream cheese mixture until the onions are just evenly distributed and still in small pieces, 5 to 10 seconds. Taste for seasoning, adding more cayenne pepper and/or salt if needed. Spoon the spread into a serving bowl and serve with bagel chips or pita crisps. If you are not serving the spread right away refrigerate it, but let it come to room temperature before serving so it's easier to spread.

BIG BATCH: *It's not easy to cook more than 4 cups of onions in a large frying pan slowly enough to caramelize them, so make this recipe one batch at a time.*

MENU

A LAST-MINUTE WINE TASTING

Call six friends and invite them over. Ask them to bring a favorite wine to sample, hopefully with a good story to share. You provide bread, cheese, and fruit— and a few appetizers for when everyone gets hungry.

FLEURIE'S CARAMELIZED ONION SPREAD
✻
GOAT CHEESE WITH CILANTRO PESTO, *page 34*
✻
RICOTTA-FILLED BRESAOLA
WITH ARUGULA AND PARMESAN SHAVINGS, *page 46*
✻
SMOKED FISH PÂTÉ, *page 52*

RECIPE REMINDERS

Made for

Prep notes

Don't forget

Special touches

Bring again

Herbed Goat Cheese Pyramid

SERVES 8 (MAKES 1 PYRAMID)

PREP: 10 MINUTES ✳ CHILL: 1 HOUR

TOTE NOTES

Tote the herbed goat cheese in its container. Tote the olive oil in a small jar and the olives and thyme sprig garnishes in separate small plastic bags. And, don't forget the grilled or toasted bread; carry it in a covered plastic container or plastic bag.

Bring a serving plate for the cheese and an attractive bowl for the bread slices.

PLAN AHEAD

You can prepare the cheese pyramid up to three days in advance. The grilled or toasted bread can be stored in a plastic bag for two to three days.

THIS RECIPE IS READY TO HIT THE ROAD! AFTER I folded chopped kalamata olives, fresh thyme leaves, and grated lemon zest into some fresh goat cheese, I eyed the plastic pyramid-shaped container in which the cheese was sold. Since I wasn't serving it until the next day, I packed the seasoned mixture back into the container and placed it in the refrigerator. The next evening with friends coming for dinner, I unmolded the cheese, turning it onto a pretty plate, and surrounded it with grilled slices of French bread. It had the most beautiful pyramid shape and bits of olive and herbs inside.

Any leftovers are delicious spread on bread and run under the broiler.

1 package (about 5 ounces) soft goat cheese (see Note)

¼ cup quartered pitted kalamata olives, plus 6 to 8 whole pitted kalamata olives, for garnish

1 tablespoon chopped fresh parsley

1 teaspoon fresh thyme leaves, plus 1 thyme sprig, for garnish

1 teaspoon minced fresh chives

½ teaspoon grated lemon zest

1 tablespoon olive oil, for garnish

Grilled or toasted bread slices, for serving

1. Run a knife around the edges of the cheese to loosen it from the package. Place the cheese in a mixing bowl and set aside the plastic box and lid of the package.

2. Place the quartered kalamata olives, parsley, thyme leaves, chives, and lemon zest in the bowl with the cheese and, using a rubber spatula, mix until well combined. Using a soupspoon, pack the cheese mixture back into its package and secure the lid. Tap the container on the kitchen counter lightly so that the cheese settles. Refrigerate the cheese for at least 1 hour.

3. When ready to serve, run a knife around the edges of the cheese to loosen it and, giving it a good shake, invert it onto a serving plate. Drizzle the olive oil down the sides of the cheese and garnish it with the whole kalamata olives and sprig of thyme. Serve with grilled or toasted bread.

NOTE: What you want is a small package of goat cheese that comes in a plastic box that looks something like a truncated pyramid; Chavrie is a commonly available example.

BIG BATCH: *Make as many of these pyramids as you need, seasoning them differently. For example, use sun-dried tomatoes, chopped basil, and minced garlic in one instead of the herbs and lemon zest.*

RECIPE REMINDERS

Made for

Prep notes

Don't forget

Special touches

Bring again

Goat Cheese with Cilantro Pesto

SERVES 8 TO 10

PREP: 20 MINUTES

TOTE NOTES

This appetizer can either be made up to two days in advance or assembled at the last minute. If made in advance, it is a little messier to transport, but it is more delicious because the goat cheese has had some time to marinate in the pesto— let the goat cheese come to room temperature so it's easier to spread.

Either way, when toting, place the cheese on a plate or in a shallow ramekin, then cover it with plastic wrap.

If you are assembling the dish when you arrive, bring the pesto in a small jar and stir or shake it to recombine before using.

Tote the olives in a small plastic bag or container and the bread crisps in a paper bag.

ONE OF THE BENEFITS OF TRAVELING ON A BOOK TOUR is that I get to talk with people I have never met before. Invariably the topic comes around to food and before long, we're swapping recipes. While on tour for my cupcake book, the idea for this book was in my head, and I asked my Dallas escort, Linda Veneto, what appetizer she loved to tote to parties. Linda described how she marinated goat cheese in a cilantro vinaigrette. That idea stuck with me, and when I got home I made a pesto using fresh cilantro. Then I poured the pesto over the top of a log of soft, fresh goat cheese and let it rest for an hour. Let me say that this combination is truly memorable, and while people might guess the pesto contains basil, once they taste a bite they are in for a delicious surprise.

> 1 large clove garlic, peeled
> 2 loosely packed cups cilantro leaves
> 2 tablespoons pine nuts
> ¼ teaspoon salt, or more to taste
> ⅓ cup extra-virgin olive oil
> 1 log (10½ ounces) mild goat cheese
> 8 to 10 pitted kalamata olives, for garnish
> Toasted French bread (see box, page 19), for serving

1. Using a food processor fitted with a steel blade, with the motor running, drop in the garlic through the feed tube and process until minced, about 5 seconds. Stop the machine. Add the cilantro, pine nuts, and salt and process in pulses until the cilantro is minced, about 10 seconds. Taste for seasoning, adding more salt if necessary.

2. With the motor running, gradually pour in the olive oil and process until the pesto comes together and thickens slightly.

3. Place the goat cheese on a pretty plate. Pour the pesto over the cheese, coating generously. Garnish with the olives and serve with toasted French bread slices.

BIG BATCH: *You can double or triple the pesto to top two or three logs of goat cheese. Or, you could create a platter of goat cheese logs, each covered with a different kind of pesto—one basil, one cilantro, one parsley.*

TEN SPEEDY TOPPERS
FOR CREAM CHEESE OR GOAT CHEESE

Start with a block of cream cheese or a round of soft, spreadable goat cheese. Spoon one of these toppings over it, then reach for the crackers.

1. Pepper jelly

2. Apricot preserves and toasted pine nuts

3. Cherry jam and chopped scallions

4. Sun-dried tomatoes and pesto

5. Black olive paste and grated lemon peel

6. Chopped smoked salmon and minced chives

7. Lump crabmeat and chili sauce

8. Mango chutney and toasted almond slices

9. Pomegranate seeds

10. Fig preserves and Thai chile sauce

Gorgonzola Cheese Ball

SERVES 12 TO 15 (MAKES ABOUT 2 CUPS)

PREP: 15 MINUTES ✳ CHILL: 1 HOUR PLUS 1 HOUR STANDING TIME

TOTE NOTES

Tote the cheese ball on a serving plate, covered with plastic wrap.

Bring along a box of wheat crackers and whole apples and pears to slice at the party so they don't discolor.

PLAN AHEAD

The cheese ball can be prepared several days in advance.

I LOVE CHEESE BALLS, AND THIS ONE IS A WINNER, PAIRING delicious blue cheese and walnuts. The recipe calls for Italian Gorgonzola, but in a pinch you can use any good blue cheese. Toasting the walnuts brings out their flavor and crunch. The cheese is great spread on crackers and on slices of pear and apple.

> ¾ cup chopped toasted walnuts (see box, page 99)
> 1 package (8 ounces) cream cheese, at room temperature
> 1 cup (4 ounces) crumbled Gorgonzola cheese
> 4 tablespoons butter (½ stick), at room temperature
> 1 can (2¼ ounces) sliced black olives, drained
> Wheat crackers, for serving
> 2 cups sliced red pear and green apple, for serving

1. Place the walnuts in a large, shallow bowl or baking dish.

2. Place the cream cheese, Gorgonzola, butter, and olives in a large bowl and blend with an electric mixer on low speed or with a wooden spoon until the mixture comes together. Form the cheese mixture into a ball and roll it in the walnuts. Refrigerate the cheese ball, wrapped in plastic wrap or on a serving plate covered with plastic wrap, for at least 1 hour.

3. Remove the cheese ball from the refrigerator an hour before serving so that it is spreadable. Place it on a serving plate, if necessary, and surround it with wheat crackers and pear and apple slices before serving.

BIG BATCH: *For a larger cheese ball, double the recipe.*

A CHEESE BOARD
FOR ROOKIES

A well-designed cheese board is something to behold. The key to success is in the presentation. Begin with a pretty surface—a nice board, a mirror, or a piece of marble or granite. Then, select the cheeses; this can easily be done at the supermarket deli, specialty food store, natural foods store, or farmers' market. Buy an odd number of cheeses (it's an old decorating trick that one or three or five of something looks better clustered together than an even number). If you want three, choose one sharp, one creamy, and one blue. For more than three, add a goat cheese and a designer cheese that is sure to generate conversation. You might even make little signs that have the name of each cheese as well as the flag of the country it comes from, but this is entirely optional and a little over the top!

If these suggestions are too much, just get one big block of something— a grand Cheddar, a creamy Brie, or an impressive chunk of Parmesan or aged Gouda. Whatever you choose, remember that cheese needs to be served at room temperature.

If it's not too cumbersome, the cheese board can be assembled ahead of time and transported covered with plastic wrap. But it's easy to assemble when you arrive, too. Bring little knives for cutting and spreading as well as crackers or crusty baguettes for slicing. Fill in the cheese board with fruit that pairs well with cheese, such as grapes and slices of apples and pears. And to really impress, decorate the cheese board with pomegranate seeds and slices of kumquat. Rookie no more!

Curried Cheese Ball Showered in Coconut, Chutney, and Cashews

SERVES 12 (MAKES ABOUT 1 POUND)

PREP: 20 MINUTES ✳ CHILL: 1 HOUR

TOTE NOTES

So that the garnishes don't slip and slide, tote the cheese ball on its platter, covered with plastic wrap. Bring the toppings in separate plastic bags and sprinkle them over the cheese ball when you get to the party.

It's even easier to tote the cheese mixture spread out in a flat disk on a serving plate. Top it with the garnishes, then cover the plate in plastic wrap.

Bring boxes of wheat crackers and a bowl or basket to put them in.

JUST IN TIME FOR THE SUPER BOWL, JERE MYERS, WHO lives in Nashville, shared her recipe for a curried cream cheese dip with me. I couldn't resist giving it a try, but I found myself wanting to add a little more Cheddar cheese and then to roll the mixture into a ball. The garnishes poured on top—mango chutney, flaked coconut, scallions, and cashews or peanuts—all add color and a bit of sweetness, saltiness, or crunch. Visually stunning, this appetizer is as much fun to look at as it is to eat. If you don't want to roll it into a ball you can simply spread the cheese out on a pretty plate and top it with the garnishes.

FOR THE CHEESE BALL

1 package (8 ounces) cream cheese, at room temperature

2 cups (8 ounces) shredded sharp Cheddar cheese

2 tablespoons curry powder

2 tablespoons Worcestershire sauce

FOR SERVING

⅓ cup mango chutney

¼ cup sweetened flaked coconut

¼ cup chopped roasted, salted cashews or peanuts

¼ cup chopped scallions, green parts only

Wheat crackers

1. Make the cheese ball: Place the cream cheese, Cheddar cheese, curry powder, and Worcestershire sauce in a large mixing bowl. Blend with an electric mixer on low speed or with a wooden spoon until the mixture comes together well. Form the cheese mixture into a ball and cover it with plastic wrap. Refrigerate the cheese ball for at least 1 hour.

2. To serve: Unwrap the cheese ball and place it on a pretty serving plate. Let it come to room temperature before serving so it's easier to spread. Pour the chutney on top, then scatter the coconut over it. Sprinkle on the nuts and scallions. Serve the cheese ball with wheat crackers on the side.

BIG BATCH: *You can double this recipe and combine the ingredients using an electric mixer or food processor. Form the mixture into two cheese balls or a single large one. Remember to double the garnishes as well.*

RECIPE REMINDERS

Made for

Prep notes

Don't forget

Special touches

Bring again

Blue Cheese Pecan Wafers

MAKES ABOUT 4 DOZEN WAFERS

PREP: 15 MINUTES ✳ CHILL: 45 MINUTES ✳ BAKE: 12 TO 15 MINUTES

TOTE NOTES

Carefully pack the cheese wafers in a pretty tin with a lid. One attractive way to serve them is on silver trays lined with doilies. Leave any leftovers and the tin behind as an extra little gift for the host to enjoy.

PLAN AHEAD

The cooled wafers can be stored at room temperature for up to one week in airtight metal or plastic containers lined with waxed paper. Cooled wafers can also be transferred to sturdy resealable plastic freezer bags and frozen for up to one month. Let them thaw on the kitchen counter.

WALNUTS MAY SEEM LIKE THE PERFECT FLAVOR mate for blue cheese, but I prefer the sweetness of pecans and the way they balance the sharp saltiness of the cheese. They are like two old friends, companions that bring out the best in each other. Use Danish, Maytag, or whatever other good blue cheese you have on hand. And if you just don't care for blue cheese, you can substitute one packed cup of shredded sharp Cheddar.

> 8 tablespoons (1 stick) unsalted butter
> 1 cup (4 ounces) crumbled blue cheese
> 1¼ cups all-purpose flour
> Dash of cayenne pepper
> ½ cup finely chopped pecans

1. Place the butter, blue cheese, flour, and cayenne in the bowl of a food processor fitted with a steel blade. Process in on and off pulses until the mixture is smooth, 15 to 20 seconds. Transfer the dough to a small mixing bowl and fold in the chopped pecans.

2. Tear off an 18-inch-long piece of waxed paper and place the dough on top, using a rubber spatula to shape it into a log about 12 inches long. Wrap the paper loosely around the log and refrigerate it until firm enough to handle, about 15 minutes.

3. Unwrap the log of dough and place it on top of the waxed paper. Using your hands, stretch the dough to create a longer log. Wrap the waxed paper securely around the dough log but do not seal the ends. Using light motions, roll the log back and forth on the work surface until it is about 1½ inches in diameter and 15 to 16 inches long. Place the log in the freezer for 30 minutes; it will be easier to slice and have more flavor.

4. About 20 minutes before you plan to bake the wafers, remove the log of dough from the freezer and preheat the oven to 375°F.

5. When ready to bake, unwrap the log of dough, slice it into ¼-inch wafers, and place these on ungreased rimmed baking sheets, 15 per baking sheet. Bake the wafers until they are golden brown, 12 to 15 minutes.

6. Using a metal spatula, transfer the wafers to wire racks to cool completely, about 20 minutes, before serving.

BIG BATCH: *You can make the dough in batches ahead of time, freeze it in logs for up to three days, and then bake the wafers all at one time. It will take about 2 hours for a log of dough to thaw enough to slice.*

Olive Cheese Puffs

MAKES ABOUT 40 PUFFS

PREP: 25 MINUTES ✳ BAKE: ABOUT 15 MINUTES

IF YOU LOVE CHEDDAR CHEESE AND OLIVES, THEN YOU'LL really enjoy these olive cheese puffs. I use the green manzanilla olives stuffed with pimiento, but you could use any pitted olives. The puffs freeze well and reheat beautifully.

> 2 cups (8 ounces) shredded sharp Cheddar cheese
> 8 tablespoons (1 stick) butter, at room temperature
> 1 cup all-purpose flour
> ¼ teaspoon salt
> ¼ teaspoon paprika
> Dash of cayenne pepper
> 40 medium-size pimiento-stuffed manzanilla olives, well drained

1. Preheat the oven to 400°F.

2. Place the cheese and butter in a large mixing bowl and blend with an electric mixer on low speed until creamy, 2 to 3 minutes, or place in a food processor fitted with a steel blade and process until smooth, about 1 minute. Add the flour, salt, paprika, and cayenne and blend well.

3. Working with 1 heaping teaspoon of dough at a time, mold the dough around an olive and place it on an ungreased rimmed baking sheet. Repeat until all the dough and olives have been used.

4. Bake the puffs until lightly browned, 13 to 16 minutes, then transfer them to a rack or serve them warm.

BIG BATCH: *You can easily double this recipe.*

Perfect Deviled Eggs

SERVES 6 (MAKES 12 DEVILED EGGS)

PREP: 35 MINUTES

YOU MIGHT AS WELL NOT STAGE A COVERED DISH supper in some parts of the country if you don't serve deviled or stuffed eggs. These delightfully filling eggs are especially good served with fried chicken, potato salad, and sliced tomatoes. It's funny how the revered simple deviled egg can be tricky to make. Be sure you don't overcook the eggs, first of all, and that you immediately run cold water over them to loosen the shells and make them easier to peel. Have fun with the filling, as this is just a basic recipe. Some people prefer dill pickle relish, others capers, and some like chopped fresh parsley, cilantro, or tarragon.

 6 large eggs
 2 tablespoons mayonnaise, or more as needed
 2 tablespoons sweet pickle relish, plus some of its liquid
  (optional)
 1 teaspoon Dijon mustard
 Salt and freshly ground black pepper
 Paprika or chopped parsley, for garnish

1. Place the eggs in a large saucepan and pour in enough cold water to cover them by a couple of inches. Place the pan over medium-high heat and bring to a boil. Cover the pan and remove it from the heat. Let the eggs stand in the hot water for 15 minutes.

2. Drain the water from the pan and immediately fill it with cold water. Remove the eggs from the pan and gently tap them on a counter to crack them. Peel the eggs under cool

TOTE NOTES

You can tote the garnished deviled eggs on a serving plate wrapped in plastic wrap. Carry the parsley in a little plastic bag. And bring along a jar of paprika.

  Or, arrange the eggs on one of those plates that have the little indentations for the deviled eggs and wrap that in plastic.

  If you want to pack the eggs in a plastic container with a lid, line the container with waxed paper first, to cushion the eggs in transit.

PLAN AHEAD

Deviled eggs taste best freshly made, but you can prepare them the night before and refrigerate them on a baking sheet, loosely covered with plastic wrap.

RECIPE REMINDERS

Made for

Prep notes

Don't forget

Special touches

Bring again

running water, starting at the large end. Slice the eggs in half lengthwise, remove the yolks with a teaspoon, and place them in a small bowl. Set aside the whites.

3. Add the mayonnaise, pickle relish, and mustard to the yolks and mix, mashing the yolks with a fork. Season with salt and pepper to taste. Add more mayonnaise or some of the sweet pickle liquid if the yolk mixture is too dry.

4. Spoon the yolk mixture into the hollows of the egg whites and place them on a serving plate. For a fancier look, spoon the egg yolk mixture into a resealable plastic bag, snip off one corner, and pipe the mixture into the hollows of the egg whites. Sprinkle the tops of the eggs with paprika or chopped parsley.

BIG BATCH: *Cook up to two dozen eggs at a time in a large saucepan to make deviled eggs for twenty-four.*

THE DEVILED EGG OF THE MONTH CLUB

W ho said all deviled eggs must be created alike? Or that they must only be served in the summertime? If you want to prepare deviled eggs each and every month of the year, here some suggestions.

JANUARY

Garnish the eggs with a dollop of caviar and sour cream and a couple of snipped chives crossed on the top.

FEBRUARY

Think Valentine red: Top the eggs with bits of smoked salmon and add a bit of chopped red onion.

MARCH

For something green for St. Patrick's Day, scatter chopped herbs like chives, dill, thyme, parsley, oregano, basil, chervil—whatever you have on hand—over the eggs. Or, top them with a tiny steamed asparagus tip.

APRIL

Add chopped niçoise olives or a spoonful of tapenade to the filling. Garnish the eggs with sprigs of fresh parsley. Put a bit of anchovy fillet on top of that and dream of a trip to Provence.

MAY

Make Cinco de Mayo eggs. Add a minced smoky chipotle pepper in adobo sauce and top the eggs with fresh cilantro. Or add some store-bought salsa and use cilantro for the garnish.

JUNE

Add some wasabi paste to the egg mixture and top the filling with a piece of cucumber and pickled ginger.

JULY

Go all-American. Choose your favorite family recipe that includes dill pickles or chopped sweet pickle relish. Garnish the eggs with small American flags.

AUGUST

It's summertime, so stir a little pesto into the yolk mixture. Top each egg with a tiny basil leaf and a pine nut.

SEPTEMBER

Add curry powder to the filling and garnish the eggs with a dollop of chutney and chives or a few chopped salted cashews.

OCTOBER

Try BLT eggs, topped with crumbled crisp bacon, a slice of cherry tomato, and a tiny green watercress leaf.

NOVEMBER

Add honey mustard when you make the egg filling and use a thin slice of country ham, prosciutto, or salami as a garnish.

DECEMBER

For a red and green theme on the party platter, add minced red and green bell pepper or a dollop each of red and green pepper jelly.

Ricotta-Filled Bresaola with Arugula and Parmesan Shavings

SERVES 8 (MAKES 16 TO 20 ROLLS)

PREP: 20 MINUTES

TOTE NOTES

Go ahead and assemble the bresaola *platter ahead of time, wrap it in plastic wrap, and place it in the refrigerator for up to 2 hours.*

If you want to assemble this on-site, carry the premade rolls in a plastic container, and tote the arugula, lemon wedges, and Parmesan shavings in separate plastic bags. Bring the olive oil in its bottle and don't forget a serving platter.

PLAN AHEAD

The bresaola *rolls can be made a day in advance. Store them in a large, flat plastic container in the refrigerator.*

ONE RECENT SUMMER MY FAMILY VISITED TUSCANY where we spent many evenings tasting the local antipasti before dinner. One of my favorites was *bresaola*—thinly sliced cured and dried beef—often served with arugula and lemon in a salad. Once home, I seasoned ricotta cheese with minced chives and placed a dab on each slice of *bresaola,* then rolled them up, turning the salad into an appetizer. To serve, I placed these rolls on a pretty platter and showered them with arugula and shavings of Parmesan. To eat them, you simply pick up a roll along with a couple of arugula leaves and a slice of Parmesan for a bite of Tuscan heaven.

> 1 packed cup skim ricotta cheese
> 1 tablespoon minced fresh chives
> Salt
> ¼ pound thinly sliced bresaola
> 2 loosely packed cups arugula leaves
> 2 to 3 tablespoons Parmesan cheese shavings
>   (see box, page 111)
> 1 large lemon, cut into wedges
> Extra-virgin olive oil, for drizzling

1. Place the ricotta and chives in a small bowl and stir to combine. Season with salt to taste.

2. There will be from 16 to 20 slices of *bresaola,* depending on how it is sliced. Place a teaspoonful of the ricotta mixture on one end of each *bresaola* slice and roll it up. Arrange the rolls in a spoke pattern on a pretty platter.

3. Scatter the arugula on top of the rolls or pile it in the center. Arrange the Parmesan shavings on top of the arugula. Place the lemon wedges attractively around the platter so that people can squeeze the juice over the *bresaola* rolls if they desire. Drizzle olive oil over everything and serve. It's unlikely you'll have any leftovers, but if you do, place them in a plastic container to enjoy for lunch the next day.

WANT TO TURN THE *BRESAOLA* INTO A SALAD? Forget the ricotta filling. Place the *bresaola* slices on a large platter. Top them with a generous amount of arugula leaves. Top these with Parmesan shavings. Arrange lemon wedges around the outside of the platter and drizzle olive oil on top. If you've got some really nice ripe tomatoes, peel and cut them into wedges and arrange them around the edge of the salad with the lemon wedges.

BIG BATCH: *Ricotta-filled* bresaola *is easy to double; just arrange the rolls on a larger platter.*

RECIPE REMINDERS

Made for

_____

_____

_____

_____

_____

Prep notes

_____

_____

_____

_____

Don't forget

_____

_____

_____

_____

Special touches

_____

_____

_____

_____

Bring again

_____

_____

Asian Chicken Lettuce Wraps

SERVES 4 TO 6 (MAKES ABOUT 12 WRAPS)

PREP: 20 MINUTES ✳ COOK: ABOUT 8 MINUTES

TOTE NOTES

Tote the chicken filling in a microwave-safe glass container. Once you arrive reheat it in the microwave (make sure one is available ahead of time) for 1 to 2 minutes on high power.

Rinse and pat the lettuce leaves dry before you leave, then pack them in a plastic bag. Pack the cilantro sprigs, if using, in a plastic bag, too.

Take a pretty platter with you as well as several soupspoons for spooning the chicken filling into the lettuce leaves.

PLAN AHEAD

The chicken filling can be refrigerated for up to two days.

THESE WRAPS ARE A LITTLE MESSY, BUT FUN, AND they are my children's favorite fast food. So, the pressure was on me to devise a recipe we could make at home. Here are the results. Begin with ground chicken cooked and seasoned with garlic, ginger, and hoisin sauce. Then, spoon the wonderful mixture into crisp iceberg lettuce leaves and eat it like a burrito. Add chopped roasted peanuts for a Thai flavor. When toting, keep the filling warm and the lettuce leaves cold, and you will be the hero when you share these wraps.

1 large head iceberg lettuce

1 tablespoon vegetable oil

1 pound ground chicken

3 medium-size cloves garlic, minced

1 cup chopped scallions, green parts only (from 1 bunch)

1 tablespoon minced peeled fresh ginger

¾ cup hoisin sauce

4 teaspoons soy sauce

1 teaspoon Asian (dark) sesame oil

¾ cup finely chopped water chestnuts

Fresh cilantro sprigs (optional), for garnish

1. Using a small paring knife, cut the core out of the head of lettuce and discard it. Rinse the lettuce under cool running water and drain it well on paper towels. Set the lettuce aside.

2. Place the oil in a large frying pan over medium heat. Combine in the chicken, breaking it up with a wooden spoon. Add the garlic and cook, stirring, until the chicken is cooked through, 4 to 5 minutes. Turn off the heat. Stir in the scallions, ginger, hoisin sauce, soy sauce, sesame oil, and water chestnuts. Cook the chicken filling over medium-low heat, stirring, until it bubbles and is heated through, 2 to 3 minutes. Keep the filling warm if you are serving it immediately.

3. When ready to serve, carefully pull apart the head of lettuce to separate the leaves. Pat the leaves dry with paper towels and pile them around the outside edge of a large platter. You should have at least 12 nice lettuce leaves (leftover lettuce can be wrapped and refrigerated for a later meal). Spoon the chicken filling into the center of the platter and garnish it with cilantro sprigs, if desired. Serve at once. To eat the wraps, spoon some of the chicken mixture into a lettuce leaf, wrap the lettuce up around it, and eat the wrap like a burrito.

BIG BATCH: *You can double this recipe with ease but you will need a very large skillet for cooking the chicken. If you don't own one, prepare the filling in two batches.*

RECIPE REMINDERS

Made for

Prep notes

Don't forget

Special touches

Bring again

Ann's Home-Smoked Salmon with Olives and Lemon

SERVES 12 TO 16 (MAKES ABOUT 2½ POUNDS)

PREP: 20 MINUTES PLUS AT LEAST 2 HOURS FOR SOAKING THE WOOD CHIPS
SMOKE: ABOUT 1 HOUR 15 MINUTES

TOTE NOTES

The best way to tote the garnished salmon is on the serving platter, covered in plastic wrap.

If you are garnishing the salmon at the party, carry the olives and lemon slices separately in plastic bags. Don't forget a bottle of olive oil for drizzling and the toasted bread or crackers.

PLAN AHEAD

The salmon can be smoked up to three days in advance. Place it in a glass baking dish, cover it with plastic wrap, and refrigerate it until you are ready to travel.

WHEN I THINK ABOUT THIS RECIPE, I SMILE because the story behind it brings such joy. My husband's cousin Ann Mills, who lives in Charlottesville, Virginia, drove south to Chattanooga for a big birthday party she and her siblings were hosting for their mother. Ann and her husband, Rick Childs, loaded their station wagon with baked Virginia hams and slabs of this just-smoked salmon. They chose to drive through the night, thinking that the food (and the drivers) might better survive the August heat in the cool night air. At the party, neither the drivers nor the salmon looked weary from the trip. Glistening with olive oil, the salmon was placed on large white oval platters and topped with thin slices of lemon and black and green olives. Once home, I called Ann for the recipe, then bought an electric smoker. My family relives that fun party every time we take a bite of the salmon.

4 cups oak, mesquite, or apple wood chips
Water
1 salmon fillet (about 2½ pounds), either with or
   without skin
1 teaspoon kosher salt
1 cup dry white wine
2 lemons, 1 cut in half, 1 thinly sliced and seeded

ELECTRIC SMOKERS

. . . .

Y ou can find electric
smokers at home
improvement and sporting
goods stores. They vary in
size and the number of bells
and whistles included. Use
my smoking time for the
salmon as a starting point and
consult the manufacturer's
instructions for specifics.

3 bay leaves

1 tablespoon whole black peppercorns

1 tablespoon table salt

¼ cup plus about 2 tablespoons extra-virgin olive oil

½ cup assorted olives, for garnish

Toasted French bread slices (see box, page 19) or soda
crackers, for serving

1. Place the wood chips in a bucket of water to soak for at
least 2 hours, or overnight.

2. When ready to smoke the salmon, season it with the kosher
salt and set it aside.

3. Remove the water pan from the electric smoker and add
14 cups of water and the wine, lemon halves, bay leaves,
peppercorns, and table salt. Place the water pan in the smoker
and plug it in. Using your hands, remove some of the soaked
wood chips from the bucket of water and carefully arrange
them around the electric coils of the smoker. Let the remaining
wood chips continue to soak.

4. If you are using a skinless salmon fillet, brush each side
with 1 tablespoon of the olive oil. If the fillet has skin on one
side, brush only the skinless side with 1 tablespoon of the olive

RECICE REMINDERS

Made for

Prep notes

Don't forget

Special touches

Bring again

oil. Arrange the salmon on the grill rack of the smoker, skin side down, if any. Place the rack in the smoker and cover it with the lid. Let the salmon smoke until it has just cooked through, about 1 hour and 15 minutes. Keep an eye on the smoke; when it begins to die down after about 40 minutes you will need to add the remaining wood chips.

5. Remove the rack with the salmon from the smoker and, using a large metal spatula or two, carefully transfer the salmon to a platter. When ready to serve, drizzle the remaining ¼ cup of olive oil over the salmon and garnish it with the lemon slices and olives, serving the toasted bread or crackers on the side.

BIG BATCH: *As long as you have the wood chips, the time, and the salmon, you can turn out batch after batch of this for a large gathering. You'll need to smoke one salmon fillet at a time.*

Smoked Fish Pâté

SERVES 6 (MAKES ABOUT 1½ CUPS)

PREP: 15 MINUTES

TOTE NOTES

Tote the pâté in a crock or ramekin, along with a box of crackers. If you want a garnish, bring a small jar of capers or chopped parsley in a small plastic bag.

FISH PATES AREN'T ANY MORE DIFFICULT TO ASSEMBLE than tuna salad. And they're easy to tote because they can be packed into a ramekin, just waiting to be spread onto crackers. This pâté begins with a chunk of smoked fish that you'll find vacuum-packed at the fish counter of the supermarket. Try alder-smoked salmon if it's available. Adding some cream cheese to the pâté makes a small piece of fish go a long way.

4 to 6 ounces smoked fish (wood-smoked salmon, trout, or bluefish)

3 ounces cream cheese, at room temperature

1 to 2 tablespoons sour cream or mayonnaise

¼ cup finely chopped celery

¼ cup chopped fresh parsley, plus more chopped parsley (optional), for garnish

2 tablespoons finely chopped red onion

Juice of half a lemon (1 tablespoon), or more to taste

Dash of hot pepper sauce, such as Cholula or Frank's RedHot, or more to taste

Salt and freshly ground black pepper

Capers (optional), for garnish

Fancy crackers, such as Bremner wafers or Carr's

1. Remove and discard any skin on the fish. Place the fish in a medium-size bowl and flake it with a fork. Add the cream cheese and 1 tablespoon of the sour cream or mayonnaise and stir until well blended, and the pâté is smooth enough to spread, adding more sour cream or mayonnaise if needed.

2. Fold in the celery, ¼ cup of parsley, and the onion. Add the lemon juice and hot pepper sauce and season with salt and pepper to taste. Taste for seasoning, adding more lemon juice and/or hot pepper sauce as necessary. Spoon the pâté into a small crock, ramekin, or bowl and cover with plastic wrap. Refrigerate until serving time.

3. To serve, garnish the pâté with chopped parsley or sprinkle capers on top, if desired. Serve with crackers.

BIG BATCH: *This recipe is easy to double or triple. The ingredients all multiply out neatly.*

PLAN AHEAD

You can make this pâté up to two days in advance; it will taste better when the flavors have a chance to mingle.

RECIPE REMINDERS

Made for

_____

_____

_____

_____

Prep notes

_____

_____

_____

_____

Don't forget

_____

_____

_____

_____

Special touches

_____

Bring again

_____

Layered Crabmeat Stack

SERVES 12 TO 15

PREP: 15 MINUTES ⁎ CHILL: 20 MINUTES

**TOTE
NOTES**

*Once it's assembled, you
can tote the stack on an
attractive shallow 9-inch
serving dish, in a footed
trifle bowl, or in a glass
dish with a snap-on
plastic lid.*

*Bring a bag or box
of chips or crackers, or
transport carrot and
celery sticks in a plastic
bag. Don't forget a couple
of small spreaders.*

*If the weather is
hot, it's a good idea to
transport the stack in
a cooler.*

*Leftovers are delicious
the next day, so be sure
and cover what remains
of the stack and return it
to the refrigerator.*

MY SISTER SUSAN BROUGHT THIS WONDERFUL DISH
to our weekend getaway in the mountains, and
kids and adults alike could not leave it alone.
Made with juicy lump crab piled on a bed of lemony
cream cheese and cocktail sauce and topped with shredded
cheese and crunchy scallions and bell pepper, it's no wonder
it was popular. Susan adapted the stack from a recipe her
friend had shared from *Southern Living* magazine. This
is a terrific appetizer to tote to the lake, the beach, or a
football game. It is as suitable for an office potluck as it
is for a black-tie New Year's Eve soiree.

1 package (8 ounces) reduced-fat cream cheese,
   at room temperature

2 tablespoons fresh lemon juice, or more to taste

1 tablespoon mayonnaise

½ teaspoon seasoned salt

½ teaspoon Worcestershire sauce

¾ cup cocktail sauce

1 pound lump crabmeat, drained and picked over
   for cartilage

1 cup (4 ounces) shredded Cheddar and Monterey Jack
   cheese blend

3 scallions, green parts only, chopped

½ green bell pepper, cored, seeded, and chopped
   (about ½ cup)

Pita or bagel chips, crackers, or carrot and celery sticks,
   for serving

1. Place the cream cheese in a mixing bowl and beat with an electric mixer on low speed until smooth, about 10 seconds. Add the lemon juice, mayonnaise, seasoned salt, and Worcestershire sauce and beat until combined. Taste for seasoning, adding more lemon juice as desired. Spoon the cream cheese mixture onto a 9-inch serving dish, cover with plastic wrap, and refrigerate for at least 20 minutes.

2. When ready to serve, spread the cocktail sauce over the cream cheese mixture. Scatter the crabmeat on top of the cocktail sauce and top it with the shredded cheese, then the scallions and bell pepper. Surround the dish with chips, crackers, or carrot and celery sticks and serve.

BIG BATCH: *You could easily double this and create a large free-form round stack on a pretty platter. Surround the stack with crackers and chips.*

PLAN AHEAD

Pick over the crab and prepare the vegetables one day in advance and store them in covered bowls in the refrigerator. Assemble the stack on the day you want to serve it.

RECIPE REMINDERS

Made for

Prep notes

Don't forget

Special touches

Bring again

Little Crisp Crab Cakes

SERVES 8 (MAKES 24 SMALL CRAB CAKES, 1½ INCHES EACH)

PREP: 20 MINUTES ✳ CHILL: 30 MINUTES ✳ COOK: 9 TO 10 MINUTES

TOTE NOTES

If it is possible to fry the crab cakes at the party, do so—they'll have the best flavor that way. Tote the unbaked crab cakes on a baking sheet.

If not, after frying and draining the crab cakes, place them on a baking sheet and cover it with plastic wrap. They can be refrigerated for up to 6 hours. At the party, preheat the oven to 350°F, unwrap the baking sheet, and bake the crab cakes until heated through and crisp, about 10 minutes.

Bring along a platter and the lemon wedges and capers or chopped parsley for garnishing (you can tote them in small plastic bags).

MY LITERARY AGENT, CHICAGOAN NANCY CROSSMAN, raved about the little crab cakes her friend would make for girls' night out parties. Since there is nothing better than a terrific crab cake recipe, Nancy begged Allyson Laackman for the recipe. The secrets are folding good lump crabmeat gently into the mix and using the Japanese bread crumbs known as *panko,* which both slightly bind the cakes and coat them before frying. Served warm, these are beautiful showered with parsley and/or capers and surrounded by lemon slices for squeezing. Set out small plates and forks or, if the crab cakes are being passed around at a larger gathering, place each on top of a toasted French bread round that is about the same size as the crab cake.

FOR THE CRAB CAKES

⅓ cup mayonnaise

2 tablespoons chopped fresh parsley

1 teaspoon coarse grain mustard

1 teaspoon Worcestershire sauce

¼ teaspoon cayenne pepper

¼ teaspoon Old Bay seasoning

1 large egg

Kosher salt and freshly ground black pepper

1 pound lump crabmeat, drained and picked over for cartilage

1 heaping cup plus 2 tablespoons panko (see Note)

¼ cup olive oil

¼ cup vegetable oil

FOR THE GARNISHES
2 lemons, cut into wedges
$\frac{1}{4}$ cup capers, drained, or chopped fresh parsley

1. Place the mayonnaise, parsley, mustard, Worcestershire sauce, cayenne pepper, Old Bay seasoning, and egg in a large mixing bowl and mix with a fork until the egg is well incorporated. Season with salt and black pepper to taste.

2. Gently fold in the crab and 2 tablespoons of the *panko* until the mixture just comes together and is still fairly loose. Form 24 small crab cakes, 1$\frac{1}{2}$ to 2 inches in diameter, and place them on a parchment paper– or waxed paper–lined baking sheet. Place the baking sheet in the refrigerator to chill for about 30 minutes.

3. When you are ready to fry the crab cakes, preheat the oven to 300°F.

4. Dust the crab cakes on both sides with the remaining heaping cup of *panko* crumbs and set aside the baking sheet. Place the olive oil and vegetable oil in a large frying pan and heat over medium-high heat until hot. Working in batches, carefully slide the crab cakes into the hot oil and cook until lightly browned on both sides, 1 to 2 minutes per side. As the crab cakes finish cooking, transfer them to paper towels to drain. Remove the parchment paper or waxed paper from the baking sheet and place the drained crab cakes on the sheet. When all of the crab cakes are cooked, place the baking sheet in the oven to keep warm, preferably for only 20 minutes but they can be kept warm for up to an hour.

5. To serve, carefully transfer the hot crab cakes to a serving platter. Garnish the platter with the lemon wedges and sprinkle capers or chopped parsley over the crab cakes.

NOTE: *Panko,* coarse Japanese bread crumbs, are similar to our dry bread crumbs but, because of their flakier texture,

RECIPE REMINDERS

Made for

Prep notes

Don't forget

Special touches

Bring again

PLAN AHEAD

You can make the crab cake mixture and form the crab cakes early in the day. Place them on a lined baking sheet, cover it with plastic wrap, and refrigerate until it's time to cook or travel.

they're a whole lot crunchier. You'll find boxes of *panko* in the supermarket aisle with the Asian ingredients.

BIG BATCH: *You can double this recipe easily. Allow additional time for dredging and frying the crab cakes.*

TO SAUCE OR NOT TO SAUCE?

My husband, John, likes a dab of sauce on top of crab cakes, whereas a squeeze of lemon juice is fine for me. For those of you, like my husband, who want the sauce, here are five based on a cup of mayonnaise.

1. CHILI SAUCE: Add 1 clove of garlic that's been pressed in a garlic press and ½ cup of chili sauce to a cup of mayonnaise.

2. CHIPOTLE SAUCE: Puree 1 canned chipotle pepper, add it to a cup of mayonnaise, and blend well.

3. REMOULADE SAUCE: Chop the green parts of 4 scallions. Add them, plus a rib of minced celery,

2 tablespoons of chopped fresh parsley, 1 teaspoon of paprika, and as much hot pepper sauce as you like to the mayonnaise.

4. TARTAR SAUCE: Add ¼ cup of chopped dill pickle (1 medium-size pickle), ¼ cup of chopped fresh parsley, 2 tablespoons of drained capers, 1 tablespoon of finely chopped onion, and 1 tablespoon of white wine vinegar to the cup of mayonnaise.

5. TARRAGON TARTAR SAUCE: Same as the tartar sauce, but use 2 tablespoons of chopped fresh parsley and 2 tablespoons of chopped fresh tarragon instead of the ¼ cup of parsley.

BLT Canapés

SERVES 8 (MAKES 24 CANAPÉS)

PREP: 30 MINUTES

WHO CAN RESIST THE FLAVORS OF BACON, LETTUCE, and tomato, especially in small canapés that are perfect for prepping ahead of time and assembling at the last minute? The base may be made from any bread you have around—rounds stamped out of good white sandwich bread or slices of a baguette. The bacon mayonnaise is easily prepared in advance so the flavors have a chance to meld. For smaller canapés, cut bread rounds about an inch in diameter and top them with slices of red or yellow grape or cherry tomatoes.

1 cup mayonnaise

8 slices bacon, cooked, drained, and crumbled

$\frac{1}{4}$ loosely packed cup chopped fresh parsley

Cayenne pepper

8 to 12 slices sturdy white sandwich bread

24 slices ($\frac{1}{4}$ inch thick) plum tomatoes
(from about 6 tomatoes), patted dry

$\frac{2}{3}$ cup shredded iceberg lettuce, or 24 small basil leaves

1. Combine the mayonnaise, bacon, and parsley in a small bowl. Season with cayenne pepper to taste. The bacon mayonnaise can be refrigerated, covered, for up to 24 hours.

2. Preheat the oven broiler.

3. Using a small biscuit or round cookie cutter, cut 24 rounds, each $1\frac{1}{2}$ inches in diameter, from the slices of bread. Place the rounds on a baking sheet and broil until lightly browned on one side, 1 to 2 minutes.

TOTE NOTES

Toasting the bread helps to keep the canapés from getting soggy but they will taste best if you assemble them after you arrive.

Tote the bacon mayonnaise in a small plastic container.

Bring the tomatoes, lettuce or basil, and bread rounds in separate plastic bags.

Don't forget—you'll need a platter.

PLAN AHEAD

The bacon mayonnaise can be made a day in advance.

4. When you are ready to serve, arrange the bread rounds on a pretty platter, browned side down. Spread 1 to 2 teaspoons of bacon mayonnaise on each bread round, then top it with a slice of tomato and garnish it with either a teaspoon of shredded lettuce or a small basil leaf. Serve at once.

BIG BATCH: *Make twice the amount of bacon mayonnaise and increase the other ingredients to make a bigger batch of canapés. For an eye-catching presentation, alternate red and yellow tomatoes.*

A DOZEN CROSTINI WITHOUT A RECIPE

Begin with a loaf of French bread. Slice it diagonally into ¼-inch-thick slices, spread these with olive oil, and bake them at 400°F until crisp, about 15 minutes. Then top the toast rounds with any of these for quick, no-fuss crostini.

1. A smear of soft goat cheese and a dab of fig preserves

2. A spoonful of caramelized onions and garlic and a scattering of shredded Parmesan cheese

3. A rubbing of garlic and a slice of roasted red pepper

4. A spoonful of ham salad and a dab of orange marmalade

5. A slice of plum tomato and a dab of pesto

6. A spoonful of sour cream and a scattering of good caviar

7. A slice of creamy blue cheese and a sliver of pear

8. A smear of soft goat cheese and a sliver of steamed asparagus

9. A dab of olive paste and a slice of yellow cherry tomato

10. A spoonful of tuna salad and a grinding of black pepper

11. A spoonful of hummus and a kalamata olive

12. A smear of herbed cream cheese and a fresh rosemary leaf

Jan's Bruschetta

SERVES 15 TO 18 (MAKES 30 TO 36 BRUSCHETTA)

PREP: 25 MINUTES

WHEN THE GIRLS GATHER FOR A DINNER OF ITALIAN food or there is a backyard dinner party, everyone looks forward to these bruschetta. Jan Ramsey of Nashville adapted a tomato sauce recipe from *The New Basics Cookbook* by Julee Rosso and Sheila Lukins to top toasted rounds of French bread, and thus, her bruschetta was born. She uses grape tomatoes because they are sweet and available year round, which means we can enjoy bruschetta anytime. *Molto bene!*

1 loaf French bread (about 10 inches long)

3 to 4 tablespoons olive oil

1 pint grape tomatoes (2 cups)

$\frac{1}{4}$ loosely packed cup chopped fresh basil

$\frac{1}{4}$ cup chopped scallions, green parts only

1 tablespoon chopped fresh oregano

2 medium-size cloves garlic, crushed in a garlic press

$\frac{1}{4}$ teaspoon kosher salt

Freshly ground black pepper

$\frac{1}{4}$ cup or more shredded Parmesan cheese

1. Preheat the broiler.

2. Cut the ends off the French bread, then cut the rest of the loaf into $\frac{1}{4}$-inch crosswise slices. You should have about 36. Place the bread slices on a rimmed baking sheet and brush them with 2 to 3 tablespoons of olive oil. Broil the bread until lightly browned, 1 to 2 minutes (you do not need to turn it). Remove the baking sheet from the oven and set aside.

TOTE NOTES

If your travel time will be less than an hour, you can make the bruschetta at home and transport them in a large rectangular plastic container with a snap-on lid.

Or, assemble the bruschetta once you're at the gathering—tote the tomato topping in a plastic container with a snap-on lid, the bread rounds in a large plastic bag, and the Parmesan in a small one.

Don't forget the platter.

PLAN AHEAD

The topping can be made a day in advance and stored in a covered bowl in the refrigerator.

3. Chop the tomatoes into ¼-inch pieces and place them in a colander to drain off as much liquid as possible. Place the chopped tomato pulp in a mixing bowl and add 1 tablespoon of olive oil and the basil, scallions, oregano, garlic, and salt. Stir to combine, then season with pepper to taste.

4. To serve, place a teaspoonful of the tomato mixture on top of each round of bread and top it with some Parmesan. Carefully transfer the bruschetta to a serving platter and serve.

BIG BATCH: *With some help with the chopping, you can double or triple this recipe for big groups. To save time, toast the bread rounds a day ahead. Keep them in plastic bags.*

**M
E
N
U**

AN ITALIAN NIGHT WITH THE GIRLS

Call your best friends, agree on a date, and gather on the screened porch for dinner. Everyone brings a dish or wine, and tonight it's Italian!

JAN'S BRUSCHETTA, *page 61*
∗
BETH'S MANICOTTI, *page 210*
∗
THE BEST CAESAR SALAD, *page 92*
∗
CRUSTY BREAD
∗
ELENA'S TIRAMISU, *page 438*

R. B.'s Grilled Pizza

SERVES 8 TO 10 (MAKES TWO 8-INCH PIZZAS)

PREP: 15 MINUTES PLUS 1 HOUR FOR THE DOUGH TO RISE
GRILL: 9 TO 10 MINUTES

MY FRIEND R. B. QUINN IS AN OUTSTANDING barbecue cook and a funny guy; he is always coming up with a new twist on an old favorite. R. B. turned us on to grilling pizza instead of baking it in the oven, and once you taste the charred yeasty crust, you'll swear you're in some old pizzeria in Rome. Made with refrigerated fresh pizza dough from the store deli, these pizzas are fun for a party because everyone can add their own toppings (see box, page 64). Take the fixings with you, or bring the finished pizzas on a board, ready to cut into squares and serve. The secret is to have a light hand with the toppings, using well-drained fresh ingredients.

1 pound fresh pizza dough

3 tablespoons olive oil

2 medium-size cloves garlic, crushed in a garlic press

½ teaspoon kosher salt

2 cups diced and drained fresh tomatoes (about 1 pound)

2 cups (8 ounces) shredded mozzarella cheese

1 loosely packed cup fresh basil leaves (optional), torn

1. Remove the dough from the refrigerator, turn it into a lightly oiled mixing bowl, and let it double in size in a warm spot. This takes about an hour.

2. Heat the grill to medium-high. Divide the dough into two pieces and, working with one at a time, punch each down with

TOTE NOTES

Grilled pizza is perfect for a party because it is meant to be shared. Take the fixings with you and prepare the pizzas when you arrive; or bring the pizzas partially cooked and assembled (with the toppings on and ready to finish grilling); or tote the finished, cooked pizzas covered in aluminum foil, ready to slice and eat.

If you're planning on grilling the pizza when you arrive, this is going to take a little coordination with your host. Make sure the grill will be available and that the host has plenty of fuel and counter space. Take the dough in a ball and roll it out when you get there. Tote the toppings in separate containers. Don't forget a rolling pin and platters large enough to hold the pizzas.

your fist on a lightly floured work surface. Roll and stretch the dough to form 2 roughly 8-inch circles. Leaving the work surface floured, carefully transfer the pizza dough to the grill and let cook on one side until the crusts hold their shape and are lightly browned on the bottom, 4 to 5 minutes. Using a spatula, remove the crusts from the grill and take them inside.

3. Arrange the crusts on the floured work surface so that the grilled side is up. In a small bowl combine the olive oil, garlic, and salt, and brush this mixture over the tops of the pizzas. Sprinkle the tomatoes and mozzarella over the pizzas, and scatter the torn basil leaves on top, if desired.

4. Reduce the grill heat to medium and carefully return the pizzas to the grill to cook toppings-side up. Cover the grill and cook the pizzas until the cheese melts and the crust has lightly browned on the bottom, about 5 minutes.

5. Using a spatula, transfer the pizzas to a cutting board and cut them into small serving pieces.

BIG BATCH: *Make as many pizzas as you like, remembering that you'll get two pizzas per pound of dough and that each pizza will generously feed four or possibly more, if it is an appetizer.*

AS YOU LIKE IT

People love to add their own toppings, so if you are grilling the pizzas at the party, bring little containers of fresh herbs, chopped marinated artichokes, crumbled feta—you name it. Just avoid a heavy tomato sauce because it will make the crust soggy.

Tea Sandwiches for Friends

MAKES 6 SANDWICHES EACH OF TOMATO, CUCUMBER, AND CHICKEN, FOR 54 TO 66 TEA SANDWICHES

PREP: 30 MINUTES

I DELIVERED A BOX OF HOMEMADE TEA SANDWICHES TO my friends Alice and Don Schwartz when Don wasn't well. Using tomatoes and cucumbers that I had on hand, and cooking some chicken breast, I easily prepared the little sandwiches and they elicited the sweetest thank-you note from Alice. She revealed that Don remembered standing on a stool at the kitchen counter when he was a boy, watching his mother make sandwiches just like these. Cut into small servings, with the crusts removed, tea sandwiches are dainty and easy to handle. They are beloved by children and anyone who adores a good tea party or a walk down memory lane.

FOR THE JAZZED-UP MAYONNAISE

1 cup store-bought mayonnaise (see Note)

2 tablespoons olive oil

1 tablespoon fresh lemon juice

¼ teaspoon paprika

FOR THE SANDWICHES

36 slices good sandwich bread, such as Pepperidge Farm

36 thin slices peeled cucumber

6 tablespoons chopped fresh mint

Salt and freshly ground black pepper

24 thin slices ripe tomato

6 tablespoons chopped fresh basil

1 to 1½ cups shredded freshly cooked chicken breast

6 tablespoons watercress, stems removed

TOTE NOTES

You can tote tea sandwiches in just about anything—a pretty basket, a plastic container, or even a cardboard shirt box lined with waxed paper. If you are taking the sandwiches to a friend, be sure you tote them in a container that doesn't have to be returned.

To keep the flavors separated, pack each kind of sandwich together.

Bring along a plate of cookies as well and you'll have the makings for a nice tea party.

PLAN AHEAD

When well wrapped, tea sandwiches can be made 4 hours in advance.

1. Prepare the jazzed-up mayonnaise: Place the store-bought mayonnaise, olive oil, lemon juice, and paprika in a small bowl and stir until well combined. Set the mayonnaise aside.

2. Make the sandwiches: Remove the crusts from the bread by holding the slices together and cutting down the sides of the loaf with a serrated knife. Place the slices of bread on a work surface and spread one side of each with about 1½ teaspoons of the mayonnaise mixture.

3. Arrange 6 slices of cucumber on top of a slice of bread. Sprinkle 1 tablespoon of the mint over the cucumber, then season it with salt and pepper to taste. Place a slice of bread, mayonnaise side down, on top of the mint and lightly press down on it. Cut the sandwich into 4 triangles by making 2 corner-to-corner cuts through it. Make 5 more sandwiches with the remaining cucumber and mint and cut them into triangles. You now have 24 cucumber tea sandwiches.

4. Arrange 4 slices of tomato on top of a slice of bread. Sprinkle 1 tablespoon of the basil over the tomato and season it with salt and pepper, if desired. Place a slice of bread, mayonnaise side down, on top of the basil and lightly press down on it. Cut the sandwich into 4 squares or 2 halves. Make 5 more sandwiches with the remaining tomato and basil and cut them into squares or halves.

5. Spoon the shredded chicken on top of 6 slices of bread, dividing it evenly among them. Sprinkle 1 tablespoon of watercress over each chicken sandwich, then top each with one of the remaining 6 slices of bread, mayonnaise side down. Lightly press down on a chicken sandwich, then cut it into 3 equal rectangular sticks. Repeat with the remaining chicken sandwiches.

6. If not serving the sandwiches immediately, line a large plastic container or two containers with waxed paper and arrange the sandwiches inside. Place a damp paper towel on top of the sandwiches. Cover the container and refrigerate the sandwiches until ready to serve; they will keep for up to 4 hours.

NOTE: There is nothing I love better than homemade mayonnaise, but it's not something I tend to make much anymore. With raw egg yolks, homemade mayonnaise is not a safe spread for sandwiches that might sit out on the party platter. Instead, begin with a good commercial mayonnaise because it has an acid content that is sufficiently high to prevent the mayonnaise from posing a food safety threat. Store-bought mayo does, however, improve with a little doctoring up. I like Duke's mayonnaise for tea sandwiches, and to give it more of a homemade taste, I add a little olive oil, lemon juice, and paprika. Duke's is available in stores only in the southeast. Hellmann's mayonnaise is a little sweeter, but it is also a good base for these sandwiches.

BIG BATCH: *Make as many sandwiches as you like, counting on one whole sandwich per person.*

SANDWICH STORAGE

The trick to keeping sandwiches fresh is one I learned from my mom. She would make a tray of sandwiches for a party and cover them with damp paper towels. Then she would cover the damp towels with plastic wrap and secure it well around the edges. The sandwiches would stay fresh and moist and not dry out in the refrigerator.

RECIPE REMINDERS

Made for

Prep notes

Don't forget

Special touches

Bring again

MAKE ANY SEASON SOUP SEASON

Soup is a terrific crowd-pleaser, but it usually isn't offered up in the "What can I bring?" mix. I hope the selections here change that. These soups are easy to prepare and tote and can serve large groups or small family gatherings.

For summer, I had to include gazpacho. During July or August, when cucumbers, tomatoes, and bell peppers are in the market and on your counter in abundance, you've got the immediate makings for this cold soup. The same is true with Julia's Chilled Zucchini Soup. It's a great way to make use of those plentiful squash from the garden. Both soups can be served in bowls at a sit-down dinner or spooned into shot glasses or demitasse cups for a large stand-around crowd.

I had to share our family's vegetable soup, since it's the ultimate response to "What can I bring?"—ready for heating up on the stove or stashing in the freezer for future meals. The hearty potato soup and Tuscan bean are also cold-weather favorites, just right for packing in a thermos and taking to a pregame tailgate party.

Don't miss the black bean soup and Missy's Chicken Tortellini Soup—my kids love it. And for spicy palates, try the Chicken Taco Soup and, of course, the chili. This is a meaty rendition, slowly baked in the oven.

Any way you serve it, be sure to bring the soup!

Summertime Gazpacho

**SERVES 14 TO 16 AS AN APPETIZER; 8 AS A FIRST COURSE;
6 AS A MAIN COURSE (MAKES 7 TO 8 CUPS)**

PREP: 25 MINUTES ✳ CHILL: AT LEAST 2 HOURS

W HEN THE HEAT OF JULY AND AUGUST LEAVES
your palate clueless as to what to eat, think
gazpacho. Make gazpacho. Tote gazpacho.
Serve gazpacho. It's very versatile. Garnish it with a dab
of sour cream, a crunch of good croutons, a smidgen of
crabmeat, or a showering of chopped fresh dill. Gazpacho
is perfect for personalizing, so feel free to adapt this to
suit your taste. Save any leftovers, as they are delicious
the next day. Plus, it makes a terrific sauce for grilled fish.

2 cups cucumber chunks, preferably Kirby or hothouse
   (seedless English; see Note)

1 cup red bell pepper chunks

3 cups coarsely chopped seeded tomatoes

½ cup minced red onion or Vidalia onion

1 large clove garlic, crushed in a garlic press

3 cups tomato juice

¼ cup extra-virgin olive oil

2 tablespoons red wine vinegar

1 teaspoon kosher salt, or more to taste

Dash of freshly ground black pepper

Dash of red pepper flakes (optional)

½ cup chopped mixed fresh herbs,
   such as parsley, dill, oregano, tarragon

1 cup sour cream, for garnish

6 to 8 pitted kalamata olives (optional),
   for garnish

**TOTE
NOTES**

*Tote the gazpacho in
glass jars or thermal
containers. Bring along
the sour cream and
olives, if desired, in
separate containers.*

   *While in transit, keep
everything well chilled in
a cooler with ice.*

PLAN AHEAD

*The gazpacho can
be made a day in
advance—in fact,
it's best that way.*

**RECIPE
REMINDERS**

Made for

Prep notes

Don't forget

Special touches

Bring again

1. Place the cucumber chunks in the bowl of a food processor fitted with a steel blade. Process until chopped but not pureed, 7 or 8 pulses. Transfer the cucumbers to a large glass bowl. Add the red bell pepper to the processor and pulse until chopped, 6 to 7 pulses, then transfer the bell pepper to the glass bowl. Add the tomatoes to the processor and pulse until chopped, 7 to 8 pulses. Transfer the tomatoes to the glass bowl.

2. Add the onion, garlic, tomato juice, olive oil, vinegar, salt, black pepper, red pepper flakes, if desired, and herbs to the glass bowl and stir to combine. Cover the bowl with plastic wrap and refrigerate for at least 2 hours, preferably overnight, before serving.

3. To serve, ladle the gazpacho into bowls or, if serving a crowd, into fun martini glasses or demitasse cups. Garnish the soup with a dollop of sour cream and an olive, if desired.

NOTE: If you use Kirby or hothouse cucumbers you won't have to seed them. You can use regular cucumbers, but if they are thick and waxed, you will need to peel as well as seed them.

BIG BATCH: *It's best to make gazpacho one batch at a time. The more you double up ingredients the less control you have over the consistency, and it is easy to overprocess (puree) some vegetables and underprocess others.*

SOUPS ON THE GO

Since the invention of the thermos, toting warm soup to school or work has been simple and welcome. I remember that smug feeling when I ate my mom's homemade vegetable soup right from the thermos at the lunchroom table, and my friends kept asking longingly what smelled so good.

But what if you want to carry a large amount of soup for a gathering? You don't so much need a thermos as you do a large cooking pot with handles, or my favorite— the slow cooker. After the soup or chili has cooked and it is still warm, ladle it into the ceramic insert of a slow cooker and top it with the lid. Then, either secure the lid with tape or wrap a clean bath towel around the container to prevent spills while you travel. Once you're at the party, you can place the ceramic container back into the slow cooker, plug it in, and set the temperature on low to keep the soup warm. Or you can ladle the soup into a cooking pot and gently reheat it on the stove.

Pour cold soups into large, clean glass jars and store them in the fridge until it's time to travel. Transport them in a cooler surrounded by ice.

And remember that when serving soup, it's fun to serve crunchy things alongside. Pass a basket of tortilla chips for chili and any Southwestern soups, try melba rounds and toasted French bread slices with cold soups, and offer hearty corn bread or garlic bread for bean and vegetable soups.

One last note—when you are bringing soup, be sure your host knows ahead of time so the soup bowls and spoons will be ready. If you plan on serving soup in something a little more playful, be sure to bring enough containers, whether they are demitasse cups or shot glasses or . . . you name it.

Julia's Chilled Zucchini Soup

SERVES 12 AS AN APPETIZER; 6 AS A FIRST COURSE (MAKES 6 CUPS)

PREP: 15 MINUTES ✳ COOK: 25 MINUTES ✳ CHILL: 6 HOURS

TOTE NOTES

Toting the soup in a thermos will keep it cool. Or, transport it in a glass jar.

Don't forget the half-and-half to stir in at the last minute; you can carry it in a small jar. And bring the chopped parsley garnish and the toast rounds or melba toast in plastic bags.

PLAN AHEAD

The soup can be refrigerated, covered, for up to two days.

MY FRIEND WYETH BURGESS IS ORIGINALLY FROM Memphis, Tennessee, and that is where this wonderful cold zucchini soup originated. Her friend Julia Maddux created it, and it has become a soothing staple to tote to new mothers, people home from the hospital, or those moving into a new home on a hot day. For bridal luncheons and small dinner parties, the soup is perfect because it is light, elegant, and refreshing, especially in the summer months.

1 quart (4 cups) low-sodium chicken broth
3 to 4 packed cups coarsely grated zucchini
    (1 pound; from 2 medium-large zucchini)
1½ cups chopped sweet onion (1 large onion)
1 package (8 ounces) cream cheese, cut into 1-inch cubes
Salt and white pepper
Hot pepper sauce
¼ cup half-and-half
2 tablespoons chopped fresh parsley, for garnish
Toasted French bread rounds (see box, page 19)
    or melba toast, for serving

1. Place the chicken broth in a large saucepan and bring to a simmer over medium heat. Add the zucchini and onion and cook, covered, until the vegetables are fork-tender, about 15 minutes. Remove the lid and, with the soup at a simmer, add the cubes of cream cheese, one at a time, whisking until they are incorporated. Let the soup simmer until thickened, about 10 minutes, then turn off the heat. Season the soup with salt, white pepper, and hot sauce to taste.

2. Working in batches, ladle the warm soup into a food processor or blender and process until almost smooth, about 15 seconds. Flecks of zucchini should still be visible. Pour the soup into a glass storage dish and refrigerate, uncovered, until cooled. Then cover the dish with plastic wrap and refrigerate at least 6 hours or overnight.

3. Just before serving, stir the half-and-half into the soup. Ladle it into demitasse cups or bowls and garnish with the parsley. Serve with toasted rounds of French bread or melba toast on the side.

BIG BATCH: *You can double this soup in a very large cooking pot; take care to thoroughly whisk in all the cream cheese so that the soup thickens evenly. Or, you can make one batch of soup at a time as the preparation time is minimal. To speed the chilling, refrigerate the soup in a shallow container, then transfer it to a larger, taller container for storage.*

RECIPE REMINDERS

Made for

Prep notes

Don't forget

Special touches

Bring again

House Favorite Vegetable Soup

SERVES ABOUT 8 AS A FIRST COURSE (MAKES ABOUT 9 CUPS)

PREP: 20 MINUTES ✶ COOK: 1 ½ HOURS

TOTE NOTES

You can tote the vegetable soup in glass or plastic containers (wait until the soup has cooled before ladling it into them). Then reheat the soup when you get to the gathering.

If the soup is a gift, attach a label with the name of the recipe, the ingredients, and instructions for bringing the soup to a boil before serving.

PLAN AHEAD

The soup can be refrigerated for up to three days.

Achapter on soups that travel well wouldn't be complete without a great vegetable soup recipe. Similar to the recipe I shared in *The Dinner Doctor,* the one here contains ground sirloin for flavor, a leek because it cooks down beautifully in soups, and some tomato sauce. The tomato sauce helps the soup thicken and contributes a little sweetness. This is an all-around soup, perfect for wintertime crowds, nice to keep in the freezer for last-minute dinners, and a comforting gift with a loaf of bread for families after the death of a loved one.

1 tablespoon olive oil

8 ounces ground beef sirloin

1 leek, white part only, cleaned well and thinly sliced

2 medium-size cloves garlic, sliced

Kosher salt and freshly ground black pepper

1 can (28 ounces) diced tomatoes, undrained

1 can (15 ounces) tomato sauce

1 can (about 14 ounces) beef broth (optional)

2 cups frozen vegetables of your choice (I use a mixture of corn, carrots, peas, and green beans)

3 bay leaves

1. Place the olive oil in a large soup pot over medium-high heat. Crumble in the ground sirloin, breaking it up with a wooden spoon. Cook, stirring, until the beef browns all over and is cooked through, about 3 minutes.

2. Stir in the leek and garlic, then season with salt and pepper to taste. Cook, stirring, 1 minute longer.

3. Stir in the diced tomatoes. Fill the diced-tomato can with water and add this to the pot. Stir in the tomato sauce and add the can of beef broth, if desired, or fill the tomato sauce can with water again and add this to the pot.

4. Stir in the frozen vegetables and bay leaves. Let the soup come to a boil, then cook, stirring, for 3 to 4 minutes. Reduce the heat to medium-low, cover the pot, and let the soup simmer until thickened, 1 to 1½ hours. Taste for seasoning, adding more salt and/or pepper if needed. Remove and discard the bay leaves before serving.

BIG BATCH: *If you have a large stock pot, this recipe doubles and triples well.*

RECIPE
REMINDERS

Made for

Prep notes

Don't forget

Special touches

Bring again

Jackie's Potato Soup

SERVES 8 TO 10 AS A MAIN COURSE (MAKES ABOUT 10 CUPS)

PREP: 45 MINUTES ✳ COOK: 15 TO 20 MINUTES

TOTE NOTES

Tote the potato soup in plastic containers and reheat it at the gathering. Bring along separate plastic bags of crumbled bacon, chopped scallions, and/or shredded cheese for garnishes, if desired.

PLAN AHEAD

The potato soup can be refrigerated for up to three days.

I F YOU'RE ASKED TO FEED A CROWD, THIS IS THE SOUP FOR the job. It is satisfying and comforting, yet colorful and fun. The recipe comes from Jackie Drake of Bardstown, Kentucky. I like to use most any potatoes I have on hand, but the best taste comes from Yukon Gold potatoes or another flavorful potato that will not fall completely apart while cooking. Garnish the soup with crumbled bacon, chopped scallion, and shredded Cheddar cheese, and people will be lining up for a serving.

FOR THE SOUP

6 cups peeled and diced (½-inch cubes) potatoes

1 cup shredded carrots (from 3 medium-size carrots)

½ cup chopped sweet onion

1 tablespoon chopped fresh parsley, or 1 teaspoon parsley flakes

2 chicken-flavored bouillon cubes

½ teaspoon salt

¼ teaspoon freshly ground black pepper

2 cups water

¼ cup all-purpose flour

3 cups 2-percent reduced-fat milk

2 cups (8 ounces) shredded Colby cheese, or 10 ounces processed American cheese, such as Velveeta

FOR THE GARNISHES

8 slices bacon (optional), cooked and crumbled

½ cup chopped scallions, green parts only (optional)

1 cup (4 ounces) shredded sharp Cheddar or Colby cheese (optional)

1. Place the potatoes, carrots, onion, parsley, bouillon cubes, salt, and pepper in a large pot. Add 2 cups of water, stir, and bring to a boil over medium-high heat. Reduce the heat and let simmer, uncovered, until the potatoes are soft, 8 to 10 minutes.

2. Meanwhile, place the flour and ½ cup of the milk in a small bowl and whisk to mix, then set aside.

3. When the potatoes are done, don't drain them; push them to one side of the pot. Working over low heat, whisk the flour and milk mixture into the potato broth. Cook, stirring, until the broth thickens. Add the remaining 2½ cups of milk and the 2 cups of cheese and cook, stirring, until the cheese is melted and smooth, 4 to 5 minutes. Then, if desired, mash the potatoes with a potato masher to help them blend into the soup.

4. When ready to serve, ladle the soup into bowls and garnish each serving with some bacon, scallions, and/or some of the 1 cup of cheese, if desired.

BIG BATCH: *You could double this recipe in a very large pot, or just make two or three batches of the soup for a crowd.*

READY, SET, SERVE

Serve soup in wide, shallow soup bowls or, for fun, in little mugs. For a casual buffet, you can ladle the soup right from the pot into the bowls. For a more festive and formal buffet, spoon the soup into nice tea cups, garnish it, and arrange the cups on a platter.

RECIPE REMINDERS

Made for

Prep notes

Don't forget

Special touches

Bring again

Tuscan White Bean Soup

SERVES 8 AS A FIRST OR MAIN COURSE (MAKES ABOUT 8 CUPS)

PREP: 20 MINUTES PLUS 1 HOUR FOR SOAKING THE BEANS ✳ COOK: 2 TO 3 HOURS

TOTE NOTES

To tote the whole batch of soup to a gathering, ladle it into the container of a slow cooker or take it in a cooking pot with handles. Wrap either of these with a clean towel to absorb any spills along the way. Reheat the soup over medium heat, stirring, for 8 to 10 minutes.

PLAN AHEAD

The bean soup can be made a day in advance and stored, covered, in the refrigerator. It also freezes well in plastic containers or in quart jars after it has cooled down. Be sure to leave an inch of space at the top of the container if you are freezing the soup, as it might expand when frozen. Thaw in the refrigerator.

I WAS RAISED ON WHITE BEAN SOUP SIMMERED ALL afternoon with ham hocks. But while the flavor of bean soup cooked with ham makes me nostalgic, I prefer to prepare bean soups with chicken stock, olive oil, and chopped vegetables. It is more Tuscan in style, and I feel it's a healthier and happier rendition. This all-season soup travels well to tailgate and Super Bowl parties and to new neighbors hungry for a comforting meal.

> 1 pound dried white (great northern) beans, picked over
> 3 to 4 cups boiling water, plus 4 cups cool water
> 3 tablespoons olive oil
> 1 cup chopped onion (1 medium-size onion)
> 1 cup chopped carrots (2 medium-size carrots)
> 4 medium-size cloves garlic, sliced
> 1 quart (4 cups) low-sodium chicken broth
> 3 chicken-flavored bouillon cubes
> 2 bay leaves
> 1 big sprig fresh rosemary (optional)
> **Salt and freshly ground black pepper (optional)**

1. Rinse the beans in a colander and place them in a large heatproof bowl.

2. Pour enough boiling water over the beans to cover them by 1 inch. Let the beans soak in the hot water for 1 hour, then rinse and drain them. Set the beans aside.

3. Place the olive oil in a large heavy pot over medium-low heat. Add the onion, carrots, and garlic and stir to combine.

Cook until the onion and carrots soften, but don't brown, stirring constantly, 5 to 6 minutes.

4. Add the soaked beans, the chicken broth, 4 cups of cool water, and the bouillon cubes, bay leaves, and rosemary sprig, if desired, to the pot and bring to a boil over medium-high heat. Reduce the heat and let the soup simmer, covered, until the beans are soft, 2 to 3 hours.

5. Taste the soup for seasoning, adding salt and/or pepper if needed. To thicken the soup, mash a quarter of the beans up against the side of the pot, using the back of a large spoon. Remove and discard the rosemary sprig, if any. Stir the soup before serving.

BIG BATCH: *You can cook two batches of the soup at one time, in a very large pot, taking care to stir the contents well. To lower the temperature of the soup quickly so that you can safely store it, refrigerate the soup first in shallow containers, then transfer it to a deeper storage container and return it to the refrigerator.*

FALL FOOTBALL TAILGATE PARTY

Crisp fall air makes you want to head to the nearest football game, pull down the car tailgate, and picnic with friends. Divvy up this menu of totable foods. The soup will stay warm in a thermos.

LAYERED CRABMEAT STACK, *page 54*
✳
CUBAN CHICKEN LEGS, *page 223*
✳
TUSCAN WHITE BEAN SOUP
✳
CHOCOLATE CHIP BROWNIES
WITH CREAM CHEESE "GOO," *page 404*

M
E
N
U

RECIPE REMINDERS

Made for

Prep notes

Don't forget

Special touches

Bring again

Weekend Black Bean Soup

SERVES 10 TO 12 AS A FIRST COURSE; 6 AS A MAIN COURSE (MAKES 10 CUPS)

PREP: 30 MINUTES ✳ COOK: 3¾ TO 4 HOURS

TOTE NOTES

Tote the bean soup in plastic containers and reheat it over medium-low heat for 8 to 10 minutes, stirring occasionally, before serving.

Take along a container of sour cream and some minced red onion and chopped cilantro in separate plastic bags for garnishing the soup, if desired.

PLAN AHEAD

The bean soup can be made ahead and refrigerated for up to three days or frozen for up to two months.

MAKE THIS SOUP ON A WEEKEND WHEN YOU'VE GOT the time to enjoy its wonderful aroma. I have tasted many variations of black bean soup, but this one has the fullest flavor. A puree of onion, bell pepper, and parsley, as well as a bit of sherry, oregano, and cumin—my favorite flavors—makes sure of that! Take this soup to a good friend. Or make a potful and invite friends for dinner. It is the perfect first course or, with crusty bread and a salad, a meal on its own. By pouring boiling water over the beans and letting them soak beforehand, you reduce the cooking time.

FOR THE SOUP

1 pound dried black beans, picked over

3 to 4 cups boiling water, plus 3 quarts cool water

3 chicken-flavored bouillon cubes

3 bay leaves

½ small onion, peeled

½ cup fresh parsley

¼ small green bell pepper, cored and seeded

2 tablespoons olive oil

6 medium-size cloves garlic, minced

1 to 2 tablespoons dry sherry

1 teaspoon dried oregano

1 teaspoon ground cumin

Salt and freshly ground black pepper

FOR THE GARNISHES

Minced red onion (optional)

Chopped fresh cilantro (optional)

Sour cream (optional)

1. Rinse the beans in a colander and place them in a large bowl.

2. Pour enough of the boiling water over the beans to cover them by 1 inch. Let the beans soak in the hot water for 20 minutes, then rinse and drain them.

3. Place the soaked beans, bouillon cubes, bay leaves, and 3 quarts of cool water in a large soup pot and stir to combine. Let come to a boil over medium-high heat. Reduce the heat to medium-low and let the beans simmer, covered, until they are nearly tender, about 3 hours.

4. Meanwhile, place the onion, parsley, and bell pepper in a blender or food processor and pulse until smooth, 8 to 10 pulses. Set the onion puree aside.

5. Place the olive oil in a large frying pan over medium heat. Add the garlic and cook until soft, about 1 minute. Add the onion puree and cook, stirring constantly until softened, 2 to 3 minutes.

6. After the beans have cooked for 3 hours, stir the garlic and onion mixture into them. Add the sherry, oregano, and cumin, then season with salt and black pepper to taste. Let the soup simmer, uncovered, over medium-low heat until the beans are tender and the soup is thick, 45 minutes to 1 hour. Remove and discard the bay leaves before serving the soup garnished with minced onion, chopped cilantro, and/or sour cream, if desired.

BIG BATCH: *This soup is best made one batch at a time. Black beans take a little longer to cook than other beans and are not as easy to double batch.*

RECIPE REMINDERS

Made for

Prep notes

Don't forget

Special touches

Bring again

Missy's Chicken Tortellini Soup

SERVES 8 AS A MAIN COURSE (MAKES 8 TO 10 CUPS)

PREP: 15 MINUTES * **COOK: 20 TO 25 MINUTES**

TOTE NOTES

Tote this soup in quart-size jars or in plastic containers with lids and reheat it over medium-low heat for 5 to 7 minutes, stirring often.

Bring along the Parmesan cheese in a plastic bag for spooning on top once the soup is hot. You can keep this soup warm in a slow cooker once you are on-site.

PLAN AHEAD

The soup can be made the day before you plan on serving it. Once it has cooled down, cover and refrigerate it.

MY TENNIS FRIEND MISSY MYERS HERE IN NASHVILLE was asking me about the book I was working on, and when I described it to her, a big smile crossed her face. "I've got to give you my chicken and tortellini soup recipe. It is my favorite dish to bring to other people." Well, Missy followed through with the recipe, and my family really enjoyed it when I tested it. We ate the soup for two nights—it's a meal in one pot, needing only some crusty bread on the side. As is my nature, I tinkered with Missy's recipe a bit, adding fresh spinach instead of frozen. As easy to prepare midweek as it is on weekends, simmer up a pot to take to a friend or make it for your own family.

2 tablespoons olive oil

1 cup finely chopped onion (1 medium-size onion)

3 medium-size cloves garlic, minced

8 cups (2 quarts) low-sodium chicken broth

1 can (28 ounces) crushed tomatoes

2 teaspoons dried Italian seasoning

4 cups shredded roast chicken (from a 3-pound whole roast chicken, skin and bones removed)

1 package (9 ounces) fresh cheese tortellini

Salt and freshly ground black pepper

1 package (5 ounces) baby spinach, stems removed

1 cup (4 ounces) shredded or grated Parmesan cheese, for serving

1. Place the olive oil in a large, heavy soup pot over medium heat. Add the onion and garlic, reduce the heat to medium-low, and cook, stirring until soft, 3 to 4 minutes. Stir in the chicken broth, tomatoes, and Italian seasoning. Cover the pot and let simmer until the flavors develop, about 10 minutes.

2. Stir in the chicken and tortellini and season with salt and pepper to taste. Let the soup simmer, uncovered until the tortellini have cooked, 7 to 8 minutes. Add the spinach, and cook, stirring, until wilted, 1 to 2 minutes. Ladle the soup into bowls and garnish it with the Parmesan.

BIG BATCH: *You can double batch this recipe; use a very large pot and, once the soup is cooked, chill it in smaller, shallow containers.*

WHAT EVERY (BUSY) GIRL WANTS: A BOWL OF SOUP OR . . .

. . . a well-stocked freezer full of homemade soups, ready for reheating or toting to friends. Seriously, the best hosts may have a calm reserve and a sense of style, but they frequently also have a full and organized freezer. One of my favorite freezer items is leftover soup, which I portion out and label for future meals. The best leftovers to freeze are vegetable and bean soups and chili. Chilled soups such as gazpacho don't freeze well.

Soups that contain a lot of potato, pasta, or rice don't taste great after freezing either.

Here is how I freeze soup: I recycle heavy-duty heat-proof and freezer-proof quart jars or buy them at the supermarket. I pack cooled soup into these jars, leaving about an inch of space at the top in case the soup expands when frozen. I seal the jars well and label them with a permanent marker. Most soups can be frozen for up to four months.

RECIPE REMINDERS

Made for

Prep notes

Don't forget

Special touches

Bring again

Chicken Taco Soup

SERVES 8 AS A MAIN COURSE (MAKES ABOUT 8 TO 10 CUPS)

PREP: 15 MINUTES ✳ COOK: 1 HOUR

PEOPLE LOVE THIS SOUP. THE FLAVORS APPEAL TO adults and teens—and children, too, as long as the seasoning isn't too spicy. The preparation time is minimal because the soup is made mostly from canned ingredients easily stocked in your pantry. When you buy canned tomatoes with chiles, select the mild kind if you are cooking for children, or just use plain diced tomatoes. If you are serving this to a crowd of adults, try one can of mild and one of hot tomatoes and chiles. The soup is perfect at any time of the year, but it fits Halloween suppers, tailgate picnics, and Super Bowl parties especially well.

2 tablespoons olive oil

1 cup chopped onion (1 medium-size onion)

2 medium-size cloves garlic, sliced

1 can (about 14 ounces) low-sodium chicken broth

1 can (15 ounces) chili-seasoned beans, undrained

1 can (about 15 ounces) black beans, undrained

1 can (about 15 ounces) corn, drained

2 cans (10 ounces each) diced tomatoes with green chiles, undrained

2 skinless, boneless chicken breast halves (8 ounces each)

2 tablespoons taco seasoning

1 cup crushed tortilla chips, plus whole tortilla chips for serving

1 cup (4 ounces) shredded Cheddar cheese, for garnish

1. Place the olive oil in a large soup pot over medium heat. Add the onion and garlic and cook, stirring, until softened but not brown, about 3 minutes. Add the chicken broth, chili-seasoned beans, black beans, corn, tomatoes with chiles, chicken breasts, and taco seasoning and stir to combine. Increase the heat to medium-high and bring to a boil, then reduce the heat to medium-low and let the soup simmer, covered, until the chicken has cooked through, 40 to 45 minutes. Remove the pot from the heat and transfer the chicken to a plate to cool for 15 minutes.

2. When the chicken is cool enough to handle, shred it and return it to the pot. Add the crushed tortilla chips and stir to mix. Cook the soup, uncovered, over medium heat until it thickens and the chips soften, about 15 minutes. Spoon the soup into bowls, garnish it with the Cheddar cheese, and serve with tortilla chips alongside.

BIG BATCH: *The soup doubles well, made in a large pot. If you do double the recipe, slice the chicken breast halves in half again before cooking so that they have a chance to cook through.*

RECIPE REMINDERS

Made for

Prep notes

Don't forget

Special touches

Bring again

Mighty Fine Texas Chili

SERVES 8 TO 10 (MAKES ABOUT 10 TO 12 CUPS)

PREP: 25 MINUTES * COOK: 2 HOURS

TOTE NOTES

Tote the chili to the gathering in a slow cooker. When you arrive, plug in the cooker and set it on low, and the chili will stay warm while people help themselves.

Don't forget the garnishes; bring the chopped red onion and cilantro in separate plastic bags and the sour cream in its container, then arrange them in small bowls on a pretty platter next to the chili.

PLAN AHEAD

If you make the chili a day or two in advance, the flavors will intensify. Store it in a large plastic container, covered, in the refrigerator.

I LOVE LE CREUSET POTS BECAUSE THEY ARE HEAVY AND keep the heat at a gentle, even temperature so food does not stick or burn. They are the best pots for cooking long-simmering soups and chilis, especially when you want to let them cook without constantly having to check the oven. This is a meaty Texas-style chili and, true to Texas tradition, the pinto beans are optional. Once the chili comes to a boil, the oven can do the magic. When the chili is done cooking, spoon it into bowls, garnish it with chopped onion, sour cream, and cilantro, and be sure to have fresh jalapeño peppers on hand for the Texans. If you don't have a Le Creuset pot, you can use a Dutch oven.

FOR THE CHILI

2 tablespoons olive oil

1¼ pounds lean coarsely ground beef

1 cup chopped onion (1 medium-size onion)

4 medium-size cloves garlic, minced

2 tablespoons chili powder

2 tablespoons all-purpose flour

2 tablespoons ground cumin

1 tablespoon dried oregano

1 quart (4 cups) beef broth

1 can (14½ ounces) diced tomatoes, undrained

1 can (10 ounces) diced tomatoes with green chiles

About 3 cans (about 15 ounces each) pinto beans (optional; see Note), rinsed and drained

FOR THE GARNISHES

Chopped red onion

Sour cream

Cilantro sprigs

1. Place a rack in the center of the oven and preheat the oven to 300°F.

2. Place the olive oil in a large, heavy soup pot over medium-high heat. Crumble in the ground beef, breaking it up with a wooden spoon. Cook, stirring, until the beef browns all over and is nearly cooked through, 2 to 3 minutes. Add the onion and garlic and cook, stirring, 2 minutes longer. Reduce the heat to medium and stir in the chili powder, flour, cumin, and oregano. Slowly add the beef broth, stirring until it is incorporated. Stir in the diced tomatoes and the tomatoes with chiles.

MENU

SUPER BOWL WITH THE NEIGHBORS

Make a pot of chili, invite the neighbors over for the game, and dig into a fun assortment of munchies. TV football can be nail-biting entertainment, so have plenty of foods to crunch and foods to dip to get rid of all that nervous energy.

TWELVE-LAYER TACO DIP, *page 16*
✳
DEBORAH'S HOT SPINACH DIP, *page 26*
✳
TORTILLA CHIPS
✳
R. B.'S GRILLED PIZZA, *page 63*
✳
MIGHTY FINE TEXAS CHILI
✳
CHOCOLATE BUTTERMILK SHEET CAKE, *page 338*

RECIPE REMINDERS

Made for

Prep notes

Don't forget

Special touches

Bring again

GREAT GO-WITHS

Don't forget these side dishes when rounding up friends for a weekend chili feast.

✳

MEXICAN CORN BREAD
(page 462)

or

CHEESY GARLIC BREAD
(page 333)

✳

JOHN'S HOMEMADE COLESLAW
(page 126)

✳

MY FAVORITE KEY LIME PIE
(page 414)

3. Cover the pot and carefully transfer it to the oven on the center rack. Bake the chili until it thickens nicely and has cooked down, about 2 hours.

4. Transfer the pot to the stove and carefully remove the lid, watching out for the escaping steam. Stir in as many cans of pinto beans as desired, then replace the lid. Cook the chili over low heat, stirring occasionally, until the beans heat through. Serve the chili garnished with red onion, sour cream, and cilantro sprigs.

NOTE: One can of pinto beans will give the chili a hint of beans. Two cans are for those who like beans in their chili. And three cans of pinto beans are for those who *must* have chili with beans.

WANT SOME MORE IDEAS FOR GARNISHES? Set out some shredded lettuce, chopped tomatoes, and shredded cheese. And, for those who like it hot, chopped fresh jalapeño peppers.

BIG BATCH: *You can make a double batch of the chili in a very large pot. Cooked on top of the stove, it will take 3 to 4 hours; stir the chili occasionally.*

WATCHING THE CLOCK?

If you are going to be out of the house for longer than two hours, this chili will cook down and taste delicious when baked for about 3 hours at 250°F. And, if you're pressed for time, you can cook the chili at a simmer on top of the stove, but be careful to stir it often. Cooked that way, the chili should be ready in an hour and a half.

THE BEST SALADS

When serving a salad with a grilled steak or a bowl of pasta, often all you need are fresh greens, a dash of salt, and a drizzle of good olive oil. And yet, when you bring a salad to a covered dish supper, dinner party, picnic, or office luncheon, you don't want a minimalist affair. You want a salad with accessories.

You want a salad that turns heads the minute you remove the plastic wrap and add the toppings. It needs to be visually exciting—with bright fresh colors like red and orange and green— and it needs to be exciting to eat, as well. The textures should vary from crunchy to luscious, and the flavors should range from sweet and tangy to salty and rich—think crisp greens, piquant vinaigrettes, creamy salty cheeses, sweet-tart fruits, and a scattering of toasted nuts.

This chapter is packed with what I think are the best salads around. I am a salad lover, and I gravitate toward the salads on restaurant menus and potluck tables alike. I adore salads on the side and salads as the main course. I like interesting greens with some real thought put into them, salads with a plan.

This chapter is filled with those salads, whether they are served along with a main course or they *are* the main course. They are totally accessorized from the greens to the vinaigrette to the topping, all in sync with one another. You'll find a Big Green Salad with Orange, Avocado, and Red Wine Vinaigrette; a Baby Blue Salad with Sweet and Spicy Pecans; Spinach Salad with Mahogany

Roasted Mushrooms and Onions; and Roasted Beet Salad with Walnuts and Blue Cheese Dressing, all perfect for potlucks. They offer bright colors, fresh flavors, and easy assembly on-site.

This chapter is also filled with "whimsical" salads I love to pull together when the ingredients are in season and the mood strikes. I make Arugula Salad with Grape Tomatoes and Parmesan Shavings when my friend Bill has a bumper crop of arugula. The Tomato, Mozzarella, and Basil Salad with Fresh Tomato Vinaigrette is just perfect when summer tomatoes are here and the basil in the garden is a foot tall. White Corn Salad with Fresh Herb Vinaigrette is best made with sweet summer corn, and Waldorf Salad is best with crisp fall apples.

And then there are salads that are neither grand nor driven by the season, but are perennial potluck favorites: sweet-and-sour broccoli salad (try my new, lighter twist), John's Homemade Coleslaw, Southern Potato Salad, Old-Fashioned Macaroni Salad, and cold gelatin salads with vegetables or fruit. People love these salads, and there is a reason they have been around for so long on our picnic tables—they are delicious! Take them to big parties where fried chicken and burgers and ribs are being served, and be ready to tote home an empty bowl.

Whether they feature the seasons' best or make us nostalgic for our childhood favorites, the salads in this chapter are easy to assemble and don't take much last-minute fussing. For green salads this means the dressing can be made in advance and stored in a jar, the toppings might be cut and placed in baggies, and the greens can be rinsed, wrapped, and chilled until serving time. Pasta salads are a great do-ahead, with everything tossed together and wrapped to go. The same goes for tabbouleh and for coleslaw, both of which improve in flavor if you make them ahead of time.

A number of these recipes came to me from friends or by word of mouth. Some may seem similar to recipes you have tried before or already love. Feel free to experiment with what's here, adding grilled salmon to the "Baby Blue" salad, layering ground beef in the taco salad, or substituting mango in the Papaya and Arugula Salad. Use the vinaigrette recipe from one salad on another. Add toppings from your pantry and your region of the country. Explore this chapter and try my recipes, then get creative with your own. Salad should be bright, fresh, and fun—an expression of your personality.

TIMETABLE FOR A GREAT SALAD

L et's say you want to create a salad for dinner. Here is a game plan to help you make the most of your time and keep the salad tasting its best.

EARLY IN THE DAY

1. Rinse the lettuce, dry it, and store it in the crisper.

2. Prepare the garnishes: Toast nuts (see page 99) and fry croutons (see page 105) early in the day—or even the night before. Put them in plastic bags once they have cooled.

Shred or crumble cheese, pack it in plastic bags, and refrigerate it.

Chop hardy vegetables that can be prepared ahead of time.

3. Make the vinaigrette. Keep it at room temperature unless the recipe suggests it be stored in the refrigerator.

4. Prepare marinated salads and slaws.

5. Dust off the salad bowl and locate the salad fork and spoon for serving.

AN HOUR OR SO BEFORE SERVING

1. Place the salad greens in the salad bowl, cover them with a damp paper towel, and cover the bowl with plastic wrap. Refrigerate the greens.

2. Place marinated salads and slaws in serving bowls, cover with plastic wrap, and refrigerate.

3. Slice tomatoes up to an hour beforehand, but do not refrigerate them because it changes their texture.

4. Arrange composed salads on serving platters, cover them with plastic wrap, and keep them in the refrigerator or in a cool place in the kitchen if they contain tomatoes.

JUST BEFORE SERVING

1. Add "soft" toppings, like fruit or cheese, to the salad.

2. Shake or whisk the vinaigrette, drizzle it over the salad, and toss.

3. Add crunchy toppings.

The Best Caesar Salad

SERVES 8 TO 12

PREP: 35 MINUTES

TOTE NOTES

Tote the croutons, dressing, and salad ingredients separately to keep the salad from getting soggy (you can bring the romaine in a covered salad bowl). Pour the dressing over the salad only when the meal is being served, shaking it well first.

PLAN AHEAD

Prepare the croutons and salad dressing a day ahead. Store the croutons in a plastic bag and refrigerate the dressing in a jar. Early on the day of the party, grate the Parmesan and rinse and dry the lettuce; it can be refrigerated until serving time in a plastic bag or in a large covered salad bowl.

W HEN IN DOUBT, BRING A GREAT CAESAR SALAD. And what makes a great Caesar? Fresh romaine; a zesty dressing of anchovies, garlic, lemon juice, and olive oil; a generous handful of shredded Parmesan cheese; and crunchy homemade croutons. Whereas many Caesar dressings contain a raw egg to enrich the dressing, this one does not need it, making this salad more suitable to feeding crowds and toting. Serve it with Italian food, burgers, or steaks.

FOR THE CROUTONS
6 slices firm sandwich bread or French bread
⅓ cup olive oil
Salt

FOR THE SALAD DRESSING
1 large clove garlic
2 anchovy fillets, chopped
1 tablespoon fresh lemon juice
2 teaspoons Dijon mustard
1 teaspoon Worcestershire sauce
¼ cup (1 ounce) grated Parmesan cheese
⅓ cup olive oil
Salt and freshly ground black pepper (optional)

FOR THE SALAD
2 heads romaine lettuce, rinsed and dried
⅓ cup (about 1 ounce) shredded Parmesan cheese, for sprinkling
Freshly ground black pepper
Anchovy fillets (optional)

1. Make the croutons: Trim the crusts from the bread and stack the slices on top of each other. Cut the bread into 1-inch cubes.

2. Place ⅓ cup of olive oil in a large frying pan over medium-high heat. When it is hot, add the bread cubes and cook, stirring, until they are browned all over, 3 to 4 minutes. Using a slotted spoon, transfer the croutons to paper towels to drain. Sprinkle the croutons with salt and set aside.

3. Make the salad dressing: With the motor running, drop the garlic through the feed tube of a food processor fitted with a steel blade and process until minced. Turn off the machine, scrape down the side of the bowl, and add the 2 anchovies, lemon juice, mustard, Worcestershire sauce, and ¼ cup of grated Parmesan. Pulse until the mixture is smooth. With the motor running, slowly pour in ⅓ cup of olive oil, and process until the dressing has thickened. Taste the dressing for seasoning, adding salt and/or pepper, if needed. Set the dressing aside.

4. Prepare the salad: Break the romaine into bite-size pieces and place it in a salad bowl. When ready to serve, add the dressing, ⅓ cup of shredded Parmesan cheese, black pepper, and the reserved croutons to the romaine and toss to mix. Season with pepper to taste. Serve the salad with anchovy fillets on the side, if desired.

HOW ABOUT A SOUTHWESTERN CAESAR? Add a smidgen of ground cumin and ground red pepper to the salad dressing. Peel and cube an avocado and a tomato and scatter them on top of the salad. If you like, add canned onion rings instead of croutons.

BIG BATCH: *The dressing doubles well in a food processor, but toss only one batch of salad at a time in a serving bowl, replenishing it as needed.*

RECIPE REMINDERS

Made for

Prep notes

Don't forget

Special touches

Bring again

Big Green Salad with Orange, Avocado, and Red Wine Vinaigrette

SERVES 8

PREP: 20 MINUTES

TOTE NOTES

Tote the vinaigrette in a glass jar; shake it well before using. Bring the toasted almonds and pieces of orange in separate plastic bags. Leave the romaine in its package; peel and cube the avocado just before serving. Don't forget— you'll need a bowl in which to toss the salad.

PLAN AHEAD

Make the vinaigrette the day before and refrigerate it. You can toast the almonds a day ahead, too. And cut up the orange early on the day of the party.

SOPHISTICATED AND SIMPLE, THIS SALAD REMINDS ME of the avocado salads my mother used to make, adding grapefruit or orange sections. The crunchy romaine is a nice counterpoint to the luscious avocado, and the sweet oranges balance the tang of the oregano-scented vinaigrette. My friend Jan gave me the vinaigrette recipe, which I have tinkered with, and it is terrific on any salad—but especially on this one. Serve the salad in the summertime with grilled shrimp or in the winter with a fillet of beef and scalloped potatoes.

FOR THE RED WINE VINAIGRETTE

¼ cup red wine vinegar

1 large clove garlic, crushed in a garlic press

¼ teaspoon salt, or more to taste

¼ teaspoon freshly ground black pepper, or more to taste

¼ teaspoon dried oregano, or more to taste

½ cup olive oil

2 tablespoons grated Parmesan cheese

FOR THE SALAD

1 bag (about 10 ounces) chopped hearts of romaine lettuce (8 packed cups)

1 large navel orange, peeled, separated into segments, and cut into 1-inch pieces (1½ cups; see box)

1 large ripe avocado, preferably Hass, peeled and cut
into 1-inch cubes (1 to 1½ cups)

¼ cup toasted sliced almonds (see box, page 99)

1. Make the red wine vinaigrette: Place the red wine vinegar,
garlic, salt, pepper, and oregano in a small mixing bowl.
Gradually whisk in the olive oil a little at a time until the
vinaigrette comes together and thickens slightly. Taste for
seasoning, adding more salt, pepper, and/or oregano as
necessary. Fold in the Parmesan and set the vinaigrette aside.

2. Prepare the salad: Place the romaine in a serving bowl.
Scatter the orange pieces and avocado on top. Pour enough of
the vinaigrette over the salad to lightly coat it when tossed; the
greens should look wet but not weighed down—you can always
add a little more vinaigrette. Top the salad with the almonds.

BIG BATCH: *The vinaigrette doubles well, but the larger
amount is easier to prepare in a blender or food processor.
Toss only one batch of salad at a time, replenishing the salad
bowl when needed.*

TO MAKE ORANGE SECTIONS

Orange sections look prettier and release more of their juice if you remove the membranes when you separate them into segments. Once you have peeled the orange, being sure to remove all of the white pith, make V-shape cuts between the membranes and cut out the orange sections to release them. It's easy to do—but not essential, if you're in a hurry.

Roasted Beet Salad with Walnuts and Blue Cheese Dressing

SERVES 6 TO 8

PREP: 60 TO 70 MINUTES

TOTE NOTES

Tote the blue cheese dressing, walnuts, beets, onion, and orange in separate containers.

Bring the romaine lettuce in the salad bowl or on the platter covered with plastic wrap, then assemble the salad at the gathering.

PLAN AHEAD

Roast the beets, chop up the orange, and make the salad dressing the day before, then refrigerate them. You can toast the walnuts then, too.

ONE OF MY FAVORITE FALL AND WINTER SALADS, THIS is hearty, almost a meal in itself, and brings together interesting flavors and colors. Although you have to roast the beets, toast the walnuts, and peel the sections of the orange, these tasks, as well as making the blue cheese dressing, can be done a day ahead. The dressing is delicious and thick and should be dolloped on top. We usually have some Stilton cheese on hand during the holidays, but feel free to use whatever blue cheese you like best. If you prefer a thinner dressing, fold crumbled blue cheese into a good homemade or bottled vinaigrette.

6 medium-size beets

2 tablespoons olive oil

1 cup walnut halves

2 large heads romaine lettuce

½ cup reduced-fat sour cream

1 tablespoon mayonnaise

1 tablespoon cider vinegar

1 tablespoon milk, or more as needed

1 cup (4 ounces) crumbled blue cheese, such as Gorgonzola or Stilton

1 medium-size red onion, cut into thin slivers

1 large navel orange, peeled, separated into segments (see box, page 95), and chopped

1. Preheat the oven to 400°F.

2. Rinse the beets and trim off the root ends and the beet greens, leaving an inch of the stems intact. Set aside the beet greens for another use. Slice the beets in half lengthwise and place them cut side up in a shallow baking dish. Drizzle the olive oil over the beets. Tent the baking dish with aluminum foil. Bake the beets until they are tender, 40 to 45 minutes.

3. Remove the baking dish from the oven; reduce the oven temperature to 350°F. Let the beets cool, then peel and cut them into bite-size pieces. Cover the beets with plastic wrap and place them in a cool spot or refrigerate them.

4. Place the walnuts on a rimmed baking sheet and bake them until they are lightly browned and the skins come off easily, 7 to 8 minutes. Set the walnuts aside to cool.

5. Meanwhile, rinse and dry the romaine, discarding any ragged, limp outside leaves. Place the romaine in clean linen or cotton kitchen towels to dry or dry it in a salad spinner, then refrigerate it in clean kitchen towels or a loosely tied bag.

6. Place the sour cream, mayonnaise, cider vinegar, and milk in a blender or food processor fitted with a steel blade and process until smooth, about 5 seconds. Add more milk as needed to achieve a pourable consistency a little thicker than heavy cream. Transfer the sour cream mixture to a glass bowl and stir in the blue cheese.

7. To serve, tear the romaine into bite-size pieces and place in a salad bowl or on a large platter. Arrange the beets on top, along with the onion and orange. Spoon the dressing over the salad, scatter the toasted walnuts on top, and serve.

BIG BATCH: *You can double this salad, just prepare twice as much lettuce, twice the amount of the toppings, and twice as much salad dressing.*

RECIPE REMINDERS

Made for

Prep notes

Don't forget

Special touches

Bring again

Theresa's Romaine and Apricot Salad

SERVES 8

PREP: 20 MINUTES

TOTE NOTES

Toss the romaine, broccoli slaw, tomatoes, and apricots in a salad bowl, cover it with plastic wrap, and refrigerate it until you are ready to travel.

Cover the measuring cup containing the vinaigrette with plastic wrap or transfer it to a jar with a lid (the vinaigrette will keep at room temperature) and tote it and the almonds separately.

When you arrive, shake the vinaigrette still in the jar and add it and the almonds to the salad bowl and toss to mix.

IT TAKES SOME CREATIVITY TO COME UP WITH THE RIGHT dish to bring, whether to a family that's new to the neighborhood or a mom who's welcoming her first baby into the world. I used to fall into the meat loaf and mashed potato rut. So I was all ears when my sister Susan told me about this salad of romaine lettuce and broccoli slaw tossed with an apricot dressing. The recipe comes from Susan's friend Theresa O'Donnell of Atlanta. It is delicious with barbecue and with roasted or grilled pork tenderloin. The dressing is also good poured over broccoli slaw mix.

FOR THE APRICOT VINAIGRETTE

3 tablespoons all-fruit apricot preserves
3 tablespoons white wine vinegar
½ cup vegetable oil
Salt and freshly ground black pepper

FOR THE SALAD

1 bag (8 ounces) chopped romaine lettuce (7 to 8 cups)
1 bag (12 ounces) broccoli slaw mix (3 cups)
1 cup cherry tomatoes, cut in half
½ cup dried apricots, cut into quarters
⅓ cup toasted sliced almonds (see box)

1. Make the apricot vinaigrette: Place the apricot preserves in a glass measuring cup and heat in the microwave oven on high power until softened, about 15 seconds. Whisk in the white wine vinegar and oil and season with salt and pepper to taste. Set the vinaigrette aside.

2. Prepare the salad: Place the romaine lettuce and broccoli slaw in a large mixing bowl and stir to combine. Add the tomatoes, apricots, and almonds and toss to mix. Add the vinaigrette and toss to coat. Transfer the salad to a large serving bowl. Serve at once.

BIG BATCH: *As long as you have an extra large bowl for tossing the salad, you can double this recipe. Or, you could make two batches of everything and replenish it as needed.*

A TOAST TO NUTS!

Toasting nuts and sesame seeds releases their fragrance and brings out their crunch. It's amazing how much flavor, texture, and color a little heat can add.

TO TOAST SESAME SEEDS, place them in a heavy skillet over medium heat and stir until they are golden brown, 1 to 2 minutes.

TO TOAST ALMOND SLICES AND SLIVERS, preheat the oven to 350°F. Spread the almonds on a rimmed baking sheet and toast them until lightly browned, 2 to 3 minutes.

TO TOAST PECAN HALVES, preheat the oven to 350°F. Spread the pecans on a rimmed baking sheet and toast them until deep golden brown, 4 to 5 minutes.

TO TOAST WALNUT HALVES, preheat the oven to 350°F. Spread the walnuts on a rimmed baking sheet and toast them until deeply browned, 8 to 10 minutes.

With all nuts and seeds, remember to spread them evenly in a single layer before toasting and watch them closely to make sure they don't burn.

RECIPE REMINDERS

Made for

Prep notes

Don't forget

Special touches

Bring again

Baby Blue Salad with Sweet and Spicy Pecans

SERVES 10 TO 12

PREP: 25 TO 30 MINUTES

TOTE NOTES

Tote everything separately to keep the salad from getting soggy. Store the pecans in a plastic bag and the vinaigrette in a jar. Place the drained mandarin oranges and the rinsed berries in separate plastic containers.

The greens should be refrigerated in the bag until serving time. Shake the vinaigrette well before using, but don't pour it over the salad until the meal is being served.

And remember to bring a salad bowl.

PLAN AHEAD

Make the toasted pecans and the vinaigrette a day ahead. Early on the day of the gathering, drain the mandarin oranges and rinse and dry the berries.

DROP-DEAD DELICIOUS, THIS SALAD IS WELL WORTH preparing for that special get-together. The toasted, seasoned pecans; from-scratch balsamic vinaigrette; and bright, fresh berries really make it a standout. It has made the rounds of my potluck circuit in the last few years, and I often tweak it to my liking. Feel free to use most any combination of salad greens you have on hand, except iceberg.

FOR THE BALSAMIC VINAIGRETTE
$\frac{1}{2}$ cup balsamic vinegar
3 tablespoons honey
3 tablespoons Dijon mustard
2 medium-size shallots, minced
2 medium-size cloves garlic, minced
$\frac{1}{4}$ teaspoon salt
$\frac{1}{4}$ teaspoon freshly ground black pepper
1 cup olive oil

FOR THE SALAD
12 ounces mixed field greens or mesclun (12 cups)
1 can ($8\frac{1}{4}$ ounces) mandarin oranges, drained
$1\frac{1}{4}$ cups blueberries ($\frac{1}{2}$ pint)
2 cups strawberries (1 pint), hulled and sliced
1 to $1\frac{1}{4}$ cups raspberries ($\frac{1}{2}$ pint)
1 cup (4 ounces) crumbled blue cheese
2 cups Sweet and Spicy Pecans (page 482)

1. Make the balsamic vinaigrette: Place the balsamic vinegar, honey, mustard, shallots, garlic, salt, and pepper in a mixing bowl and stir to combine. Gradually whisk in the olive oil, a little at a time, until the vinaigrette comes together and thickens.

2. Prepare the salad: Place the field greens in a serving bowl. Top with the mandarin oranges, blueberries, strawberries, and raspberries. Scatter the blue cheese and Sweet and Spicy Pecans over the top. Pour enough vinaigrette over the salad to lightly coat the greens and refrigerate any remaining vinaigrette.

BIG BATCH: *The vinaigrette doubles well, but preparing it in a blender or food processor will make assembly easier. Toss only one batch of salad at a time and replenish as needed.*

GRAB AND GO: SALAD IN A BAG

The rinsed, chopped salad that comes in plastic bags has changed our lives, allowing us to offer salads 24-7 to family and friends. But for those special occasions when you don't want it to appear that you have just ripped open a bag and dumped it into a bowl, here are ways to disguise bagged greens and dress the salad up a bit.

1. Mix and match greens. Add spinach leaves to chopped romaine. Add mâche or curly endive to field greens.

2. Remove the stems from spinach.

3. Add matchstick slices of carrots and bell pepper to slaw mix.

4. Make your own croutons; you'll find directions on page 105.

5. Use a quick homemade vinaigrette instead of dressing from a jar. Fragile greens need a light dressing. More substantial greens, such as romaine and iceberg, can handle mayonnaise-based and thick Caesar dressings.

RECIPE REMINDERS

Made for

Prep notes

Don't forget

Special touches

Bring again

A GLOSSARY OF GREENS

What goes into the salad bowl? Take your pick.

✳ Arugula (or rocket)—beloved in Italy, arugula is delicious on its own with salt and good olive oil. Its peppery flavor is addictive. Add sliced ripe tomatoes and Parmesan shavings for a real feast.

✳ Belgian endive—these slender, long pale green leaves are pricey and precious. Snip a few into a salad for a pleasantly bitter flavor and a decided crunch.

✳ Bibb lettuce—smaller than Boston, Bibb lettuce has leaves that are slightly firmer. Use it as you would Boston lettuce.

✳ Boston (or butter) lettuce—Boston lettuce's large, soft, deep-green leaves are delicate and fragile. They are pretty lined up on a platter, filled with sliced tomatoes, or coated with a vinaigrette.

✳ Curly endive (or chicory)—these spiky leaves are delightfully bitter to the taste, and they mix well with milder greens.

✳ Escarole—a hearty lettuce, save the escarole heart for small gatherings and mix the outer leaves with romaine in a wintry salad.

✳ Iceberg—the all-American, all-purpose lettuce is at home on burgers and also cut into wedges and served with a thick blue cheese dressing.

✳ Leaf lettuce—loose, leafy garden lettuces are fresh and light and summery, but they wilt quickly. Once rinsed and dried, use them soon. Spoon a light vinaigrette on top just before serving. Red leaf lettuce is especially pretty on the plate.

✳ Mâche (or lamb's leaf)—these small spoon-shaped pale green leaves are adorable to look at and fun to add to other greens in a mixed salad.

✳ Radicchio—this reddish-purple hearty green looks like cabbage but doesn't taste like cabbage at all. Radicchio is bold and peppery and mixes well with other greens.

✳ Romaine—the perennial Caesar salad favorite. A good keeper, romaine may be rinsed and dried and stored for several days. Its crunchy texture holds up well to thicker dressings.

✳ Spinach—deep green, hearty spinach can be enjoyed on its own with mushrooms and a slightly sweet dressing or mixed with other greens. Trim off the stems before serving. Buy spinach in the bag, if possible, to avoid the three or four rinsings often needed to get the sand and grit off loose spinach leaves.

✳ Watercress—the dark green, small round watercress leaf is peppery—nice with oranges and milder greens and delicious on sandwiches.

Spinach Salad with Mahogany Roasted Mushrooms and Onions

SERVES 6

PREP: 30 MINUTES

W HEN A GREAT SPINACH SALAD COMES ALONG, I remember it. That's because far too many of the spinach salads I have eaten were heavy on the bacon, too sweet, or just tasted bland. This salad, on the other hand, is full of flavor because the mushrooms and onions are roasted ahead of time in a sweet balsamic vinegar and olive oil mixture. You toss them with the spinach right from the bag and garnish the salad with goat cheese croutons. Spinach salad doesn't get any better.

3 slices sturdy sourdough bread

2 ounces soft goat cheese

$\frac{1}{3}$ cup plus 1 tablespoon olive oil

$\frac{1}{3}$ cup balsamic vinegar

1 tablespoon light brown sugar

Salt

8 ounces mushrooms, lightly rinsed and patted dry (12 mushrooms)

1 cup onion slivers (1 medium-size onion)

1 bag (10 ounces) spinach (6 to 7 cups), rinsed and drained well, stems removed

1. Preheat the broiler to high.

2. Place the bread on a cutting board and spread it with the goat cheese. Cut the bread into 1-inch cubes and place in a

---

TOTE NOTES

Put the croutons in a small plastic bag.

When it's time to leave, place the mushrooms and onions in the bottom of a serving bowl, pile the spinach on top, and cover the bowl with plastic wrap.

Don't forget to take along the dressing in a microwave-safe container.

When you arrive, warm the dressing, covered with a paper towel, in the microwave on high power for 15 seconds, then toss it with the salad and garnish with the croutons.

shallow metal baking dish. Drizzle 1 tablespoon of the olive oil over the bread cubes, then broil until the cheese bubbles up, 2 to 3 minutes. Set the croutons aside. Reduce the oven temperature to 425°F.

3. Place the balsamic vinegar, brown sugar, and ¼ teaspoon of salt in a medium-size mixing bowl and stir to combine. Whisk in the remaining ⅓ cup of olive oil.

4. Trim off and discard the tips of the mushroom stems. Add the mushrooms and onions to the bowl with the balsamic vinegar dressing and stir to coat well. Using a slotted spoon, transfer the mushrooms and onions to a small cast-iron skillet or glass baking dish, setting aside the dressing. Bake the mushrooms and onions until they are golden, 12 to 15 minutes, stirring once.

5. Using a slotted spoon, transfer the baked mushrooms and onions to a serving bowl. Pour the reserved dressing into the hot skillet or baking dish and stir until the heat from the skillet or dish warms it.

6. Add the spinach to the serving bowl and stir to combine with the mushrooms and onions. When you are ready to serve, toss the dressing with the spinach and season with salt to taste. Garnish the salad with the goat cheese croutons.

IN A HURRY? Skip the croutons and garnish the spinach salad with ¼ cup of Parmesan cheese shavings (see page 111).

BIG BATCH: *The dressing and roasted veggies double easily. Prewashed spinach comes in 20-ounce bags!*

CROUTONS

At our house you had better lock up the homemade croutons or they are going to be nibbled before the salad makes it to the table. Store-bought croutons are handy, but they do not compare in flavor to freshly made ones. And croutons are so easy to make. Here's how.

✳ Choose whatever sturdy bread you have on hand—a loaf of French bread, sourdough, or a supermarket sandwich white like Pepperidge Farm. Cut French bread and sourdough into 1-inch cubes, leaving the crust on. Remove the crust from the slices of sandwich bread, then stack the slices one on top of another and cut them into 1-inch cubes.

✳ Heat a generous amount of olive oil in a frying pan over medium heat. Add a sliced clove of garlic to the pan to perfume the oil if you like, removing the garlic when it is lightly browned.

✳ Add the bread to the hot oil and cook, stirring with a slotted spoon, until the croutons are lightly browned on all sides, 3 to 4 minutes.

✳ Transfer the croutons to paper towels to drain, and season them lightly with salt and pepper, if desired. You can also get a bit fancy and add dried oregano, seasoning salt, and Parmesan cheese. Once the croutons have cooled, store them in a plastic bag.

RECIPE REMINDERS

Made for

Prep notes

Don't forget

Special touches

Bring again

Spinach Salad with Curried Apple and Cashew Dressing

SERVES 8 TO 10

PREP: 25 MINUTES

TOTE NOTES

Tote the dressing in a glass jar (if you want to make it the day before, it can be stored at room temperature). Don't forget to give the dressing a stir or shake before using it.

Chop the apple an hour or so before you plan to serve the salad and toss it with some lemon or orange juice so that it does not discolor. Tote the apple, cashews, cranberries, scallions, and sesame seeds in separate plastic bags.

Leave the romaine and spinach in their packages, refrigerating them until you're ready to travel. And bring a serving bowl.

THIS WONDERFUL SALAD RECIPE CAME TO ME FROM a friend of a friend, as great recipes often do. It's from Amy Benson of Atlanta, who is in a supper club with my sister Susan. Susan made the salad and toted it to our weekend getaway in the mountains. She packed the dressing in a plastic container, left the spinach and romaine in their bags, brought along an apple ready to cut into pieces, and the cashews, cranberries, and chopped scallions. Assembly was a breeze—we just opened, poured, tossed, and served. The salad is a little exotic, which makes it perfect for serving with such simple foods as grilled chicken, fried chicken, or ham, those mainstays of the potluck table.

FOR THE SALAD DRESSING

2 tablespoons white wine vinegar

1 tablespoon dry white wine

2 teaspoons Dijon mustard

1 teaspoon soy sauce

3 tablespoons sugar, or more to taste

½ teaspoon curry powder

½ teaspoon salt, or more to taste

¼ teaspoon freshly ground black pepper, or more to taste

½ cup vegetable oil

FOR THE SALAD

- 1 package (about 10 ounces) chopped romaine lettuce (about 8 loosely packed cups)
- 1 package (5 ounces) spinach leaves, rinsed and drained well, stems removed (4 to 5 loosely packed cups)
- 1 medium-size Granny Smith apple, cored and chopped into $\frac{1}{2}$-inch pieces
- $\frac{1}{3}$ cup cashews
- $\frac{1}{4}$ cup dried cranberries
- 2 scallions, green parts only, chopped
- 1 tablespoon sesame seeds, toasted (see box, page 99)

1. Make the dressing: Place the white wine vinegar, wine, mustard, soy sauce, sugar, curry powder, salt, and pepper in a medium-size bowl. Gradually add the oil, a little at a time, whisking to combine until the dressing has thickened. Taste for seasoning, adding another tablespoon of sugar and more salt and/or pepper as needed. Set the dressing aside.

2. Prepare the salad: Place the romaine and spinach in a large salad bowl and toss to combine. Top with the apple, cashews, cranberries, scallions, and sesame seeds.

3. Stir the salad dressing to recombine, then pour half of it over the salad and toss to coat well. Taste for seasoning and add more dressing if needed. (Any leftover dressing can be refrigerated for up to two weeks.) Serve at once.

BIG BATCH: *You can easily double and triple the dressing, but toss only one recipe's worth of salad at a time, replenishing the salad bowl as needed.*

Papaya and Arugula Salad

SERVES 6

PREP: 20 TO 25 MINUTES

**TOTE
NOTES**

*Go ahead and place the
arugula, papaya, olives,
and onion on the platter
and cover it with plastic
wrap to tote.*

 *Pour the walnut or
olive oil in a small glass
jar with the lime or
lemon juice, if desired,
and bring it separately.*

PLAN AHEAD

*The platter of salad can
be refrigerated for up to
6 hours. Season it with
salt and pepper and
drizzle the oil and lemon
juice, if using, over it just
before serving.*

PAPAYA IS NOT AS SWEET AS MANGO OR PEACHES BUT it gives a salad great texture, flavor, and color. And peppery arugula is a perfect flavor mate. This is a wonderful salad to serve when people are serious about the wine they drink because there is no vinegar in the dressing to spoil the wine's flavor, just walnut oil and a little lime or lemon juice, if you like. It is delicious with grilled flank steak, salmon, or Cuban-seasoned pork and chicken dishes.

  1 package (5 to 6 ounces) arugula (about 6 loosely
   packed cups)
  3 cups cubed ripe papaya (½-inch or bite-size chunks;
   half of 1 large or 2 small papayas)
  8 to 12 pitted kalamata olives
  ¼ cup finely slivered red onion
  Kosher salt and freshly ground black pepper
  2 or 3 tablespoons walnut or olive oil
  Juice of ½ lime or lemon (about 1 tablespoon; optional)

1. Arrange the arugula on a pretty platter or in a shallow bowl. Arrange the papaya cubes on top of the arugula. Scatter the olives and onion slivers on top.

2. Just before serving, season the salad with salt and pepper and drizzle the walnut or olive oil over it. If desired, squeeze some lime or lemon juice on the salad. Serve at once.

BIG BATCH: *This salad is quite easy to double and triple, just replenish it as needed and dress the salad each time. Or, make two or three platters—or one very large platter—of salad.*

NOT A FAN OF THE BAG?
HOW TO RINSE AND STORE GREENS

· ·

Store-bought romaine too chopped and slaw mix too coarse? Salad in the bag is convenient, but often it's hard to find the greens you are looking for, or the lettuce may be past its prime, and no longer crunchy. So, if you need a particular type of greens or don't like a bag's looks (fragile leafy greens often don't bag well), go back to the basics and buy lettuce by the head or bunch. Yes, head and bunch lettuces must be washed and dried, so they're more time-consuming, but they're also easier on the wallet. In fact, for a crowd, head lettuce is the most economical choice.

To prepare most greens, except iceberg lettuce, separate the head or bunch into leaves and rinse them in several changes of cold water. You can do this in a large colander or in a clean sink. For iceberg, remove the core and then run water through the whole head, from bottom to top; turn the lettuce right side up to drain.

Drying lettuce is the more challenging step. But it's pretty straightforward if you have a salad spinner: While the lettuce whizzes around in the colander part of the spinner, the water from the leaves is thrown off and drains away. It's possible to mimic a salad spinner by enclosing lettuce leaves in a large clean cotton or linen kitchen towel and shaking the towel back and forth to cast as much water off the leaves as possible. Or, you can spread kitchen towels on a counter, line them with paper towels, and arrange the rinsed lettuce leaves on top. Use the paper towels to blot up as much water as possible, then discard the paper towels and roll the kitchen towels up around the lettuce. You can place the bundle of lettuce and towels in the refrigerator crisper for a couple of hours. Or, let the lettuce dry in the refrigerator, then transfer it to a loose plastic bag lined with paper towels.

It is best to rinse such fragile greens as leafy lettuces, arugula, and baby spinach on the day you plan to use them. Romaine and iceberg are more forgiving, and you can store them in rolled-up towels or in a loosely closed plastic bag for a day or so.

Arugula Salad with Grape Tomatoes and Parmesan Shavings

SERVES 4 TO 6

PREP: 15 MINUTES

TOTE NOTES

Arrange the arugula, tomatoes, and Parmesan on the platter and cover it with plastic wrap for toting. Bring along some kosher salt, the pepper mill, and the olive oil and lemon wedges to season the salad just before serving.

PLAN AHEAD

The platter of salad can be refrigerated for up to 2 hours.

ONE OF MY FONDEST FOOD MEMORIES OF OUR FAMILY'S trip to Italy is of the crisp arugula salads. This may not sound all that spectacular, but if you get a chance to taste the fresh arugula there, how intensely peppery it is compared to the blander arugula in our supermarkets, I'm sure you'll agree. Most often the salad was arugula alone; we'd drizzle olive oil on top, season it with a little salt, and squeeze some fresh lemon juice over it. Sometimes large shavings of Parmesan cheese lay on top. But my favorite rendition was at a little restaurant in Rome, not far from the Piazza Navona, where the arugula was surrounded by ripe tomatoes *and* topped with Parmesan. I have been able to duplicate this at home by using grape tomatoes, sliced in half, because they are the most consistently sweet and ripe tomatoes in our marketplace. Serve this salad with anything; it's simple and good.

1 package (5 to 6 ounces) arugula
  (about 6 loosely packed cups)

1 cup grape tomatoes, sliced in half lengthwise

1 cup Parmesan shavings (about 4 ounces; see box)

Kosher salt and freshly ground black pepper

¼ cup extra-virgin olive oil

1 lemon, cut into wedges

1. Arrange the arugula on a pretty platter. Arrange the grape tomato halves around the arugula and place the Parmesan shavings on top of the greens.

2. Just before serving, season the salad with salt and pepper. Drizzle the olive oil over the salad. Serve the lemon wedges on the side for squeezing over the salad.

BIG BATCH: *You can make multiples of this salad. It is easy to replenish, and it is a buffet-supper breeze because the last bite tastes as delicious as the first.*

SHAVING PARMESAN

To make large Parmesan shavings, you need a wedge of good Parmesan cheese. Run it down the slicing side of a metal box grater. It is easier to make shavings of cheese when the cheese is at room temperature.

RECIPE REMINDERS

Made for

_____

_____

_____

_____

_____

Prep notes

_____

_____

_____

_____

Don't forget

_____

_____

_____

_____

Special touches

_____

_____

_____

_____

Bring again

_____

Cucumber and Tomato Salad with Sweet Dill Vinaigrette

SERVES 8

PREP: 25 MINUTES

**TOTE
NOTES**

*This salad can be a little
messy to tote, so place it
on a platter that has a lip
and cover it with plastic
wrap, then place the
platter in a towel-lined
box or bin for traveling.*

PLAN AHEAD

*The flavor of the
cucumbers improves
when they marinate,
so the salad will taste
better if you pour
the vinaigrette over it
ahead of time. It can
be refrigerated for up
to 4 hours. If you want
to include avocado,
don't add it until just
before serving, so it
keeps its fresh green
color.*

CUCUMBER SALAD IS OFTEN OVERLOOKED BECAUSE it's not flashy. And yet it is an indispensable part of the buffet table, offering a refreshing cold crunch when so many dishes can be warm and heavy. This salad is especially nice when mild cucumbers are in the market or when your garden is yielding a bumper crop. I like to pair cucumbers with tomatoes and green onions. You might like to pair them with sweet Vidalia onions. Any way they are delicious in a sweet vinaigrette made with rice wine vinegar. Fresh dill is a natural, so I always add some. And if I want to make the salad more substantial, I add sliced avocado at the last minute, along with chilled shrimp or crabmeat.

FOR THE SWEET DILL VINAIGRETTE

1/3 cup rice wine vinegar

1 tablespoon sugar

1/2 cup olive oil

2 tablespoons chopped fresh dill

Salt and freshly ground black pepper

FOR THE SALAD

3 cucumbers (about 2 pounds), rinsed

4 medium-size ripe tomatoes, peeled

3 scallions, green part only, chopped (about 1/2 cup)

Salt and freshly ground black pepper

Avocado slices (optional), for garnish

$\frac{1}{2}$ cup peeled steamed shrimp, sliced in half lengthwise, or $\frac{1}{2}$ cup lump crabmeat (optional)

Dill fronds, for garnish

1. Make the vinaigrette: Place the rice wine vinegar and sugar in a small mixing bowl. Gradually whisk in the olive oil, a little at a time, until the vinaigrette thickens slightly. Add the dill and season with salt and pepper to taste. Set the vinaigrette aside.

2. Make the salad: Peel the cucumbers in strips, so that stripes of dark skin and light green flesh alternate down the sides. Cut

SUMMER PICNIC WITH FRIENDS

The ultimate potluck, a summer picnic is a wonderful excuse for "What can I bring?" It begs you to pull together a regional menu based on the foods of the season. Here is a summer medley we enjoy on the patio Down South.

HOME-FRIED CHICKEN TENDERS WITH
BLUE CHEESE SAUCE, *page 226*

＊

SQUASH CASSEROLE WITH SWEET ONIONS
AND CHEDDAR, *page 288*

＊

CUCUMBER AND TOMATO SALAD WITH
SWEET DILL VINAIGRETTE

＊

DOUBLE-CRUST BLACKBERRY COBBLER, *page 428*

＊

SIXTY-MINUTE CARAMEL CAKE, *page 359*

M E N U

**RECIPE
REMINDERS**

Made for

Prep notes

Don't forget

Special touches

Bring again

TOMATO TALK

The fun of any tomato salad is that you get to choose which tomatoes to use. Think sliced red and yellow tomatoes. Think a multicolored array of heirloom tomatoes. Toss in a few sliced grape tomatoes to play with different sizes. Tomato salads should appeal to the palate and the eye.

off and discard the ends and cut the cucumbers into ¼-inch-thick slices. Slice the tomatoes ⅓ inch thick. On a round platter (it will need to be about a foot wide), arrange the cucumber slices in a ring around the rim. Arrange the tomato slices inside of the cucumbers. Scatter the chopped scallions on top and season with salt and pepper to taste.

3. To serve, pour the vinaigrette over the cucumbers and tomatoes. Arrange avocado slices and/or spoon shrimp or crabmeat in the center of the platter, if desired. Garnish the salad with fronds of fresh dill.

BIG BATCH: *To make enough salad for sixteen, double the vinaigrette and slice twice as many cucumbers and tomatoes. Arrange the salad on two large platters.*

TEN VINAIGRETTE VARIATIONS

Vinaigrette is the basic black dress of the food world. Like a dress, which you can reaccessorize with a new scarf, belt, or handbag, the flavor of a vinaigrette can be changed simply by adding different ingredients to the basic recipe. Here's the standard recipe and ten ways to dress it up.

FOR THE VINAIGRETTE

Stir together 2 tablespoons of red wine vinegar, ¼ teaspoon of salt, and ¼ teaspoon of freshly ground black pepper. Whisk in 4 tablespoons of olive oil, continuing to whisk until thickened slightly. The vinaigrette will dress 3 to 4 cups of salad greens.

FOR THE FLAVORINGS

1. Add a clove of garlic that has been crushed in a garlic press.

2. Add a crushed clove of garlic, 1 tablespoon of shredded Parmesan cheese, and ¼ teaspoon of dried oregano.

3. Add a crushed clove of garlic, a pinch of sugar, and 3 tablespoons of crumbled Gorgonzola cheese.

4. Use white wine vinegar instead of red.

5. Use white wine vinegar rather than red and walnut oil instead of olive oil.

6. Use rice wine vinegar in place of red wine vinegar and add 1 tablespoon of sugar and 1 tablespoon of chopped fresh dill.

7. Use rice wine vinegar, not red wine vinegar, and add 1 tablespoon of sugar and a dash of soy sauce; use 2 tablespoons of Asian (dark) sesame oil and 2 tablespoons of olive oil.

8. Use balsamic vinegar rather than red wine vinegar and add a crushed clove of garlic to the dressing.

9. Use lemon juice instead of red wine vinegar.

10. Use lemon juice in place of red wine vinegar and add a crushed clove of garlic and 1 tablespoon of grated Parmesan cheese.

Sliced Tomato Salad with Basil and Buttermilk Dressing

SERVES 6 TO 8

PREP: 20 MINUTES

 TOTE NOTES

To tote, slice the tomatoes just before you're ready to go, arrange them on a platter with the lettuce, and cover with plastic wrap.

Spoon the dressing over the salad just before serving.

PLAN AHEAD

You can make the dressing up to a day ahead; refrigerate and tote it in a plastic container with a lid.

MAKE THIS SALAD WHEN RIPE SUMMER TOMATOES are in season or when you find some of those great greenhouse tomatoes with lots of flavor. It is beautiful to look at and a nice departure from plain sliced tomatoes on a plate. If you wish, serve the dressing on the side, but it's much prettier when it cascades down the tomato slices and onto the lettuce. For even more drama, use two yellow tomatoes and two red tomatoes and alternate the slices on the platter.

FOR THE BASIL AND BUTTERMILK DRESSING

1 packed cup fresh basil leaves
1 scallion, chopped (2 tablespoons)
$\frac{1}{3}$ cup buttermilk
2 tablespoons mayonnaise
Salt and freshly ground black pepper

FOR THE SALAD

3 cups salad greens of your choice
    (Boston or Bibb lettuce, arugula, or spinach)
4 large ripe tomatoes, peeled and sliced

1. Make the dressing: Place the basil, scallion, buttermilk, mayonnaise, and a dash each of salt and pepper in a food processor fitted with a steel blade or in a blender. Process until the basil and scallion are well minced and the dressing is smooth. Spoon the dressing into a glass bowl, cover it with plastic wrap, and refrigerate it until time to serve.

2. Prepare the salad: Place the salad greens on a medium-size platter. Arrange the tomato slices attractively on top of the greens. Pour the dressing over the tomatoes in a wavy line so that it doesn't completely cover the tomatoes. Serve as soon as possible.

BIG BATCH: *You can easily double the salad dressing in a food processor or blender. Buy double the salad greens and tomatoes.*

RECIPE REMINDERS

Made for

Prep notes

Don't forget

Special touches

Bring again

Tomato, Mozzarella, and Basil Salad with Fresh Tomato Vinaigrette

SERVES 8

PREP: 30 MINUTES PLUS 2 HOURS STANDING TIME

TOTE NOTES

Cover the salad platter with plastic wrap and tote the vinaigrette in a glass jar.

PLAN AHEAD

The vinaigrette can be made early in the day and kept at room temperature. Up to an hour before you plan to leave, prepare the tomatoes, mozzarella, and basil and arrange them and the olives on the platter. When it's time to serve, sprinkle the salad with kosher salt and pour the vinaigrette on top.

ONE OF MY FAVORITES FOR SERVING AT HOME AND away, this Italian salad is composed of fresh mozzarella, tomatoes, and basil. And one of the prettiest ways to present it is to alternate slices of mozzarella, tomato, and fresh basil leaves on a long platter. Sprinkled with salt and drizzled with good olive oil, this salad can easily feed a crowd. Should you want to take the salad one step further and give it real pizzazz, follow the recipe here. Prepare a simple vinaigrette made with fresh tomatoes and olive oil to spoon on top, and garnish the platter with pitted kalamata olives.

FOR THE FRESH TOMATO VINAIGRETTE

3 medium-size tomatoes

1 medium-size clove garlic, crushed in a garlic press

$\frac{1}{2}$ cup extra-virgin olive oil

1 tablespoon fresh lemon juice, or more to taste

Salt and freshly ground black pepper

FOR THE SALAD

2 cups arugula or Bibb lettuce leaves (optional)

1 pound fresh mozzarella, sliced into 16 slices ($\frac{1}{4}$ inch thick)

3 to 4 large ripe tomatoes, peeled and sliced into $\frac{1}{3}$-inch slices (16 to 20 slices)

16 large fresh basil leaves
16 pitted kalamata olives
Kosher salt

1. Make the fresh tomato vinaigrette: Peel the medium-size tomatoes and cut them in half. Squeeze the tomato halves as you would a lemon into a sieve set over a medium-size glass mixing bowl. You will need to press on the seeds to release the juice. Transfer the tomato halves to a cutting board and cut them into small pieces. You should have about 1 cup of chopped tomatoes. Add these tomatoes to the bowl with the tomato juice and add the garlic and olive oil. Stir to blend. Add the lemon juice and season with salt and pepper to taste. Taste for seasoning, adding more lemon juice as needed. Let the vinaigrette stand, covered with plastic wrap or waxed paper, at room temperature for at least 2 hours.

2. Prepare the salad: Place the arugula or Bibb lettuce leaves, if using, on a long pretty platter. Alternate slices of mozzarella and tomatoes, placing a basil leaf on top of each tomato slice. Scatter the olives around the edge of the platter and sprinkle the salad with kosher salt. When ready to serve, pour the vinaigrette over the salad.

BIG BATCH: *Double the amount of vinaigrette and buy more tomatoes and mozzarella. It's also easy to cut this recipe in half to serve four people: Use 8 ounces mozzarella, 2 large tomatoes, and just a cup of basil. Go ahead and prepare the same amount of vinaigrette. Whatever is left can be refrigerated and used in a couple of days on green salads.*

RECIPE REMINDERS

Made for

Prep notes

Don't forget

Special touches

Bring again

Fresh Green Bean Salad with Crumbled Feta Vinaigrette

SERVES 8

PREP: 25 MINUTES

THERE IS NOTHING MORE SATISFYING THAN A marinated green bean salad served with a grilled leg of lamb, a roast chicken, or a good steak. And this salad is spectacular because it marries thin green beans with the Mediterranean flavors of oregano, feta, and walnuts. The salad can be made in advance and garnished with the toasted walnuts at the last minute.

$\frac{1}{3}$ cup olive oil

2 teaspoons dried oregano

Salt and freshly ground black pepper

2 pounds thin green beans, trimmed

$\frac{1}{2}$ cup finely chopped red onion

$\frac{1}{4}$ cup finely chopped red bell pepper

2 tablespoons balsamic vinegar

$\frac{1}{4}$ cup (about 2 ounces) crumbled feta cheese

$\frac{1}{2}$ cup chopped toasted walnuts (see box, page 99)

$\frac{1}{4}$ cup chopped parsley (optional), for garnish

1. Place the olive oil and oregano in a large mixing bowl and stir to combine. Season with salt and black pepper to taste. Set the seasoned olive oil aside.

2. Bring a large pan of water to a boil over high heat. Add the green beans and 1 teaspoon of salt and cook, uncovered, until the beans turn bright green and are crisp but tender, 3 to 4 minutes. Drain the beans immediately, then run cold water over them to cool them down. Pat the beans dry with paper towels and set aside.

3. Place the onion and bell pepper in the bowl with the seasoned olive oil and stir to combine. Stir in the balsamic vinegar and feta cheese. Toss the beans with the feta vinaigrette.

4. Just before serving, top the salad with the toasted walnuts and parsley, if desired.

BIG BATCH: *This salad can be doubled and tripled. Cook the green beans one batch at a time and cool them down quickly so you don't overcook them.*

MENU

SPRING MEDITERRANEAN SUPPER

The crisp spring air makes everyone hungry for the flavors of the Mediterranean. So get friends to help you serve this meal, featuring creamy goat cheese, grilled lamb, and bright salads.

HERBED GOAT CHEESE PYRAMID, *page 32*

✳

GRILLED LEG OF LAMB WITH GREEK
CHIMICHURRI SAUCE, *page 248*

✳

FRESH GREEN BEAN SALAD WITH
CRUMBLED FETA VINAIGRETTE

✳

SLICED TOMATO SALAD
WITH BASIL AND BUTTERMILK DRESSING, *page 116*

✳

COCONUT ALMOND MACAROONS, *page 390*
AND LEMON SORBET

RECIPE
REMINDERS

Made for

Prep notes

Don't forget

Special touches

Bring again

Jess's Broccolini Salad

SERVES 8 TO 10

PREP: 20 MINUTES

TOTE NOTES

The toasted ramen noodles, almonds, and sesame seeds can be transported in a plastic bag (after they're toasted they'll keep for two to three days).

Bring the romaine and chopped broccolini in a separate plastic bag—but don't forget the serving bowl.

Tote the dressing in a glass jar, giving it a good shake before using.

When you arrive, toss the romaine and broccolini in the serving bowl, then add the dressing and the ramen mixture.

OUR FRIENDS JESS AND MOE HILL HAD US TO DINNER and served this terrific salad along with baked salmon. The salad was fresh and light, perfect for a summer night. It's an ideal potluck salad because it feeds a lot of people and the flavors improve after it sits awhile. Jess came up with the recipe because her three children don't like the cabbage in slaw. The sweet dressing is similar to that used on ramen salads, except in this recipe the ramen-noodle flavor packet is omitted (feel free to add it if you like). To make the salad even more kid-friendly, skip the almonds.

2 tablespoons (¼ stick) butter

1 package (3 ounces) ramen noodles (any flavor)

⅓ cup sliced almonds

2 tablespoons sesame seeds

⅓ cup red wine vinegar

⅓ cup sugar

2 medium-size cloves garlic, crushed in a garlic press

1 teaspoon Dijon mustard

½ teaspoon salt

½ cup olive oil

1 bag (8 ounces) chopped romaine lettuce, or 2 heads romaine lettuce, chopped (7 to 8 cups)

1 bunch broccolini, trimmed and chopped (about 2½ cups; see Note)

1. Melt the butter in a large frying pan over medium-low heat. Open the package of ramen and remove and discard the seasoning packet. Chop the noodles into small pieces and add them to the frying pan along with the almonds and sesame seeds. Cook the ramen, almonds, and sesame seeds, stirring, until they turn golden brown, 3 to 4 minutes. Set aside to cool.

2. Place the vinegar, sugar, garlic, mustard, and salt in a medium-size mixing bowl. Gradually whisk in the olive oil, a little at a time, until the dressing thickens slightly.

3. To serve, toss the romaine with the broccolini in a large serving bowl. Pour enough of the dressing over the salad to coat, then toss well. Spoon the toasted ramen, almonds, and sesame seeds on top and toss again to coat.

NOTE: Broccolini, a hybrid of the cabbage family, is a cross between broccoli and Chinese kale and has a flavor that is slightly sweeter than broccoli.

BIG BATCH: *This recipe is easily doubled for big groups. Buy the bagged romaine to save time rinsing and chopping.*

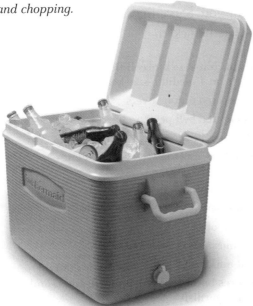

RECIPE REMINDERS

Made for

Prep notes

Don't forget

Special touches

Bring again

My Sweet and Sour Broccoli Salad

SERVES 5 TO 6

PREP: 25 MINUTES

TOTE NOTES

Transfer the salad to a serving bowl, but don't garnish it with the bacon. Cover the bowl with plastic wrap and refrigerate it until you're ready to leave. Carry the bacon separately in a small plastic bag and scatter it over the salad just before serving.

PLAN AHEAD

Washed and separated into florets, the broccoli can be stored in a plastic bag in the refrigerator for up to three days. Slice the onion and bell pepper a day ahead and refrigerate them. Fry the bacon early on the day of the gathering and store it, covered, at room temperature.

RAW BROCCOLI SALAD MADE WITH MAYONNAISE, raisins, and bacon is a potluck staple, but it has never been a favorite of mine. It always seems the salad is swimming in mayonnaise and loses its fresh appeal after sitting out on a buffet table for a couple of hours. But knowing how many people like this salad, I realized how much it needed to be a part of this book, so I decided to try my hand at lightening it up without losing any of the ingredients. Here is a recipe that is an improvement on the original and one that I know is better for you. Serve the salad with sliced ham, grilled fish, or fried chicken.

4 cups bite-size broccoli florets
   (from 1 medium-size head)
½ cup red onion slivers
½ cup red bell pepper slivers
¼ cup yellow raisins
3 tablespoons toasted sliced almonds
   (see box, page 99)
¼ cup white wine vinegar
2 tablespoons light brown sugar
¼ cup olive oil
2 tablespoons mayonnaise
Salt and freshly ground black pepper
2 slices bacon, cooked, drained, and crumbled,
   for garnish

1. Place the broccoli, onion, bell pepper, raisins, and almonds in a large mixing bowl and toss to combine. Set the broccoli mixture aside.

2. Place the white wine vinegar and brown sugar in a small mixing bowl and whisk to combine. Gradually whisk in the olive oil, a little at a time, until the dressing thickens slightly. Stir in the mayonnaise and season with salt and black pepper to taste.

3. Pour the dressing over the broccoli mixture and toss to coat. Spoon the salad into a serving bowl and garnish with the crumbled bacon. Serve at once.

BIG BATCH: *You can double and triple the broccoli salad.*

RECIPE REMINDERS

Made for

Prep notes

Don't forget

Special touches

Bring again

John's Homemade Coleslaw

SERVES 6 TO 8

PREP: 20 MINUTES

MY HUSBAND, JOHN, MAKES TERRIFIC COLESLAW because he loves everything about it, from shredding the fresh cabbage right into the bowl, to seasoning it just so with sweet pickle juice, to spooning it onto his plate! I shared his method in *The Dinner Doctor,* but no potluck book would be complete without a great slaw recipe, so here it is again, this time with fresh radishes for their color and sweet peppery flavor. Yes, you can use a one-pound bag of slaw mix instead of shredding your own cabbage and carrots, but John prefers it this way—his homemade version.

1 small head of cabbage (1½ pounds), trimmed, cored, and quartered

2 large carrots

3 radishes

½ cup chopped sweet onion

½ cup chopped green bell pepper

½ cup mayonnaise

¼ cup sweet pickle juice

3 tablespoons pickle relish

3 tablespoons sugar, or more to taste

1 teaspoon seasoned salt, such as Lawry's, or more to taste

1. Rinse the cabbage in cold water and let it drain well in a colander. Using a box grater, shred the cabbage into a large mixing bowl. You will have about 8 cups. Trim and peel the carrots and shred them into the mixing bowl. Trim the radishes and shred them into the bowl. Add the onion and bell pepper and stir to combine.

2. Make a well in the center of the slaw mixture and add the mayonnaise, pickle juice, pickle relish, sugar, and seasoned salt. Stir with a fork to mix the dressing and then, using a wooden spoon, stir the dressing and the slaw mixture to combine. Taste for seasoning, adding more sugar or seasoned salt if needed.

BIG BATCH: *For larger quantities, shred the cabbage, carrots, and radishes using a food processor. The coleslaw doubles and triples well.*

**M
E
N
U**

JULY FOURTH CELEBRATION

Whether the main dish is crowd-pleasing ribs or catfish, it will be fun because you're gathering with friends and family on this all-American day. Let everyone bring a favorite side dish, adding baked beans or green beans or casseroles, breads, and especially homemade ice cream to the menu.

EASY BARBECUED RIBS, *page 238*
or
CATFISH FRY WITH HOMEMADE TARTAR SAUCE, *page 220*
✳
SOUTHERN POTATO SALAD, *page 131*
✳
JOHN'S HOMEMADE COLESLAW
✳
WATERMELON BOAT WITH SUMMER FRUITS,
page 160
✳
MEXICAN CORN BREAD, *page 462*
✳
PEACH AND BLUEBERRY CRISP, *page 430*

**RECIPE
REMINDERS**

Made for

Prep notes

Don't forget

Special touches

Bring again

Asian Slaw with Peanut Dressing

SERVES 6 TO 8

PREP: 35 TO 40 MINUTES

TOTE NOTES

Tote this slaw in its serving bowl covered with plastic wrap, but carry the peanuts and cilantro sprigs separately in little plastic bags to add as garnishes.

PLAN AHEAD

The dressed slaw can be kept for up to 6 hours, but don't garnish it until just before serving.

FOR SEVERAL YEARS A GROUP OF MOMS I KNOW HAS been meeting together to share dinner. It started when our daughters were fifth graders and now the girls are almost in college. We celebrate birthdays, housewarmings—any milestone we can think of—and if we can't think of one, we just gather to try out a new restaurant. We discuss our lives, our children, and often cooking. One night at dinner everyone was talking about this slaw recipe. Our friend Kren Teren had made it for a weekend getaway to the lake, and everyone begged her for the recipe. Now that I've tasted it, I agree with the group—it's yummy! This is a fun and festive slaw with an Asian twist. It works best made with freshly shredded cabbage, although if you are using a slaw mix, choose the coarsely shredded variety, not angel hair.

1 small head of cabbage (1½ pounds), trimmed, cored, and quartered

2 cups shredded carrots

2 cups finely chopped red bell pepper

1 cup chopped scallions (about 4 scallions)

1 loosely packed cup fresh cilantro leaves, plus cilantro sprigs for garnish

6 tablespoons rice wine vinegar

⅓ cup creamy peanut butter

3 tablespoons vegetable oil

3 tablespoons Asian (dark) sesame oil

3 tablespoons soy sauce

3 tablespoons light brown sugar

1 piece (2 inches) fresh ginger, peeled and grated
(about 2 tablespoons)

2 large cloves garlic, crushed in a garlic press

½ cup lightly salted dry-roasted peanuts

1. Rinse the cabbage in cold water and let it drain well in a colander. Using a box grater, shred the cabbage into a large mixing bowl. You will have about 8 cups. Add the carrots, bell pepper, scallions, and cilantro leaves and stir to combine. Refrigerate the cabbage mixture; it will keep as long as overnight.

2. Combine the rice wine vinegar, peanut butter, vegetable and sesame oil, soy sauce, brown sugar, ginger, and garlic in a mixing bowl and whisk to combine. Pour the dressing over the cabbage mixture and toss to coat well.

3. To serve, transfer the slaw to a serving bowl and garnish it with the peanuts and cilantro sprigs.

BIG BATCH: *Using a food processor, you can shred enough cabbage to double this recipe. You'll need a very large mixing bowl to toss the slaw with the dressing.*

RECIPE REMINDERS

Made for

Prep notes

Don't forget

Special touches

Bring again

Carrot and Raisin Salad

SERVES 6 TO 8

PREP: 20 MINUTES

THE FUN OF THE POTLUCK TABLE IS THAT IT FEATURES a mix of old and new. You'll find those friendly nostalgic dishes you haven't tasted since you were a child and eclectic cutting-edge creations that make you beg for the recipe. This familiar salad falls into the first camp. It is sometimes called carrot slaw, but I've always known it as carrot and raisin salad. Sweet and good, it was surely invented by some mom who wanted her kids to eat more carrots. It works!

6 large or 8 medium-size carrots, peeled
½ cup finely chopped celery
½ cup chopped apple
⅓ cup dark raisins
¼ cup mayonnaise, or more as needed
¼ cup plain yogurt
1 tablespoon sugar (optional)

Using a box grater, shred the carrots into a large bowl. Or, use a food processor fitted with a steel blade to shred them, then transfer the carrots to a large bowl. Stir in the celery, apple, and raisins, followed by the mayonnaise and yogurt. Taste for sweetness and add the sugar, if desired. Transfer the carrot salad to a serving bowl, cover it with plastic wrap, and refrigerate it until serving time.

BIG BATCH: *You can double this recipe, and you might be tempted to use preshredded carrots, but they are not as good as freshly shredded. You can use the food processor to shred a dozen carrots quickly.*

Southern Potato Salad

SERVES 8

PREP: 45 MINUTES

M Y HEART GETS HEAVY THINKING ABOUT MY MOM'S potato salad: I miss sneaking a taste from the bowl when she made it for all of us. And I recall with affection all those picnics and potlucks of my past where her potato salad was the star. The secret? Nothing extraordinary, for potato salad isn't exotic. But, it is exacting. You need waxy potatoes that stand up to boiling. You mustn't overcook them. You need to season the potatoes while they are warm. And then you need some add-ins, such as onion and celery and maybe hard-cooked egg, but add-ins are personal and regional, too. Here is a blueprint for a good potato salad. Try your hand at it, varying it as you like. Homemade potato salad will always be fondly remembered.

3 pounds waxy potatoes such as Yukon Gold or
    red potatoes
Salt
1 tablespoon olive oil
2 tablespoons white wine vinegar or lemon juice
Freshly ground black pepper
1 cup thinly sliced celery
½ cup finely chopped sweet onion
1 cup mayonnaise, or ½ cup mayonnaise and
    ½ cup plain yogurt
Chopped parsley (optional), for garnish
Ripe tomato wedges (optional), for garnish

1. Scrub the potatoes and cut them in half or quarters so that the pieces are the same size and about 2 inches across.

TOTE NOTES

Tote the potato salad in its serving bowl covered with plastic wrap. Keep it chilled in a cooler en route. Bring the garnishes in small containers.

PLAN AHEAD

You can make the potato salad the night before, cover it with plastic wrap, and refrigerate it until it's time to travel.

Made for

Prep notes

Don't forget

Special touches

Bring again

Place the potatoes in a medium-size saucepan and add cold water to cover and 1 teaspoon of salt. Bring to a boil over medium-high heat. Reduce the heat to low and let simmer, covered, until the potatoes are barely tender and easily pierced with a fork, 15 to 20 minutes. Potatoes continue to cook as they cool, so be careful not to overcook them.

2. Drain the potatoes and, as soon as they are just cool enough to handle, remove and discard the skins. Cut the potatoes into 1-inch cubes and place them in a large mixing bowl.

3. Add the olive oil and vinegar or lemon juice to the potato cubes, tossing to combine, then season with salt and pepper to taste. Add the celery and onion and toss to combine.

4. When the potatoes have cooled completely, fold in the mayonnaise or the combination of mayonnaise and yogurt. Taste for seasoning, adding more salt and/or pepper as needed. Spoon the potato salad into a serving bowl and serve it at once or refrigerate it, covered with plastic wrap. If desired, garnish it with parsley and tomato wedges, just before serving.

WANT TWO MORE WAYS TO MAKE POTATO SALAD? Add 2 chopped hard-cooked eggs along with the onion and celery, then add a pinch of sugar to the mayonnaise and ¼ cup of sweet pickle relish, if you like.

Or, use ¼ cup of chopped chives instead of the onion. Add ½ cup of chopped parsley and a very finely minced clove of garlic along with the celery, chives, and parsley.

BIG BATCH: *You can double and triple the potato salad, but work in two or three separate batches—use separate pots for cooking the potatoes and separate bowls for mixing. I have found that when too many potatoes are in a large pot they are more likely to overcook or cook unevenly.*

Warm Potato Salad with Rosemary and Camembert

SERVES 8

PREP: 35 MINUTES

MY COUSIN MARY GRISSIM BROUGHT THIS POTATO salad to an Easter lunch. She is a good and inventive cook, and we appreciated her break from the usual. Pretty and fragrant, this warm salad is a fun departure from mayonnaise-based potato salads. It complements ham, roast pork, and roast beef.

3 pounds red-skinned potatoes

Salt

2 tablespoons rice wine vinegar

1 medium-size clove garlic, crushed in a garlic press

¼ cup olive oil

Freshly ground black pepper

8 ounces Camembert cheese, cut into 1-inch pieces

2 tablespoons fresh rosemary leaves

1. Scrub the potatoes and, if necessary, cut them in half so that the pieces are the same size and about 2 inches across. If they are small new potatoes, leave them whole. Place the potatoes in a large saucepan and add cold water to cover and 1 teaspoon of salt. Bring to a boil over medium-high heat. Reduce the heat to low and let simmer, covered, until the potatoes are barely tender and easily pierced with a fork, 15 to 20 minutes. Potatoes continue to cook as they cool, so be careful not to overcook them.

TOTE NOTES

This potato salad was meant to be served warm; in any case it needs to be served the same afternoon it's made. Do not refrigerate it; just spoon it into a serving bowl and cover it with plastic wrap to tote.

For a fresher look, don't add the rosemary leaves until just before serving; scatter them on top of the salad right after you unwrap it.

PLAN AHEAD

Although it won't be warm, the salad can sit at room temperature for up to 3 hours—it will still be delicious.

2. Drain the potatoes and, as soon as they are cool enough to handle, remove and discard the skins. Cut the potatoes into 1-inch cubes and place them in a large mixing bowl.

3. Add the rice wine vinegar, garlic, and olive oil to the potatoes, then season them with salt and pepper to taste, tossing to coat. Fold in the cheese and rosemary and serve at once, if possible.

BIG BATCH: *You can double this recipe, but cook the potatoes in two pans and use a light hand when folding in the cheese. Serve the salad on a large platter and use the rosemary as a garnish.*

Quick Tabbouleh

SERVES 8 TO 10

SOAK: 30 MINUTES ✳ PREP: 40 MINUTES

TOTE NOTES

Tabbouleh makes a great do-ahead salad. Just cover the serving bowl with plastic wrap, and the salad is ready to tote.
Bring the crumbled feta cheese, if using, and mint sprigs in separate plastic bags and garnish the tabbouleh just before serving.

TABBOULEH IS A MIDDLE EASTERN SALAD COMBINING bulgur wheat with parsley, tomatoes, lemon juice, and olive oil. It is one of the most refreshing salads in warm weather. I came to love the convenience of tabbouleh salad mixes, which require just thirty minutes to soak, because I could have tabbouleh on the spur of the moment. The only problem is that when you fold in the seasoning packet of dried herbs and spices the tabbouleh tastes like something out of a package— which it is! So, I came up with a recipe that combines the best of both worlds—the quick bulgur from two boxes of tabbouleh salad mix and just one seasoning packet, plus a lot of chopped fresh parsley, mint, scallions, cucumbers, and tomatoes to add freshness. You can do the chopping while the bulgur wheat soaks.

> 2 packages (5¼ ounces each) tabbouleh (or tabouli) salad mix (about 2 cups bulgur wheat)
>
> 2 cups boiling water
>
> 5 tablespoons olive oil
>
> 3 tablespoons fresh lemon juice (2 medium-size lemons)
>
> 1 teaspoon salt, or more to taste
>
> Freshly ground black pepper
>
> 1 cup chopped fresh parsley
>
> 1 cup chopped tomato (1 medium-size tomato)
>
> 1 cup finely chopped cucumber (½ large cucumber)
>
> ½ cup chopped fresh mint, plus mint sprigs, for garnish
>
> ¼ cup chopped scallions
>
> ⅓ cup (about 1½ ounces) crumbled feta cheese (optional), for garnish

1. Place the bulgur wheat from the tabbouleh salad mixes and the contents of one of the salad mix's spice packet in a large heatproof mixing bowl and stir to combine (discard the second spice packet). Add the boiling water, cover with plastic wrap, and let soak in the refrigerator for 30 minutes.

2. Remove the bowl from the refrigerator and stir the bulgur wheat. Stir in the olive oil and lemon juice and season with salt and pepper to taste. Fold in the parsley, tomato, cucumber, mint, and scallions. Transfer the tabbouleh to a serving bowl and serve at once, garnished with the feta cheese, if desired, and the mint sprigs.

BIG BATCH: *You can double and triple this recipe. Make each batch in a separate bowl to ensure that the boiling water soaks through and cools down in the refrigerator.*

RECIPE REMINDERS

Made for

Prep notes

Don't forget

Special touches

Bring again

Greek Pasta Salad

SERVES 8

PREP: 40 TO 45 MINUTES

TOTE NOTES

Tote this salad right in its serving bowl and bring the optional garnish of peppers or shrimp in a separate container, if you like. Cover the serving bowl with plastic wrap that sticks securely to the rim of the bowl to make traveling less messy.

If possible, let the salad come to room temperature before serving. Then stir the salad again and top it with the garnish, if using.

I LOVE THIS PASTA SALAD; IT'S SO STRAIGHTFORWARD IN flavor, easy to prepare, and pretty to look at. And, it's interesting enough on the buffet table that it doesn't get overlooked. Use whatever short pasta you've got in the pantry—shells, penne, or spirals. What makes the salad Greek is the seasonings—garlic, oregano, and mint—as well as the add-ins of kalamata olives, cucumbers, feta cheese, and tomatoes. Serve the salad from a nice ceramic bowl, and garnish it with pickled banana or cherry peppers or whole steamed and peeled shrimp. Or, just let the salad speak for itself.

1 pound medium-size shell or other short pasta (4 cups)

Salt

⅔ cup olive oil

2 tablespoons fresh lemon juice (1 lemon)

2 small cloves garlic, crushed in a garlic press

1 teaspoon dried oregano

Freshly ground black pepper

2 cups cherry or grape tomatoes, cut in half

1½ cups chopped cucumber
   (2 medium-size or 1 large cucumber)

1 cup chopped red onion (1 medium-size onion)

1 cup (4 ounces) crumbled feta cheese

½ cup chopped pitted kalamata olives

¼ cup chopped fresh mint or parsley

Pickled banana or cherry peppers or steamed shrimp
   (optional), for garnish

1. Bring a large pot of water to a boil over high heat. Stir in the pasta and 1 teaspoon of salt, reduce the heat to medium-high, and cook the pasta, uncovered, according to the package directions until just done, 8 to 9 minutes.

2. Meanwhile, place the olive oil, lemon juice, garlic, and oregano in a large mixing bowl and whisk to combine. Season with salt and black pepper to taste. Set the salad dressing aside.

3. Drain the pasta well in a colander, shaking it to remove the excess water. Transfer the pasta to the large mixing bowl with the dressing. Stir to coat and let the pasta come to room temperature, about 20 minutes.

4. When the pasta is cool, fold in the tomatoes, cucumbers, onion, feta cheese, olives, and mint or parsley. Stir to combine well. Taste for seasoning, adding more salt and/or black pepper if needed. Transfer the salad to a serving bowl and serve at once garnished with the banana peppers or shrimp, if desired, or cover and refrigerate the salad until serving time.

BIG BATCH: *This salad is easy to double or triple, but cook the pasta a pound at a time, and mix the salad one batch at a time.*

RECIPE REMINDERS

Made for

Prep notes

Don't forget

Special touches

Bring again

Orzo and Spinach Salad with Lemon-Cranberry Vinaigrette

SERVES 8

PREP: 20 MINUTES

DRIED SWEETENED CRANBERRIES, BABY SPINACH, crumbled feta, toasted pecans, soft orzo, and a lemon and olive oil dressing make this salad light and pleasing. Orzo is that wonderful rice-shaped pasta that doesn't stick together after cooking, making it a good candidate for pasta salad. This is a cross between a spinach salad and a pasta salad, for those who like a little of both.

8 ounces orzo pasta (2 cups)
Salt
1 package (5 ounces) baby spinach, rinsed and
    drained well
1 cup (4 ounces) crumbled feta cheese
½ cup dried sweetened cranberries or cherries, chopped
½ teaspoon grated lemon zest (1 lemon)
2 tablespoons fresh lemon juice (1 lemon)
⅓ cup olive oil
Freshly ground black pepper
½ cup chopped toasted pecans (see box, page 99)
    or Sweet and Spicy Pecans (page 482), for garnish

1. Bring a medium-size pot of water to a boil over high heat. Stir in the orzo and ½ teaspoon of salt, reduce the heat to medium-high, and cook the orzo, uncovered, according to package directions until just done, 7 to 8 minutes.

2. Meanwhile, place the spinach, feta cheese, and cranberries or cherries in a large mixing bowl and stir to combine. Set the spinach mixture aside.

3. Place the lemon zest and juice in a small mixing bowl and gradually whisk in the olive oil, a little at a time, until the lemon dressing thickens slightly. Season the dressing with salt and pepper to taste.

4. Drain the orzo well in a fine sieve, not a colander (the pieces of orzo are so small they often fall through the holes of a colander). Shake the orzo well to remove the excess water. Transfer the orzo to the bowl with the spinach mixture and toss.

5. Pour the lemon dressing over the orzo mixture and toss again to coat well. Transfer the salad to a serving bowl and garnish with the chopped pecans right before serving.

BIG BATCH: *You can double and triple the salad, but cook only 1 pound of orzo at a time so it doesn't overcook and become gummy.*

Antipasto Pasta Salad

SERVES 10 TO 12

PREP: 30 MINUTES

TOTE NOTES

Cover the serving bowl with plastic wrap that sticks well to the rim of the bowl and this salad will be ready to travel. Toss it again just before serving.

Take the basil leaves in a small plastic bag and garnish the salad at the last minute.

PLAN AHEAD

The pasta salad can be refrigerated, covered with plastic wrap, for up to 24 hours.

THIS SALAD FROM MY SISTER SUSAN IN ATLANTA IS perfect for serving a large group. It incorporates all the flavors of an antipasto platter. Use penne, bow tie, or spiral pasta, and feel free to improvise on the salad add-ins by using other veggies, such as mushrooms and cherry tomatoes. The salad is great served with grilled or fried chicken, steaks, or burgers.

1 pound penne, bow tie, or spiral pasta (4 cups)

¼ teaspoon salt

4 ounces hard salami or pepperoni, cut into ¼-inch strips

1 jar (12 ounces) roasted red peppers, drained and cut into strips (1½ cups)

1 jar (12 ounces) or 2 jars (6 ounces each) marinated artichoke hearts, drained and halved

1 cup (4 ounces) diced provolone cheese

1 cup sliced black olives

½ cup chopped red onion

⅓ loosely packed cup chopped fresh basil, plus basil leaves, for garnish

⅔ cup bottled vinaigrette such as red wine, Caesar, or Italian salad dressing, or more as necessary

1. Bring a large pot of water to a boil over high heat. Stir in the pasta and salt, reduce the heat to medium-high, and cook the pasta, uncovered, according to the package directions until just done, 8 to 10 minutes.

2. Meanwhile, place the salami or pepperoni strips, red pepper strips, artichoke hearts, provolone cheese, olives, onion, and chopped basil in a large serving bowl and toss to mix. Set the salami mixture aside.

3. Drain the pasta well in a colander, shaking it to remove the excess water. Let the pasta cool slightly, then transfer it to the mixing bowl with the salami mixture. Pour ⅔ cup of the vinaigrette over the pasta and toss until well coated. Add more vinaigrette as needed to moisten the salad. Garnish the salad with basil leaves just before serving.

BIG BATCH: *This is a great salad for doubling and tripling. Cook the pasta in 1-pound batches, drain it well, and toss it with a little oil or a little of the dressing so it doesn't stick together. Then combine it with the add-ins in a large bowl.*

THE SALAD BOWL?

Salad bowl or salad plate? Much depends on what goes into the salad, because the ingredients determine how it should be served. For example, leafy salads with vinaigrettes are best served in a bowl that catches the dressing and makes serving easier. Glass bowls are the right container for layered salads because you can see the layers through the side of the bowl, making for a pretty presentation. Wooden bowls, on the other hand, are best for Caesar salads and salads where you want to impart the flavor of garlic before adding other ingredients. Simply run a cut garlic clove around the inside of the bowl to perfume it. And shallow bowls and platters make composed salads of layered tomatoes or chunky salads of pasta or corn look dramatic.

RECIPE REMINDERS

Made for

Prep notes

Don't forget

Special touches

Bring again

Old-Fashioned Macaroni Salad

SERVES 8

PREP: 25 MINUTES * CHILL: 1 HOUR

TOTE NOTES

Tote the macaroni salad in a serving bowl covered with plastic wrap or place it in a nice large plastic bowl with a snap-on lid and serve right from that bowl.

The salad needs no last minute garnishing, just give it a quick stir before serving to combine ingredients that might have settled.

PLAN AHEAD

This salad tastes its very best when it has been refrigerated all day.

C AN YOU IMAGINE AN ALL-AMERICAN POTLUCK without a classic macaroni salad? That's as bleak an image as New Year's Eve without a kiss. While I wasn't raised on this salad—my mother favored potato salad—I loved to spoon it onto my plate at church suppers. I still do any chance I get. It is cool and refreshing and the peppers, onions, carrots, and celery provide just the right amount of crunch. You can chop the vegetables while the macaroni cooks, and feel free to add more adventuresome seasoning as you like. This salad is just delicious.

1 pound elbow macaroni (4 cups)
Salt
1 cup finely chopped green bell pepper
1 cup finely chopped carrots
1 cup finely chopped celery
1 cup finely chopped red onion
　(1 medium-size onion)
2 cups mayonnaise
½ cup sweet pickle relish
2 tablespoons cider vinegar
1 teaspoon Dijon mustard
Freshly ground black pepper

1. Bring a large pot of water to a boil over high heat. Stir in the macaroni and ½ teaspoon of salt, reduce the heat to medium-high, and cook the macaroni, uncovered, according to the package directions until just done, 7 to 8 minutes.

2. Meanwhile, place the bell pepper, carrots, celery, and onion in a large serving bowl. Set the vegetable mixture aside.

3. Drain the macaroni well in a colander, shaking it to remove the excess water. Let the macaroni cool slightly, then transfer it to the bowl with the vegetables and stir to combine.

4. Add the mayonnaise, pickle relish, cider vinegar, and mustard to the macaroni mixture and stir to combine well. Taste for seasoning, adding salt and black pepper as needed. Cover the bowl with plastic wrap and refrigerate for at least 1 hour, preferably all day.

BIG BATCH: *As long as you have some help with the chopping, this salad doubles well.*

Curried Rice and Artichoke Salad

SERVES 8

PREP: 20 MINUTES

TOTE NOTES

A highly totable salad, this is perfect for traveling because it does not shift around in the bowl. Transport it in the serving bowl covered with plastic wrap.

PLAN AHEAD

You can prepare the salad a day or so ahead of time; its flavor will grow richer as it refrigerates.

I CANNOT IMAGINE DOING WITHOUT THIS NOSTALGIC favorite at a potluck gathering. Through the years I have updated it to add more crunch and use less mayonnaise. In the traditional recipe, you add the marinade from the jars of artichokes as well, but I think this makes the salad too greasy. So far I have been unsuccessful at substituting plain white rice for the Rice-A-Roni typically used in the old standard. Sometimes a classic recipe's core ingredient just has to stay the same.

2 packages (6.9 ounces each) chicken-flavor Rice-A-Roni

Olive oil, for cooking the Rice-A-Roni

6 scallions, green parts only, trimmed and chopped (about ½ cup)

½ cup finely chopped red or green bell pepper

½ cup sliced green olives

¼ cup chopped fresh parsley

1 jar (12 ounces) or 2 jars (6 ounces each) marinated artichoke hearts

½ cup mayonnaise

2 teaspoons curry powder

½ cup toasted sliced almonds (see box, page 99), for garnish

1. Prepare the Rice-A-Roni following the instructions on the package and using olive oil. Cook the rice until it tests done and the liquid has evaporated, about 15 minutes. Let cool.

2. Meanwhile, place the scallions, bell pepper, olives, and parsley in a large mixing bowl. Drain the artichoke hearts, chop them into pieces, and add them to the mixing bowl.

3. Whisk the mayonnaise and curry powder together in a small bowl and set the curry mayonnaise aside.

4. Add the Rice-A-Roni to the bowl with the artichokes. Spoon the curry mayonnaise on top of the rice and stir until well coated. To serve the salad cold, cover the bowl with plastic wrap and refrigerate for at least 1 hour. Or, transfer the salad to a pretty, shallow serving bowl and serve at once. Garnish the salad with the almonds just before serving.

BIG BATCH: *For best results, cook no more than two packages of Rice-A-Roni at a time and prepare the salad in batches.*

RECIPE REMINDERS

Made for

Prep notes

Don't forget

Special touches

Bring again

White Corn Salad with Fresh Herb Vinaigrette

SERVES 6 TO 8

PREP: 40 MINUTES

TOTE NOTES

Tote the salad in the serving bowl covered with plastic wrap.

PLAN AHEAD

The salad is best freshly made, but you can prepare it a day ahead and keep it refrigerated.

A S FOOD EDITOR OF *THE ATLANTA JOURNAL-CONSTITUTION* years ago, I wrote stories about a farmer in Georgia named Jep Morgan and the fresh herbs he grew. Jep shared a fabulous corn salad recipe with me; for a long time that was the only way I prepared fresh corn and I committed the recipe to memory. Years pass and memory fades—as I planned this chapter of the book, I longingly recalled that salad and tried to find the recipe to no avail. But the method stayed with me, and I tried it out again in my Nashville kitchen, serving the salad to my family, who gave it a hearty thumbs-up. The trick is to sauté the vegetables first in olive oil and then add white wine to the pan and let it cook down. This becomes the vinaigrette for the fresh corn, and to this base you can add fresh herbs and seasoning. Make the salad using the freshest summer corn and whatever fresh herbs you have on hand.

6 ears white or yellow corn, or a mix of the two, shucked

½ cup olive oil

2 cups chopped scallions, both white and green parts (1 bunch)

1 cup finely chopped red onion (1 medium-size onion)

1 cup finely chopped red bell pepper

2 medium-size cloves garlic, minced

½ cup dry white wine

1 tablespoon sugar

1 cup chopped fresh parsley or a mix of parsley,
     fresh oregano, and thyme leaves
Salt and freshly ground black pepper

1. Hold an ear of corn upright on a cutting board and, using a sharp knife, cut down close to the cob to slice off the kernels. Repeat with the remaining ears of corn. You should have about 4 cups of corn. Set it aside.

2. Place the olive oil in a large frying pan over medium heat. Add the scallions, onion, bell pepper, and garlic. Reduce the heat to low and cook, stirring, until the onions soften and begin to caramelize, 6 to 7 minutes. Add the wine to the pan and let simmer until reduced by about half, about 3 minutes.

3. Stir in the sugar and the corn kernels and cook, stirring, over low heat until the corn has just cooked through, 4 to 5 minutes. Turn off the heat and stir in the parsley or the mix of parsley, oregano, and thyme. Season with salt and black pepper to taste. Transfer the corn salad to a serving dish and serve at room temperature. Or, let the corn come to room temperature, then cover it with plastic wrap and refrigerate. Let the salad return to room temperature before serving.

BIG BATCH: *Working one batch at a time, you can double and triple this recipe.*

RECITE
REMINDERS

Made for

_____

_____

_____

_____

_____

Prep notes

_____

_____

_____

_____

Don't forget

_____

_____

_____

_____

Special touches

_____

_____

_____

_____

Bring again

_____

_____

Tina's Corn and Black Bean Salad

SERVES 8

PREP: 45 MINUTES ✳ CHILL: 2 TO 3 HOURS

TOTE NOTES

You can tote the salad on a serving platter or in a serving bowl covered with plastic wrap. Bring the tortilla chips in a separate plastic bag.

PLAN AHEAD

If you would like to prepare this salad the night before, omit the lettuce and cilantro; they should be folded in just before serving. Spoon the salad into a large serving bowl, cover it with plastic wrap, and refrigerate it until it's time to leave. Tote the lettuce and cilantro separately in plastic bags, along with the chips, and assemble the dish at the gathering.

TINA OSCHMAN OF KNOXVILLE, TENNESSEE, HOSTED a party for a group of teens who had traveled through Europe together over the summer. She served grilled burgers and bratwursts and loaded the dining room table with a variety of salads. Tina made the most wonderful corn salad with black beans and lima beans and Mexican flavors. She piled it on a big ceramic platter; I loved the salad's freshness and its bright, vibrant yellow, red, and green colors. Since Tina sent me the recipe, it has become a mainstay in my kitchen.

4 ears white or yellow corn, or a mix of the two, shucked
Salt
¼ cup all-fruit apricot preserves
3 tablespoons fresh lime juice
   (1 large or 2 medium-size limes)
1 tablespoon olive oil
½ teaspoon ground cumin or chili powder
Freshly ground black pepper
½ head iceberg lettuce, thinly sliced (about 2 cups)
1 red bell pepper, cored, seeded, and chopped
1 can (about 16 ounces) black beans, rinsed and drained
1 can (about 15 ounces) lima beans, rinsed and drained
1 fresh jalapeño pepper, seeded, deveined, and
   finely chopped
¼ cup chopped fresh cilantro
2 cups large tortilla chips, for garnish

1. Fill a large pot with 3 to 4 inches of water and bring to a boil over medium-high heat. Add the corn and ½ teaspoon of salt, reduce the heat to low, and let the corn simmer until it is just done and still crisp, 3 to 4 minutes. Remove and drain the corn, then set it aside to cool.

2. Place the apricot preserves, lime juice, olive oil, and cumin or chili powder in a large glass bowl and whisk to combine. Season with salt and black pepper to taste. Set the salad dressing aside.

3. When the corn is cool enough to handle, hold an ear upright on a cutting board and, using a sharp knife, cut down close to the cob to slice off the kernels. It is fine if some of the kernels stay together in pieces. Repeat with the remaining ears of corn. Set the corn aside.

4. Add the lettuce, bell pepper, black beans, lima beans, jalapeño, and cilantro to the bowl with the dressing. Toss to combine, then fold in the corn kernels.

5. Refrigerate the salad for 2 to 3 hours, either in the mixing bowl or transferred to a serving platter or bowl and covered with plastic wrap. When ready to serve, transfer the salad to a serving dish, if necessary, and arrange the tortilla chips around the edge.

WHAT ABOUT A SUCCOTASH SALAD? Add chopped fresh tomatoes to the beans and garnish the top with crumbled bacon.

BIG BATCH: *Double this recipe, boiling enough corn as needed. Take care not to overcook the corn, so the kernels still have some crunch to them.*

RECIPE REMINDERS

Made for

Prep notes

Don't forget

Special touches

Bring again

Chicken Taco Salad with Cilantro-Lime Vinaigrette

SERVES 8

PREP: 35 TO 40 MINUTES

TOTE NOTES

Tote the chicken salad in its plastic-wrapped salad bowl. Bring the tortilla chips in a plastic bag and the vinaigrette in a pretty bowl covered with plastic wrap. Just before serving, uncover the salad. Give the vinaigrette a stir to recombine, then pour some of it over the salad. Top the salad with the tortilla chips and serve the rest of the vinaigrette on the side.

PLAN AHEAD

You can make the salad as early as the night before; refrigerate it and the vinaigrette until you're ready to travel.

W HEN YOU LOOK AT A LAYERED SALAD, YOU THINK a lot of work must have gone into preparing it, what with all those ingredients and the fancy presentation. But it is really all about the stunning glass bowl, a great vinaigrette, and a selection of ingredients that complement one another visually and taste-wise. Take this salad—it's flavorful and pretty to look at, yet the lettuce comes from a bag, the beans and corn from a can, the cheese is already shredded, and the chicken roasted in the supermarket deli. The only work you do is chop an onion and a few tomatoes and turn on the blender for the vinaigrette. To save a step and serve the salad as a side, just omit the chicken.

FOR THE SALAD

1 bag (about 10 ounces) chopped hearts of romaine lettuce (8 packed cups)

1½ cups chopped ripe tomato (1 large or 2 medium-size tomatoes)

1 can (about 15 ounces) black beans, rinsed and drained

1 cup chopped red onion or sweet white onion (1 medium-size onion)

2 cups (8 ounces) shredded Mexican blend cheese

1 can (about 15 ounces) corn kernels, drained

1 can (6 ounces) sliced black olives, drained

2 cups (about 8 ounces) shredded roast chicken breast (see Note)

FOR THE CILANTRO-LIME VINAIGRETTE

⅓ cup chopped fresh cilantro leaves

½ cup fresh lime juice (3 medium-size limes)

½ cup olive oil

½ cup reduced-fat sour cream

1 teaspoon sugar

Salt and freshly ground black pepper

2 cups lightly crushed tortilla chips, for serving

1. Make the salad: Place the lettuce in the bottom of a large glass salad bowl. Arrange the tomatoes in a layer on top of the lettuce. Spoon the beans on top of the tomatoes, then add the onion, cheese, corn, olives, and chicken in layers. Cover the bowl with plastic wrap and refrigerate until chilled and ready to serve.

2. Make the cilantro-lime vinaigrette: Place the cilantro, lime juice, olive oil, sour cream, and sugar in a blender or food processor fitted with a steel blade. Process in on and off pulses until the vinaigrette is smooth, 10 to 15 seconds. Season with salt and pepper to taste.

3. To serve, pour a little of the vinaigrette over the salad and top it with the tortilla chips. Serve the remaining vinaigrette on the side.

NOTE: For even more flavor, instead of buying a roast chicken, cook 2 skinless, boneless chicken breasts (8 to 10 ounces) in a slow cooker for 4 to 6 hours with a packet of taco (Mexican) seasoning. You won't need to add any liquid.

BIG BATCH: *You can double the ingredients of the salad and layer them in two separate salad bowls instead of one larger one.*

RECIPE REMINDERS

Made for

Prep notes

Don't forget

Special touches

Bring again

Tarragon Chicken Salad with Celery Shavings

SERVES 4

PREP: 40 MINUTES (INCLUDES THE TIME TO COOK THE CHICKEN)

WHETHER IT'S STUFFED INTO A RIPE TOMATO, spread onto soft bread, or spooned on lettuce leaves, homemade chicken salad is a treat. My family loves it in the summertime when anything hot seems too heavy, and it makes a nice gift for new neighbors because most everyone eats chicken salad. Although it may seem like adding an unneccessary step, I urge you to use chicken from home-cooked bone-in chicken breasts. They're easy to prepare, and the chicken has more flavor and is more tender. You may want to add a cup of grapes to the salad, too—go ahead if you like. I tend to be more of a purist, happy with well seasoned, properly cooked chicken and the crunch of the thinly sliced celery and chopped pecans.

2 cups (about 8 ounces) chopped or shredded cooked chicken breast (see Note)

Onion salt

½ cup very thinly sliced celery

⅓ cup mayonnaise

¼ cup reduced-fat sour cream

2 tablespoons fresh lemon juice (1 medium-size lemon)

1 tablespoon fresh tarragon leaves

Table salt and freshly ground black pepper

Lettuce leaves (optional), for serving

½ cup chopped toasted pecans (see page 99)

1. Place the chicken in a medium-size mixing bowl and season well with onion salt. Add the celery and toss to combine. Add the mayonnaise, sour cream, and lemon juice and stir to combine. Fold in the tarragon and season to taste with table salt and pepper. Cover the bowl with plastic wrap and refrigerate it.

2. When you are ready to serve, transfer the chicken salad to a serving plate lined with lettuce leaves, if desired, and garnish with the pecans.

NOTE: To cook the chicken, place 2 bone-in chicken breasts, 12 ounces to 1 pound, with their skin, in a medium-size saucepan and add water to cover. Add salt and pepper and a little sliced onion. Bring the water to a boil over medium-high heat, then reduce the heat, cover the pan, and let the chicken simmer until it tests done, 20 to 25 minutes. As soon as the chicken is cool enough to handle, remove the meat from the bones, and discard the bones and skin. Chop or shred the chicken. You'll need about 2 cups for this recipe.

WANT ANOTHER WAY TO SERVE THIS CHICKEN SALAD? The salad looks festive stuffed into little cherry tomatoes as an hors d'oeuvre. It's also good spread on sandwiches, in which case you'll want to stir the toasted pecans in first.

BIG BATCH: *I kept this recipe small on purpose because people tend to make and eat chicken salad on the same day, so there are no leftovers. But should you want to serve eight or twelve or sixteen, you can easily multiply the recipe times two or three or four. Count on two chicken breasts to feed four people. When cooking in quantity, be sure to chill the salad quickly for safety. Place it in a shallow glass dish, cover, and refrigerate.*

RECIPE REMINDERS

Made for

Prep notes

Don't forget

Special touches

Bring again

Chicken and Basmati Rice Salad

SERVES 6 TO 8

PREP: 25 MINUTES

TOTE NOTES

Tote the salad in a plastic container, bring the lettuce separately in a plastic bag, and don't forget the platter.

If you want to take the chicken salad to a friend, pack it in a plastic bowl with a snap-on lid and bring along a loaf of good bread.

WHEN YOU ARRIVE

Just before it's time to serve, line the platter with lettuce, then pile on the salad.

JUST LIKE THE GAME TELEPHONE, RECIPES MAKE THEIR rounds and change a little each step along the way. My version of this popular chicken salad uses basmati rice and red grapes. I also like to fold in toasted nuts, such as the Sweet and Spicy Pecans if I have the time to prepare them ahead, or just toasted sliced almonds if I don't. This is perfect picnic food and a great weekend salad to keep in the refrigerator.

1 cup basmati rice

2 cups chicken broth, or 2 cups water

Salt

4 cups (about 1 pound) cooked shredded or chopped chicken (see Note)

½ cup mango chutney

⅓ cup chopped scallions (about 3 scallions)

½ cup chopped toasted almonds (see box, page 99), or Sweet and Spicy Pecans (page 482)

½ cup finely chopped celery

2 cups sliced red grapes

1 cup mayonnaise

Freshly ground black pepper

Bibb or red-leaf lettuce leaves, for serving

1. Place the basmati rice, 2 cups of chicken broth or water, and ½ teaspoon of salt in a saucepan and bring to a boil over medium-high heat. Reduce the heat to medium-low, cover the pot, and let the rice simmer until cooked through and the liquid is absorbed, 18 to 20 minutes. (You can also make the salad with brown rice, but you will need to increase the liquid by ¼ cup and cook the rice longer, for up to 40 minutes.)

2. Place the chicken, chutney, scallions, nuts, celery, and grapes in a large mixing bowl. Add the rice, followed by the mayonnaise and stir to mix well. Season with salt and pepper to taste. Cover the bowl with plastic wrap and refrigerate it until chilled (it can be refrigerated overnight).

3. To serve, line a platter with lettuce leaves, then pile on the salad.

NOTE: You can buy roast chicken from the deli or you can cook your own. If you use skinless, boneless chicken breasts, don't overcook them. Simmer them in water for just 15 minutes, then turn off the heat and let them rest in the water for 10 minutes longer. When the chicken is cool enough to handle, shred it with your hands or chop it into pieces.

BIG BATCH: *You can easily double and triple Chicken and Basmati Rice Salad to feed a crowd.*

RECIPE REMINDERS

Made for

Prep notes

Don't forget

Special touches

Bring again

Chilled Shrimp Rémoulade Salad

SERVES 6 TO 8

PREP: 45 MINUTES ✳ CHILL: 1 HOUR

TOTE NOTES

You can assemble the shrimp salad, cover the platter with plastic wrap, and refrigerate it until it's time to tote. If the weather is warm, transport the salad in a cooler.

PLAN AHEAD

The shrimp salad can be refrigerated overnight.

WHEN YOU GET OUT OF THE HABIT OF COOKING your own shrimp you forget how wonderful it smells steeping in lemon and seasonings, or how easily a colander of freshly cooked shrimp turns into a marvelous salad. Sure, you can prepare this recipe using already-cooked shrimp from the supermarket, but be sure to try it from scratch at least once. Save a little time by buying large shrimp so you have fewer to peel, devein, and chop. If your market carries those shrimp in the shell that are the "easy peel" variety, buy those. They haven't been peeled, but they have been deveined, saving you a step. Shrimp salad is a treat, so serve it on pretty lettuce leaves and with good tomatoes.

FOR THE SHRIMP

½ lemon

2 tablespoons shrimp or crab boil seasoning

1 teaspoon salt

4 quarts water

2 pounds large fresh shrimp in their shells

1 cup finely chopped celery

¼ cup finely chopped onion

FOR THE RÉMOULADE

1 cup mayonnaise

3 tablespoons ketchup

1 tablespoon fresh lemon juice

1 medium-size clove garlic, crushed in a garlic press

1 teaspoon dry mustard

1 teaspoon Worcestershire sauce

Hot pepper sauce (optional)

FOR SERVING

2 cups Bibb or Boston lettuce leaves

2 tomatoes, cut into wedges

$\frac{1}{4}$ cup chopped fresh parsley, for garnish

1 tablespoon finely chopped dill pickle (optional),
   for garnish

1. Prepare the shrimp: Place the lemon half, shrimp or crab boil seasoning, and salt in a large pot. Add the water, cover, and bring to a boil. When the water is boiling, add the shrimp, stir, re-cover the pot, then remove it from the heat. Let the shrimp sit in the hot liquid until they turn bright pink and the shells loosen, about 10 minutes. Transfer the shrimp immediately to a colander in the sink, let cool for 5 minutes, then refrigerate them for at least 1 hour.

2. Remove and discard the shells from the shrimp and devein them, if necessary. Cut each shrimp in thirds (you can keep them whole if you prefer) and place them in a medium-size mixing bowl. Add the celery and onion, stir, and refrigerate.

3. Make the rémoulade: Place the mayonnaise, ketchup, lemon juice, garlic, dry mustard, and Worcestershire sauce in a small mixing bowl and whisk to combine. Season with hot pepper sauce to taste, if desired.

4. Pour the rémoulade over the shrimp and stir to mix well. Cover the salad with plastic wrap and refrigerate it until chilled, at least 1 hour.

5. To serve, line a platter with the lettuce leaves. Spoon the shrimp salad into the middle of the platter, partially covering

RECIPE REMINDERS

Made for

Prep notes

Don't forget

Special touches

Bring again

REMOULADE REDUX

Creamy, tangy rémoulade does excellent double duty as a dip or slather. Make an extra batch of it and try it alongside chilled, steamed asparagus spears or thin green beans, with crab cakes or seared scallops, or spread on a fish sandwich in place of tartar sauce.

the lettuce. Arrange the tomato wedges on the lettuce around the shrimp salad. Garnish the salad with parsley and chopped dill pickle, if desired.

WANT A FUN ISLAND VARIATION? Use jerk seasoning instead of the shrimp seasoning to cook the shrimp. Substitute lime juice for lemon juice in the rémoulade, thinly slice an avocado and/or mango and arrange it around the platter with the tomatoes, and omit the dill pickle garnish.

BIG BATCH: *You can boil up to 4 pounds of shrimp in a large pot. To save time, use frozen cooked shrimp, but be sure that you thaw and drain them well before using.*

MENU

GRADUATION LUNCH

Mark the milestone with a festive lunch you pull together with the help of others. Keep it casual and friendly—it's time to celebrate, so there's no need to be too serious.

JULIA'S CHILLED ZUCCHINI SOUP, *page 72*

✳

CHILLED SHRIMP RÉMOULADE SALAD, *page 156*

✳

BROCCOLI BRAG CASSEROLE, *page 260*

✳

LELIA'S EASY CHOCOLATE POUND CAKE, *page 347*

LETTUCE GET TOGETHER

A salad potluck is a fun *What Can I Bring?* theme for a casual meal, lunch with friends, a book club dinner, or an investment club meeting. For years, alums of the Pi Beta Phi sorority have enjoyed something they call a "Lettuce Get Together for Lunch" party. Here's how you can organize one of your own.

You (the host) provide a nice assortment of salad greens and salad dressings. You ask each guest to bring one topping for the salad; you might provide some suggestions on the invitation. Arrange the toppings in little ice cream bowls surrounding the great big bowl of greens. Or, place the toppings in chip and dip plates, on trays to the side, or even in wooden salad bowls—anything that lends an organized smorgasbord feel to the table. You should also have on hand some good bread, a light dessert, and a beverage that suits the occasion: wine, water, iced tea, lemonade—whatever you like.

Here are some salad topper ideas.

* Sliced vine-ripened tomatoes

* Yellow grape tomatoes

* Sliced cucumbers tossed with salt, sugar, and white wine vinegar

* Steamed, chilled thin green beans

* Sautéed zucchini with garlic slivers

* Steamed asparagus

* Grilled eggplant slices

* Roasted red pepper slices

* Marinated mushrooms or artichoke hearts

* Fresh strawberries

* Dried sweetened cranberries, cherries, or blueberries

* Mandarin oranges

* Sliced mango

* Toasted pecans, walnuts, pine nuts, or sunflower seeds

* Crumbled blue cheese or feta cheese

* Soft goat cheese cubes and fresh basil drizzled with olive oil

* Homemade croutons (see box, page 105)

* Freshly fried bacon, crumbled

* Slices of grilled chicken

* Steamed shrimp

* Crab cakes

* Smoked salmon or trout

* Anchovies

* Slices of rare grilled steak

Watermelon Boat with Summer Fruits

SERVES 18

PREP: 1 HOUR

MY MOTHER WAS A CREATIVE COOK WHO LOVED TO serve beautiful food. One of her signature summer salads was this grand watermelon boat, filled with melon balls, fresh pineapple, strawberries, and either blueberries or grapes. As children we marveled at the boat and its construction. When she wanted something more elaborate, she would cut a basket out of the watermelon, leaving a top strip of rind intact for the basket's handle. Through the years I have made this boat or basket for my kids, and it is really so easy. The fruits here will hold up well on the summer buffet table for four or five hours. You can even rewrap the boat and chill it overnight, although the fruits at the bottom get pretty soggy. The only fruit I don't recommend using is fresh peaches because they darken quickly. If you're timid about cutting the watermelon, draw an outline with a fine-tip marker first, then follow that with your knife. This is a real crowd-pleaser.

1 large watermelon, 12 to 16 inches long and about 15 pounds
1 large cantaloupe
1 medium-size honeydew melon
1 jumbo fresh pineapple
1 pint blueberries
3 cups strawberries (about 1½ pints)
Mint sprigs, for garnish

1. Rinse the watermelon and dry it with a kitchen towel. Place the watermelon on its side on a work surface. Cut out a large oval-shaped piece, cutting about one-third of the way down into the melon to create a boat shape. Using a sharp knife, trim the watermelon flesh off the lid piece of watermelon and place it in a large bowl, discarding the rind. Using the knife and a large spoon, cut around the inside of the rind of the larger piece of watermelon and transfer the flesh to the large bowl. It will take a while to cut and scoop out all the watermelon flesh. What will remain is the shell of the watermelon—the watermelon boat. Swab up the juice from the bottom of the boat with paper towels. Lightly cover the boat with plastic wrap and place it in the refrigerator.

2. If the watermelon has seeds, remove and discard them. Cut the watermelon into 1- to 2-inch pieces and return these to the large bowl. Cover the bowl with plastic wrap and refrigerate it.

3. Cut the cantaloupe and the honeydew melon in half and remove the seeds with a large spoon. Using a 1-inch melon ball scooper, scoop out balls of cantaloupe and honeydew and place them in a second large bowl. You will have about 6 cups of cantaloupe balls and 4 to 5 cups of honeydew, depending on the size of the melons. Cover this bowl with plastic wrap and refrigerate it.

4. Using a sharp knife, cut off the top of the pineapple and discard it. Cut down the side of the pineapple and across the bottom to remove the skin. Slice the pineapple off the core by standing the pineapple pulp on its end and making cuts straight down to remove the flesh. Cut each long piece of pineapple into 1-inch chunks. Place the chunks in a medium-size bowl, cover it with plastic wrap, and refrigerate it.

5. Rinse the blueberries and let them drain in a colander. Rinse the strawberries, let them drain on paper towels, then remove the hulls. Cut the strawberries in half if they are large.

BABY BOATS

Instead of making one large boat, you can use smaller melons to make mini boats. Or, cut a large watermelon in half lengthwise, then cut the half melons in half lengthwise so you have four long pieces. Cut each of these into four or six lengths to form individual boats. Scoop out the watermelon flesh so that a little remains on the sides—enough to keep the fruits in the boats. Then, following the recipe, add the rest of the fruits.

If you'd like, use construction paper, wooden skewers, and a glue stick to make sails for the boats.

Place the drained blueberries and strawberries in a large bowl, cover it with plastic wrap, and refrigerate it.

6. When you are ready to finish the boat, you can use a sharp paring knife to create a scalloped or a sawtooth edge around the top of it. Or, just leave the edge plain. Remove the fruits from the refrigerator and place them randomly in the boat. You may not use all the watermelon. The strawberries should be placed in the top third so they add visual interest. And, half of the blueberries should be reserved for scattering on top. Garnish the sides with some mint sprigs and serve at once or cover with plastic wrap and refrigerate until serving time. Before you add the strawberries to the boat, keep them separate from the melon and pineapple because the berries will bleed into the other fruits and cause them to turn pink.

BIG BATCH: *If you must, make two boats. But this salad feeds a crowd, and the bigger the watermelon, the bigger the boat!*

M E N U

BURGERS IN THE BACKYARD

Summer always seems so short, so turn to the grill on as many warm nights as you can, cooking up last-minute meals with the neighbors and their kids.

TURKEY BURGERS ON THE GRILL
WITH PESTO MAYONNAISE, *page 232*

✳

TINA'S CORN AND BLACK BEAN SALAD, *page 148*

✳

WATERMELON BOAT WITH SUMMER FRUITS,
page 160

✳

BEBE'S CHESS CAKE, *page 402*

Waldorf Salad

SERVES 8

PREP: 20 MINUTES

REMEMBER WALDORF SALAD? IT WAS SOMETHING of a sixties phenomenon, a wonderful crunchy salad of apples and celery and often walnuts and purple grapes, tossed with a mayonnaise dressing. The recipe has been around a long time, originating at the Waldorf-Astoria hotel in New York in the late 1800s. High time for a Waldorf salad renaissance, I think.

½ cup mayonnaise

½ cup applesauce

3 tablespoons honey

1 tablespoon fresh lemon juice

5 cups chopped crisp apples (Granny Smith or Golden Delicious; 4 to 5 large apples), unpeeled

1½ cups seedless purple grapes

1½ cups finely chopped celery

1 cup walnuts

Bibb lettuce leaves (optional), for garnish

1. Place the mayonnaise, applesauce, honey, and lemon juice in a small bowl and stir to combine.

2. Place the apples, grapes, celery, and walnuts in a large mixing bowl, add the mayonnaise mixture, and stir until well incorporated. Refrigerate the salad covered with plastic wrap until ready to serve, then spoon it onto a platter lined with Bibb lettuce leaves, if desired, or in a serving bowl.

BIG BATCH: *Waldorf salad doubles well.*

TOTE NOTES

Prepared early in the day, transferred to a serving bowl, and covered with plastic wrap, the salad can be refrigerated until you're ready to tote it as is.

Or, refrigerate the salad in a large plastic bowl with a snap-on lid and take this, along with a platter and Bibb lettuce leaves in a plastic bag, and you can assemble the salad at the party.

RECIPE REMINDERS

Made for

Prep notes

Don't forget

Special touches

Bring again

Margaret's
Black Cherry Salad

SERVES 12 TO 16

PREP: 25 MINUTES ✳ CHILL: 5 TO 6 HOURS

**TOTE
NOTES**

*If you are not traveling
far, you can place the
salad on the lettuce-lined
platter and cover it with
plastic wrap to tote.*

*If you are traveling a
bit longer, leave the salad
in the mold or baking
dish and unmold it when
you arrive. Bring the
lettuce in a plastic bag
and don't forget the
platter.*

*When the weather
is warm, you'll want to
transport the salad in
a cooler.*

PLAN AHEAD

*Make the salad and
refrigerate it, covered in
the pan, for up to two
days.*

I'M ALWAYS ON THE LOOKOUT FOR A GREAT SALAD TO update holiday meals, so when Nashville resident Margaret Boyd brought this black cherry salad to the house, I was thrilled to taste it. Dramatic in color—dark red with bits of green and gold peeking through—its flavor is complex, combining the tart apples with sweet cherries and crunchy walnuts. The salad goes well with ham, turkey, or roast pork. Make it in a large ring mold if you have one, or simply use a 13 by 9–inch dish. The salad is pretty served cut up into squares and placed on a large platter or tray lined with lettuce leaves.

1 can (20 ounces) crushed pineapple
1 can (15 ounces) pitted black cherries, packed in syrup
2 packages (3 ounces each) black cherry gelatin
1 packed cup chopped Granny Smith apple
  (1 large apple)
⅔ cup chopped walnuts
Vegetable oil spray, for misting the mold
Red leaf lettuce, for serving

1. Drain the pineapple in a sieve over a medium-size bowl, setting aside the liquid. Spoon the pineapple back into the can and refrigerate it.

2. Drain the cherries in a sieve over a medium-size bowl, setting aside the liquid. Spoon the cherries back into the can and refrigerate them.

3. Pour the liquid from the pineapple into a measuring cup. Add enough of the cherry liquid and/or water to measure 3 cups of liquid, then pour this into a medium-size saucepan and bring to a boil over medium-high heat. When the liquid is boiling, remove the pan from the heat, add the gelatin, and stir with a fork until completely dissolved.

4. Pour the hot gelatin mixture into a large glass bowl, let cool for 5 minutes, then refrigerate it, uncovered, until it is the consistency of egg whites, 1 to $1\frac{1}{2}$ hours.

5. Remove the gelatin from the refrigerator and add the drained pineapple and cherries and the apple and walnuts, stirring until they are well blended.

6. Lightly spray an 8-cup ring mold or 3-quart glass baking dish with vegetable oil. Transfer the gelatin mixture to the mold or baking dish and cover with plastic wrap. Refrigerate until set, at least 4 hours, preferably overnight. The ring mold will take longer to set than the baking dish.

7. When ready to serve, if using a ring mold, fill the sink with 1 inch of hot water. Let the ring mold sit in the water for a few seconds. Run a sharp knife around the edge of the mold, then gently shake it to loosen the salad. Invert the salad onto a platter lined with lettuce leaves. If using a baking dish, run a knife around the edges of the dish, cut the salad into servings, and using a metal spatula, transfer them to a platter lined with lettuce leaves. Either way, the unmolded salad will keep for 3 to 4 hours.

BIG BATCH: *You can certainly make two or three batches of the cherry salad in separate molds. Don't mix more than a single batch at a time in one bowl or the gelatin might not set properly.*

RECIPE REMINDERS

Made for

Prep notes

Don't forget

Special touches

Bring again

Ladies' Lunch Tomato Aspic

SERVES 8 TO 12

PREP: 50 MINUTES ✳ CHILL: 4 HOURS

TOTE NOTES

To tote the aspic, unmold it on a serving platter and cover it with plastic wrap. Carry the dill sprigs and lemon wedges separately in small plastic bags and garnish the aspic at the gathering.

If the weather is warm, transport the aspic in a cooler.

PLAN AHEAD

The aspic can be prepared a day ahead; refrigerate it until you're ready to travel.

WHEN I PICTURE A LADIES' LUNCHEON, A BRIDAL shower, a baby shower, even an Easter lunch, I see tomato aspic on the table. Yes, it's retro and harkens back to a time when moms supposedly wore shirtwaist dresses and pearls to fix dinner, but it's also incredibly delicious with today's food. Try tomato aspic with a grilled steak. Pile shrimp salad into the middle. Or serve Chilled Shrimp Rémoulade Salad or Tarragon Chicken Salad with Celery Shavings alongside. Tomato aspic gets more exciting when you discover all the goodies and seasonings inside—cucumber and dill here—or add hot pepper sauce, or even quartered artichoke hearts. The aspic can be made in a two-quart glass baking dish or a mold.

2 envelopes unflavored gelatin

⅓ cup water

4 cups (32 ounces) tomato juice

1 medium-size sweet onion, thinly sliced

⅓ cup chopped celery leaves

1 tablespoon sugar

1 teaspoon salt

½ teaspoon freshly ground black pepper, or more to taste

¼ cup fresh lemon juice (1 large lemon), plus lemon wedges, for garnish

1 tablespoon chopped fresh dill, plus dill sprigs,
   for garnish

1 large cucumber, peeled, seeded, and finely chopped
   into ¼-inch pieces (1½ cups; optional)

Vegetable oil spray, for misting the mold

1. Place the gelatin and water in a small bowl and stir until
the gelatin is dissolved, then set it aside.

2. Place the tomato juice, onion, celery leaves, sugar, salt, and
pepper in a large saucepan. Bring to a boil over high heat,
reduce the heat to low, and simmer for 10 minutes, stirring
occasionally. Remove the pan from the heat and strain the
juice through a sieve into a large bowl. Add the gelatin mixture

---

BEST FRIEND BRIDAL SHOWER

What a nice way to pay tribute to your good friend,
the bride-to-be, with this luncheon for family and
friends. The menu is ladylike, the type of food you're
not served every day. So get out the heirloom china,
polish the silver, and serve her in style.

TARRAGON CHICKEN SALAD
WITH CELERY SHAVINGS, *page 152*

or

CHILLED SHRIMP RÉMOULADE SALAD, *page 156*

✳

LADIES' LUNCH TOMATO ASPIC

✳

CINDY'S CHILE CHEESE GRITS, *page 326*

✳

WHOLE WHEAT REFRIGERATOR ROLLS, *page 460*

✳

LEMON SQUARES, *page 395*

**RECIPE
REMINDERS**

Made for

Prep notes

Don't forget

Special touches

Bring again

TEN WAYS TO DRESS UP TOMATO ASPIC

1. *Chopped artichoke hearts*

2. *Fennel fronds and fresh tarragon*

3. *Chopped green olives with pimientos*

4. *Chopped roasted red peppers*

5. *Minced celery*

6. *Chopped steamed asparagus*

7. *Cubed hearts of palm*

8. *Cubed avocado*

9. *Chopped cooked shrimp*

10. *Use Bloody Mary mix instead of tomato juice*

and stir until it is incorporated. Stir in the lemon juice and chopped dill. Taste for seasoning, adding more pepper as necessary. Let the tomato juice mixture cool on the counter for 15 to 20 minutes, then place the bowl, uncovered, in the refrigerator. Chill the aspic until it just begins to set, $1\frac{1}{2}$ to 2 hours.

3. Fold the cucumber into the aspic, if desired. Lightly spray a 4- to 6-cup mold or 2-quart dish with vegetable oil. Pour the aspic into the mold and refrigerate it until firmly set, about 2 hours.

4. When ready to serve, fill the sink with 1 inch of hot water. Dip the mold in the water for a few seconds, then invert the aspic onto a serving platter. Garnish it with dill sprigs and lemon wedges.

BIG BATCH: *You can double the aspic and prepare it in a larger baking dish or an 8-cup ring mold. To find out how much a mold will hold, measure it by seeing how many cups of water are needed to fill it.*

CROWD-PLEASING MAIN DISHES

I wonder if main dishes at a potluck feel neglected? Cutting-edge appetizers, fancy green salads, and drop-dead delicious desserts get all the fanfare; who much notices the main dish? But it is the heart of the meal. Barbecues, fish fries, shrimp boils, and turkey at Thanksgiving are the reasons for the party. The main dish sets the tone and lets all the other recipes take the spotlight.

When I planned this chapter, I knew I had to have turkey and beef tenderloin and plenty of casseroles, but which recipes and how to organize them? It dawned on me that potluck main dishes are either the take-along kind, such as casseroles, or they're the "you're hosting the party" kind, like turkey or barbecued ribs.

The mains you tote, like the ones in the beloved 13 by 9-inch baking dish, appear first here. Among others, you'll find Currey's King Ranch Chicken, Black Bean Tortilla Bake, and Creamy Macaroni and Beef Casserole, a few of my favorites. Dishes I cook for friends in my home follow, such as skewers of lemon and garlic grilled shrimp, Grilled Chicken for a Crowd, and oven-baked pork tenderloins.

Main dishes are the mainstay of every successful meal. I hope you enjoy the recipes I've shared with you here.

Parmesan Chicken Rolls

SERVES 6 TO 8

**PREP: 15 MINUTES ✳ BRINE: 3 HOURS ✳ BAKE: 1 HOUR
PLUS 20 MINUTES RESTING TIME**

**TOTE
NOTES**

*To tote the chicken rolls,
cover the baking dish
with aluminum foil and
carry the chicken in it.
If you want to serve the
chicken rolls warm,
reheat them in a 300°F
oven for 20 minutes when
you get to the gathering.*

   *Chicken rolls are
also delicious cold. Once
they've cooled down,
cover the baking dish
with plastic wrap and
refrigerate them—you
can tote them when
they're chilled. They look
pretty when sliced and
arranged on a nice platter
garnished with arugula
and tomato slices.*

PLAN AHEAD

*You can bake the chicken
rolls a day in advance;
refrigerate them, covered.*

MY MOTHER USED TO BAKE CHICKEN THIS WAY, AND WE especially enjoyed it the next day, served cold along with potato salad and sliced tomatoes. It's odd that a recipe as simple as this could give me trouble, but I ended up testing it a half-dozen times before I came up with the best method. The problem is that boneless chicken breasts vary in size and tenderness. I found that if you soak them in cold salted water in the refrigerator (what's known as brining) and then bake them, they are a lot more tender, no matter the size. And I found that an hour's cooking time was right, so I baked the chicken at a little hotter temperature in the beginning to get the crumbs to brown for good flavor and color, then reduced the heat slightly to keep the chicken moist as it cooked through. You can adapt this recipe as you see fit by adding chopped fresh herbs and your favorite seasonings. And try the "piccata" version for adventuresome taste buds when the menu is Italian.

6 skinless, boneless chicken breast halves
   (about 2¼ pounds)

2 teaspoons kosher salt

3 to 4 slices good sturdy white bread, such as sourdough
   or Pepperidge Farm white bread

1 large clove garlic, peeled

¼ loosely packed cup fresh parsley leaves

1 cup (4 ounces) grated Parmesan cheese

⅓ cup olive oil

1. Rinse the chicken and place it in a large bowl. Add cold water to cover and stir in the kosher salt. Refrigerate the chicken for at least 3 hours before baking.

2. Place a rack in the center of the oven and preheat it to 350°F.

3. Remove the chicken breasts from the brine, pat them dry with paper towels, and set aside.

4. Tear the bread into pieces and place in a food processor fitted with a steel blade. Add the garlic and parsley and process until you have crumbs, about 20 seconds. Transfer the crumbs to a shallow pan and stir in the Parmesan cheese.

5. Pour the olive oil in a shallow bowl. Dip the chicken breasts into the olive oil, then dredge them in the crumb and cheese mixture. Roll up the chicken breasts, beginning at the short end, and place the rolls side-by-side in a 13 by 9–inch glass or ceramic baking dish. If desired, you can secure the rolls with half a wooden skewer. Scatter any of the remaining crumb mixture over the top of the chicken and drizzle any remaining oil over the crumbs.

6. Bake the chicken until the crumb topping has browned, about 30 minutes, then reduce the heat to 325°F and bake until the chicken has cooked through, about 30 minutes longer. Remove the chicken from the oven, let it rest for 20 minutes, then slice and serve.

WHAT ABOUT PARMESAN CHICKEN ROLLS PICCATA? Once you remove the chicken from the oven, squeeze the juice of 1 lemon—about 2 tablespoons—over it. Garnish the chicken with 2 tablespoons of drained capers and ¼ cup of chopped fresh parsley.

BIG BATCH: *You can double, triple, or quadruple this recipe, baking the chicken rolls on a large sheet pan for a big party.*

RECIPE REMINDERS

Made for

Prep notes

Don't forget

Special touches

Bring again

Slow-Cooker Chicken and Dressing

SERVES 8 TO 10

PREP: 25 TO 30 MINUTES

COOK: 3 TO 4 HOURS ON HIGH HEAT, OR 7 HOURS ON LOW

TOTE NOTES

Tote the chicken to the party in the slow cooker. It will stay warm that way. When you arrive, plug the cooker back in and set it on low to keep the chicken warm.

DON'T YOU JUST LOVE THE SLOW COOKER? IT TRULY is the busy cook's best friend. And this recipe is a great one for the winter holidays when you need to bring a main dish to a potluck supper. Or, it's wonderful for family get-togethers when the folks like something warm and comforting. This dish tastes like Thanksgiving dinner all in one pot, and it comes from the people at Oxmoor House publishing and *Southern Living* magazine. We collaborated on a Christmas cookbook, and they shared this recipe from their test kitchen. It's a dandy!

4 cups shredded cooked chicken
  (about 1 pound; from 1 rotisserie chicken)
6 cups coarsely crumbled corn bread
8 slices firm white bread, torn into pieces
2 cans (about 14 ounces each) chicken broth
2 cans (10¾ ounces each) cream of chicken soup
1 cup chopped onion (1 medium-size onion)
3 ribs celery, chopped (about ¾ cup)
4 large eggs, lightly beaten
1 teaspoon ground sage
½ teaspoon coarsely ground black pepper
¼ teaspoon salt
Vegetable oil spray, for misting the cooker
8 tablespoons (1 stick) butter, at room temperature

1. Place the chicken, corn bread, white bread, chicken broth, cream of chicken soup, onion, celery, eggs, sage, pepper, and salt in a large mixing bowl. Stir to combine well.

2. Mist a 5-quart round slow cooker with vegetable oil spray and add the chicken mixture to the cooker. Dot the top with the butter. Cover the cooker and cook until the eggs are done, 3 to 4 hours on high heat or 7 hours on low heat. Stir the chicken before serving.

BIG BATCH: *It's not possible to double this recipe in one slow cooker. If you need to make more, use a second slow cooker.*

FOUR HEARTY RECIPES FOR ROOM IN THE INN

To help the homeless, communities feed and house them in churches and civic centers with the help of such organizations as Room in the Inn. Here are some recipes that are nourishing, heartening, and travel well when you are feeding a crowd.

SLOW-COOKER CHICKEN AND DRESSING
✳
CURREY'S KING RANCH CHICKEN, *page 180*
✳
JUDY'S MOM'S MEAT LOAF, *page 190*
✳
CREAMY MACARONI AND BEEF CASSEROLE, *page 206*

MENU

RECIPE REMINDERS

Made for

Prep notes

Don't forget

Special touches

Bring again

Susan's Chicken Potpie

SERVES 6

**PREP: 15 TO 20 MINUTES ✳ BAKE: 27 TO 34 MINUTES
PLUS 10 MINUTES RESTING TIME**

TOTE NOTES

You can cover the potpie and tote it while it's still warm from the oven.

PLAN AHEAD

Bake the potpie the night before, then cover and refrigerate it. Take the chilled pie with you and reheat it at the gathering in a 350°F oven for about 20 minutes.

WHEN ASKED TO BRING A DISH, MY SISTER SUSAN makes her signature potpie. It's a hit with all ages because the ingredients are fresh and the taste is soothing. Susan doesn't fuss with making homemade piecrust, relying, instead, on the convenience of a refrigerated crust. I know I shared this recipe with you in *The Dinner Doctor*, but it had "What can I bring?" written all over it and begs repeating here.

1 package (2 rounds; 15 ounces) refrigerated
    pastry rounds

2 tablespoons (¼ stick) butter

1½ cups chopped frozen or fresh vegetables
    of your choice (see Note)

2 cups (about 8 ounces) shredded cooked chicken

3 tablespoons all-purpose flour

Salt and freshly ground black pepper

2 cups low-sodium chicken broth

1. Place a rack in the center of the oven and preheat the oven to 450°F.

2. Set one pastry round aside. Place the other round in a 9-inch pie pan that is 2 inches deep. Crimp the edge of the pastry with a fork, then prick the bottom a few times. Bake the pastry until it is well browned, 7 to 8 minutes. Remove the pie pan from the oven and set it aside. Reduce the oven temperature to 350°F.

3. While the crust for the pie bakes, melt the butter in a large skillet over medium heat. Add the vegetables and cook, stirring, for about 1 minute. Add the chicken and cook, stirring for about 1 minute longer. Sprinkle the flour over the vegetables and chicken, then season with salt and pepper to taste. Cook, stirring, until the flour is incorporated, about 1 minute longer. Add the broth to the skillet, increase the heat to medium-high, and cook, stirring constantly, until the mixture thickens slightly, 1 to 2 minutes.

4. Pour the chicken mixture into the baked piecrust. Cover the top with the remaining pastry round. Turn the edge of the top pastry under the crimped edge of the bottom crust with your fingertips. Press around the edge with a fork to seal the two together. Make several vents in the top pastry with a sharp knife.

5. Bake the pie on top of a baking sheet until the crust is golden brown and the juices are bubbling, 20 to 25 minutes. If the juices are bubbling but the top has not browned, place the potpie under the broiler until it turns golden. Let the potpie rest for 10 minutes, then slice it and serve.

NOTE: You can use frozen peas, carrots, lima beans, and green beans, or mixed vegetables. Fresh asparagus tips, peas, green beans, mushrooms, and slices of summer squash would also be good, just be sure to cut them into small pieces so they cook all the way through.

BIG BATCH: *This is a great recipe to double; just remember you need two crusts for each pie. Bake both pies at the same time.*

RECIPE REMINDERS

Made for

Prep notes

Don't forget

Special touches

Bring again

Creole Chicken Spaghetti

SERVES 12

PREP: 25 MINUTES ＊ COOK: 30 MINUTES

TOTE NOTES

Tote the spaghetti topped with cheese in the baking dish covered with aluminum foil. At the gathering, bake the spaghetti in a 350°F oven until it is heated through and the cheese melts, 15 to 20 minutes.

PLAN AHEAD

You can make the sauce a day or two in advance and refrigerate it covered—the flavors will improve. Reheat the sauce on the stove just before you boil the spaghetti and finish making the dish.

Or, you can boil the spaghetti up to 2 hours ahead. Toss it with olive oil once it's drained. Reheat the spaghetti and sauce topped with the cheese in a 350°F oven for 25 to 30 minutes.

I HAVE WONDERFUL MEMORIES OF ATTENDING CHURCH suppers as a child and being served something called chicken spaghetti. It sounded pretty exotic to me, considering my mother never added anything to spaghetti sauce but ground beef. Chicken spaghetti isn't really Italian, but more a mix of Italian, Creole, and Tex-Mex, which makes it really interesting. I came across this recipe years ago and it's a keeper, a perfect covered dish supper entrée, something to tote or serve to guests at home. Vary the seasonings as you like.

1/4 cup olive oil

2 cups sliced onions (2 medium-size onions)

2 cups (8 ounces) sliced mushrooms

1 to 1 1/4 cups chopped green bell pepper

3/4 cup chopped celery (3 ribs)

4 medium-size cloves garlic, minced

1 jar (32 ounces) pasta sauce

1 can (14 1/2 ounces) diced tomatoes with their juices

2 tablespoons sugar, or more to taste

2 tablespoons Worcestershire sauce

1 tablespoon chili powder

2 teaspoons ground cumin

Salt and freshly ground black pepper

4 cups shredded cooked chicken (about 1 pound; from 3 large chicken breasts or 1 rotisserie chicken)

1 pound spaghetti

2 cups (8 ounces) shredded cheddar cheese

1. Place the olive oil in a large saucepan over medium-low heat. Add the onions, mushrooms, bell pepper, celery, and garlic and cook, stirring, until the onions soften and the mushrooms begin to lose their liquid, 4 to 5 minutes. Add the pasta sauce and tomatoes with their juices and stir to combine. Add the sugar, Worcestershire sauce, chili powder, and cumin. Taste for seasoning, adding more sugar as needed and salt and black pepper to taste. Reduce the heat to low, cover the pan, and let simmer until the sauce thickens slightly, about 20 minutes. Remove the pan from the heat and stir in the chicken. Cover and keep warm.

2. Bring a large pot of water to a boil over high heat. Break the spaghetti noodles in half. Stir in the spaghetti and 1 teaspoon of salt, reduce the heat to medium-high, and cook the spaghetti, uncovered, according to the package directions until just done, 6 to 7 minutes.

3. Drain the spaghetti well in a colander, shaking it to remove the excess water, then return it to the pot. Pour the sauce on top of it and stir to combine well, then reheat gently over low heat. Transfer the sauced spaghetti to a serving platter, top it with the cheese, and serve at once. Or, if you'd like the cheese melted, spoon the spaghetti and sauce into a 13 by 9–inch glass or ceramic baking dish, top it with the cheese, and loosely cover it with aluminum foil. Bake the spaghetti in a 350°F oven until the cheese melts, about 15 minutes, then serve it straight from the baking dish.

BIG BATCH: *If you need to double or triple the spaghetti, make the sauce in a large pot, then divide it into two or three containers and refrigerate it until needed.*

RECIPE REMINDERS

Made for

Prep notes

Don't forget

Special touches

Bring again

Chicken Enchiladas

SERVES 8 TO 10

PREP: 25 MINUTES ✳ BAKE: 25 TO 30 MINUTES
PLUS 10 MINUTES RESTING TIME

**TOTE
NOTES**

*You can tote the filled
tortillas and bake them
when you arrive. Or, go
ahead and bake the
tortillas and keep them
warm by wrapping the
baking dish first with
heavy-duty aluminum foil
and then a towel to hold
in the heat.*

PLAN AHEAD

*The filled tortillas can
be refrigerated for a
day or kept frozen in a
resealable plastic freezer
bag for several weeks. Let
them thaw before baking.*

W HAT MAKES THIS CASSEROLE A LITTLE DIFFERENT
is that the sauce is not creamy. It is essentially
just a chile, salsa, broth, and herb combination
that is pureed and poured over the enchiladas. This keeps
the tortillas very moist, and it makes a great dish that
holds well on the buffet table. Serve whatever toppings
you like—sour cream, chopped tomatoes, avocado cubes,
and shredded iceberg lettuce—on the side.

Vegetable oil spray, for misting the pan

2 tablespoons olive oil

1 cup thinly sliced onion (1 medium-size onion)

½ cup chopped red bell pepper

2 to 3 cups (8 to 12 ounces) shredded or chopped
   cooked chicken

1 teaspoon ground cumin

4 ounces (half an 8-ounce package) reduced-fat cream
   cheese, cut into cubes

Salt and freshly ground black pepper

2 cans (4½ ounces each) chopped green chiles,
   undrained

2 medium-size cloves garlic, peeled

½ loosely packed cup fresh parsley or cilantro leaves

2 teaspoons dried oregano

1 cup low-sodium chicken broth

1 cup tomato salsa

10 flour tortillas (6 to 7 inches each)

2½ cups (10 ounces) shredded Mexican-style cheese blend

1. Place a rack in the center of the oven and preheat the oven to 375°F. Lightly mist a 13 by 9–inch glass or ceramic baking dish with vegetable oil spray and set it aside.

2. Place the olive oil in a large skillet over medium-low heat. Add the onion and bell pepper and cook, stirring, until the onion is soft, 4 to 5 minutes. Remove the skillet from the heat and stir in the chicken and cumin. Add the cream cheese and place the skillet back over the heat. Cook, stirring, until the cream cheese melts and creates a sauce. Season with salt and black pepper to taste and set the filling aside.

3. Place the chiles, garlic, parsley or cilantro leaves, and oregano in a food processor or blender and process until nearly smooth, about 30 seconds. Add the chicken broth and salsa and process until well combined, another 30 seconds. Season with salt and black pepper to taste. Spoon a third of the sauce in the prepared baking dish and set aside.

4. Place the tortillas on a work surface and spoon some of the chicken mixture down the center of each tortilla, dividing it evenly. Set aside 2 cups of the cheese for the topping, then sprinkle the remaining ½ cup of cheese over the chicken, dividing it evenly among the 10 tortillas. Roll up the tortillas and place them seam side down in the baking dish, squeezing them in if needed. Spoon the remaining sauce over the tortillas and sprinkle the reserved 2 cups of cheese on top.

5. Bake the enchiladas until the cheese melts and the sauce is bubbly, 25 to 30 minutes. Let the enchiladas rest for 10 minutes, then serve with the toppings of your choice.

BIG BATCH: *You can double this recipe and put the enchiladas in a larger pan, such as a roasting pan. Bake the larger batch at 350°F until bubbly; it will take nearly an hour.*

RECIPE REMINDERS

Made for

Prep notes

Don't forget

Special touches

Bring again

Currey's King Ranch Chicken

SERVES 12

PREP: 30 MINUTES ✳ **COOK: ABOUT 34 MINUTES**
BAKE: 55 MINUTES TO 1 HOUR PLUS 5 MINUTES RESTING TIME

**TOTE
NOTES**

*If the casserole is going to
be served within 2 hours
of the time it finishes
baking, let it rest for
5 minutes, then wrap it
in a clean kitchen towel
to keep it warm. Tote it
wrapped up in the towel.*

*If you want to bake
the chicken more than
2 hours ahead, let it cool,
then cover it with plastic
wrap and refrigerate it.
Once you arrive at the
gathering, reheat the
chicken, covered with
aluminum foil, in a
350°F oven for about
20 minutes.*

V ARIATIONS OF THIS TEXAS RECIPE HAVE BEEN
around for years. This version comes from my
friend Currey Thornton of Nashville, who used
to cater and knows how to serve crowds successfully. It's
an ample casserole of chicken, peppers, spicy tomatoes,
and flour tortillas in a creamy cheese sauce and goes well
with a green salad or a fruit salad.

4 skinless, boneless chicken breast halves
(about 1½ pounds)

1 teaspoon Italian seasoning

1 teaspoon ground cumin

1 teaspoon salt

¼ teaspoon freshly ground black pepper

Vegetable oil spray, for misting the pan

2 tablespoons (¼ stick) butter

1 medium-size green bell pepper, cored, seeded,
and chopped (1 cup)

1 medium-size onion, chopped (1 cup)

3 medium-size cloves garlic, sliced

2 cans (10 ounces each) chopped tomatoes with
green chiles, such as Ro-Tel, undrained

1 can (10¾ ounces) cream of mushroom soup, undiluted

1 can (10¾ ounces) cream of chicken soup, undiluted

12 small (6-inch) flour tortillas, cut into quarters

3 cups (12 ounces) Mexican-style shredded cheese

1. Place the chicken in a medium-size saucepan and add water to cover. Add the Italian seasoning, cumin, salt, and black pepper. Bring the water to a boil over medium-high heat, then reduce the heat to low and let simmer, covered, for about 15 minutes. Turn off the heat and let the chicken sit in the cooking liquid for about 15 minutes longer. Using a slotted spoon, remove the chicken from the pan and drain it (set the chicken broth aside for another use). When the chicken is cool enough to handle, pull it into shreds. You should have about 4 cups of chicken. Set the chicken aside.

2. Place a rack in the center of the oven and preheat the oven to 350°F. Lightly mist a 13 by 9–inch glass or ceramic baking dish with vegetable oil spray and set it aside.

3. Place the butter in a large skillet over medium heat. Add the bell pepper, onion, and garlic and cook until soft, 3 to 4 minutes. Remove the pan from the heat and add the tomatoes with chiles and mushroom and cream of chicken soups. Stir until well combined.

4. Ladle 1 cup of this sauce on the bottom of the prepared baking dish. Place a third of the tortilla quarters in the baking dish. Top that with a third of the chicken and sprinkle a liberal layer of cheese over it. Repeat the layers ending with the remaining cheese. Cover the baking dish with aluminum foil.

5. Bake the chicken until the sauce is bubbly, about 45 minutes, then uncover the casserole and let it brown on top, 10 to 15 minutes longer. Let the chicken rest for 5 minutes before serving.

BIG BATCH: *This is a large casserole; bake two if you are feeding a really big group.*

RECIPE
REMINDERS

Made for

Prep notes

Don't forget

Special touches

Bring again

Tex-Mex Chicken Spaghetti

SERVES 8 TO 10

PREP: 50 MINUTES ✴ BAKE: 30 TO 35 MINUTES

TOTE NOTES

Tote the spaghetti casserole covered with aluminum foil and wrapped in a clean kitchen towel to keep it warm; the casserole can sit a while and still taste good.

Bring the chopped onion in a small plastic bag.

PLAN AHEAD

You can bake the spaghetti casserole the night before. Cover the baking dish with aluminum foil and refrigerate it. Reheat the casserole, covered, in a 350°F oven for about 20 minutes before serving.

I CAME ACROSS THIS RECIPE IN MY MOTHER'S RECIPE files. It was not something I remembered her making, but it seemed like a dish my kids would love. And it sounded vaguely similar to King Ranch chicken casserole (see page 180), except that this recipe contains thin spaghetti and the King Ranch uses flour tortillas. So I gave it a try, adding some cumin for flavor, using a thinner spaghetti than the original recipe called for, and serving chopped sweet onion on the side for crunch. Everyone loved this spaghetti—it was hearty and filling and a little spicy, too; perfect for potlucks. If you're not into using canned soup and Velveeta, then move on to another recipe.

4 skinless, boneless chicken breast halves
    (about 1$\frac{1}{2}$ pounds; see Note)

1 chicken-flavored bouillon cube

1$\frac{1}{2}$ teaspoons salt

$\frac{1}{4}$ teaspoon freshly ground black pepper

12 ounces thin spaghetti

1 can (10 ounces) chopped tomatoes with green chiles,
    such as Ro-Tel, undrained

1 pound Velveeta cheese, cubed

1 can (10$\frac{3}{4}$ ounces) cream of mushroom soup

$\frac{1}{2}$ teaspoon ground cumin

1 cup (4 ounces) shredded Cheddar cheese

1 cup finely chopped onion (1 medium-size onion),
    for serving

1. Place the chicken in a medium-size saucepan and add water to cover. Add the bouillon cube and ½ teaspoon of salt and the pepper. Bring the water to a boil over medium-high heat, then reduce the heat to low and let simmer, covered, for about 15 minutes. Turn off the heat and let the chicken sit in the cooking liquid for about 15 minutes longer. Using a slotted spoon, remove the chicken from the pan. Measure 1 cup of the chicken broth and set aside, reserving the remaining broth for another use. When the chicken is cool enough to handle, pull it into shreds. You should have about 4 cups of chicken. Set the chicken aside.

2. Place a rack in the center of the oven and preheat the oven to 350°F.

3. Bring a large pot of water to a boil over high heat. Break the spaghetti noodles in half. Stir in the spaghetti and 1 teaspoon of salt, reduce the heat to medium-high, and cook the spaghetti, uncovered, according to the package directions until just done, 6 to 7 minutes. Drain the spaghetti well in a colander, shaking it to remove excess water, then set it aside.

4. Place the pot back on the stove and add the tomatoes with chiles, Velveeta cheese, mushroom soup, cumin, and the reserved 1 cup of broth. Cook, stirring, over low heat until the cheese has melted and the mixture is smooth, 6 to 7 minutes. Fold in the chicken and the drained spaghetti and stir to combine well. Spoon the mixture into a 13 by 9–inch glass or ceramic baking dish. Sprinkle the Cheddar cheese over the top.

5. Bake the spaghetti casserole until the cheese has melted on top and the casserole is bubbling around the edges, 30 to 35 minutes. Remove the baking dish from the oven and serve with the chopped onion on the side.

NOTE: No time to cook your own chicken? Buy a roast chicken from the supermarket deli and remove the skin.

RECIPE REMINDERS

Made for

Prep notes

Don't forget

Special touches

Bring again

CANNED SOUP IN THE CUPBOARD

Don't knock it—those old-favorite "cream of" soups help make easy, tasty sauces in casseroles and stews. Keep a few on hand (mushroom, chicken, asparagus, and tomato, for example). Next time you ask "What can I bring?" you'll be glad they're there.

Pull the meat from the bones and use 4 cups of shredded or chopped chicken. Use 1 cup of canned low-sodium chicken broth in place of the cooking liquid.

BIG BATCH: *Double the ingredients and divide them between two casseroles. Bake both at the same time.*

HOW TO DRESS UP
A 13 BY 9-INCH BAKING DISH

Casseroles—you either love them or hate them, right? Could the problem be the ho-hum baking dish in which they rest? Does that glass casserole have bland written all over it? Let's dress it up.

1. Buy an inexpensive basket in which to put the casserole dish.

2. Buy a fun painted casserole holder at a specialty store so you don't see the glass dish.

3. Use oval baking dishes; a three-quart one will hold as much as a 13 by 9–inch baking dish.

4. Look for ceramic casseroles with handles.

5. Place the baking dish on a tray and surround it with flowers, fruit, or little votive candles.

Turkey Tetrazzini

SERVES 8 TO 10

PREP: 30 MINUTES ∗ BAKE: 25 TO 30 MINUTES PLUS 10 MINUTES RESTING TIME

THIS IS THE CASSEROLE OF MY CHILDHOOD, THE DISH my mother made using leftover Thanksgiving or Christmas turkey. It is seasoned lightly with sherry and topped with pecans and green olives, and it can go well with something as simple as a green salad and rolls. Make it for an office potluck lunch, bridal shower, or Easter brunch. Vary the seasonings as you like; you can use chicken instead of turkey.

8 ounces thin spaghetti

Salt

3 cups (about 12 ounces) chopped or shredded cooked turkey

4 tablespoons (½ stick) butter

2 cups (8 ounces) sliced mushrooms

½ cup chopped onion

½ cup chopped celery

3 tablespoons all-purpose flour

2 cups low-sodium chicken broth

1 cup heavy (whipping) cream

2 tablespoons sherry

Freshly ground black pepper

1 cup (4 ounces) grated Parmesan cheese

½ cup chopped pecans, for topping

¼ cup sliced green olives, for topping

1. Bring a large pot of water to a boil over high heat. Break the spaghetti noodles in half. Stir in the spaghetti and 1 teaspoon

TOTE NOTES

Tote the baked Turkey Tetrazzini covered with aluminum foil and wrapped in a towel to keep it warm.

Covered with aluminum foil, the casserole can be kept warm in a 200°F oven or a warming drawer.

A refrigerated casserole can be reheated, covered, in a 350°F oven for 20 minutes.

of salt, reduce the heat to medium-high, and cook the spaghetti, uncovered, according to the package directions until just done, 6 to 7 minutes. Drain the spaghetti well in a colander, shaking it to remove excess water, then place it in a large mixing bowl, add the turkey, and toss to combine. Set the turkey and spaghetti mixture aside.

2. Place a rack in the center of the oven and preheat the oven to 375°F.

3. Place the butter in a large pot over medium heat. Add the mushrooms, onion, and celery and cook, stirring, until softened, 3 to 4 minutes. Reduce the heat to medium-low and add the flour. Cook, stirring, for 1 minute. Add the chicken broth and cook, stirring, until it begins to thicken, 1 to 2 minutes. Add the cream and stir until combined. Add the sherry, season with salt and pepper to taste, and cook, stirring, until the mixture comes just to a boil, about 2 minutes. Remove the pot from the heat and stir in ½ cup of the Parmesan cheese. Pour the sauce into the bowl with the spaghetti and turkey and stir to combine well.

4. Transfer the turkey mixture to a 13 by 9–inch glass or ceramic baking dish and sprinkle the remaining ½ cup of Parmesan over it. Sprinkle the pecans and olives over the Parmesan. Bake the casserole until it is bubbling, 25 to 30 minutes. Let the casserole rest for 10 minutes, then serve.

BIG BATCH: *You can double or triple this recipe, but bake each batch in a single 13 by 9–inch baking dish.*

Barb's Taco Ring

SERVES 8

PREP: 20 MINUTES

BAKE: 20 TO 25 MINUTES ✳ **COOL: 3 TO 4 MINUTES**

BUSY MOM BARBARA GILL, WHO LIVES IN NASHVILLE, was talking to me one day about this taco ring and how her kids begged for it and how she garnished it like a big taco with shredded lettuce and cheese and chopped tomatoes. It must have been near lunchtime because I was about to faint from hunger hearing her description. So, I made her taco ring, and then I made it again, and the next time, I garnished it with such fanfare that I decided this is one great recipe to take with you. You can prep it but not bake it until you arrive at the party or potluck. For a crowd, make two or three. They will all disappear.

FOR THE TACO RING

2 tablespoons olive oil (optional)

1½ pounds ground lean turkey or beef (see Notes)

2 packages (1¼ ounces each) low-sodium taco seasoning mix

1 cup water

2 packages (8 ounces each) refrigerated crescent rolls (regular or reduced-fat; see Notes)

FOR SERVING

Reduced-fat sour cream

Shredded iceberg lettuce

Chopped tomatoes

Shredded Cheddar cheese

Guacamole

TOTE NOTES

Tote the unbaked taco ring on its baking sheet, covered with plastic wrap, and bake it when you get to the party; it will be crisp and fragrant.

Place the lettuce, tomatoes, and Cheddar cheese in little plastic bags and bring the sour cream and guacamole in separate containers.

Don't forget a platter or wooden board for serving.

PLAN AHEAD

The unbaked taco ring can be covered with plastic wrap and refrigerated a day ahead.

**PRONTO
PLATTER**

*If you can't find a plate
or platter large enough
for the taco ring, don't
worry. Cut a piece of
sturdy cardboard that
is as large as the ring
plus a 2-inch margin
on all sides. It might
be a square, circle, or
rectangle. Cover the top
with aluminum foil and
tuck the ends of foil
underneath to conceal
them, then carefully
arrange the baked taco
ring on top.*

1. Place a rack in the center of the oven and preheat the oven
to 375°F.

2. Place the olive oil, if using, in a large skillet over medium
heat. Add the turkey or beef, breaking it into bits with a
wooden spoon. Cook, stirring, until cooked through, 3 to 4
minutes. Add the taco seasoning and stir to mix evenly, then
add the water. Increase the heat to medium-high and cook,
stirring, until the liquid has nearly evaporated, 4 to 5 minutes.
Set the turkey mixture aside.

3. Unroll the crescent rolls; you will have 16 triangles of
dough. Place an ungreased baking sheet or pizza stone, about
14 by 16 inches, on a work surface. Arrange the dough with
the large sides of the triangles facing the center of the baking

**M
E
N
U**

SWEET SIXTEEN BIRTHDAY BASH

Your baby is sixteen. Save your tears for another night
because this meal's upbeat and the food is *fun*. Have her
friends or the other parents bring a salsa, dip, or fruit. You
bake the taco ring and garnish it like crazy. The dessert
might be a surprise; hide it in the freezer. The party will
be sweet and unforgettable—just like your child.

COWBOY CAVIAR, *page 20*
*
TORTILLA CHIPS
*
BARB'S TACO RING, *page 187*
*
FRESH FRUIT OF THE SEASON
*
CHOCOLATE PEPPERMINT ICE CREAM CAKE, *page 344*

sheet and the points hanging over the edge. Leave a 3- to 4-inch empty space in the center of the baking sheet. Press the dough together where the triangles meet to connect them.

4. Spoon the turkey or beef mixture in a ring on top of the joined dough, leaving the center empty (you can put a bowl of sour cream there when serving). Carefully pull up the points of the crescent rolls, twisting them together to seal them over the filling. Don't get too fussy with this because after the taco ring bakes, it looks gorgeous no matter whether the filling is completely covered by the rolls.

5. Bake the taco ring until it is golden brown, 20 to 25 minutes, then let it cool for 3 to 4 minutes. Transfer the ring to a serving plate. Place a bowl of sour cream in the space you left in the center and arrange the lettuce, tomatoes, Cheddar cheese, and guacamole in little bowls attractively around the taco ring.

NOTES: I like to use a little more than a pound of meat. Barb likes to use 2 pounds because she says her kids are really hungry after they get in from school and sports. Suit yourself. A pound seems a little skimpy to me, but 2 pounds is packed.

As for the crescent rolls, I have used both regular and reduced fat, but the regular are definitely flakier and taste better in the taco ring.

BIG BATCH:
It's just as easy to make two taco rings as it is to prepare one.

RECIPE REMINDERS

Made for

Prep notes

Don't forget

Special touches

Bring again

Judy's Mom's Meat Loaf

SERVES 6 TO 8

PREP: 10 MINUTES * BAKE: 55 MINUTES TO 1 HOUR
PLUS 20 MINUTES RESTING TIME

TOTE NOTES

Leave the meat loaf in the pan, cover it with aluminum foil, then wrap a kitchen towel around it to keep it warm en route. Or, when you arrive you can reheat the meat loaf in a 300°F oven for about 15 minutes.

PLAN AHEAD

You can bake the meat loaf up to 2 hours in advance and keep it at room temperature. Or, bake it the night before or early on the day of the gathering and refrigerate it, covered. Either way you'll want to reheat it before serving.

JUDY WRIGHT IS A GENEROUS COOK WHO PREPARES meat loaf for the charity organization Room in the Inn. She recalled one time she made a nine-and-a-half-pound meat loaf in a deep roasting pan, brought it to serve, and every bit was gone in less than thirty minutes. Judy's meat loaf secret is her mother's meat loaf secret—Lipton onion soup mix. She has adapted the recipe on the box, adding brown sugar, mustard, and extra ketchup. And I have adapted hers slightly, soaking the bread in milk, which is one secret to a great meat loaf, and the other—using extra ketchup for the glaze. If there is any meat loaf left over, my family loves it at any temperature, especially cold the next day, sliced on a sandwich with a little ketchup, a little mayo, and a slice of dill pickle.

2 cups bread cubes (4 to 5 slices of sturdy white bread)
¾ cup milk or water
1 envelope (1 ounce) onion soup mix
2 large eggs, lightly beaten
1 cup ketchup
2 tablespoons Dijon mustard
2 tablespoons light brown sugar
2 pounds ground beef (I use sirloin)

1. Place a rack in the center of the oven and preheat the oven to 350°F.

2. Place the bread cubes, milk or water, and onion soup mix in a large mixing bowl. Stir to combine. Add the eggs, $\frac{1}{2}$ cup of the ketchup, and the mustard and brown sugar and stir well. Using your fingers, break apart the ground beef and distribute it in the mixing bowl. Still using your hands, work the ground beef into the bread mixture until just combined; don't overwork it as this will toughen the meat. Transfer the meat mixture to a 13 by 9–inch glass or ceramic baking dish and shape it into a loaf. Drizzle the remaining $\frac{1}{2}$ cup of ketchup over the top of the meat loaf.

3. Bake the meat loaf until the top has browned and the loaf has cooked through, 55 minutes to 1 hour. Transfer the meat loaf to a serving platter and let it rest for at least 20 minutes before slicing.

BIG BATCH: *You can double and triple this recipe. Bake two or three meat loaves at the same time, but shape each into a 2-pound loaf so that it bakes through in an hour.*

MORE THAN TWO POUNDS OF BEEF IN THE PACKAGE?

If you've got a package of ground beef that weighs more than the two pounds called for in the meat loaf recipe here, pinch off the extra and place it in a resealable freezer bag. The frozen ground beef will keep for two to three months. Thaw the meat later and brown it to add to vegetable soup or spaghetti sauce.

RECIPE REMINDERS

Made for

Prep notes

Don't forget

Special touches

Bring again

January Lamb Stew

SERVES 6 TO 8

PREP: 25 TO 30 MINUTES ✳ COOK: 1 HOUR, 15 MINUTES

**TOTE
NOTES**

*Once the stew has cooled,
transfer it to clean quart
jars or plastic storage
containers.*

   *Or, tote the stew
right in the cooking pot.
Le Creuset pans are
wonderful for both
cooking and toting
because the lids are
heavy and secure so
nothing leaks out in
transit.*

   *When you arrive,
reheat the stew on
site over medium-low
heat, stirring it until
it comes to a boil,
10 to 15 minutes.*

CORABEL AND MARTIN SHOFNER HOSTED A FUN
Twelfth Night dinner party one cold January
night. When we arrived, the aroma of rosemary
and lamb wafted out of the kitchen door. A magnificent
lamb stew simmered on the stove, and we gobbled it
down with crusty bread. This is an entrée both to serve
at home—ask others to bring a green salad, some crusty
bread, a good bottle of red wine, and a chocolate or
cherry dessert—and to tote to another location. The stew
can be made ahead and packed in quart-size glass jars to
take with you.

2 tablespoons olive oil

2 pounds lean leg of lamb, cubed (about 4 cups)

2 medium-size onions, chopped (about 2 cups)

8 medium-size cloves garlic, minced

1 quart low-sodium chicken or beef broth

2 cups canned white beans, rinsed and drained

4 carrots, peeled and cut into 1-inch pieces (about 3 cups)

1 tablespoon fresh rosemary leaves, crushed in your hand

1 bay leaf

Salt and freshly ground black pepper

1. Place the olive oil in a large, heavy saucepan over medium
heat. Add the lamb and brown well on all sides, 4 to 5 minutes.
To avoid crowding, you may need to do this in batches, adding
only enough lamb to cover the bottom of the pan, then removing
it and browning more. Set all of the browned lamb aside.

2. Add the onions and garlic to the saucepan and cook, stirring, until they begin to brown, about 3 minutes. Add the broth and let it come to a simmer, scraping the bottom of the pan to loosen the cooked bits. Add the reserved lamb, white beans, carrots, rosemary, and bay leaf. Cover the pan and reduce the heat as needed to let the stew simmer until the meat is cooked through and tender, about 1 hour.

3. Season the stew with salt and pepper to taste and remove and discard the bay leaf before serving.

BIG BATCH: *You can easily double and triple the stew, using a large pot or Dutch oven.*

BABY, IT'S COLD OUTSIDE

Stack the logs on the fire, put on a Perry Como CD, and gather together with close friends over a warm winter's dinner.

JANUARY LAMB STEW
*
BIG GREEN SALAD WITH ORANGE, AVOCADO, AND RED WINE VINAIGRETTE, *page 94*
*
CRUSTY BREAD
*
CRANBERRY TART, *page 423*

M
E
N
U

RECIPE REMINDERS

Made for

Prep notes

Don't forget

Special touches

Bring again

Ham and Cheese Overnight Soufflé

SERVES 10 TO 12

PREP: 15 MINUTES ✳ CHILL: OVERNIGHT
BAKE: 55 MINUTES TO 1 HOUR

TOTE NOTES

Tote the unbaked soufflé, wrapped in plastic wrap, and bake it when you arrive at the gathering.

Mix the cracker crumbs and the melted butter together before you leave home and carry them in a small plastic bag, then sprinkle them over the soufflé just before baking.

PLAN AHEAD

You can prepare the soufflé a day in advance; don't bake it, just cover it and put it in the refrigerator. Make the topping at the same time and set it aside at room temperature until you are ready to bake.

FOR ALL OF YOU BUSY WORKER BEES—YOU KNOW who you are, working all day and staying up until midnight catching up on housework and getting a head start on a party dish you're toting the next day— well, this dish is for you. It should be made the night before and tucked in your refrigerator so you can go snooze. The next day it will bake up puffed and golden, like some precious soufflé. The only secret is to use soft bread. I have made this with crusty sourdough, the dense kind sold at a bakery here, and it's good but not fluffy and light. When I made it with the supermarket deli bread that is much lighter, my kids liked it better, and I'll admit it was more ethereal, more like a classic soufflé. Serve it with a green salad, a fruit salad, and perhaps some grilled or roasted asparagus for brunch.

Vegetable oil spray, for misting the baking dish

10 slices soft Italian-style white bread,
   cut into ½-inch cubes (4 cups)

4 ounces thinly sliced ham, cut into 1-inch pieces
   (about 1 cup)

3 cups (12 ounces) shredded sharp Cheddar cheese

2 tablespoons minced onion

6 large eggs

3 cups milk

1 teaspoon Dijon mustard

1 cup crushed buttery round crackers,
   such as Ritz (about 16 crackers)

5 tablespoons unsalted butter, melted

1. Lightly mist a 13 by 9–inch glass or ceramic baking dish with vegetable oil spray. Scatter half of the bread cubes in the baking dish. Top with the ham, Cheddar, and onion, then the remaining bread cubes. Set the baking dish aside.

2. Place the eggs, milk, and mustard in a medium-size bowl and whisk to combine. Pour the egg mixture over the bread cubes and press down on them so they are immersed in the liquid. Cover the baking dish with plastic wrap and refrigerate it overnight.

3. When ready to bake, place a rack in the center of the oven and preheat the oven to 350°F.

4. Toss the cracker crumbs and melted butter together in a small bowl. Using your fingers, scatter the crumb mixture over the top of the soaked bread cubes. Bake the soufflé until it puffs up and is golden, 55 minutes to 1 hour. Serve at once.

BIG BATCH: *Make two or three soufflés at one time to feed a crowd.*

RECIPE REMINDERS

Made for

Prep notes

Don't forget

Special touches

Bring again

Lou Ann's Spinach, Prosciutto, and Mushroom Midnight Strata

SERVES 8 TO 12

PREP: 15 TO 20 MINUTES ✳ BAKE: 45 MINUTES

TOTE NOTES

Stratas are best eaten within 10 to 15 minutes of being taken out of the oven because they sink a little—not as much as a soufflé, but enough to notice. So tote the unbaked strata, wrapped in plastic wrap, in a wide basket or a shallow box and bake it when you arrive.

PLAN AHEAD

The unbaked strata can be refrigerated, covered, for 24 hours.

A STRATA—THE FANCY NAME FOR A BREAD, MILK, and egg casserole—is a wonderful way to use up leftovers. It's an even better do-ahead because it can linger in the refrigerator for a day before you bake it. Then, it puffs up golden and important looking. Lou Ann Brown, who lives in Nashville, dreamed up this inviting combination of mushrooms, prosciutto, and fresh spinach. Use the softest, squishiest Italian-style bread you can find. Lou Ann took the *strata* with her to a New Year's party. She stashed it in the refrigerator for most of the evening and placed it in the oven around 11:00 P.M. so it would be ready at the stroke of midnight.

Vegetable oil spray, for misting the baking dish
1 large (1 pound) loaf soft Italian-style white bread
2 tablespoons olive oil
4 loosely packed cups baby spinach (4 to 5 ounces), rinsed and drained well
2 cups (8 ounces) sliced mushrooms
2 medium-size cloves garlic, sliced
6 ounces prosciutto, chopped
6 large eggs
4 cups milk
2 tablespoons Dijon mustard

2 cups (8 ounces) shredded fontina cheese

1 cup (4 ounces) shredded Parmesan cheese

1. Place a rack in the center of the oven and preheat the oven to 350°F. Lightly mist a 13 by 9–inch glass or ceramic baking dish with vegetable oil spray and set it aside.

2. Cut the bread into 1-inch cubes and set them aside.

3. Place the olive oil in a large skillet over medium heat. Add the spinach, mushrooms, and garlic and cook, stirring with a wooden spoon, until the spinach wilts and the mushrooms begin to lose some of their liquid, 3 to 4 minutes. Set the spinach mixture aside.

4. Scatter half of the bread cubes in the prepared baking dish. Spoon the spinach mixture over the bread. Scatter the chopped prosciutto over the spinach mixture. Scatter the remaining bread cubes on top.

5. Place the eggs, milk, and mustard in a small bowl and beat with a fork until the eggs are lemon colored, about 1 minute. Fold in the fontina and Parmesan cheeses. Pour the cheese and egg mixture over the bread cubes, taking care to distribute the cheese evenly. Bake the *strata*, uncovered, until golden brown, about 45 minutes. Serve at once.

BIG BATCH: *You can assemble two or three* stratas *at once. Vary the fillings to make them more interesting, using different cheeses and adding fresh herbs.*

RECIPE REMINDERS

Made for

Prep notes

Don't forget

Special touches

Bring again

Mushroom and Gruyère Cheesecake

SERVES 8 TO 10

**PREP: 25 MINUTES ✳ BAKE: 1 HOUR AND 15 MINUTES
PLUS 1 HOUR RESTING TIME IN THE OVEN ✳ COOL: 30 TO 40 MINUTES**

TOTE NOTES

Once the cheesecake has cooled, wrap it in aluminum foil while it's still in the springform pan. Then wrap a kitchen towel over the foil and place the cheesecake in a shallow box to make it easy to carry.

PLAN AHEAD

This cheesecake tastes best baked within an hour or so of eating. Yet, you can plan ahead and streamline the process by prepping in advance: Prebake the crust. Let the cream cheese come to room temperature. And shred the Gruyère cheese, drain the spinach, and chop the scallions and mushrooms.

MY FRIEND JUDY WRIGHT IS A FABULOUS COOK, so you know if you are invited to her house, there is nothing to bring except yourself. Seriously, Judy knows her way around the kitchen. We all asked if we could bring something to a prewedding luncheon in October but she said no. And it looked as if her lunch was effortless—the salad was made and tossed on the side table and the most glorious-looking cheesecake was cooling next to it. As it turned out, this cheesecake was savory and our main dish, and it was crammed with mushrooms, spinach, and Gruyère cheese. It's one of Judy's favorites for entertaining friends.

FOR THE CRUST

1 tablespoon unsalted butter, at room temperature, for greasing the springform pan
1⅓ cups fine bread crumbs
5 tablespoons unsalted butter, melted

FOR THE FILLING

3 packages (8 ounces each) cream cheese, at room temperature
¼ cup heavy (whipping) cream
Salt
¼ teaspoon ground nutmeg
¼ teaspoon ground cayenne pepper

4 large eggs

1 cup (4 ounces) shredded Gruyère cheese

1 package (10 ounces) frozen chopped spinach,
     thawed and drained well

2 tablespoons chopped scallions, green parts only

3 tablespoons unsalted butter

2 cups (8 ounces) mushrooms, finely chopped

Freshly ground black pepper

1. Make the crust: Place a rack in the center of the oven and preheat the oven to 350°F. Rub a 9-inch springform pan with the tablespoon of butter and set the pan aside.

2. Spread out the bread crumbs on a rimmed baking sheet and place them in the oven to toast as it preheats, 8 to 10 minutes.

3. Transfer the toasted bread crumbs to a small mixing bowl. Pour the melted butter over them and stir to combine. Press the crumb mixture firmly into the bottom and up the side of the prepared springform pan. Bake the crust until golden brown, 8 to 10 minutes. Let the crust cool while you prepare the filling. Reduce the oven temperature to 325°F.

4. Make the filling: Place the cream cheese, cream, $\frac{1}{2}$ teaspoon of salt, nutmeg, and cayenne in a blender or food processor fitted with a steel blade and process until smooth. Add the eggs and process to mix. Divide the cream cheese mixture evenly between 2 bowls. Stir the shredded Gruyère cheese into one bowl and set it aside. Add the drained spinach and scallions to the second bowl and stir to combine. Spoon the spinach mixture into the cooled crust and set it aside.

5. Place the 3 tablespoons of butter in a large skillet over medium-high heat. Add the mushrooms and cook, stirring, until the liquid cooks out of the mushrooms, 8 to 10 minutes. Season the mushrooms with salt and black pepper to taste.

**RECIPE
REMINDERS**

Made for

Prep notes

Don't forget

Special touches

Bring again

CREATIVE CARRIERS

Take a look around your house and you'll find you've got baskets and boxes in which this cheesecake can travel. Line a basket with a clean kitchen towel, and cover the top of the springform pan with another towel or plastic wrap. Transported in a pretty basket, this cheesecake is just right for taking to picnics and tailgate brunches.

6. To assemble the cheesecake, spoon the mushrooms over the spinach filling in the springform pan. Carefully pour the Gruyère cheese filling over the top. Set the springform pan on a baking sheet and place in the oven. Bake the cheesecake until just set, about 1 hour and 15 minutes. Turn off the oven and open the oven door slightly, inserting a kitchen towel to keep the door ajar. Let the cheesecake rest in the oven for 1 hour. Then, place the cheesecake on a wire rack to cool to room temperature, 30 to 40 minutes, before serving.

BIG BATCH: *Bake two cheesecakes at once. If you like, you can vary the seasoning, adding 1 cup of chopped cooked broccoli instead of the spinach and using a cup of grated Cheddar cheese in place of the Gruyère.*

White Bean and Spinach Lasagna

SERVES 8 TO 10

PREP: 25 MINUTES ☀ BAKE: 40 TO 45 MINUTES
PLUS 20 MINUTES RESTING TIME

I FIND THAT MOST LASAGNA IS BORING. AND, WHAT WITH sitting and being reheated, the thick and slippery noodles often grab all the moisture from the sauce, making the lasagna dry. This well-seasoned version with white beans and fresh spinach is an exception; it has plenty of sauce and cheese to make it moist. It reminds me of the lasagnas in Italy. While not very Italian, substituting egg roll wrappers for the typical noodles helps. Thin and understated, the wrappers are easy to layer in the pan.

FOR THE SAUCE

2 tablespoons olive oil

8 ounces ground turkey or lean ground beef

2 medium-size cloves garlic, sliced

1 jar (32 ounces) tomato-based pasta sauce

1 can (15 to 16 ounces) white beans, drained

1 teaspoon dried oregano

FOR THE LASAGNA

1 container (15 ounces) whole or skim milk ricotta cheese

3 cups (12 ounces) shredded mozzarella cheese

½ cup (2 ounces) grated Parmesan cheese

2 large eggs

12 egg roll wrappers (about half of a 16-ounce package; see Note)

2 loosely packed cups fresh spinach (about 2 ounces), rinsed and drained well

---

TOTE NOTES

You can tote the lasagna right out of the oven; cover it with aluminum foil and keep it warm by wrapping it in towels or newspaper.

If you prefer, reheat the lasagna in a 300°F oven for 20 minutes once you arrive. (Any leftover slices of lasagna can be reheated, loosely covered with paper towels or waxed paper, in the microwave oven, on high power for 45 seconds to 1 minute.)

PLAN AHEAD

The lasagna can be assembled a day in advance—cover it with plastic wrap and refrigerate it until you're ready to bake. Tote the lasagna straight from the refrigerator and you can bake it in a 350°F oven when you arrive at the gathering. Refrigerated lasagna will take 10 to 15 minutes longer to bake, 55 minutes to 1 hour.

1. Make the sauce: Place the olive oil in a large pan over medium-low heat. Add the ground turkey or beef and garlic and cook, stirring, until the meat browns and cooks through, 3 to 4 minutes. Reduce the heat to low and add the pasta sauce, beans, and oregano. Let the mixture simmer until thickened, about 10 minutes. Set the sauce aside.

2. Make the lasagna: Place the ricotta, 1 cup of the mozzarella, and the Parmesan cheese in a medium-size bowl and stir to combine. Add the eggs and stir until mixed well. Set the cheese mixture aside.

3. Preheat the oven to 350°F.

4. Spoon 1 cup of the sauce in the bottom of a 13 by 9–inch glass or ceramic baking dish and spread it out with a rubber spatula. Place 4 egg roll wrappers on top of the sauce, cutting 2 of the wrappers as needed to completely cover the bottom of the baking dish. Spread a third of the cheese mixture over the wrappers. Cover this with 1 cup of the spinach, then top with a third of the remaining sauce.

5. Add 4 more egg roll wrappers on top of the sauce, cutting them as necessary to cover. Spread half of the remaining cheese mixture over the wrappers and top this with half of the remaining sauce. Arrange the remaining last 4 egg roll wrappers on top and spread the remaining cheese mixture over them. Top the cheese mixture with the remaining cup of spinach and spoon the remaining sauce on top. Scatter the remaining 2 cups of mozzarella over the lasagna.

6. Bake the lasagna, uncovered, until it bubbles around the edges and browns slightly, 40 to 45 minutes. Let the lasagna rest for about 20 minutes, then cut it into squares and serve. (If you're serving the lasagna at home, you can keep it hot in a 200°F oven until your guests arrive.)

NOTE: You'll find egg roll wrappers in the refrigerated case of the supermarket's produce section. The recipe uses about half of a 16-ounce package. Wrap the remaining wrappers well and freeze them for another use.

BIG BATCH: *When you need to feed a crowd, you can bake two lasagnas at the same time.*

Mexican "Lasagna" Stack

SERVES 8 TO 10

**PREP: 20 MINUTES ✳ BAKE: 25 TO 30 MINUTES
PLUS 10 MINUTES RESTING TIME**

**TOTE
NOTES**

*Tote the "lasagna" stack
in the springform pan,
covered with aluminum
foil and wrapped in a
towel.*

*Bring the tomato,
cilantro, and lettuce
garnishes in separate
plastic bags.*

*If necessary, the
"lasagna" stack can be
gently reheated in a
300°F oven for about
20 minutes. Just before
serving, unmold the
stack by placing the
springform pan on
a round platter and
unfastening the side.
Garnish the stack and
you're ready to serve.*

SIMILAR TO THE MEXICAN "LASAGNA" THAT APPEARED
in the *Dinner Doctor,* this easy crowd-pleaser is
a little larger and so it serves more people than
the earlier version. Baking the "lasagna" in a springform
pan makes it easy to transport and, when you unmold it,
creates a dramatic presentation. Place it on a platter and
shower it with tomatoes, shredded lettuce, and fresh
cilantro. You can use flour or corn tortillas; I prefer the
milder flavor of flour tortillas when I'm serving a crowd.

FOR THE LASAGNA
Vegetable oil spray, for misting the skillet
1½ pounds lean ground beef or ground turkey
2 cups salsa
9 flour tortillas (10 inches each)
1 can (16 ounces) refried beans, preferably fat-free
1½ cups reduced-fat sour cream
3 cups (12 ounces) shredded Mexican-style cheese blend

FOR THE GARNISH
Chopped fresh tomatoes
Cilantro sprigs
Shredded iceberg lettuce

1. Place a rack in the center of the oven and preheat the oven
to 400°F.

2. Place a large skillet over medium heat and mist it with
vegetable oil spray. Add the ground beef or turkey and cook,

stirring and breaking up the lumps with a wooden spoon, until the meat browns all over and is cooked through, 4 to 5 minutes. Stir in 1 cup of the salsa. Set the meat mixture aside.

3. Spread the remaining salsa in the bottom of a 10-inch springform pan. Top it with 3 of the tortillas. Dollop a third of the beans over the tortillas, then a third of the meat mixture, $\frac{1}{2}$ cup of the sour cream, and then 1 cup of the cheese. Top with 3 more tortillas, half of the remaining beans and half of the meat mixture, $\frac{1}{2}$ cup sour cream, and 1 cup of cheese. Top this with the remaining 3 tortillas, beans, meat mixture, $\frac{1}{2}$ cup sour cream, and 1 cup of cheese. Cover the pan with aluminum foil.

4. Bake the "lasagna" until it has heated through and the cheese has melted, 25 to 30 minutes. Remove the "lasagna" from the oven, let it rest for 10 minutes, then remove the side of the springform pan. Cut the "lasagna" into wedges and serve it garnished with the chopped tomatoes, cilantro sprigs, and shredded lettuce.

BIG BATCH: *You can double this recipe and bake it in a larger springform pan. The tortillas don't have to fit exactly; cut them to fit the pan. Remember that the larger the pan, the lower the oven temperature needs to be and the longer the stack will take to heat through: Bake it at 375°F for 45 minutes to an hour.*

RECIPE REMINDERS

Made for

Prep notes

Don't forget

Special touches

Bring again

Creamy Macaroni and Beef Casserole

SERVES 8

**PREP: 30 MINUTES * BAKE: 30 TO 35 MINUTES
PLUS 10 MINUTES RESTING TIME**

TOTE NOTES

Cover the baked casserole with aluminum foil to keep it warm en route, or reheat it, covered, in a 350°F oven for 15 to 20 minutes, when you arrive.

PLAN AHEAD

After you scatter the cheese over the top of the casserole, you can cover the baking dish with aluminum foil and refrigerate it overnight. Then, uncover and bake the casserole right from the refrigerator; it will take about forty minutes.

WHEN YOU BRING THIS CASSEROLE ALONG, NOT A smidgen will be left in the pan. It is one of my family's favorite recipes, a tangy, creamy blend of tomato sauce, noodles, and cheese. Serve the macaroni casserole with a green salad, such as The Best Caesar Salad (see page 92), and garlic bread.

> 2 cups elbow macaroni
> Salt
> 2 tablespoons olive oil
> Vegetable oil spray, for misting the pan
> 1½ pounds lean ground beef or ground turkey
> 1 cup chopped onion (1 medium-size onion)
> 3 medium-size cloves garlic, sliced
> 1 teaspoon ground cumin
> Freshly ground black pepper
> 1 can (15 ounces) tomato sauce
> 2 tablespoons tomato salsa
> 3 ounces reduced-fat cream cheese (see Note), at room temperature
> 1 cup reduced-fat sour cream
> 2 cups (8 ounces) shredded sharp cheddar cheese

1. Bring a large pot of water to a boil over high heat. Stir in the macaroni and ½ teaspoon of salt, reduce the heat to medium-high, and cook the macaroni, uncovered, according to the package directions until just done, 7 to 8 minutes. Drain the macaroni well in a colander, shaking it to remove excess water, then toss it with 1 teaspoon of the olive oil and set aside.

2. Place a rack in the center of the oven and preheat the oven to 375°F. Lightly mist a 13 by 9–inch glass or ceramic baking dish with vegetable oil spray and set it aside.

3. Place the remaining 5 teaspoons of olive oil in a large frying pan over medium heat. Add the ground beef and cook, stirring, until cooked through, 3 to 4 minutes. Add the onion and garlic and cook, stirring, until soft, 2 to 3 minutes. Add the cumin and season with salt and pepper to taste. Add the tomato sauce and salsa and cook, stirring, until the mixture bubbles and thickens a bit, about 5 minutes.

4. Place the cream cheese and sour cream in a small mixing bowl. Using a wooden spoon or a fork, stir to combine. Set the cream cheese mixture aside.

5. Transfer the drained macaroni to the prepared baking dish. Spoon the sauce evenly over the macaroni and smooth out the top with the back of the spoon. Dollop the cream cheese mixture on top of the sauce and, using a rubber spatula, spread it out so that it is smooth. Scatter the cheddar cheese over the top of the casserole.

6. Bake the casserole until it bubbles around the edges, 30 to 35 minutes. Let it rest 10 minutes before serving.

NOTE: You can cut 3 ounces off a larger 8-ounce block of cream cheese, or you can purchase the cream cheese in a small 3-ounce package.

BIG BATCH: *You'll need to bake two or three casseroles when you want to feed a crowd.*

RECIPE REMINDERS

Made for

Prep notes

Don't forget

Special touches

Bring again

Baked Penne with Mozzarella and Basil

SERVES 6

PREP: 20 MINUTES ✳ BAKE: ABOUT 25 MINUTES

TOTE NOTES

Cover the baking dish with aluminum foil to take the pasta with you. You may want to bring along some fresh basil leaves in a small plastic bag to use as a garnish before serving.

When you arrive, keep the pasta warm on a warming tray or in a 200°F oven until it's time to serve.

WHEN I HAD LUNCH WITH KATIE WORKMAN in New York several years ago we talked about being busy moms and how challenging it can be to get a nice dinner on the table. Katie told me about this pasta, claiming that not only did her two children love it but so did company. Everything can be assembled the night before, and you can vary the ingredients as the seasons change, keeping it simple in the summer but adding cubes of ham in the winter and possibly shrimp in the spring. A green salad makes a good accompaniment.

1 pound penne, ziti, or bow tie pasta
1 teaspoon salt
1 jar (16 ounces) vodka-flavored tomato sauce
1 pound fresh mozzarella, cubed
½ cup loosely packed chopped fresh basil
½ cup (2 ounces) shredded Parmesan cheese

1. Place a rack in the center of the oven and preheat the oven to 400°F.

2. Meanwhile, bring a large pot of water to a boil over high heat. Stir in the pasta and salt, reduce the heat to medium-high, and cook the pasta, uncovered, according to package directions until just done, 6 to 7 minutes.

3. Drain the pasta well in a colander, shaking it to remove the excess water, then return it to the pot. Stir in the tomato sauce, mozzarella cubes, and basil. Transfer the pasta mixture to a 2-quart baking dish and top it with the Parmesan.

4. Bake the pasta until the sauce is creamy and bubbly and begins to brown, 23 to 25 minutes. Keep the pasta warm until ready to serve.

BIG BATCH: *Double the recipe by using two large pots to boil the penne and combine the ingredients, then bake the pasta in two baking pans.*

RECIPE REMINDERS

Made for

Prep notes

Don't forget

Special touches

Bring again

Beth's Manicotti

SERVES 6 TO 8

**PREP: 45 TO 50 MINUTES * BAKE: 35 TO 40 MINUTES
PLUS 15 MINUTES RESTING TIME**

**TOTE
NOTES**

*Cover and tote the baked
manicotti while it's still
warm. If necessary, you
can reheat it in a 350°F
oven for 15 minutes when
you get to the gathering.*

PLAN AHEAD

*The unbaked manicotti
can be refrigerated,
covered with aluminum
foil, for a day. Or, cover
the baking dish with
heavy-duty aluminum foil
and freeze the unbaked
manicotti for up to two
weeks. Let the manicotti
thaw before baking.
When baking it right
from the refrigerator,
increase the baking time
to 45 to 50 minutes.*

MY FRIEND BETH MEADOR ALWAYS HAS A GREAT
recipe up her sleeve, and this is one she makes
to feed a group. For our Italian supper night
she made this entrée, and we enjoyed it with a wonderful
salad, good bread, wine, and Chocolate Zuccotto Cake
(see page 372). For a change of pace, bring this instead
of lasagna to a potluck supper. It is worth the extra effort.

FOR THE SAUCE

1 tablespoon olive oil

1 pound ground beef round

2 cans (6 ounces each) tomato paste

½ cup chopped onion

1 can (3 ounces) sliced mushrooms, drained

3 tablespoons chopped fresh parsley

2 teaspoons dried oregano

1 medium-size clove garlic, crushed in a garlic press

1½ teaspoons salt

1 teaspoon sugar

FOR THE SHELLS AND FILLING

Vegetable oil spray, for misting the baking dish

8 manicotti shells

Salt

3 cups (24 ounces) ricotta cheese

2 large eggs

¾ cup (3 ounces) grated Parmesan cheese

¼ cup chopped fresh parsley

2 cups (8 ounces) shredded mozzarella cheese

1. Make the sauce: Place the olive oil in a large, deep skillet over medium heat and add the ground beef. Brown the beef, stirring, 3 to 4 minutes. Drain off the fat. Add the tomato paste, onion, mushrooms, parsley, oregano, garlic, salt, sugar, and 2 cups of water. Let the sauce come to a boil, stirring, then reduce the heat to low and let simmer, covered, until thickened, about 30 minutes. Set the meat sauce aside.

2. Prepare the shells and filling: Place a rack in the center of the oven and preheat the oven to 350°F. Lightly mist a 13 by 9–inch glass or ceramic baking dish with vegetable oil spray.

3. Bring a large pot of water to a boil over high heat. Stir in the manicotti shells and ½ teaspoon of salt, reduce the heat to medium-high, and cook the manicotti, uncovered, according to the package directions until just done, 8 to 9 minutes. Drain the shells well in a colander, then rinse them in cold running water and drain again. Set the manicotti aside.

4. Place the ricotta, eggs, ½ cup of the Parmesan, the parsley, and ½ teaspoon of salt in a medium-size bowl and stir to combine well. Using a teaspoon, stuff each manicotti with ⅓ to ½ cup of the ricotta mixture.

5. Ladle a third of the meat sauce in the prepared baking dish, spreading it out evenly. Arrange the stuffed manicotti shells in a row on top of the sauce. Pour the remaining sauce over the shells and cover the baking dish with aluminum foil. Bake the manicotti until bubbly, 30 to 35 minutes.

6. Remove the baking dish from the oven and sprinkle the manicotti with the mozzarella and the remaining ¼ cup of Parmesan. Turn off the oven. Place the baking dish back in the oven only long enough for the cheese to melt, 3 to 4 minutes. Let the manicotti rest for about 15 minutes, then serve.

BIG BATCH: *You can triple this recipe by tripling the ingredients and using two boxes of manicotti shells. They come twelve to a box.*

RECIPE REMINDERS

Made for

Prep notes

Don't forget

Special touches

Bring again

Black Bean Tortilla Bake

SERVES 8 TO 10

PREP: 30 MINUTES * BAKE: 35 TO 40 MINUTES

THIS IS A GREAT VEGETARIAN ENTREE TO BRING TO potlucks because it's a hit with adults and kids alike. Meat eaters like it, too; the hearty sauce with black beans is substantial and delicious. You control the heat by adding, or not adding, the jalapeño pepper and deciding whether to use the original Ro-Tel tomatoes, which are spicy, or the milder version. This bakes in a 13 by 9–inch baking dish, and when you serve it, you might want to put the dish on a tray with decorative little bowls on the side filled with the garnishes—shredded lettuce, cilantro, lime wedges, and sour cream.

FOR THE TORTILLA BAKE

2 tablespoons vegetable oil

1 large red bell pepper, cored, seeded, and chopped (1 cup)

1 medium-size onion, chopped (1 cup)

3 medium-size cloves garlic, minced

1 fresh jalapeño pepper (optional), cored, seeded, deveined, and chopped

1 can (14½ ounces) diced tomatoes, undrained

1 can (10 ounces) chopped tomatoes with green chiles, such as Ro-Tel, undrained

1 can (about 15 ounces) black beans, rinsed and drained

1 tablespoon ground cumin

6 flour tortillas (7 to 8 inches each)

4 cups (1 pound) shredded Cheddar and Monterey Jack cheese blend

FOR SERVING

Shredded iceberg lettuce

Chopped fresh cilantro

Sour cream

Lime wedges

1. Place a rack in the center of the oven and preheat the oven to 350°F.

2. Place the vegetable oil in a large pan over medium heat. Add the bell pepper, onion, garlic, and jalapeño, if desired. Cook, stirring, until the onion softens, 2 to 3 minutes. Add both types of tomatoes, the black beans, and cumin and let simmer, stirring occasionally, uncovered, until the sauce is slightly reduced, 7 to 8 minutes.

3. Spread about 2 cups of the sauce in the bottom of a 13 by 9–inch glass or ceramic baking dish. Place 2 tortillas on top, overlapping them, then sprinkle 1½ cups of the cheese over the tortillas. Spoon half of the remaining sauce over the cheese, top it with 2 tortillas, and 1½ cups of cheese. Repeat with the remaining sauce, 2 tortillas, and 1 cup of cheese. Cover the baking dish with aluminum foil.

4. Bake the casserole until it has cooked through and the cheese has melted, 35 to 40 minutes. Transfer the tortilla bake to a tray and serve it with the lettuce, cilantro, sour cream, and lime wedges on the side.

BIG BATCH: *Make two casseroles instead of one extra-large one—they will take less time to bake and be easier to tote.*

RECIPE REMINDERS

Made for

Prep notes

Don't forget

Special touches

Bring again

YOU MAKE THE MAIN, THEY BRING THE SIDES

You know the drill—come up with a rib-sticking or party-themed main course and ask everyone else to bring a side dish or another part of the meal. On the one hand, it's daunting because the entrée you choose sets the tone of the gathering. But on the other hand, once you've decided what you want to prepare, your job is nearly done.

Say you're feeding a crowd. You'll find a recipe here for a Lowcountry-style shrimp boil and another one that makes so much marinade that you can marinate as many as twenty-four chicken breasts and grill them ahead of time. Pork tenderloin? It's here. As is a wonderful grilled leg of lamb, a twenty-pound oven-roasted turkey, and a slow-cooked brisket of beef.

Not feeding a crowd? Try my grilled shrimp on skewers with an avocado salsa, the eighteen-minute salmon baked in the oven, or a catfish fry. If you don't feel like serving seafood, you'll find barbecued pork ribs and grilled flank steaks with a delicious dry rub.

Whether the gathering is a big deal—an occasion calling for grilled beef tenderloin with horseradish sauce—or quite casual—think turkey burgers—these recipes are so solid they help put the *main* in main dish. Of course, once you issue your invitation, friends and family are sure to ask "What can I bring?" To help you have an answer ready, with each main dish that follows you'll find menu suggestions for side dishes that will deliciously round out the meal.

Lowcountry Shrimp Boil

SERVES 10 TO 12

PREP: 25 MINUTES ✳ COOK: ABOUT 15 MINUTES

I FIRST ATTENDED A SHRIMP BOIL OUTSIDE SAVANNAH when I was a young food writer. It was exhilarating to be in that warm sea air and to eat the freshest shrimp, briefly boiled, served with potatoes, corn, and smoked sausage. You can create a shrimp boil at your house if you can find some really fresh shrimp in the shell. The rest is easy—a boiling pot, either inside or outdoors, plenty of napkins, and cold beer or tea.

⅓ cup seasoned salt, such as Lawry's,
  or ⅓ cup seafood seasoning, such as Old Bay

3 bay leaves

4 pounds small red-skinned potatoes, scrubbed

2 pounds smoked sausage, cut into 2-inch pieces

6 ears corn, shucked and cut in half

4 to 5 pounds fresh large shrimp in their shells

Lemon wedges, for garnish

Cocktail sauce, for serving

1. Place a large stockpot half filled with water over medium-high heat. Add the seasoned salt and bay leaves. Cover the pot and bring to a boil.

2. Add the potatoes and sausage and cook until the potatoes are nearly tender, 12 to 15 minutes. Add the corn and shrimp, re-cover the pot, and let return to a boil. Cook the shrimp until they turn bright pink, 3 minutes—no more.

3. Using a slotted spoon, transfer the shrimp, potatoes, sausage, and corn to a large platter. Garnish with the lemon wedges. Serve with cocktail sauce.

WHAT CAN THEY BRING?

JOHN'S HOMEMADE COLESLAW,
page 126

✳

CHEESY GARLIC BREAD,
page 333

✳

LEMON ICEBOX CHEESECAKE WITH A GINGERSNAP CRUST,
page 370

RECIPE REMINDERS

Made for

Prep notes

Don't forget

Special touches

Lemon Garlic Shrimp with an Avocado Salsa

SERVES 8 TO 10

PREP: 30 MINUTES ✳ MARINATE: 3 HOURS ✳ GRILL: ABOUT 20 MINUTES IN ALL

WHAT CAN THEY BRING?

ROASTED ASPARAGUS
WITH OLIVE OIL
AND SALT,
page 256
✳
FRESH CORN PUDDING,
page 270
✳
TRES LECHES CAKES
PILED WITH
STRAWBERRIES,
page 365

PLAN AHEAD

You can grill the shrimp early in the day and refrigerate them until your guests arrive. Let the shrimp come to room temperature on a platter before serving.

THIS RECIPE IS A LITTLE FUSSIER THAN A SHRIMP boil, but for the dinner-party group it is perfect. First you marinate peeled shrimp in lemon and olive oil, then you grill them. Have the shrimp on the skewers ready to grill when everyone arrives and have the salsa chilling. You can vary this as you wish, adding chunks of fish such as tuna or snapper to the skewers. The salsa, too, can be adapted by adding grapefruit or mango instead of the orange.

FOR THE SHRIMP

60 large shrimp (about 3 pounds), peeled and deveined, tails on

2 lemons

6 tablespoons olive oil

4 medium-size cloves garlic, crushed in a garlic press

¼ cup chopped fresh parsley

Dash of cayenne pepper

Salt and freshly ground black pepper

FOR THE AVOCADO SALSA

2 navel oranges, peeled, sectioned, and membranes removed (see box, page 95), chopped into ½-inch pieces (about 2 cups)

1 large ripe avocado, peeled, pitted, and chopped into ½-inch pieces (about 1½ cups)

½ cup finely chopped red onion

¼ cup rice wine vinegar

1 tablespoon sugar
⅓ cup olive oil
Salt and freshly ground black pepper
2 tablespoons chopped fresh cilantro (optional)

YOU'LL ALSO NEED
10 wooden skewers

1. Prepare the shrimp: Place the shrimp in a large glass bowl and set aside. Cut the lemons in half and squeeze them over a sieve set atop a medium-size bowl to catch the seeds. Whisk in the 6 tablespoons of olive oil until thickened, then fold in the garlic, parsley, and cayenne pepper. Season with salt and black pepper to taste. If you like, you can grate the zest from the lemon halves and fold this in, too. Pour the marinade over the shrimp, cover the bowl with plastic wrap, and refrigerate for at least 3 hours.

2. Make the avocado salsa: Place the oranges, avocado, and onion in a medium-size bowl and toss lightly to mix.

3. In a separate bowl, whisk together the rice vinegar and sugar, then whisk in the ⅓ cup of olive oil until combined. Season with salt and black pepper to taste. Pour the vinaigrette over the avocado mixture and toss to coat. Add the cilantro, if desired. Cover the bowl with plastic wrap and refrigerate until chilled.

4. Thread the shrimp onto wooden skewers, placing 6 shrimp on each skewer. Spoon a little of the marinade over the shrimp and set the skewers aside.

5. When ready to cook, preheat the grill to medium-high heat.

6. Place the skewers of shrimp on the grill and cook until just done, 2 to 3 minutes per side. The shrimp will turn pink and be just firm to the touch. Transfer the skewers to a serving platter as the shrimp is finished grilling and serve at room temperature with the salsa.

RECIPE REMINDERS

Made for

Prep notes

Don't forget

Special touches

Eighteen-Minute Salmon with a Fresh Ginger Glaze

SERVES 6

PREP: 5 MINUTES ✳ BAKE: 18 MINUTES

WHAT CAN THEY BRING?

Jess's
Broccolini Salad,
page 122

✳

Creamy
Scalloped Potatoes,
page 282

✳

Cranberry Tart,
page 423

A HOST'S DREAM, THIS DISH IS QUICK TO ASSEMBLE AND ready to place on the buffet table straight from the oven. The recipe is also very flexible: I have made it with whole fillets of salmon that weighed between a pound and a half and two pounds, and I have used smaller pieces, less than a pound—both with the same amount of glaze. I have let the salmon soak in the glaze for a few hours in the refrigerator before cooking, and I have placed it right into the oven without marinating it. Any way you prepare it, people rave about it. Thanks to Jess Hill and Sally Bailey of Nashville for the recipe, which Sally adapted from a chicken recipe in *The Barefoot Contessa Cookbook.*

1 salmon fillet (about 1½ pounds)
⅓ cup reduced-sodium soy sauce
⅓ cup honey
2 tablespoons grated peeled fresh ginger
2 medium-size cloves garlic, crushed in a garlic press

1. Place the salmon in a 13 by 9–inch glass or ceramic baking dish and set it aside. Place the soy sauce, honey, ginger, and garlic in a small mixing bowl and stir to combine. Pour the soy sauce mixture over the salmon, lifting it up with a fork so that the marinade can run underneath and coat the salmon well. If you have the time, cover the baking dish with plastic wrap and refrigerate it for up to 2 hours. Or set the salmon aside while the oven preheats.

2. Place a rack in the center of the oven and preheat the oven to 400°F.

3. Uncover the salmon and bake it until the soy sauce mixture forms a glaze and the fish flakes around the edges, about 18 minutes. If the fillet is thicker in the center than at the edges, the center will cook less quickly; add a few minutes more baking time if needed. If you cut the salmon into pieces, the edges will be less likely to overcook. Remove the pieces of salmon from the oven as they test done. Or, do as we do in my house—cook the salmon all at once, saving the edges for the kids and the more rare center for the adults who prefer it that way. The salmon is also delicious served cold.

RECIPE REMINDERS

Made for

Prep notes

Don't forget

Special touches

Catfish Fry with Homemade Tartar Sauce

SERVES 6 TO 8

PREP: 30 MINUTES ✳ COOK: 35 TO 40 MINUTES

WHAT CAN THEY BRING?

JOHN'S HOMEMADE COLESLAW, *page 126*

✳

SLICED TOMATO SALAD WITH BASIL AND BUTTERMILK DRESSING, *page 116*

✳

MEXICAN CORN BREAD, *page 462*

✳

PEACH AND BLUEBERRY CRISP, *page 430*

SEVERAL YEARS BACK A GROUP OF NASHVILLE'S FOOD writers gathered on my friend Mindy's patio to entertain Tom Parker-Bowles, son of Camilla Parker-Bowles. Tom wanted to eat local food on his tour through the United States, and on that patio he was served our version of fish and chips—the crispiest fried catfish imaginable and good old-fashioned tartar sauce. Outdoor fish frying is the way to go because you keep the aroma and mess out of your kitchen. Use a turkey fryer, or a heavy twelve-inch-wide Dutch oven or deep cast-iron skillet, and fit a frying basket into it so you can lift up the fish as it cooks. You can just as easily use an electric fryer, which will keep the oil temperature constant— important for successful frying. So pick a pretty day, find some fresh fish, and take your time. It's much better to fry smaller batches of fish so that the oil doesn't lose too much heat, and besides, when you keep people waiting for that second taste, they'll only enjoy it more.

FOR THE TARTAR SAUCE

1 cup mayonnaise

2 tablespoons finely chopped shallot (1 medium-size shallot)

¼ cup sweet pickle relish

2 tablespoons chopped drained capers

2 tablespoons chopped fresh parsley

Hot pepper sauce

FOR THE FISH

1¾ cups white cornmeal (see Note)

¼ cup all-purpose flour

4 teaspoons seasoned salt, such as Lawry's

Freshly ground black pepper

4 large eggs

2 tablespoons water

3 pounds catfish or other white fish fillets, cut into thirds, rinsed, and patted dry with paper towels

48 ounces (6 cups) vegetable oil, such as canola or peanut

FOR THE GARNISH

Fresh parsley sprigs

2 lemons, cut into wedges

Capers

1. Make the tartar sauce: Place the mayonnaise, shallot, pickle relish, chopped capers, parsley, and a little hot sauce in a small bowl and stir to combine. Cover the bowl with plastic wrap and refrigerate until serving time.

2. Prepare the fish: Combine the cornmeal, flour, and seasoned salt in a shallow bowl. Season with pepper to taste.

3. Place the eggs and water in another shallow bowl and whisk to combine. Dredge each piece of fish in the egg mixture followed by the cornmeal mixture, then dredge it in the eggs, followed by the cornmeal again. Place the coated fish on a baking sheet and let rest a few minutes for the breading to adhere.

4. When ready to cook, heat the oil in a large, heavy Dutch oven over medium-high heat until it registers 360°F on a candy thermometer. Fry the fish until golden brown, from 4 to 5 minutes, adding enough pieces to the pan, one at a time, to fill but not crowd it. The thinner tail-end strips will take less time. Test for doneness by making a small slit in the fish with a

RECIPE REMINDERS

Made for

Prep notes

Don't forget

Special touches

**OUT OF THE
FRYING PAN . . .
OTHER IDEAS**

*Catfish not in your market?
Choose the freshest, mildest
fish fillets you can find—
snapper, tilapia, or
mahimahi. When it's
summertime, try dredging
small, whole okra pods and
fry them as well.*

knife; the fish will look white and creamy. Transfer the fish to
a rack set on a baking sheet that has been lined with paper
towels. Use the thermometer to check the oil temperature. You
want it to be constant; make sure the temperature is 360°F
before adding another batch of fish.

5. Serve the fish as it is fried, garnished with parsley, lemon
wedges, and capers and with the tartar sauce on the side.

NOTE: White cornmeal is usually more finely ground and is
preferred in the South, but yellow will work fine, too.

FRYING OUTDOORS

You have several options for turning the outdoors into a kitchen. You can cook the catfish over a hot gas grill in a Dutch oven or a cast-iron skillet that is three to four inches deep. You can use a portable propane burner as your heat source; just be sure it will heat to 360°F. Or, you can buy a turkey fryer kit—this is what's used for cooking Cajun fried turkey. They are available at hardware and home-improvement stores.

Cuban Chicken Legs

SERVES 8

PREP: 10 MINUTES ✳ **MARINATE: 3 HOURS** ✳ **BAKE: ABOUT 40 MINUTES**

Y FRIENDS MINDY AND R. B. KEPT RAVING ABOUT a dinner party where the Cuban host served grilled chicken legs along with a salad made with papaya and arugula. Those chicken legs benefited from the Cuban-inspired marinade of lemon juice, garlic, oregano, and olive oil. They'll feed a crowd because you can buy the big party packs of legs and marinate as many as you need in plastic bags before baking. To serve, place the salad in the center of a large, pretty platter, then arrange the chicken legs around the greens in a spoke pattern. The secret to this recipe? "Too much" garlic.

15 to 16 chicken legs (about 4 pounds)

1½ cups fresh lemon juice (from 6 to 8 lemons), plus 1 or 2 lemons, thinly sliced and seeded

½ cup olive oil

15 medium-size cloves garlic, chopped

2 chicken-flavored bouillon cubes, crumbled

1 tablespoon kosher salt

1 tablespoon dried oregano, or a small handful of fresh oregano

1 teaspoon freshly ground black pepper

Papaya and Arugula Salad (page 108), for serving

1. Rinse the chicken legs under cold running water and pat them dry with paper towels. Place the lemon juice, olive oil, garlic, bouillon cubes, salt, oregano, and pepper in a jumbo (2½-gallon) resealable plastic bag or large nonreactive bowl— glass, plastic, ceramic, or stainless steel. Add the chicken legs.

WHAT CAN THEY BRING?

ROAST POTATOES
FOR A CROWD,
page 278

✳

CHEESY GARLIC BREAD,
page 333

✳

MY FAVORITE
KEY LIME PIE,
page 414

WANT TO TOTE
THE CHICKEN
LEGS?

*Arrange the chicken legs on
a platter with the papaya
salad, cover the platter with
plastic wrap, and you're
ready to go.*

RECIPE
REMINDERS

Made for

_____

_____

_____

Prep notes

_____

_____

_____

_____

Don't forget

_____

_____

_____

_____

Special touches

_____

_____

_____

_____

Seal the bag or cover the bowl with plastic wrap and let the
chicken marinate for a few hours or as long as overnight.

2. When ready to cook, place a rack in the center of the oven
and preheat the oven to 400°F.

3. Remove the chicken from the marinade and discard the
marinade. Place the chicken on a large rimmed baking sheet.
Scatter the lemon slices over the chicken. Bake the chicken
until it is cooked through, tender, and lightly browned, about
40 minutes.

4. Place the Papaya and Arugula Salad in the middle of a large
platter. Arrange the chicken legs with the baked lemon slices
around the salad. The chicken can be served warm or chilled.
If you'd like to make the chicken legs ahead of time, they'll
keep for 24 hours; you can reheat them in a 400°F oven for
10 minutes, if you want to serve them warm.

BIG BATCH: *It's easy to make more than one batch—double or
triple the recipe by buying a lot of chicken legs and placing them
in two or three separate marinating bags. You'll probably be able
to fit fifteen to sixteen legs in one bag.*

MAKING A MAIN DISH IN NO TIME

If only we had a magic wand and "poof," dinner was ready at once. But wishful thinking aside, you can still cook at home and enjoy a main dish with little fuss. Think and cook fast with these recipe ideas; the finished dishes are ideal for toting or serving from your own kitchen.

* **QUICK POACHED SALMON:** Place a 1½- to 2-pound fillet of salmon skin side down on a baking sheet, season it with salt and pepper, drizzle olive oil over it, and place a piece of parchment paper right on top of the fish. Bake the salmon in a 450°F oven until just done, 12 to 15 minutes. Serve the salmon on a pretty platter surrounded by lemon slices and whatever garnish you have in the refrigerator.

* **SHRIMP AND VEGGIE PLATTER:** Pile peeled, steamed shrimp from the supermarket deli on a platter. Add cut up vegetables from your crisper—celery, carrots, zucchini, cherry tomatoes. Make a really quick dip of mayonnaise seasoned with fresh lemon juice and zest, paprika, and garlic crushed in a garlic press. Spoon this into a pretty dish and place it in the center of the platter.

* **CHICKEN PARMESAN PRONTO:** Buy 1 pound (just 1 pound is plenty, not 2) of fried chicken tenders from the supermarket deli. Slice them on the diagonal into three or four pieces and place these in a 13 by 9–inch glass or ceramic baking dish. Spoon store-bought tomato sauce over the chicken and dollop it with pesto if you have it. Top this with a thick layer of shredded mozzarella and Parmesan cheese. Cover the baking dish loosely with aluminum foil and bake the chicken at 350°F until the sauce bubbles, the cheese melts, and the chicken has heated through, 25 to 30 minutes.

Home-Fried Chicken Tenders with Blue Cheese Sauce

SERVES 8

PREP AND CHILL: 30 TO 75 MINUTES
COOK: 25 TO 30 MINUTES

WHAT CAN THEY BRING?

SOUTHERN POTATO SALAD,
page 131

*

DAVID'S GRILLED ARTICHOKES WITH ROASTED TOMATO VINAIGRETTE,
page 253

*

SQUASH CASSEROLE WITH SWEET ONIONS AND CHEDDAR,
page 288

*

GEORGIA PECAN PIE,
page 408

UNLIKE ANYTHING YOU BUY AT A FAST-FOOD DRIVE-IN or "fern bar," these crisp little chicken tenders are bites of heaven. They are crunchy, not greasy; succulent and full of real chicken, not processed bits. And the blue cheese sauce is similar to that famous chicken-wing sauce from Buffalo, New York. (For kids, serve the chicken with a bottled honey-mustard sauce.) I know, frying can be a mess, but you can fry these ahead of time, and you can use an electric fryer, too.

FOR THE BLUE CHEESE SAUCE

1 cup mayonnaise

½ cup reduced-fat sour cream

2 medium-size cloves garlic, crushed in a garlic press

2 tablespoons fresh lemon juice

½ cup (2 ounces) crumbled blue cheese

FOR THE CHICKEN TENDERS

2 pounds chicken tenders (about 24)

1 cup all-purpose flour

1 tablespoon seasoned salt, such as Lawry's

2 large eggs

2 tablespoons milk

48 ounces (6 cups) vegetable oil, such as canola or peanut

FOR SERVING

2 cups celery sticks

Hot pepper sauce (optional)

1. Make the blue cheese sauce: Place the mayonnaise, sour cream, garlic, and lemon juice in a small bowl and stir to combine. Fold in the blue cheese, cover the bowl with plastic wrap, and refrigerate it.

2. Prepare the chicken tenders: Rinse the chicken tenders under cold running water and pat them dry with paper towels. Combine the flour and seasoned salt in a wide, shallow bowl. Combine the eggs and milk in a bowl and beat with a fork to blend well. Dredge the chicken tenders in the flour mixture, dip them in the egg mixture, and then dip them again in the flour, generously coating each piece. Place the chicken tenders on a baking sheet and refrigerate them for at least 15 minutes or up to 1 hour (this helps the coating dry out and adhere better).

3. When ready to cook, heat about 1-inch of oil in a deep 12-inch skillet until it registers 360° to 370°F on a candy thermometer. Fry a few pieces of chicken at a time; do not crowd the skillet. Adding too much cold chicken at once will make the oil temperature plummet; that's how you get greasy chicken. Cook the tenders until their internal temperature registers 160°F on an instant-read meat thermometer, or until the juices run clear when pricked with the tip of a sharp knife, 6 to 7 minutes. Turn the chicken a few times while frying. A mesh splatter guard really helps keep the mess manageable. Place the cooked chicken tenders on a rack set over a paper towel-lined baking sheet (this will keep the chicken crisp all over) or drain them on brown paper bags. (The chicken tenders can be cooked up to 2 hours ahead.)

4. To serve, arrange the chicken tenders and celery sticks on a round serving plate and place the blue cheese sauce in a small bowl in the center for dipping. If desired, add a small bowl of hot sauce for dunking.

WANT TO TOTE THE CHICKEN TENDERS?

To tote the chicken tenders, line a plastic container with waxed paper or parchment paper, then place the tenders in it on end, so that they will stay crisp. Lightly tent the top of the container with aluminum foil.

Bring the blue cheese sauce in a small plastic container and tote the celery sticks in a plastic bag. If you like, bring along a bottle of hot sauce.

RECIPE REMINDERS

Made for

_____

_____

Prep notes

_____

_____

Don't forget

_____

_____

Special touches

_____

_____

_____

Grilled Chicken for a Crowd

SERVES 12

PREP: 10 MINUTES ✳ MARINATE: 12 TO 24 HOURS
GRILL: 30 MINUTES IN ALL

**WHAT CAN
THEY BRING?**

**THE BEST
CAESAR SALAD,**
page 92
✳
**GREEN BEANS WITH
A SPICY TOMATO SAUCE,**
page 276
✳
SPINACH AND FETA PIE,
page 286
✳
**BAKED MACARONI
AND CHEESE,**
page 330

✳
**AUNT ELIZABETH'S
BANANA PUDDING,**
page 434

THE MARINADE FOR THIS CHICKEN IS GREAT BECAUSE you can throw it together in minutes in the food processor and marinate as much chicken as you like overnight. The tomato soup and vinegar make the marinade tangy and keep the chicken moist and sweet. This recipe explains how to cook boneless chicken breast pieces, but you could just as easily cook bone-in breasts. They will take longer, and you might want to baste them with the marinade as they cook. Do the grilling at the last minute, or do it the day before for delicious cold grilled chicken.

1 can (10¾ ounces) condensed cream of tomato soup
1 cup olive oil
¾ cup vegetable oil
¾ cup cider vinegar
¾ cup sugar
2 tablespoons chopped onion
1 tablespoon Worcestershire sauce
2 medium-size cloves garlic, peeled
1 teaspoon dry mustard
12 skinless, boneless chicken breast halves
    (about 3 to 4 pounds)

1. Place the tomato soup, olive oil, vegetable oil, sugar, onion, Worcestershire sauce, garlic, and dry mustard in a blender or food processor fitted with a steel blade and blend until smooth, about 45 seconds. You will have more marinade than you need for 12 chicken breast halves (see Note).

2. Rinse the chicken breasts under cold running water and pat them dry with paper towels. Cut the chicken breasts in half and, using a meat pounder or a heavy skillet, pound them to an even ½-inch thickness. Arrange the pounded chicken in a single layer in two 13 by 9–inch glass or ceramic baking dishes and pour 2 cups of the marinade over the chicken (1 cup per baking dish). Cover the baking dishes with plastic wrap and marinate the chicken in the refrigerator overnight.

3. When ready to cook, preheat the grill to medium heat.

4. Remove the chicken from the marinade, discarding the marinade. Grill the chicken pieces until the juices run clear when pricked with the tip of a sharp knife, 4 to 5 minutes per side, turning once. Once the chicken is done, place it on a serving platter and tent it with aluminum foil to keep warm if serving at once. If desired, heat some of the unused marinade to boiling and serve it in a small pitcher alongside the chicken breasts. The chicken is equally good served cold.

NOTE: This recipe makes about a quart of marinade and can be used to marinate up to 24 chicken breast halves. Any marinade you don't use can be stored in a glass jar in the refrigerator for up to two weeks. Heat the extra marinade and serve it as a sauce for the chicken. Or, you can use the marinade as a vinaigrette for salad.

RECIPE REMINDERS

Made for

Prep notes

Don't forget

Special touches

Roast Turkey in the Bag

SERVES 16 TO 20

**PREP: 15 TO 20 MINUTES ∗ ROAST: 2½ TO 3 HOURS
PLUS 45 MINUTES RESTING TIME**

WHAT CAN
THEY BRING?

**SWEET POTATO
CASSEROLE WITH
PECAN CRUNCH,**
page 292

∗

**MY FAVORITE TURKEY
DRESSING,**
page 316

∗

**SPICED CRANBERRY
SAUCE,**
page 314

∗

**THANKSGIVING
PUMPKIN PIE,**
page 418

I HAVE BECOME SO ACCUSTOMED TO, AND SPOILED BY, this method of cooking turkey that I just don't see myself roasting the bird any other way again. Turkey cooks more quickly in the bag, which frees up oven space, letting me pop in the side dishes. No basting is needed, so if I want, I can put the bird in the oven before church on Christmas Eve and it is ready when we get home. Plus, the turkey turns out brown and gorgeous and all those drippings are caught in the bag, making clean-up a breeze. And it jump-starts a turkey hash or soup for the next day.

1 tablespoon all-purpose flour

1 turkey (20 pounds; see Note)

1 medium-size onion, cut in half

1 lemon, cut in half

1 bunch fresh thyme or parsley

1 teaspoon salt

½ teaspoon freshly ground black pepper

4 tablespoons (½ stick) butter, melted

2 teaspoons seasoned salt, such as Lawry's

Fresh herbs, for garnish

Purple grapes, for garnish

YOU'LL ALSO NEED

1 turkey-size oven-cooking bag (14 by 20 inches)

1. Place a rack in the center of the oven and preheat the oven to 350°F. Place the flour in the oven-cooking bag and shake it. Place the oven bag in a large roasting pan that is at least 2 inches deep.

2. Remove the giblets and neck from the turkey and set them aside for another use or discard them. Rinse the turkey under cold running water and pat dry with paper towels. Place the onion, lemon, thyme or parsley, salt, and pepper in the cavity of the turkey. Brush the outside of the turkey with the melted butter and sprinkle the seasoned salt all over it. Place the turkey in the oven bag, and gather the bag loosely around the turkey, allowing room for heat circulation. Secure the bag with its nylon tie. Cut four or five 1-inch slits in the top of the bag so that steam can escape. Tuck the ends of the bag in the roasting pan.

3. Roast the turkey until an instant-read meat thermometer placed in the thickest part of the inner thigh registers 180°F, 2½ to 3 hours. (If you stuff the turkey, you will need to add another 30 minutes cooking time.)

4. Remove the roasting pan from the oven and place it on the stovetop. Let the turkey rest in the bag for about 15 minutes. Carefully remove the turkey from the bag and transfer it to a platter to rest for about 30 minutes before carving. Gently tent the turkey with aluminum foil to keep it warm while it rests. Garnish the turkey with herbs and grapes before serving.

NOTE: My family adores leftover turkey for sandwiches, so we like to roast a big one. The general rule is a pound of turkey for every person, and this should give you leftovers. I have learned to buy a slightly larger bird so that there are even more leftovers, plus I like to send sliced turkey home with folks as well.

RECIPE REMINDERS

Made for

Prep notes

Don't forget

Special touches

Turkey Burgers on the Grill with Pesto Mayonnaise

SERVES 8

PREP: 25 TO 30 MINUTES ✷ GRILL: ABOUT 10 MINUTES

WHAT CAN THEY BRING?

TINA'S CORN AND BLACK BEAN SALAD,
page 148

✷

SUMMERTIME RATATOUILLE,
page 304

✷

WATERMELON BOAT WITH SUMMER FRUITS,
page 160

✷

SEVEN-LAYER BARS,
page 400

WE STARTED GRILLING TURKEY BURGERS YEARS ago on a whim. The recipe I found looked inviting and a lot more flavorful than a boring beef burger. Now my kids prefer turkey burgers, and I like them, too, because these are packed with garlic and parsley and cook effortlessly on the backyard grill. Plus, any leftovers are delicious the next day. But, I realize that some people won't buy this, so I say try these turkey burgers and make traditional beef burgers, as well. Stir together the easy pesto mayo, slice some ripe summertime tomatoes, and you are in for fine eating, whatever kind of burger you choose.

FOR THE BURGERS

2 pounds lean ground turkey (see Note)

$\frac{1}{2}$ cup soft bread crumbs

$\frac{1}{2}$ cup finely minced onion

$\frac{1}{2}$ cup chopped fresh parsley

2 medium-size cloves garlic, crushed in a garlic press

2 egg whites

1 teaspoon salt

$\frac{1}{2}$ teaspoon freshly ground black pepper

Vegetable oil spray, for misting the grill

FOR SERVING

1 cup mayonnaise

2 tablespoons pesto sauce

Hamburger buns

Sliced tomatoes

Lettuce leaves

Sliced onions

Mustard and ketchup

Both dill and sweet pickles

1. Place the turkey in a mixing bowl and add the bread crumbs, onion, parsley, garlic, egg whites, salt, and pepper. Mix with a wooden spoon or your hands until the ingredients are just incorporated. Form the turkey mixture into 8 patties about ⅓-inch thick, then set them aside.

2. Place the mayonnaise and pesto in a small bowl and stir to combine. Set the pesto mayonnaise aside.

3. Preheat the barbecue grill to medium-high heat. Mist the grate with vegetable oil spray so the burgers won't stick.

4. Grill the burgers until they are firm to the touch and the juices run clear, 4 to 5 minutes per side, turning once. Transfer the burgers to a platter or buns and serve with the pesto mayonnaise and tomato slices, lettuce, onions, mustard, ketchup, and pickles on the side.

NOTE: Ground turkey is often sold with a fat content of 7 or 15 percent. This recipe works beautifully with either, even the lower-fat version.

RECIPE REMINDERS

Made for

Prep notes

Don't forget

Special touches

Anita's Oven-Baked Pork Tenderloins

SERVES 16

PREP: 20 MINUTES ⁎ BAKE: 2 HOURS PLUS 20 MINUTES RESTING TIME

WHAT CAN THEY BRING?

SPINACH SALAD
WITH MAHOGANY
ROASTED MUSHROOMS
AND ONIONS,
page 102

⁎

WALDORF SALAD,
page 163

⁎

CINDY'S CHILE
CHEESE GRITS,
page 326

⁎

IRON SKILLET
APPLE TART,
page 421

ANITA BARGER, WHO LIVES IN ATLANTA, GOT THIS recipe from her mother, Carol Nichols of Pine Bluff, Arkansas, who got the recipe from a longtime friend, Joan Thompson of Hot Springs Village, Arkansas. It is a wonderful way to cook pork tenderloins for a crowd. You can also cook these honey-glazed tenderloins on the grill—you'll find directions following the recipe. For smaller gatherings, make half the recipe, baking two tenderloins. If there are leftovers, they make delicious sandwiches the next day.

½ cup honey
½ cup ketchup
2 tablespoons (¼ stick) butter
2 tablespoons light brown sugar
2 tablespoons fresh lemon juice
Garlic powder (see Note)
4 to 5 pounds pork tenderloin (4 tenderloins)
Salt and freshly ground black pepper
⅓ cup Dijon mustard

1. Place a rack in the center of the oven and preheat the oven to 325°F.

2. Place the honey, ketchup, butter, brown sugar, lemon juice, and ¼ teaspoon of garlic powder in a small saucepan over low heat. Let the honey glaze simmer, stirring, until the flavor develops, about 5 minutes, then remove it from the heat.

3. Rinse the pork tenderloins under cold running water and pat them dry with paper towels. Place the pork in a large roasting pan or two 13 by 9–inch glass or ceramic baking dishes. Sprinkle the pork on all sides with salt, pepper, and garlic powder. Generously brush the tops of the tenderloins with the Dijon mustard.

4. Bake the pork, uncovered, for 15 minutes, then brush it with some of the honey glaze. Continue baking the pork until tender, about 2 hours in all, brushing it with more glaze every 15 minutes. Let the tenderloins rest for 20 minutes before serving.

NOTE: If you prefer, you can substitute 1 medium-size clove of garlic, crushed in a garlic press, for the ¼ teaspoon of garlic powder in the honey glaze. You'll still need to use the garlic powder to season the outside of the pork tenderloins.

WANT TO GRILL THE PORK TENDERLOINS? Season the tenderloins with salt, pepper, and garlic powder and brush them with a little Dijon mustard, but not too much. Place them on a medium-high grill and close the lid. Grill the pork for 5 to 7 minutes. Turn the pork, and grill it, covered, another 5 to 7 minutes. Brush the pork with the glaze several times as it grills, making sure the grill temperature is low enough to keep the glaze from burning. Turn off the heat and let the pork sit on the grill for 5 to 10 minutes longer, until it is cooked through and registers an internal temperature of 160°F on an instant-read meat thermometer.

RECIPE REMINDERS

Made for

Prep notes

Don't forget

Special touches

Braised Pork Loin
with Prunes and Almonds

SERVES 8 TO 10

PREP: 20 MINUTES ✳ BAKE: 2 HOURS PLUS 30 MINUTES RESTING TIME

**WHAT CAN
THEY BRING?**

BIG GREEN SALAD
WITH ORANGE,
AVOCADO, AND
RED WINE
VINAIGRETTE,
page 94

✳

BEREAVEMENT CORN,
page 266

OR

CREAMY
SCALLOPED POTATOES,
page 282

✳

SWEET AND SAVORY
BAKED APRICOTS,
page 312

✳

FRESH APPLE CAKE
WITH CARAMEL GLAZE,
page 356

COSTUME SUPPERS FOR ADULTS ARE SURELY NOT
something you want to pass up, especially when
a friend invites you to a murder-mystery dinner
party. My friends Beth and Bill Meador planned a hilarious
murder-mystery party set in ancient Rome, and this recipe
was the main dish. Beth clipped it from the party kit, and
I have tweaked it a bit. This is a delicious way to cook
a large pork loin for a crowd of eight to ten. Once the
roast has cooked thoroughly, you can tent the pan with
aluminum foil and keep the pork warm until time to serve.

FOR THE PORK
3 to 4 pounds boneless pork loin
1 tablespoon olive oil
Salt and freshly ground black pepper

FOR THE GLAZE
¾ cup low-sodium chicken broth
½ cup pitted prunes
½ cup slivered almonds
2 medium-size cloves garlic, peeled
2 tablespoons dry red wine
1 tablespoon olive oil
1 tablespoon honey
1 teaspoon freshly ground black pepper
1 teaspoon fennel seed
1 teaspoon dried oregano
½ teaspoon ground cumin

1. Place a rack in the center of the oven and preheat the oven to 350°F.

2. Rinse the pork loin under cold running water and pat it dry with paper towels. Place the pork in a 13 by 9–inch glass or ceramic baking dish and drizzle the 1 tablespoon of olive oil over it. Generously season the pork with salt and pepper. Bake the pork until lightly browned and almost cooked through, about 1 hour and 15 minutes.

3. Meanwhile, prepare the glaze: Place the chicken broth, prunes, almonds, garlic, red wine, 1 tablespoon of olive oil, honey, pepper, fennel seed, oregano, and cumin in a food processor fitted with a steel blade or a blender and pulse until the prunes, almonds, and garlic are finely chopped, 30 to 45 seconds.

4. When the pork has cooked for 1 hour and 15 minutes, pour the glaze over it. Return the pork to the oven and bake it until well browned and cooked thoroughly, about 45 minutes longer. Tent the pork with aluminum foil and let it rest for about 30 minutes before slicing and serving. Pour the pan drippings into a small saucepan and bring to a boil. Serve this as a sauce on the side.

RECIPE REMINDERS

Made for

Prep notes

Don't forget

Special touches

Easy Barbecued Ribs

SERVES 6

PREP: 15 MINUTES ✳ BAKE: 1½ HOURS ✳ GRILL: ABOUT 10 MINUTES
PLUS 20 MINUTES RESTING TIME

**WHAT CAN
THEY BRING?**

TOMATO, MOZZARELLA,
AND BASIL SALAD WITH
FRESH TOMATO
VINAIGRETTE,
page 118

✳

POTLUCK BAKED BEANS,
page 318

✳

CHEESY GARLIC BREAD,
page 333

✳

NASHVILLE FUDGE PIE,
page 412,
AND ICE CREAM

EVERYONE LOVES BARBECUED RIBS, AND HERE IS A supereasy way to prepare them. You precook the seasoned ribs in oven-cooking bags, then brush them with your choice of barbecue sauce and cook them long enough on the grill for the glaze to set. Pork baby back ribs are the meatiest and most tender of the pork ribs. Look for supermarket specials where you can buy them on sale, then freeze the ribs until warm weather comes and it's time to barbecue.

> 5 pounds (2 racks) pork baby back ribs
>
> 3 to 4 tablespoons seasoned salt such as Lawry's
>
> 1 tablespoon all-purpose flour
>
> ¼ cup water
>
> 1 cup barbecue sauce (see Note),
>   or more as needed
>
> **YOU'LL ALSO NEED**
>
> 1 large oven-cooking bag (14 by 20 inches)

1. Place a rack in the center of the oven and preheat the oven to 325°F.

2. Cut the ribs into 3- to 4-rib sections and rub them all over with seasoned salt. Place the flour in the oven-cooking bag and shake it. Put the bag in a large roasting pan and arrange the ribs inside in a single layer, then add the water. Gather the ends of the bag together and secure them with a nylon tie. Cut six ½-inch slits in the top of the bag so that steam can escape.

3. Bake the ribs until they are browned and cooked through, about 1½ hours. Remove the pan from the oven and carefully cut open the bag. Transfer the ribs to a platter and set aside.

4. When ready to cook, preheat the barbecue grill to medium-high heat.

5. While the grill is preheating, brush the ribs on both sides with the barbecue sauce. Place the ribs on the hot grill and cook 4 to 5 minutes per side. Reduce the heat to low. Baste the ribs with more barbecue sauce, if desired, and grill them until the sauce has formed a glaze, 1 or 2 minutes per side longer. Let the ribs rest about 20 minutes, loosely tented with aluminum foil, then serve.

NOTE: Use your favorite ketchup-based barbecue sauce. Sticky Fingers and KC Masterpiece are both good choices.

WANT TO GRILL WHEN IT'S COLD OUTSIDE?
When you cook with a gas grill, the length of cooking time varies with the weather. When it is cold outside, the grill takes longer to heat up, and if you open the lid, the heat of the grill plummets and the food cooks more slowly. So, allow more time for grilling when the weather is cold and don't be in a hurry. Also, look for visual signs for doneness instead of relying on how long it should take for the food to be done.

RECIPE REMINDERS

Made for

Prep notes

Don't forget

Special touches

John's Grilled Beef Tenderloin

SERVES 8

PREP: 10 MINUTES ✳ GRILL: 25 MINUTES PLUS 1 HOUR RESTING TIME

WHAT CAN THEY BRING?

BABY BLUE SALAD WITH SWEET AND SPICY PECANS,
page 100

✳

ROASTED ASPARAGUS WITH OLIVE OIL AND SALT,
page 256

✳

BOURSIN POTATO GRATIN,
page 284

✳

CHOCOLATE PEPPERMINT ICE CREAM CAKE,
page 344

HERE IS MY SECRET RECIPE WHEN I WANT TO SERVE company no matter what the season: grilled whole beef tenderloins. Please don't tell my husband, but I love this recipe because he cooks it on the grill, and I am free to get the house cleaned, the table set, and the side dishes arranged—maybe a dessert made. John is pretty meticulous about grilling, and he loves rare beef tenderloin, so he takes care with this recipe. People are always wowed, and that makes me even happier. I keep my eyes open for whole beef tenderloins going on sale throughout the year; I buy a couple and put them in my freezer. We trim our own tenderloins, removing fat and loose strips of meat for a lean, tapered look. John can tell when the tenderloin is done just by pressing down on it with his fingertips. He says if it is still a little soft, it is still a little rare. But you can also use a meat thermometer to tell when it's time to take the meat off the grill. Then, cover the tenderloin with aluminum foil and know that your entrée is waiting. You can relax and enjoy the evening with family and friends.

FOR THE SOUR CREAM HORSERADISH SAUCE

1 cup prepared horseradish

½ cup mayonnaise

½ cup sour cream

2 tablespoons Dijon mustard

FOR THE BEEF

1 whole beef tenderloin, 6 to 7 pounds, untrimmed

3 tablespoons browning sauce, such as Kitchen Bouquet

1 tablespoon Worcestershire sauce

1 tablespoon low-sodium soy sauce

1 tablespoon vegetable oil

6 medium-size cloves garlic, peeled

1 teaspoon kosher salt

1. Make the horseradish sauce: Place the horseradish, mayonnaise, sour cream, and mustard in a small mixing bowl and stir to combine. Cover the bowl with plastic wrap and refrigerate until ready to serve.

2. Prepare the beef: Trim the tenderloin of all fat and loose pieces of meat or have the butcher do this for you. (Ask to keep the trimmings or have them ground to use in chili. You can freeze them in plastic freezer bags and turn them into beef stew or vegetable soup on another day.) Place the tenderloin in a 13 by 9–inch glass or ceramic baking dish.

3. Place the browning sauce, Worcestershire sauce, and soy sauce in a small bowl and stir to mix. Brush the tenderloin all over with this mixture, followed by the vegetable oil.

4. Mince the garlic on a cutting board. Add the salt to the garlic and, using the flat side of a knife, press the salt into the garlic to form a paste. Rub the garlic paste onto the tenderloin.

5. Preheat the grill to medium-high heat.

6. Grill the tenderloin, turning to cook all sides, until done to taste; when cooked to rare, about 25 minutes, the internal temperature will register 120°F on an instant-read meat thermometer inserted in the middle or thickest part. If you are using a charcoal grill, you will need to bank the coals around the edge of the grill and set the cover ajar, allowing smoke to escape. If you are using a gas grill, the amount of

RECIPE REMINDERS

Made for

Prep notes

Don't forget

Special touches

TOO MUCH
TENDERLOIN?

*My nephews say there is
never too much tenderloin
and they may be right. We
slice leftovers thinly and
place them on top of salads
the next day. We tuck slices
along with sautéed onions
and peppers into* panini.
*And, the most delicious
beef and vegetable soup
begins with cubes of beef
tenderloin.*

heat the grill puts out will depend on the outside temperature. If it is cold, you will need to cook the beef covered. If it is a hot day, you can cover it for a little while, then remove the cover and watch the heat closely so you don't burn the outside of the tenderloin, just create a nice browned crust.

7. Transfer the beef to a serving platter, loosely tent it with aluminum foil, and let it rest for at least 1 hour; it will continue to cook as it rests. Serve the tenderloin warm after an hour or at room temperature after up to 3 hours, with the horseradish sauce on the side.

WANT INDOOR ROAST BEEF? No grilling master on hand to cook the beef? No problem. Preheat the oven to 475°F. Rub the outside of the beef tenderloin with 4 tablespoons of soft butter, season it with garlic salt, and place it in a roasting pan. Bake the tenderloin for about 15 minutes, then turn off the oven and let the beef sit in the oven for about 15 minutes. Remove the tenderloin from the oven, loosely tent it with aluminum foil, and let rest for about 30 minutes before carving. It will be a perfect medium-rare.

HAM IT UP

L ately it seems that hams are disappearing. They look smaller at the typical supermarket meat counter, and while you'll see a spiral-sliced ham in practically every holiday food catalog, there is little ham of any variety available between May and November. That doesn't mean that we should stop preparing succulent hams in our own kitchens. Boneless home-cooked ham is delicious, versatile, and easy on the wallet. Here are some suggestions to get the juices flowing.

SPIRAL-SLICED HAM: Pretty on the platter, spiral-sliced hams have a crunchy brown sugar topping and are easy to serve since the slices pull effortlessly off the bone. If you buy one, take care to use it within a few days and to keep it well wrapped in the refrigerator. You can remove the leftover slices from the bone and freeze them in plastic bags for up to two months. And you can use the bone to make split pea or black bean soup if you do this within two or three days.

CURED HAM FROM THE SUPERMARKET: A little boring, but less expensive, cured ham is often your only choice. How to make it more interesting? Spread a paste of ½ cup of Dijon mustard and 6 tablespoons light brown sugar over it. Bake the ham at 350°F until the glaze puffs up and browns. Let the ham rest an hour, before slicing and serving it.

Or, bake the ham the way my mother did. Buy as large a boneless half ham as you can find—5 to 7 pounds—and place it on a sheet of heavy-duty aluminum foil that has been misted with vegetable oil spray. Pack light brown sugar over the top of the ham and pour a cup of Coca-Cola or apple juice over it. Bring the foil up around the ham to enclose it and turn the edges of the foil under to seal the ham in a large packet, then place the ham in a roasting pan. Bake the ham in a 325°F oven for about 3 hours (figure 30 minutes per pound). Let the ham cool in the foil, then slice it and serve.

✳

For a pretty way to serve ham, pull out your grandmother's platter and surround the ham with curly parsley. Or, use an Italian platter and garnish the ham with sage sprigs and kumquats. One more serving option: Place the ham on a cutting board surrounded by little pots of interesting mustards, chutneys, and pickles.

Grilled Dry-Rub Flank Steaks

SERVES 8

**PREP: 10 MINUTES ✳ CURE: OVERNIGHT ✳ GRILL: 10 MINUTES
PLUS 30 MINUTES RESTING TIME**

WHAT CAN THEY BRING?

FRESH GREEN BEAN SALAD WITH CRUMBLED FETA VINAIGRETTE, *page 120*

✳

TWICE-BAKED POTATOES, *page 280*

✳

CARROT CAKE WITH MAPLE CREAM CHEESE FROSTING, *page 362*

UESTS COMING FOR DINNER TOMORROW? WHAT could be easier than grilling some flank steaks, especially if you have planned ahead and rubbed those steaks with spices and let them cure overnight. As my friend R. B. says, as long as you place the holy trinity of dry rub on the meat—equal parts kosher salt, coarse black pepper, and paprika—you can add any other seasonings you like to the rub. So open the spice drawer and get creative! Two flank steaks will feed eight people, and you might have leftovers for sandwiches or quesadillas if you are lucky.

1 tablespoon kosher salt
1 tablespoon coarsely ground black pepper
1 tablespoon paprika
1 teaspoon garlic powder
1 teaspoon dry mustard
2 teaspoons chili powder
2 teaspoons ground cumin
2 flank steaks (1½ pounds each)
About ¼ cup vegetable oil
Sliced limes, for garnish

1. Combine the salt, pepper, paprika, garlic powder, dry mustard, chili powder, and cumin in a small bowl. Rub the flank steaks with about 1 tablespoon of dry rub per side. Place each steak in a plastic resealable bag and refrigerate overnight.

2. When ready to cook, preheat the grill to high heat.

3. Rub the steaks generously on all sides with oil, about 1 tablespoon per side (this will help the flank steak develop a nice charred crust). Grill the flank steaks until done to taste, about 5 minutes per side for medium-rare. When grilled to medium-rare, an instant-read meat thermometer will register an internal temperature of 125°F.

4. Transfer the steaks to a cutting board, cover them loosely with aluminum foil, and let them rest for about 30 minutes. Thinly slice the flank steaks across the grain, angling the knife blade away from the meat. Serve the steak slices on a platter, pouring the steak juices over the meat. Garnish the platter with lime slices.

EASY MARINADE FOR FLANK STEAKS

Open a 16-ounce bottle of Italian dressing made with balsamic vinegar. Place the dressing in a blender or food processor along with a dash of hot pepper sauce, 2 tablespoons of reduced-sodium soy sauce, and 3 peeled garlic cloves. Process until the marinade is smooth. Pour the marinade over 2 flank steaks and let marinate, covered, overnight in the refrigerator. Then, remove the steaks from the marinade, pat them dry, and place them on the grill to cook as directed above.

RECIPE REMINDERS

Made for

Prep notes

Don't forget

Special touches

Oven-Barbecued Beef Brisket

SERVES 12 TO 16

PREP: 10 MINUTES ✴ BAKE: 4 HOURS PLUS 30 MINUTES RESTING TIME

WHAT CAN THEY BRING?

SOUTHERN POTATO SALAD, *page 131*

✴

JOHN'S HOMEMADE COLESLAW, *page 126*

✴

BROCCOLI BRAG CASSEROLE, *page 260*

✴

HOT CURRIED FRUIT, *page 309*

✴

MEXICAN CORN BREAD, *page 462*

✴

ORANGE MARMALADE CAKE, *page 353*

FOR FEEDING LARGE GROUPS, YOU CANNOT BEAT BEEF brisket cooked until tender and thinly sliced. You'll have a satisfying entrée, meat for sandwiches, or a wonderful beginning for homemade chili. But the trick is cooking brisket long enough to make it tender. Of course you could cook it in a slow cooker, but another great option is to take advantage of something we all use just about every day—the oven. If you bake the brisket in a covered roasting pan on a bed of sliced onions with a little salt, pepper, brown sugar, and barbecue sauce on top, after three and a half to four hours, you have fall-apart tender beef fit for a crowd.

1 large onion, very thinly sliced

One 5- to 6-pound flat beef brisket (see Note)

2 tablespoons seasoned salt, such as Lawry's

Table salt and freshly ground black pepper

3 tablespoons light brown sugar

1½ cups barbecue sauce, plus more as needed for serving

1. Place a rack in the center of the oven and preheat the oven to 325°F.

2. Place the onion slices on the bottom of a large roasting pan that is 2 to 3 inches deep. Season the beef brisket all over with the seasoned salt. Place the brisket in the roasting pan and season it with table salt and pepper to taste. Scatter the brown sugar over the top of the brisket and pour the barbecue sauce over the brown sugar. Cover the pan tightly with aluminum foil.

3. Bake the brisket for about 3½ hours, then remove the aluminum foil, taking care not to let the steam burn you. Bake the brisket, uncovered, until the juices reduce and the top becomes glazed, about 30 minutes longer.

4. Let the brisket rest for about 30 minutes. Transfer the meat to a cutting board and, when it is cool enough to handle, trim off any surface fat. Slice the brisket on the diagonal into thin slices. To make the sauce, degrease the cooking juices from the roasting pan, place them in a saucepan, and let come to a simmer over medium heat. Add more barbecue sauce to the pan as needed (you'll want at least 2 cups of pan sauce to serve 12), then serve the sauce with the brisket.

NOTE: The "flat" cut beef brisket has less fat than the "point" cut. Both need a long, slow cooking to tenderize them.

RECIPE REMINDERS

Made for

Prep notes

Don't forget

Special touches

Grilled Leg of Lamb with Greek Chimichurri Sauce

SERVES 10

**PREP: 15 MINUTES ✳ MARINATE: 8 HOURS
GRILL: 1¾ TO 2 HOURS PLUS 15 MINUTES RESTING TIME**

WHAT CAN THEY BRING?

CUCUMBER AND
TOMATO SALAD
WITH SWEET DILL
VINAIGRETTE,
page 112

✳

ROAST POTATOES
FOR A CROWD,
page 278

✳

SPINACH AND FETA PIE,
page 286

✳

COCONUT ALMOND
MACAROONS,
page 390
AND
LEMON SQUARES,
page 395

INSTEAD OF THE USUAL EASTER HAM, WHY NOT COOK A leg of lamb? It's a wonderful springtime entrée that is a real divide-and-conquer meal, attracting all sorts of interesting side dish contributions from others. This lamb is well seasoned with fresh garlic, rosemary, and lemon slices; it marinates in the refrigerator overnight. Then you can grill it on a rotisserie or directly on the grill until it's done just to taste. You can also roast it in the oven; you'll find directions on page 250. When lamb grills or roasts it tends to crisp up, cooking more on the edges while remaining rare in the center. Since everyone likes lamb at a different degree of doneness, there is something delicious here for everybody. And save those bits of lamb with the bone to simmer in January Lamb Stew (see page 192)—even if it's not January!

1 bone-in leg of lamb (5 to 7 pounds)

1 whole bulb garlic, separated into cloves, peeled, large cloves cut into slivers

2 tablespoons kosher salt

1 tablespoon freshly ground black pepper

1 tablespoon dried thyme, plus fresh thyme sprigs (optional) for garnish

1 tablespoon dried oregano, plus fresh oregano sprigs (optional) for garnish

3 lemons, thinly sliced and seeded, plus lemon wedges for serving

4 stalks (8 inches long) fresh rosemary,
   plus rosemary sprigs (optional), for garnish

2 to 3 tablespoons olive oil

Greek Chimichurri Sauce (recipe follows),
   for serving

1. Using the tip of a sharp knife, cut evenly spaced small slits about ½ to 1 inch deep all over the lamb. Insert pieces of garlic clove in the slits. You should have 20 or more slits.

2. Place the salt, pepper, dried thyme, and dried oregano in a small bowl and stir to combine.

3. Tear off a piece of aluminum foil large enough to completely wrap the leg of lamb and place it on a work surface. Arrange a large piece of plastic wrap on top of it. Place the garlic-studded leg of lamb on top of the plastic wrap. Rub the herb mixture all over the leg of lamb. Arrange the lemon slices and stalks of rosemary all over the lamb. placing some underneath the leg and some on top. Wrap the lamb tightly with the plastic wrap, then with the aluminum foil. Refrigerate the lamb until ready to cook, at least 8 hours, preferably overnight.

4. When ready to cook, unwrap the lamb and remove the lemon slices and rosemary sprigs and discard them. Rub the lamb lightly with olive oil.

5. Preheat the grill to medium-high heat.

6. Skewer the lamb on the rotisserie spit, if using, and grill according to the manufacturer's instructions until cooked to taste, 1¾ to 2 hours. When done to medium-rare the internal temperature of the lamb will read 125°F on an instant-read meat thermometer (take care not to touch the bone when inserting the thermometer). When done to medium-well the temperature will register 140°F. You can also grill the leg of lamb on a medium-high grill over indirect heat, turning it often; it will be done after 1¾ to 2 hours.

RECIPE REMINDERS

Made for

Prep notes

Don't forget

Special touches

7. Remove the lamb from the rotisserie spit, if using, and place it on a platter to rest for about 15 minutes before carving. Or, let the lamb cool completely, wrap it in aluminum foil, and refrigerate it. Rewarm the lamb by opening up the foil on top and placing the lamb in a 350°F oven for about 30 minutes before serving.

8. Carve the lamb into slices. Garnish the platter with sprigs of fresh thyme, oregano, rosemary, if desired, and lemon wedges. Serve the Greek Chimichurri Sauce on the side.

Greek Chimichurri Sauce

SERVES 10 (MAKES ABOUT 1½ CUPS)

PREP: 10 MINUTES

Here, Argentina's beloved garlicky sauce is infused with the traditional Greek flavors of mint and oregano.

> 1 cup coarsely chopped red onion (1 medium-size onion)
> 1 cup pitted kalamata olives
> 1 cup loosely packed fresh mint leaves
> 1 cup loosely packed flat-leaf or curly parsley
> ½ cup loosely packed fresh oregano
> 1 medium-size clove garlic, peeled
> 1 tablespoon fresh lemon juice, or more to taste
> Pinch of salt

Place the onion, olives, mint, parsley, oregano, garlic, lemon juice, and salt in a food processor fitted with a steel blade. Process until finely chopped and well blended, about 1 minute. Taste for seasoning, adding more lemon juice as needed. Spoon the chimichurri sauce into a small glass bowl, cover it with plastic wrap, and refrigerate until serving time.

SENSATIONAL SIDES

Be it a dinner party, a grand buffet, a potluck lunch, or a Thanksgiving feast, when side dishes are full of personality they often steal the spotlight away from the main dish. Easter ham? If you've got green beans, squash casserole, hot rolls, and deviled eggs on your plate, who needs anything else? Summer chicken on the grill? Yawn. Bring on the ratatouille, tomato pie, and potato salad. Thanksgiving turkey? Save room for the sweet potatoes, cranberry sauce, and corn pudding.

Think how boring meals would be without side dishes. Sides have stories to tell—like the way your mother cooked corn. They bring the foods of other countries to life and can open your eyes to new ways to prepare a favorite vegetable. Take artichokes—

I love them steamed and fried, but when my friend David grilled artichokes and served them with a smoky fresh tomato sauce, he introduced me to a recipe I just had to share.

It's not always possible to cook fresh and in season, so I like to keep chopped spinach in the freezer and cans of those big Italian green beans, which are great for simmering with olive oil and brown sugar. The recipes here are mostly based on vegetables, but you'll find several outstanding fruit dishes and a garlic bread. Many are comforting casseroles that ring a nostalgic tone. There are also newer twists on simple foods: roast asparagus seasoned with just kosher salt, Roast Potatoes for a Crowd, and assorted grilled veggies beautifully arranged on a platter. Hardly wallflowers, side dishes can be the main attraction.

WHAT GOES WITH WHAT?
MATCHING THE SIDE TO THE MAIN

What with all of the deliberations people go through trying to decide what sides go with the rest of the menu, I've learned that practice does make perfect. The trial and error method works best in matching foods—you know what combinations are right the first time you fork into them. Commit those recipes and menus to memory and they become the birthday dinners, anniversary celebrations, Thanksgivings, and summer barbecues that your family will enjoy year after year.

Of course there are flavor mates that work regardless of the season—ham and corn, beef and potatoes, fish and rice, and chicken with just about anything. But, for those new to planning a menu, here are a few things I have learned on the job.

✳ Figure out the main dish first, then choose the sides.

✳ Select a starch next, be it potato, rice, pasta, or grits. Let the season help you with this choice. If it is summertime, you might opt for potato salad or roasted potatoes,

rice salad, or a light pasta. When the weather is cooler, go for a creamy potato dish, or possibly a corn pudding or soufflé, or a cheesy vegetable casserole.

✳ Then, add something crunchy, such as a green salad or a vegetable salad; in summer, fruit salad is a good choice.

✳ Now, add a vegetable—in the summer, a green vegetable lightly roasted or grilled, or maybe ratatouille. And in the fall, possibly simmered green beans or sautéed zucchini.

✳ For larger buffets, include another colorful side or two that's a bit of fun, such as the Fresh Tomato Pie (page 296), the Spinach and Feta Pie (page 286), or Curried Corn and Bell Peppers (page 268).

✳ Then add bread and at least one dessert. Lemon works well after fish. Chocolate follows beef—and just about anything else. When it's the season, choose a fresh fruit pie or cobbler. For holidays, let tradition be your guide.

David's Grilled Artichokes with Roasted Tomato Vinaigrette

SERVES 8

**PREP: 20 MINUTES ✳ COOK: 45 MINUTES ✳ COOL: 20 MINUTES
GRILL: ABOUT 25 MINUTES**

MY FRIEND DAVID PATTERSON IS A WONDERFUL cook who travels to Italy frequently, watches the TV food shows, and goes all out for a great recipe. David came up with this unique and delicious way to prepare artichokes when they come into season. It is as suitable for a large buffet as it is for a small dinner party because each artichoke half feeds one and is an ideal appetizer. You make a vinaigrette from fresh grill-charred tomatoes and spoon it into the hollow of the artichoke that's formed after the choke is removed.

4 large artichokes

Olive oil

4 medium-size tomatoes

2 to 3 cloves garlic, minced

1 cup chopped scallions, green parts only (from 1 bunch)

¼ cup minced shallots (4 medium-size shallots)

2 tablespoons red wine vinegar

Salt, cayenne pepper, and freshly ground black pepper

1. Bring a tea kettle of water to a boil.

2. Trim the tough outer leaves off the artichokes, leaving the stems attached. Stand the artichokes up side by side in a large

TOTE NOTES

Tote the artichokes on a large platter covered with plastic wrap. Bring the vinaigrette in a plastic container with a lid.

When you arrive, remove the plastic wrap from the serving platter and spoon the vinaigrette into the artichokes.

PLAN AHEAD

The artichokes can be grilled up to 6 hours ahead of time. You can make the tomato vinaigrette a day before and refrigerate it in a plastic container; let it return to room temperature before serving.

GRILL TIP

If you're using a gas grill, once you're finished grilling the food, keep the burners on for an additional 15 to 30 minutes to burn off any bits that might have gotten stuck to the grate.

pot. Add enough boiling water to come a third of the way up the side of the artichokes. Cover the pot and let the artichokes simmer over low heat until tender and a leaf pulls out easily, about 45 minutes.

3. Drain the artichokes and let them sit until they are cool enough to handle, about 20 minutes, then slice them in half lengthwise, through the stem. Using a soupspoon, scoop out the choke from the center of each artichoke half. Brush the artichokes all over with olive oil and set them aside.

4. Preheat the grill to high heat.

5. When ready to cook, brush the tomatoes with a little olive oil and place them on the hot grill. Let the tomatoes cook until charred on one side, then turn them with tongs and cook until that side is charred; repeat turning the tomatoes with tongs until they are lightly charred all over and the skin blisters, 15 to 20 minutes in all, or about 5 minutes per side. Set the tomatoes aside. Leave the fire burning.

6. Place the artichoke halves on the grill, cut side down, cover the grill, and let cook until grill marks form, 3 to 4 minutes. Turn the artichokes cut side up and let cook until grill marks form, 3 to 4 minutes longer. Set the artichokes aside.

7. Skin and core the tomatoes, leaving them whole. Place $1/3$ cup of olive oil in a large frying pan over medium heat. Add the garlic, scallions, and shallots. Cook until the vegetables soften, 5 to 6 minutes, stirring. Add the tomatoes to the pan and press down on them to flatten them. Let the tomato pulp cook until it blends with the olive oil and forms a sauce, 3 to 4 minutes. Add the red wine vinegar and season with salt, cayenne pepper, and black pepper to taste. Let the sauce come to a simmer, then turn off the heat.

8. When ready to serve, place the artichoke halves on a large platter—a white one will look dramatic. Spoon $1/4$ cup of the tomato vinaigrette into the hollow of each artichoke half. To eat, pull off the leaves and dip them into the vinaigrette, then using a knife and fork, cut the artichoke bottom into pieces.

BIG BATCH: *Knowing that each artichoke serves two people, you can prepare as many artichokes as you need and make more than one batch of tomato vinaigrette. Don't worry if you have leftover vinaigrette. It is delicious on just about anything—pasta, grilled cheese sandwiches, or grilled fish.*

**M
E
N
U**

TWENTY-FIFTH ANNIVERSARY PARTY

Has it really been twenty-five years? Whether those years have been spent at a job or in marriage, celebrate! This menu is a little fancy because it's a special occasion, so divide and conquer, letting others (but not the honoree) make a dish.

DAVID'S GRILLED ARTICHOKES
WITH ROASTED TOMATO VINAIGRETTE, *page 253*
✳
JOHN'S GRILLED BEEF TENDERLOIN, *page 240*
✳
ROASTED ASPARAGUS
WITH OLIVE OIL AND SALT, *page 256*
✳
BOURSIN POTATO GRATIN, *page 284*
✳
CHOCOLATE ZUCCOTTO CAKE, *page 372*

**RECIPE
REMINDERS**

Made for

Prep notes

Don't forget

Special touches

Bring again

Roasted Asparagus with Olive Oil and Salt

SERVES 8

PREP: 10 MINUTES * BAKE: 15 TO 20 MINUTES

TOTE NOTES

Carry the asparagus on a pretty platter, covered with plastic wrap.

Bring the Parmesan shavings and the lemon wedges separately, in small plastic bags, if desired, and garnish the asparagus just before serving.

PLAN AHEAD

The roasted asparagus can be kept at room temperature for several hours. While it can be refrigerated, covered, for up to two days, it is best freshly roasted.

NO SIDE DISH IS AS SIMPLE OR AS ELEGANT AS ROASTED asparagus. It is the ultimate do-ahead side dish, and it complements foods from fried chicken to grilled fish to burgers. Of course, it's best in the spring when you can find fresh thick asparagus in the market at a good price. Save the slender asparagus for steaming— roasting produces a meaty taste, and you need the thicker asparagus to stand up to it. Depending on the size of the asparagus you use, the cooking time will vary. Season it with nothing more than olive oil and salt, or add a showering of Parmesan cheese shavings and some lemon wedges for garnish, if you feel so moved. Don't season the asparagus with lemon juice or vinegar ahead of time, for it will turn that bright green color into a dingy green.

2 pounds thick asparagus (16 to 24 spears per pound)
¼ cup extra-virgin olive oil
Kosher salt
¼ cup Parmesan cheese shavings
   (optional; see box, page 111), for garnish
1 lemon (optional), cut into wedges, for garnish

1. Place a rack in the center of the oven and preheat the oven to 400°F.

2. Snap off and discard the tough ends of the asparagus. Place the asparagus spears in a colander and rinse under cold running water. Pat the asparagus dry with paper towels and place it on a large sheet pan or in a shallow roasting pan. Drizzle the olive oil over the asparagus and toss to coat, using your hands or a spatula. Arrange the asparagus in a single layer on the pan and sprinkle the spears with salt.

3. Bake the asparagus until still bright green and just tender when poked with the tip of a small paring knife, 15 to 20 minutes. Let the asparagus cool slightly, then pile it on a serving platter. Serve the asparagus warm or at room temperature, garnished with Parmesan and/or lemon wedges, if desired.

BIG BATCH: *You can double and triple this recipe, but take care not to overcrowd the baking pan. The asparagus needs to roast in a single layer. Use two pans, if necessary.*

TEN QUICK TABLE TOPPERS

What? You've organized the menu but forgotten the serving table? Here are some last-minute decorating suggestions.

1. Votive candles

2. Little seasonal pumpkins and squash

3. Small vases with flowers

4. Fortune cookies in a festive Chinese-carryout container

5. Bowls of miniature horoscopes

6. A pot of pretty flowers from the nursery

7. Fresh herbs in small pots

8. Little photographs in frames

9. Seashells in a glass bowl

10. Asparagus spears in a vase filled with water

RECIPE REMINDERS

Made for

Prep notes

Don't forget

Special touches

Bring again

Steamed Asparagus with a Light Ginger and Sesame Sauce

SERVES 8 TO 12

PREP: ABOUT 15 MINUTES ✳ COOK: ABOUT 5 MINUTES

TOTE NOTES

Tote the asparagus in a covered plastic container. Bring the chopped scallions and the sesame seeds, if desired, separately in small plastic bags, and don't forget the platter.

PLAN AHEAD

The asparagus can be refrigerated in the baking dish, covered with plastic wrap, for up to 24 hours. Its color is at its brightest when served freshly made, but the asparagus becomes more delicious as it marinates.

LIGHT AND FRESH, PERFECT FOR BRUNCH OR A DINNER party, this is another wonderful way to prepare asparagus. And again, it is a great do-ahead dish. I love this with ham or grilled fish or alongside an omelet. Make a batch of steamed asparagus and take it to the office potluck when you need a green vegetable to round out all of the starchy salads and fried foods. The timing for this dish is based on using slender asparagus, so if your asparagus is thicker, you'll need to increase the cooking time—it should cook until it is just barely tender and still bright green.

2 pounds thin asparagus (60 to 75 spears per pound)

2 tablespoons reduced-sodium soy sauce

2 tablespoons sugar

2 teaspoons grated peeled fresh ginger

2 teaspoons Asian (dark) sesame oil

2 teaspoons sweet red chile sauce (see Note), or a generous dash of hot pepper sauce

2 tablespoons vegetable oil

¼ cup finely chopped scallions, both white and green parts, for garnish

1 teaspoon toasted sesame seeds (optional; see box, page 99), for garnish

1. Snap off and discard the tough ends of the asparagus. Place the asparagus spears in a colander and rinse under cold running water. Pat the asparagus dry with paper towels.

2. Fill a large frying pan with 1 inch of water and bring to a boil over medium-high heat. Add half of the asparagus and cook until bright green and just tender, 2 to 3 minutes. Drain the asparagus immediately and place it in a 13 by 9–inch glass or ceramic baking dish. Repeat with the remaining asparagus, then set aside.

3. Place the soy sauce and sugar in a small mixing bowl and whisk until the sugar dissolves. Stir in the ginger, sesame oil, and chili or hot sauce. Whisk in the vegetable oil until the vinaigrette thickens slightly. Pour the vinaigrette over the asparagus and toss gently to combine. When ready to serve, transfer the asparagus and vinaigrette to a serving platter and garnish with the scallions and sesame seeds, if desired.

NOTE: You'll find sweet red chile sauce in the section of the supermarket where Thai foods are sold.

BIG BATCH: *As long as you steam the asparagus in batches so that it does not overcook, you can double and triple this recipe.*

RECIPE REMINDERS

Made for

Prep notes

Don't forget

Special touches

Bring again

Broccoli Brag Casserole

SERVES 12

PREP: ABOUT 10 MINUTES ✴ BAKE: ABOUT 50 MINUTES ✴ COOL: 10 MINUTES

**TOTE
NOTES**

*Tote the broccoli
casserole by wrapping
it in aluminum foil
and keep it warm
when you arrive on
a warming tray or
in a warming drawer.*

PLAN AHEAD

*You can bake the
casserole a day ahead;
let it cool down, then
wrap it in plastic wrap
and refrigerate it.
Rewarm the casserole,
covered with aluminum
foil, in a 300°F oven for
about 20 minutes.*

WE OFTEN SPEND THANKSGIVING IN CHATTANOOGA
with my husband's family. And we look
forward to the broccoli casserole that cousin
Pemy Patten prepares. Called Broccoli Brag, she makes
it with frozen chopped broccoli and eggs, Cheddar, and
cottage cheese. The recipe has circulated throughout
Chattanooga and was originally featured in the Junior
League cookbook called *Dinner on the Diner*. My version
calls for ricotta cheese and a little less flour than the
original recipe. You can certainly substitute small curd
cottage cheese for the ricotta, and feel free to season the
casserole as you like, adding more hot sauce or a little
ground nutmeg.

Vegetable oil spray, for misting the baking dish
2 packages (10 ounces each) frozen chopped broccoli
4 tablespoons (½ stick) butter, melted
6 large eggs, beaten
1 container (15 ounces; 2 cups) skim ricotta cheese
2 cups (8 ounces) shredded Cheddar cheese
¼ cup all-purpose flour
1 teaspoon salt, or more to taste
¼ teaspoon hot pepper sauce, or more to taste
Freshly ground black pepper

1. Place a rack in the center of the oven and preheat the oven
to 325°F. Lightly mist a 13 by 9–inch glass or ceramic baking
dish with vegetable oil spray and set the dish aside.

2. Place the broccoli in a large microwave-safe glass bowl and microwave on high power until thawed, 1½ to 2 minutes. Leaving the broccoli in the bowl, drain it over the sink, pressing on it with a fork to extract as much liquid as possible.

3. Add the butter, eggs, ricotta, 1 cup of the Cheddar cheese, and the flour, salt, and hot pepper sauce. Taste for seasoning, adding black pepper to taste and more salt and/or hot pepper sauce as desired. Stir to combine well. Transfer the broccoli mixture to the prepared baking dish and scatter the remaining 1 cup of cheddar cheese evenly over the top.

4. Bake the casserole until it turns golden brown and bubbles around the edges, 48 to 52 minutes. Let the casserole cool for at least 10 minutes before cutting it into squares to serve.

BIG BATCH: *You can make two or three broccoli casseroles in separate baking dishes.*

RECIPE REMINDERS

Made for

Prep notes

Don't forget

Special touches

Bring again

Broccoli Corn Bread

SERVES 8 TO 10

PREP: 15 MINUTES ✳ BAKE: ABOUT 25 MINUTES

TOTE NOTES

You can bake the corn bread ahead of time, wrap it in aluminum foil, then rewarm it in a 300°F oven for 15 minutes with good results. But, for the best results, this should be served freshly baked. So, prepare the batter, place it in the baking dish, cover it with plastic wrap, and refrigerate it until it's time to travel. When you get to the gathering, preheat the oven to 400°F, uncover the batter, and bake it.

PLAN AHEAD

The corn bread batter can be refrigerated for several hours before baking. It will warm up in transit, but if you are baking it straight from the fridge, add about 5 minutes to the cooking time.

JUST WHEN YOU THINK YOU'VE HEARD OF OR TASTED every recipe, well, you discover you haven't. This happened to me recently when Holly Westcott of Nashville raved about a corn bread recipe from her old hometown of Florence, South Carolina, that had a cultlike following. There, you could always count on at least one pan of Broccoli Corn Bread at covered dish suppers. Holly says this recipe is at its best right out of the oven, and I agree. If there is a way you can bake on site, do so. If the gathering is at your house, all the better—pop the corn bread into the oven as everyone mingles before supper, and it's ready when they are. Sort of a bread, sort of a vegetable side, this recipe falls into that delicious gray zone. Try it and you'll see what I mean.

Vegetable oil spray, for misting the baking dish

8 tablespoons (1 stick) butter, cut into pieces

1 package (10 ounces) frozen chopped broccoli, thawed and drained well

½ cup finely chopped onion

4 large eggs, lightly beaten

¾ cup (6 ounces) 2 percent milk-fat small curd cottage cheese

½ teaspoon salt

1 package (8½ ounces) corn muffin mix

1. Place a rack in the center of the oven and preheat the oven to 400°F. Lightly mist a 13 by 9–inch glass or ceramic baking dish with vegetable oil spray and set the dish aside.

2. Place the butter in a large microwave-safe glass bowl and microwave on high power until melted, 50 seconds to 1 minute. Stir in the broccoli, onion, eggs, cottage cheese, and salt. Stir in the corn muffin mix, pressing out the big lumps with a fork. Pour the batter into the prepared baking dish.

3. Bake the corn bread until it is lightly browned and springs back when you press it with your finger, about 25 minutes. Let the corn bread cool slightly before serving.

BIG BATCH: *You can double this recipe—put it in a slightly deeper 3-quart baking dish. It will be lightly browned after 35 to 40 minutes.*

RECIPE REMINDERS

Made for

Prep notes

Don't forget

Special touches

Bring again

Braised Red Cabbage with Apples and Wine

SERVES 8

PREP: 30 MINUTES * COOK: 45 TO 50 MINUTES

TOTE NOTES

Tote the cabbage in the cooking pot or place it in a pretty ceramic casserole. If you're concerned about the lid staying on, place a kitchen towel over it to hold it in place.

You can serve the cabbage at room temperature or briefly reheat it in the microwave oven (be sure the container is microwave safe) or over low heat on the stovetop.

PLAN AHEAD

You can prepare the cabbage a day ahead and refrigerate it, covered.

THE REAL PLEASURES OF THE FALL TABLE ARE THE root vegetables and cabbages. And while I was not raised eating braised red cabbage, now I cannot imagine pork roast without it, especially when you cook down the cabbage with onion, sugar, apples, red wine, and chicken broth. Take this to fall barbecues and winter dinners and springtime grilled sausage parties. Serve the cabbage hot from the pan or at room temperature.

4 tablespoons (½ stick) butter

1 large onion, sliced

2 tablespoons sugar, or more to taste

2 tablespoons balsamic vinegar

2 to 3 pounds red cabbage, outer leaves removed, sliced into quarters, then cut in ¼-inch slices (12 to 16 cups)

2 tart apples, peeled, cored, and thinly sliced

1 can (14½ ounces) chicken broth, or about 1½ cups chicken broth

½ cup dry red wine

1 bay leaf

1 teaspoon salt, or more to taste

Freshly ground black pepper

1. Melt the butter in a large, heavy pot over medium-low heat. Add the onion and cook, stirring, until softened, 4 to 5 minutes. Reduce the heat to low and stir in the sugar and balsamic vinegar. Add the cabbage and apples and stir to coat well. Stir in the chicken broth, wine, bay leaf, and salt and season with pepper to taste. Increase the heat to medium and let come to a boil. Cover the pot, reduce the heat to low, and let the cabbage simmer until tender, 40 to 45 minutes, stirring occasionally.

2. Taste the cabbage for seasoning, adding more salt and/or sugar, as needed. Remove and discard the bay leaf before serving.

BIG BATCH: *Using a soup pot, you can double this recipe. Enlist a friend—or a food processor—to help you slice all the cabbage.*

RECIPE REMINDERS

Made for

Prep notes

Don't forget

Special touches

Bring again

Bereavement Corn

SERVES 8

PREP: 15 MINUTES ✳ COOK: 10 MINUTES

NANCY BRADSHAW CREATED THIS RECIPE—SHE WAS always taking the corn to people who had lost a loved one. The recipe has made its way around Nashville, and I can tell you the side dish is comforting, as suitable in those sad times as it is at a happy gathering with friends. Pair the corn with fried chicken, grilled fish, roasted chicken—just about any main course. While it's best made with fresh white corn, in a pinch you can substitute frozen shoepeg corn. The frozen doesn't have that fresh corn milkiness, so you'll need to increase the liquid a bit.

8 ears white corn, such as Silver Queen,
    shucked

8 tablespoons (1 stick) unsalted butter

1 can (5 ounces) evaporated milk,
    or a scant ¾ cup heavy (whipping) cream

1 tablespoon cornstarch

1 teaspoon sugar, or more to taste

Scant ¾ cup water

Salt and freshly ground black pepper

1 tablespoon minced fresh chives,
    for garnish

Sliced ripe tomatoes (optional), for garnish

1. Hold an ear of corn upright on a cutting board and, using a sharp knife, cut down close to the cob to slice off the kernels. Repeat with the remaining ears of corn. You will have about 4 cups of kernels.

2. Melt the butter in a large skillet over medium-high heat. Add the corn kernels, followed by the evaporated milk or cream, cornstarch, and sugar and stir to combine. If using evaporated milk, fill the can with water and add this to the corn mixture or add the scant ¾ cup of water. Season the corn with salt and pepper to taste.

3. Cook the corn, stirring, until the liquid just comes to a boil, making sure that the cornstarch dissolves completely. Reduce the heat to medium-low and let simmer, uncovered, stirring occasionally, until thickened, 6 to 7 minutes. Taste for seasoning, adding more sugar, salt, and/or pepper as needed. Spoon the corn onto a serving platter and garnish it with the chives and tomatoes, if desired.

BIG BATCH: *You can double the corn recipe, using a large pot instead of a skillet.*

M
E
N
U

A COMFORTING MEAL FOR FRIENDS

Sometimes everyone needs a meal prepared by a close friend, and we crave the conversation that a small dinner party affords. Here is a down-home way to entertain friends when they need food for the body and the soul.

JOHN'S HOMEMADE COLESLAW, *page 126*
✳
JUDY'S MOM'S MEAT LOAF, *page 190*
✳
BEREAVEMENT CORN
✳
AUNT ELIZABETH'S BANANA PUDDING, *page 434*

RECIPE REMINDERS

Made for

Prep notes

Don't forget

Special touches

Bring again

Curried Corn and Bell Peppers

SERVES 8

PREP: 15 TO 20 MINUTES ✻ COOK: ABOUT 10 MINUTES

TOTE NOTES

Tote the corn and peppers straight from the stove in a pretty, shallow serving bowl covered with plastic wrap—the corn can be kept at room temperature for up to an hour before serving.

Take along some fresh cilantro or parsley in a small plastic bag for a garnish, if desired.

PLAN AHEAD

Although the color of the bell peppers is at its brightest when they are freshly cooked, you can prepare this side dish a day in advance and refrigerate it. Tote it right from the refrigerator, then spoon it into a saucepan and reheat it upon arrival.

A N UNUSUAL SIDE DISH, THIS IS A RECIPE I HAVE made for years. It is distinctive and memorable because the combination of corn and bell peppers gives it a vibrant color, and the curry flavor is exotic. Just the right side dish for grilled chicken or fish, it's tasty in the summer, with a garnish of cilantro, and festive on the holiday table instead of the usual scalloped potatoes. If you want the heat, add a few hot peppers, and for even more color, use a green bell pepper instead of the yellow.

6 ears white or yellow corn, or a mix of the two, shucked (see Note)
4 tablespoons (½ stick) butter
1 cup chopped onion (1 medium-size onion)
1 large red bell pepper, cored, seeded, and sliced
1 large yellow bell pepper, cored, seeded, and sliced
Salt and freshly ground black pepper
1 to 2 teaspoons good-quality curry powder
1 cup heavy (whipping) cream
Chopped cilantro or parsley (optional), for garnish

1. Hold an ear of corn upright on a rimmed baking sheet and, using a sharp knife, cut down close to the cob to slice off the kernels. Then, run the knife down the ear again to extract the milk and any remaining bits of corn kernels. Repeat with the remaining ears of corn. When done, you will have about 3 cups of corn kernels. Set them aside.

2. Melt the butter in a large skillet over medium heat. Add the onion and cook, stirring, until soft, about 3 minutes. Add the red and yellow bell peppers, season with salt and black pepper to taste, and cook, stirring, until the bell peppers are soft, 2 to 3 minutes.

3. Stir in the corn kernels and liquid, curry powder, and cream. Cook, stirring, until the cream bubbles up, 1 to 2 minutes. Reduce the heat to low and let simmer until slightly thickened, 3 to 4 minutes longer. Serve the corn and peppers garnished with cilantro or parsley, if desired.

NOTE: In a pinch, you can use frozen corn, but it won't have that natural fresh flavor and creaminess. You'll need 3 cups of kernels.

BIG BATCH: *This recipe is easily doubled and tripled if you are willing to cut that much fresh corn from the cob!*

Made for

Prep notes

Don't forget

Special touches

Bring again

Fresh Corn Pudding

SERVES 8 TO 10

PREP: 20 TO 25 MINUTES ✳ BAKE: 50 TO 55 MINUTES

TOTE NOTES

Corn pudding is best served warm; bake it at home, let it cool for 10 minutes, then cover it with aluminum foil. Wrap the baking dish in a clean kitchen towel to keep the heat in as you travel.

When you arrive, remove the towel and place the corn pudding in a warming drawer set on low or in a 200°F oven; the pudding will hold for up to 30 minutes.

YOU CAN FIND ALL SORTS OF VARIATIONS OF CORN pudding around—some based on canned corn, some made with canned creamed corn—but this one relies on fresh corn. It is best made in the summer when you can buy sweet corn grown close to home. Pick six nice big ears, peel back the husks, and remove the silks. By scraping down close to the cobs with a sharp knife it's easy to trim off the kernels. You need about three cups of corn kernels for this recipe; you've probably got the rest of the ingredients on hand.

6 tablespoons (¾ stick) butter

6 ears white or yellow corn, or a mix of the two, shucked

2 cups whole milk

4 large eggs

3 tablespoons all-purpose flour

2 tablespoons sugar

Salt and freshly ground black pepper

Cayenne pepper

1. Place a rack in the center of the oven and preheat the oven to 350°F. Place 2 tablespoons of butter in a 13 by 9–inch glass or ceramic baking dish and place it in the oven while it preheats until the butter melts, then set the baking dish aside.

2. Hold an ear of corn upright on a rimmed baking sheet and, using a sharp knife, cut down close to the cob to slice off the kernels. Then, run the knife down the cob again to extract the milk and any remaining bits of corn kernels.

Repeat with the remaining ears of corn. When done, you will have about 3 cups of corn kernels. Set them aside.

3. Warm the milk in a small saucepan over low heat.

4. Meanwhile, separate the eggs, placing the whites in a large mixing bowl and the yolks in another large mixing bowl. Beat the egg whites at high speed with an electric mixer until stiff peaks form, 2 to 3 minutes. Set the egg whites aside.

5. Place the remaining 4 tablespoons of butter in a glass measuring cup and microwave on high power until melted, about 1 minute. Beat the egg yolks with a fork until lemon colored. Whisk in the flour and sugar until well combined. Whisk in the warm milk and the 4 tablespoons of melted butter and season with salt and black and cayenne pepper to taste.

6. Fold in the corn kernels, then fold in the egg whites until just combined. Spoon the corn mixture into the prepared baking dish and bake until the top is golden and the pudding is just set, 50 to 55 minutes.

BIG BATCH: *This recipe is not easy to double. Just make two batches and bake them in separate baking dishes.*

RECIPE REMINDERS

Made for

Prep notes

Don't forget

Special touches

Bring again

Eggplant Parmesan with Fresh Basil

SERVES 12

PREP AND COOK: ABOUT 25 MINUTES ✳ BAKE: 35 TO 40 MINUTES PLUS 5 MINUTES RESTING TIME

TOTE NOTES

Keep the eggplant Parmesan warm when you tote it by covering the top of the baking dish with a snap-on plastic lid and placing the dish in a casserole carrier.

When you arrive, remove the plastic cover, tent the baking dish with aluminum foil, and place it in a warming drawer.

Or, you can bake the eggplant halfway through at home—about 20 minutes—and then finish baking it once you arrive.

DINNER DOCTOR READERS WILL RECOGNIZE THIS recipe—that's where I first shared it. But honestly, I could not write a book about dishes to tote without this one, which I have doubled to serve twelve and changed a bit by adding fresh basil leaves. You fry eggplant slices that have been dipped in egg. Then, as they bake they meld with a good pasta sauce enhanced with red wine. It makes a great vegetarian main course, too.

2 jars (26 ounces each) tomato-based pasta sauce

¼ cup dry red wine

4 medium-size cloves garlic, crushed in a garlic press

½ loosely packed cup torn fresh basil leaves

1 cup vegetable or olive oil, or more as needed

4 large eggs

Salt and freshly ground black pepper

2 large eggplants (3 pounds total), peeled and sliced crosswise ¼ inch thick

2 packages (8 ounces each; 4 cups total) shredded mozzarella and Parmesan cheese blend

1. Place a rack in the center of the oven and preheat the oven to 375°F.

2. Place the pasta sauce, wine, garlic, and basil in a 2-quart saucepan. Bring the sauce to a simmer over medium heat, stirring occasionally. Let simmer while you prepare the eggplant.

3. Heat ½ cup of the oil in a heavy skillet over medium-high heat. Crack the eggs into a wide, shallow bowl, season them with salt and pepper to taste, and lightly beat them with a fork. Arrange a double thickness of paper towels on a counter near the skillet. Place 2 to 3 slices of eggplant in the beaten egg and turn them to coat. Using a fork, transfer the eggplant slices to the hot oil and cook until golden brown and puffy but not cooked through, about 1 minute per side, then drain them on the paper towels. Repeat with the remaining slices of eggplant, wiping out the pan and adding more oil as necessary.

4. Place half of the eggplant slices in the bottom of a 13 by 9–inch glass or ceramic baking dish. Pour half of the pasta sauce over the eggplant, spreading it out evenly with a spatula. Scatter 2 cups of the cheese over the sauce. Repeat with the remaining eggplant, pasta sauce, and cheese. Cover the baking dish with aluminum foil and bake the casserole until it is bubbling and the cheese has melted, 35 to 40 minutes. Remove the aluminum foil and let the eggplant rest for 5 minutes, then slice and serve.

BIG BATCH: *Make a second or third casserole and you can feed twenty-four or thirty-six people. The only chore is frying the eggplant.*

EXCEPTIONAL EGGPLANT

Try to select eggplant that are firm, heavy, shiny, and very fresh. These will contain fewer seeds and be less bitter than older eggplant and will not need to be salted and drained before cooking. For the freshest eggplant, buy them in the summer and early fall from local markets. Use them within a day or two of purchase.

RECIPE REMINDERS

Made for

Prep notes

Don't forget

Special touches

Bring again

Bebe's Green Beans

SERVES 10 TO 12

PREP: ABOUT 5 MINUTES * COOK: 45 MINUTES TO 1 HOUR

MY MOTHER WAS KNOWN FOR THE WAY SHE COOKED green beans, a delicious departure from the old Southern method that uses ham or bacon. She cooked green beans in olive oil along with brown sugar and onion, and the results were sweet and tangy, not greasy. This is a recipe I use all the time when I'm cooking midweek family meals and for holidays when all the relatives are on hand. If you've got fresh pole beans, the big flat green beans that are known as Kentucky Wonder, by all means rinse and string them and cook them with these same seasonings. But if pole beans aren't available, don't fret, because I rely on the canned "Italian" green beans all the time.

4 cans ($14\frac{1}{2}$ ounces each) cut Italian green beans, drained (see Note)
1 cup chopped onion (1 medium-size onion)
$\frac{1}{4}$ cup olive oil
$\frac{1}{4}$ packed cup light brown sugar
Salt and freshly ground black pepper

1. Place the beans in a large saucepan. Add enough water to cover the beans by half. Add the onion, olive oil, brown sugar, 1 teaspoon of salt, and $\frac{1}{4}$ teaspoon pepper and stir to combine. Cover the pan and bring to a boil over medium-high heat, then reduce the heat to low and let the beans simmer until they are tender and the onion has cooked down, 45 minutes to 1 hour.

2. Taste the beans for seasoning, adding more salt and/or pepper as needed. Drain the beans and spoon them into a serving bowl or tureen for serving.

NOTE: If you can't find canned cut Italian green beans, you can use frozen ones. You'll need five 9-ounce packages.

BIG BATCH: *You can easily double this recipe, cooking the beans in a larger pot. Take care that you allow the beans to cool, then chill them well if you prepare them ahead of time. Always bring the beans back to a boil before serving.*

M
E
N
U

MEET THE NEIGHBORS

Fess up. You've been putting it off. Go ahead and invite the new family next door for dinner. To make conversation and the workload easier to handle, ask other neighbors to come, too, and have them bring a side dish or comforting dessert such as a cobbler.

ANITA'S OVEN-BAKED PORK TENDERLOINS, *page 234*
✳
FRESH CORN PUDDING, *page 270*
✳
BEBE'S GREEN BEANS
✳
DEEP DISH CHERRY COBBLER, *page 425*
AND VANILLA ICE CREAM

RECIPE REMINDERS

Made for

Prep notes

Don't forget

Special touches

Bring again

Green Beans with a Spicy Tomato Sauce

SERVES 6 TO 8

PREP: 20 MINUTES ✳ COOK: 45 TO 50 MINUTES

TOTE NOTES

Tote the green beans and tomato sauce in separate plastic containers. Bring the Parmesan and parsley sprig garnishes in small plastic bags and don't forget the serving platter.

When you arrive, reheat the tomato sauce on top of the stove over medium-low heat; it will take about 5 minutes. Then, fold in the green beans and let them cook for a few minutes before spooning them onto the platter and garnishing them.

I'VE MADE THESE GREEN BEANS FOR YEARS, AND WHAT I love about them most is the fresh tomato sauce seasoned with basil, garlic, and hot peppers that you spoon on top just before serving. This is a wonderful dish that improves if you make it a day in advance, and it becomes a main course easily with the addition of a cup of chopped smoked ham. Serve it with fried chicken, grilled steak—even hamburgers.

1 pound thin green beans
Salt
¼ cup olive oil
1 dried chile pepper, broken into thirds
5 to 6 cups chopped fresh tomatoes
   (6 medium-size tomatoes, peeled and seeded;
   see Note)
2 medium-size cloves garlic, crushed in a garlic press
¼ loosely packed cup chopped fresh parsley,
   plus parsley sprigs for garnish
2 tablespoons chopped fresh basil
½ teaspoon dried thyme
½ teaspoon dried oregano
Freshly ground black pepper
¼ cup shredded Parmesan cheese, for garnish

1. Snap the ends off the green beans, leaving the beans whole. Rinse the beans under cold running water, then drain them.

Place the beans in a large saucepan, add enough water to cover and 1 teaspoon of salt. Bring to a boil over medium-high heat, then reduce the heat to medium. Let the beans simmer, uncovered, until tender but crisp, 5 to 6 minutes. Drain the beans and set them aside.

2. Place the olive oil in a large frying pan over medium heat and add the chile pepper. Cook the pepper until it darkens, 1 to 2 minutes, then remove and discard it. Add the tomatoes, garlic, chopped parsley, basil, thyme, and oregano and season with salt and black pepper to taste. Cook, stirring, until the tomato sauce comes to a boil, then reduce the heat to low and let simmer, partially covered, until the tomatoes have lost much of their liquid and have thickened, 35 to 40 minutes.

3. If you want to serve the dish immediately, remove the pan from the heat and fold the drained beans into the sauce. Reheat them gently, over medium-low heat, 3 to 4 minutes. Transfer the beans and sauce to a serving platter, garnish with the Parmesan cheese and parsley sprigs, and serve.

NOTE: In a pinch or if good ripe tomatoes are not available, you can substitute slightly drained canned diced tomatoes for the fresh tomatoes.

WANT ANOTHER WAY TO SERVE THE GREEN BEANS? Reheat the beans in 2 tablespoons of water. Then, place the beans on a platter and spoon the warm sauce over them. Garnish the beans with Parmesan and parsley and serve at once.

BIG BATCH: *You can easily double the green bean recipe and serve it on a large platter to a crowd.*

RECIPE REMINDERS

Made for

Prep notes

Don't forget

Special touches

Bring again

Roast Potatoes for a Crowd

SERVES 8 TO 10

PREP: 10 MINUTES ✳ BAKE: 20 TO 25 MINUTES

TOTE NOTES

You can tote the potatoes in a disposable aluminum pan covered with aluminum foil and bring the platter on the side. You might want to reheat them, uncovered, in a 400°F oven for about 10 minutes. Then transfer them to the platter for serving.

MY DAUGHTER KATHLEEN USED TO RAVE ABOUT the roast potatoes she had at the Henrys' house, so I called Melissa Henry and asked for her secret. It could not be simpler, she explained— cubed Yukon Gold potatoes, olive oil, and some kind of seasoned salt, baked in a 400°F oven. So I tried her easy formula with a variety of seasonings: Lawry's, McCormick's Montreal Chicken Grill Mates, jerk seasoning, taco seasoning, and the wonderful Rendezvous barbecue seasoning from Memphis. No matter which, everyone cleaned the potato platter. These are great for accompanying grilled steaks and burgers or roast pork and chicken.

> 4 to 5 pounds Yukon Gold potatoes, scrubbed
> 2 to 3 tablespoons olive oil
> 1 teaspoon seasoned salt of your choice
> Fresh rosemary sprigs (optional), for garnish

1. Place a rack in the center of the oven and preheat the oven to 400°F.

2. If desired, peel the potatoes—or you can leave them unpeeled. Cut the potatoes into 1-inch cubes and place them on a rimmed baking sheet. Drizzle olive oil over the potatoes and sprinkle them with the seasoned salt. Using a spatula, toss the potatoes until they are well coated with the olive oil and salt, then spread them out in a single layer.

3. Bake the potatoes until they are crisp and lightly browned on the bottom and cooked through, 20 to 25 minutes. Using a spatula, transfer the potatoes to a serving platter. Garnish the platter with rosemary sprigs, if desired, and serve.

BIG BATCH: *Roast as many potatoes as you like, estimating a half pound of potatoes per person. Make sure they bake in one layer in the pan so they get brown and crisp on all sides.*

Twice-Baked Potatoes

SERVES 8

PREP: 15 TO 20 MINUTES ✳ BAKE: ABOUT 1 HOUR AND 20 MINUTES

TOTE NOTES

You have a couple of good options here, as these potatoes are easy to tote. Prepare them up to the second baking and transport them in a metal baking dish, covered with plastic wrap. When you arrive, uncover the baking dish or, better yet, transfer the potatoes to a baking sheet to spread them out, then bake them in a 400°F oven until the cheese melts, 15 to 18 minutes.

Or, you can completely bake the potatoes, place them in a shallow ceramic or glass dish, and cover it with waxed paper and aluminum foil. Wrapped in a towel or transported in an insulated bag, the potatoes will stay warm for up to 1 hour.

Either way, take the bacon and minced chive or scallion garnishes in separate plastic bags.

SOMETIMES IN OUR FAMILY WE TAKE "WHAT CAN I BRING?" outside the city limits. We tote food to Chattanooga for Thanksgiving, and my sister Susan in Atlanta will bring food with her to Nashville. It's not that we can't prepare it all, it's just that we like Susan's cooking and welcome her repertoire of recipes. She started toting Twice-Baked Potatoes several years ago. This is a great recipe to make ahead and freeze, and the potatoes can be packaged in big zipper-lock plastic bags and placed in a cooler on ice for the trip. Even if you are serving the potatoes in your home, they're wonderful to prep ahead and freeze. Season them as you like—with chives, cheese, crumbled bacon—it's really up to you.

4 large baking potatoes, scrubbed

2 teaspoons olive oil

Kosher salt

4 tablespoons (½ stick) butter

Freshly ground black pepper

½ cup milk

1 cup sour cream

2 cups (8 ounces) shredded sharp Cheddar cheese

2 tablespoons finely chopped fresh chives or scallions, plus more for garnish (optional)

8 slices bacon (optional), cooked, drained, and crumbled, for garnish

1. Place a rack in the center of the oven and preheat the oven to 400°F.

2. Rub the potatoes with the olive oil, sprinkle salt over them, and place them on a baking sheet. Bake the potatoes until soft, 55 minutes to 1 hour. Reduce the oven temperature to 350°F.

3. When the potatoes are cool enough to handle but still warm inside, cut them in half lengthwise. Using a soupspoon, scoop out the warm pulp and place it in a mixing bowl. Put the potato skins back on the baking sheet and set them aside. Add the butter to the potato pulp and mash with a fork until it melts. Season with salt and pepper to taste. Add the milk and stir until the potato mixture is stiff, then add the sour cream, 1 cup of the Cheddar cheese, and the chives or scallions and stir until well mixed.

4. Using a soupspoon, scoop the seasoned potato mixture into the potato skins, taking care not to pack it down and distributing it evenly among the skins. Place 2 tablespoons of the Cheddar cheese on top of each potato half, pressing down on it gently so that it sticks to the potato.

5. Bake the potatoes until the cheese melts and the potato filling sets, 15 to 18 minutes. Garnish the potatoes, if desired, with the crumbled bacon and more chives or scallions.

BIG BATCH: *Double and triple the potatoes for large crowds.*

PLAN AHEAD

Freeze stuffed potatoes without the cheese topping by placing them in a pan in the freezer. Once they're frozen, transfer them to a plastic freezer bag; they can be stored for up to three months. To finish baking, thaw the potatoes overnight in the refrigerator. Once thawed, top the potatoes with the cheese and bake until bubbly.

RECIPE REMINDERS

Made for

Prep notes

Don't forget

Special touches

Bring again

Creamy Scalloped Potatoes

SERVES 8

PREP: 15 MINUTES

BAKE: 35 TO 40 MINUTES ✳ PLUS 5 MINUTES RESTING TIME

**TOTE
NOTES**

*To tote the potatoes, let
them rest uncovered for
about 5 minutes after
baking. Then, cover
the baking dish with
aluminum foil, wrap it
in a clean towel, and
place it in a shallow box
or bin to carry it.*

*Or, the aluminum
foil–covered baking dish
can be transported in a
casserole carrying case.*

YOU CAN GO TO A LOT OF TROUBLE ASSEMBLING A POTATO casserole, slicing potatoes razor thin and layering them in the pan with warm cream . . . or you can open a bag of frozen hash browns. This recipe is a favorite of mine from *The Dinner Doctor,* and no one ever believes that it contains frozen potatoes. Let the potatoes cook down until creamy and you'll find that with the garlic and Parmesan, this is a great recipe for last-minute miracles. To dress up the dish you can garnish it with a little parsley; either scatter chopped parsley over the top or arrange parsley sprigs in the corners of the baking dish.

> 1 package (32 ounces) frozen cubed hash brown
> potatoes, slightly thawed
> ½ cup (2 ounces) shredded Parmesan cheese
> 2 to 3 cloves garlic, sliced
> Salt and freshly ground black pepper
> 2 cups heavy (whipping) cream
> Paprika

1. Place a rack in the center of the oven and preheat the oven to 400°F.

2. Spoon half of the hash browns in an even layer in a 13 by 9–inch glass or ceramic baking dish. Break the hash browns apart with your hands if they are still mostly frozen. Sprinkle the Parmesan cheese and garlic slices evenly over the top. Season with salt and pepper to taste.

3. Spoon the remaining hash browns in an even layer on top of the Parmesan. Pour the cream over the potatoes. Cover the baking dish with aluminum foil.

4. Bake the potatoes until the cream bubbles and has thickened and the potatoes are tender, 35 to 40 minutes. Let the potatoes rest for about 5 minutes, then sprinkle them with paprika. If you are not serving them right away, the potatoes may be kept warm in a 200°F oven or in a warming drawer.

BIG BATCH: *You can double and triple this recipe as needed. If you are baking a large batch in one dish, increase the time to 1 hour.*

TEN WAYS TO SEASON ROASTED POTATOES

Peel some nice starchy potatoes and cut them into 1-inch cubes. Place them in a baking dish and toss with olive oil. Season with any seasonings listed here, then bake them in a 400°F oven until they're crisp around the edges and soft in the center, about 20 to 25 minutes.

1. Seasoned salt

2. Minced garlic, kosher salt, and chopped fresh rosemary

3. Chili powder, ground cumin, and salt

4. Shredded Parmesan cheese and black pepper

5. Lemon juice and dried oregano

6. Jerk seasoning

7. Barbecue seasoning

8. Kosher salt and paprika

9. Asian curry powder and salt

10. Minced fresh or freeze-dried chives and a little onion salt

RECIPE REMINDERS

Made for

Prep notes

Don't forget

Special touches

Bring again

Boursin Potato Gratin

SERVES 8 TO 10

PREP: 20 MINUTES * BAKE: 45 TO 50 MINUTES

**TOTE
NOTES**

*Bake 1 or 2 hours ahead
of time, and tote the
gratin covered with
aluminum foil. Reheat
it in a 350°F oven for
15 minutes.*

*If you like, take the
chopped parsley along
in a small plastic bag
for garnish.*

YES, I'M SHARING ANOTHER POTATO CASSEROLE recipe, but I couldn't omit this one because it is completely over the top and perfect for that big-deal meal. Pair the potatoes with roast fillet of beef during the holidays or serve them alongside roast chicken to dress up weekend dinners with friends. This recipe came from Mary Eleanor McKenzie of Nashville, who got it from Sylvia Bradbury, which is usually the way with terrific recipes—they make the rounds. It's your choice whether to peel the potatoes. I think the peels interfere with the creamy rich texture, so I take that extra step, and for a bit of topping, I add shredded Parmesan cheese.

2 cups heavy (whipping) cream

1 package (about 5 ounces) Boursin cheese with
   black pepper

2 tablespoons minced shallots (2 medium-size shallots)

2 medium-size cloves garlic, crushed in a garlic press

2 teaspoons olive oil

2½ pounds Yukon Gold or red-skinned potatoes,
   peeled and sliced ⅓ inch thick (about 8 cups)

Salt and freshly ground black pepper

2 tablespoons minced fresh chives

½ cup (2 ounces) shredded Parmesan cheese (optional)

2 tablespoons chopped fresh parsley (optional), for garnish

1. Place a rack in the center of the oven and preheat the oven to 400°F.

2. Place the cream, Boursin, shallots, and garlic in a medium-size saucepan over low heat. Cook, stirring until the Boursin melts and the mixture thickens, 4 to 5 minutes.

3. Meanwhile, brush a 13 by 9–inch glass or ceramic baking dish with the olive oil. Arrange half of the potato slices in the baking dish, overlapping them as needed. Season the potatoes with salt and pepper to taste and sprinkle 1 tablespoon of the chives on top.

4. Pour half of the Boursin mixture over the potatoes. Arrange the remaining potato slices on top, season them with salt and pepper, and scatter the remaining 1 tablespoon of chives over them. Pour the remaining Boursin mixture over the potatoes. Scatter the Parmesan cheese over the top, if desired.

5. Bake the gratin, uncovered, until it is deeply browned and the potatoes are tender, 45 to 50 minutes. You can serve the gratin at once, garnished with chopped parsley, if desired, or let it rest 15 to 20 minutes before serving.

BIG BATCH: *Use two or three baking dishes to prepare a double or triple batch of the gratin for a crowd. Get some help with peeling and slicing the potatoes.*

RECIPE REMINDERS

Made for

Prep notes

Don't forget

Special touches

Bring again

Spinach and Feta Pie

SERVES 8 TO 10

PREP: ABOUT 20 MINUTES ✳ BAKE: 50 TO 55 MINUTES ✳ COOL: 20 MINUTES

**TOTE
NOTES**

*You can tote the pie
placed on a plate and
wrapped loosely with
aluminum foil. Or, carry
the sliced pie covered in
its baking dish.*

*When you arrive,
gently reheat the pie in a
350°F oven for 5 minutes
to recrisp the pastry.*

I HAVE ALWAYS LOVED SPANAKOPITAS, THE GREEK SPINACH and feta cheese pastries made with phyllo dough. And I would prepare them more often if folding and brushing the phyllo leaves wasn't so much busywork. This pie has all the great spinach and feta flavor—plus sautéed onion and Parmesan cheese—but with less hassle. You just line a pie plate with the phyllo sheets, pile in the filling, pull the phyllo up over it, and bake.

> 2 tablespoons olive oil
>
> 2 cups chopped onion (2 medium-size onions)
>
> 3 packages (10 ounces each) frozen chopped spinach, thawed and well drained
>
> 4 large eggs, beaten
>
> 8 ounces feta cheese, crumbled
>
> $\frac{1}{2}$ cup (2 ounces) shredded Parmesan cheese
>
> $\frac{1}{3}$ cup toasted pine nuts (see box)
>
> $1\frac{1}{2}$ teaspoons kosher salt
>
> Freshly ground black pepper
>
> 6 tablespoons butter ($\frac{3}{4}$ stick), melted
>
> 8 sheets frozen phyllo dough, thawed

1. Place a rack in the center of the oven and preheat the oven to 375°F.

2. Place the olive oil in a large skillet over medium heat. Add the onion and cook, stirring, until soft, 3 to 4 minutes. Spoon the cooked onion into a large mixing bowl. Add the spinach, eggs, feta and Parmesan cheese, pine nuts, and salt. Season with pepper to taste.

3. Brush a 9-inch glass pie plate with some of the melted butter. Place a sheet of phyllo dough in the pie plate, letting the ends overlap the side. Brush the phyllo with some of the butter. Repeat with 5 more sheets of phyllo, then spoon the spinach filling in the center of the pie plate. Pull the edges of the phyllo up over the filling to almost cover it. Place 1 of the remaining 2 sheets of phyllo on top and brush it with some of the butter. Cover this with the remaining sheet of phyllo, tucking the ends under so that they form a round. Brush the phyllo with the remaining butter.

4. Bake the pie until it is browned all over, 50 to 55 minutes. Let the pie cool for about 20 minutes before slicing.

BIG BATCH: *If you are feeding a crowd, make two or three of the pies. Or, use more phyllo sheets to line a 13 by 9–inch baking dish. You'll need sixteen sheets of phyllo for a baking dish of this size. Arrange twelve phyllo sheets in six layers (lay two sheets together, then butter them) to cover the bottom of the dish. Then using the same amount of filling as for the smaller pie, spoon the filling over them. Cover the filling with four sheets of phyllo in two layers. Bake the pie until it's browned, 40 to 45 minutes.*

TOASTING PINE NUTS

Toasting pine nuts intensifies their flavor. It's easy to do: Scatter the pine nuts in a single layer on a rimmed baking sheet and bake them at 350°F until they are golden brown, 5 to 7 minutes. Watch them closely, shaking the baking sheet once or twice as the pine nuts toast to prevent them from burning.

Squash Casserole with Sweet Onions and Cheddar

SERVES 10 TO 12

PREP AND COOK: 40 MINUTES ✳ BAKE: 30 TO 35 MINUTES

TOTE NOTES

You can keep the squash casserole warm in transit by covering it with aluminum foil and wrapping it in clean kitchen towels.

When you arrive, place the casserole in a warming drawer or on a warming tray. If needed, you can reheat the casserole, uncovered, in a 350°F oven for 15 minutes.

THE SQUASH CASSEROLE IS A PERENNIAL FAVORITE ON buffet tables throughout the South. It is a cross between a sauté and a soufflé and is best made with fresh small yellow crookneck squash and sweet Vidalia onions. Cook the squash on the stove only until just done, season it with a light hand, and top the casserole with good Cheddar cheese and cracker crumbs before baking. If you can't find freshly picked squash, buy the smallest squash you can find in the supermarket, or substitute zucchini for the yellow squash.

3 pounds small yellow crookneck squash

2 cups chopped sweet onion (2 medium-size onions)

1 cup water

Salt and freshly ground black pepper

8 tablespoons (1 stick) butter, plus more for greasing
   the baking dish (optional)

2 teaspoons sugar (optional)

2 large eggs

½ cup milk

Vegetable oil spray (optional), for misting the baking dish

1 cup (4 ounces) shredded sharp Cheddar cheese

1 cup crushed buttery round crackers (about 24),
   such as Ritz

1. Place a rack in the center of the oven and preheat the oven to 350°F.

2. Rinse the squash under cold running water, then trim off and discard the ends. Cut the squash crosswise into 1-inch slices and place them in a medium-size pot with 1 cup of the onion and the cup of water. Season with salt and pepper to taste. Bring to a boil over medium-high heat, then reduce the heat, cover the pot, and let simmer until the squash is just fork tender, 20 to 25 minutes. Immediately drain the squash and onions and set aside.

3. Return the pot to the stove over medium heat and add the butter. When it melts, stir in the remaining 1 cup of onion and reduce the heat to medium-low. Cook the onion, stirring, until it softens, 4 to 5 minutes. Stir in the reserved cooked squash and onion mixture and the sugar, if desired. Cook until any water clinging to the squash evaporates, 1 to 2 minutes, then remove the pot from the heat.

4. Place the eggs and milk in a small bowl and whisk to mix. Stir the egg mixture into the squash mixture. Season with salt and pepper to taste.

5. Lightly mist a 13 by 9–inch glass or ceramic baking dish with vegetable oil spray or rub it with softened butter. Spoon the squash mixture into the baking dish. Scatter the cheese on top and scatter the cracker crumbs over the cheese. Bake the casserole until it bubbles around the edges and the cracker crumbs are lightly browned, 30 to 35 minutes.

BIG BATCH: *You can make two casseroles at a time, if your oven will fit the separate dishes. And you can halve this recipe as well, cooking half as much and baking the casserole in a 2-quart baking dish.*

RECIPE REMINDERS

Made for

Prep notes

Don't forget

Special touches

Bring again

Butternut Squash and Tomato Gratin

SERVES 12

PREP: 15 MINUTES * BAKE: 20 TO 25 MINUTES

TOTE NOTES

Once the gratin has cooled a little, cover it with plastic wrap and wrap it in a towel to keep warm en route.

Or, you can reheat the gratin, covered with aluminum foil, in a 350°F oven for 10 to 15 minutes .

PLAN AHEAD

The baked squash can be kept at room temperature for up to 3 hours or refrigerated, covered, for two days.

MY MOTHER USED TO PREPARE THIS SIMPLE GRATIN to rave reviews. Her friend Ella passed along the recipe to her, and it is delicious with turkey or ham. My mom used plain canned tomatoes, while I prefer the tomatoes with seasoning—you can take your pick. The recipe is amazingly totable and resilient, looks great after traveling, and tastes wonderful no matter the occasion. So, "What can I bring?" is written all over it.

> 1 large or 2 medium-size butternut squash (4 pounds)
>
> 2 tablespoons olive oil
>
> 2 cans (14½ ounces each) diced tomatoes or tomatoes with basil, garlic, and oregano, drained
>
> 2 cups (8 ounces) shredded Cheddar cheese

1. Place a rack in the center of the oven and preheat the oven to 400°F.

2. Using a sharp knife, trim off and discard the ends of the squash, then slice it in half lengthwise. Scoop out the seeds with a spoon and discard them. Place the squash halves, cut side up, in a microwave oven, cover them with a piece of waxed paper, and cook on high power until soft yet still firm enough to cut into cubes, 8 to 9 minutes.

3. Place the squash on a large cutting board and let cool enough to handle, then peel and cut it into 1-inch cubes. Place the squash in a 13 by 9–inch glass or ceramic baking dish, drizzle the olive oil on it, then scatter the tomatoes followed by the Cheddar cheese evenly on top.

4. Bake the gratin until the cheese melts and the squash and tomatoes are heated through, 20 to 25 minutes.

BIG BATCH: *Double the gratin by making it in two baking dishes. But microwave the 8 pounds of butternut squash in batches to cook it until tender.*

READY, SET, FREEZE!

You gotta love casseroles for their one-dish ease and their ability to be assembled, frozen, and baked later. "Later" meaning when you are rushed and have only the time and patience to thaw and bake, not shop and cook. Casseroles taste best when you freeze them before baking, so once prepared, let them cool to room temperature, then cover them with heavy-duty aluminum foil and place them in the freezer. It's smart to label them as to the contents and the date you made them.

Casseroles that freeze well include eggplant Parmesan and those made with broccoli, squash, and sweet potatoes. Twice-Baked Potatoes can go from the freezer right into the warm oven. But don't freeze such roasted and grilled vegetables as asparagus or artichokes. And, don't freeze sautéed zucchini. These all turn mushy when thawed.

Freeze sides in their baking dishes or in disposable aluminum pans, covered with aluminum foil. These are especially convenient when you are toting a side like the grits on page 326, or the creamed corn on page 266, to a friend, and you don't want the friend to have to return your baking dish.

RECIPE REMINDERS

Made for

Prep notes

Don't forget

Special touches

Bring again

Sweet Potato Casserole with Pecan Crunch

SERVES 8

PREP AND COOK: 35 TO 40 MINUTES ✳ BAKE: 25 TO 30 MINUTES

MY FRIEND JENNY MANDEL AT WORKMAN PUBLISHING raved about a sweet potato casserole she enjoyed at family Thanksgiving dinners in Brooklyn. So I pressed her for the recipe, thinking it might be a New York version of the sweet potato casserole we know Down South. When Jenny searched for the source of that recipe she found out it was a Southern recipe after all. Here's just such a Southern casserole, filled with mashed sweet potatoes and topped with a crunchy brown sugar and pecan topping.

FOR THE SWEET POTATOES

2 pounds sweet potatoes, scrubbed

Salt

Vegetable oil spray, for misting the baking dish

1 cup granulated sugar

8 tablespoons (1 stick) butter, melted

⅓ cup milk

2 large eggs, beaten

1 teaspoon pure vanilla extract

1 teaspoon grated orange zest, or ½ teaspoon ground cinnamon (optional)

FOR THE PECAN CRUNCH TOPPING

¾ cup finely chopped pecans

¾ packed cup light brown sugar

¼ cup all-purpose flour

3 tablespoons butter, melted

1. Prepare the sweet potatoes: Peel and quarter the sweet potatoes. Place them in a saucepan, add cold water to cover and a pinch of salt. Bring to a boil over medium-high heat, then reduce the heat, cover the pan, and let simmer until the potatoes are tender, 20 to 25 minutes. Drain the potatoes, then mash them with a potato masher.

2. Place a rack in the center of the oven and preheat the oven to 350°F. Lightly mist a 13 by 9–inch glass or ceramic baking dish with vegetable oil spray and set the dish aside.

3. Place the mashed sweet potatoes, granulated sugar, 8 tablespoons of melted butter, milk, eggs, vanilla, and either orange zest or cinnamon, if desired, in a large mixing bowl. Beat with an electric mixer on medium-low speed until just combined, about 2 minutes. Spoon the sweet potato mixture into the prepared baking dish and smooth the top with a spoon or spatula.

4. Make the pecan crunch topping: Place the pecans, brown sugar, flour, and 3 tablespoons of melted butter in a small bowl and stir with a fork to combine. Scatter the pecan mixture evenly over the top of the sweet potatoes.

5. Bake the sweet potatoes until the pecan topping begins to brown and the potatoes are bubbly, 25 to 30 minutes.

BIG BATCH: *Boil twice as many sweet potatoes and double the remaining ingredients to make two casseroles.*

Mike's Sweet Potato "Soufflé"

SERVES 8

PREP: 35 TO 40 MINUTES * BAKE: 25 TO 30 MINUTES

TOTE NOTES

Tote the sweet potato "soufflé" warm from the oven in a thermal casserole carrier or cover it with aluminum foil and keep in a warm place in the kitchen until serving time.

WE OFTEN TRAVEL TO CHATTANOOGA TO SPEND Thanksgiving with my husband's family. It's only two hours down the road but the food is deliciously different from what my family serves. In Chattanooga, I fork into creamy scalloped oysters and this most spectacular sweet potato casserole from one of the cousins, Mike Patten. Mike took the best of two recipes from the much-loved Chattanooga cookbook by Helen Exum and turned them into this dish. The secret is using fresh mashed sweet potatoes. The "soufflé" is topped with big fat marshmallows that puff up in the oven and completely cover the top of the casserole like huge clouds. This is totally sixties retro cuisine, and I love it, but if you're in the mood for a simpler rendition, try sprinkling bread crumbs drizzled with melted butter on top of the casserole instead.

6 large sweet potatoes (about 3 pounds), scrubbed

4 tablespoons butter (½ stick), cut into tablespoons, plus more for buttering the baking dish (optional)

Vegetable oil spray (optional), for misting the baking dish

⅓ packed cup light brown sugar, or more to taste

2 tablespoons fresh orange juice

1 tablespoon dry sherry, or more to taste

1 teaspoon salt

½ teaspoon ground cinnamon

2 large eggs

¼ cup raisins

18 large marshmallows

1. Peel and quarter the sweet potatoes, then place them in a 3-quart saucepan. Add cold water to cover and bring to a boil, covered, over medium-high heat. Reduce the heat and let the potatoes simmer until they are tender, about 20 minutes. Drain the sweet potatoes and let cool briefly.

2. Meanwhile, place a rack in the center of the oven and preheat the oven to 350°F. Lightly mist a 13 by 9-inch glass or ceramic baking dish with vegetable oil spray or rub it with softened butter. Set the baking dish aside.

3. Place the 4 tablespoons butter in a large mixing bowl with the sweet potatoes on top. Add the brown sugar, orange juice, sherry, salt, and cinnamon. Beat with an electric mixer on low speed until the potatoes are fluffy and the butter has melted, about 1 minute. Add the eggs and beat until incorporated, 30 to 45 seconds. Fold in the raisins. Transfer the sweet potato mixture to the prepared baking dish.

4. Arrange the marshmallows on top of the sweet potatoes; they can be placed 3 across and 6 down, or whatever pattern works for you. Bake the sweet potatoes until the marshmallows are well browned and the casserole is bubbly, 25 to 30 minutes.

BIG BATCH: *Doubled, the sweet potato "soufflé" can be baked in two baking dishes.*

RECIPE REMINDERS

Made for

Prep notes

Don't forget

Special touches

Bring again

Fresh Tomato Pie

SERVES 6 TO 8

PREP: 25 MINUTES ✳ BAKE: 50 TO 55 MINUTES ✳ COOL: 20 MINUTES

TOTE NOTES

You can tote the pie, lightly covered with plastic wrap, in a basket or pie carrier. Slice it just before serving.

PLAN AHEAD

If you bake the pie earlier in the day, let it cool to room temperature and serve.

COMBINE FRESH TOMATOES WITH BASIL AND mozzarella and you have a Caprese salad. Combine the tomatoes with bacon and lettuce and you have a BLT. Combine some of these flavors with tomatoes in a crust, and you have this wonderful pie, which is perfect served at picnics and spring gatherings, summer barbecues, and even at tailgate parties in the fall. Use the best tomatoes you can find: If you slice, salt, and let the tomatoes drain ahead of time, they lose some of the moisture that might make the pie soggy. And they hold on to that great tomato taste.

3 medium-size tomatoes, peeled and cut into
    15 to 16 slices total
Kosher salt
1 deep-dish pie crust (9 inches), thawed if frozen
½ loosely packed cup chopped fresh basil
½ cup chopped scallions, green parts only
1 cup (4 ounces) shredded mozzarella cheese
½ cup (2 ounces) shredded Cheddar cheese
3 tablespoons mayonnaise
Dash of cayenne pepper
½ cup crumbled cooked bacon (optional)

1. Place a rack in the center of the oven and preheat the oven to 375°F.

2. Place the tomato slices on a baking rack placed in a sink or over a sheet pan. Lightly salt the tomato slices and let them sit until they give up some of their juice, about 15 minutes.

3. Meanwhile, prick the bottom and side of the pie crust with a fork a few times (see Note). Bake the crust until it just begins to brown, 5 to 6 minutes. Let the crust cool for about 15 minutes. Leave the oven on.

4. Pat the tomato slices dry with paper towels. When the crust has cooled, arrange half of the tomato slices in the bottom. Scatter ¼ cup each of the basil and scallions over them. Add the rest of the tomato slices and top these with the remaining ¼ cup each of basil and scallions.

5. Combine the mozzarella and Cheddar cheese, mayonnaise, cayenne, and bacon, if desired, in a small bowl. Spoon the cheese mixture over the tomatoes and, using a knife, spread it out as evenly as you can.

6. Bake the tomato pie until browned, 30 to 35 minutes. Then, carefully arrange a loose tent of aluminum foil over the top of the pie to shield the crust from overbrowning. Continue to bake the pie until the cheese has browned and the filling has firmed up, about 15 minutes longer. Remove the pie from the oven and let it cool at least 20 minutes before slicing and serving.

NOTE: If you prefer a more homemade look, transfer a store-bought pie crust to a glass or metal pie pan. Press the top edge down with a fork to attach the crust to the pan, then prick it with a fork and bake it.

BIG BATCH:
You can bake two pies at a time on a single rack in the oven.

RECIPE REMINDERS

Made for

Prep notes

Don't forget

Special touches

Bring again

Sautéed Zucchini with Garlic Slivers

SERVES 6 TO 8

PREP: 10 MINUTES
COOK: ABOUT 8 MINUTES PER BATCH, ABOUT 16 MINUTES IN ALL

M Y CHILDREN REQUEST THIS RECIPE ALL THE TIME, and if they beg for a green vegetable then I am more than happy to prepare it. I can't recall when I started cooking it for company. I think it was after I realized you could sauté the zucchini ahead of time and keep it at room temperature for up to an hour or so. The zucchini goes well with steaks and fillet of beef, grilled chicken, and all kinds of pasta—so I guess that's why it became a standby. The trick is to use small zucchini and to fry only a panful at a time so as to let them get a little crisp and browned. If you overcrowd the pan, the zucchini will become soggy. Use as much or as little garlic as you like. I adore the sautéed garlic and can eat it right out of the pan. Yum!

3 pounds small zucchini
3 to 4 tablespoons olive oil, or more as needed
5 to 6 cloves garlic, sliced
Kosher salt and freshly ground black pepper
Chopped fresh oregano, mint, or parsley, for garnish

1. Rinse the zucchini and trim off and discard the ends. Cut the zucchini crosswise into slices about ¼ inch or a little thicker. You will have about 9 cups. Set the sliced zucchini aside.

2. Place 2 tablespoons of olive oil in a large frying pan over medium heat and add the garlic. Cook, stirring with a wooden spoon, until the garlic is lightly browned. Using a slotted spoon, transfer the garlic to a large plate and set aside.

3. Place half of the sliced zucchini in the pan and increase the heat to medium-high. Cook the zucchini until lightly browned, 7 to 8 minutes in all. You will need to shake the pan vigorously and stir the zucchini with a wooden spoon to move it around. Reduce the heat to medium if the zucchini is browning too quickly. Using a slotted spoon, transfer the zucchini to the plate with the garlic.

4. Add more olive oil as needed to the pan and brown the remaining zucchini the same way.

5. Return the rest of the cooked zucchini and the garlic to the pan and cook it over low heat. Season with salt and pepper to taste. Spoon the zucchini onto a medium-size serving platter and garnish it with chopped oregano, mint, or parsley. It can be served warm or at room temperature.

BIG BATCH: *It's tough to double batch this recipe because you run the risk of overcooking the zucchini and making it soggy. However, you can cut up 6 pounds of zucchini and fry it in batches in two frying pans.*

RECIPE REMINDERS

Made for

Prep notes

Don't forget

Special touches

Bring again

Roasted Spring Vegetables

SERVES 8 TO 10

PREP AND COOK: 15 TO 20 MINUTES ✳ BAKE: 35 TO 40 MINUTES

TOTE NOTES

Tote the vegetables on their platter covered with plastic wrap. Bring the dressing in a plastic container with a lid and the minced chives and chive blossoms, if available, separately in small plastic bags.

PLAN AHEAD

If you like, you can roast the vegetables a day in advance and refrigerate them. In fact, you can go ahead and arrange them on a pretty platter and cover it with plastic wrap. Let the vegetables come to room temperature before serving.

PART SIDE DISH, PART SALAD, A MEDLEY OF ROASTED vegetables is suitable for lunch or dinner and can be served hot, warm, or at room temperature. It is like your best friend, ready when you are. Although this assortment of veggies is geared to springtime, you can substitute most any vegetable you like that is in season— zucchini, eggplant, peppers, even sweet potatoes. Roast the potatoes separately from the other veggies because they need a longer cooking time. And serve the dressing on the side or spooned over the vegetable medley.

> 1½ pounds small new potatoes, scrubbed and cut in half
> ½ cup olive oil
> Kosher salt
> 1 pound medium-size asparagus
> 1 medium-size fennel bulb, trimmed and cut lengthwise
>   into ½-inch slices
> 8 ounces sugar snap peas, trimmed
> 1 tablespoon Dijon mustard
> Table salt and freshly ground black pepper
> 2 tablespoons minced fresh chives, for garnish
> Whole chive blossoms (optional; see Note), for garnish

1. Preheat the oven to 400°F.

2. Place the potatoes and 2 tablespoons of the olive oil in a 13 by 9–inch glass or ceramic baking dish and season with kosher salt to taste. Using a spoon, toss the potatoes to coat, then bake until they begin to crisp around the edges, about 20 minutes.

3. Meanwhile, snap off and discard the tough ends of the asparagus. Place the asparagus spears in a colander and rinse under cold running water. Pat the asparagus dry with paper towels and place it in a large mixing bowl. Add the fennel and 2 tablespoons of the olive oil and season with kosher salt to taste. Using a spoon, toss the asparagus and fennel to coat, then transfer them to another 13 by 9–inch baking dish.

4. Once the potatoes have baked for 20 minutes, place the baking dish with the asparagus in the oven alongside the potatoes. Bake the vegetables until the potatoes are well browned and the fennel and asparagus are cooked through and lightly browned, 15 to 20 minutes. Let the vegetables cool to room temperature.

5. Bring 1 inch of water to a boil in a small saucepan over medium-high heat. Add the sugar snap peas and cook until bright green and still crisp, 1 to 2 minutes. Drain the sugar snap peas in a colander.

6. Place the mustard and remaining ¼ cup of olive oil in a small mixing bowl and whisk to combine. Season with table salt and pepper to taste.

7. When ready to serve, arrange the potatoes, asparagus, and fennel on a large serving platter. Scatter the sugar snap peas on top and spoon the mustard dressing over them. Garnish the vegetable platter with the minced chives and whole chive blossoms, if available.

NOTE: Chive blossoms can be found at farmers' markets and some produce shops that specialize in fresh herbs. Or, ask a friend with a summer herb garden to save them for you.

BIG BATCH: *To feed a crowd, roast a lot of vegetables in separate baking dishes in more than one oven or in several batches. Take care not to crowd the vegetables; spread them out in a single layer so they roast on all sides.*

RECIPE REMINDERS

Made for

Prep notes

Don't forget

Special touches

Bring again

Grilled Vegetable Platter with Pesto Vinaigrette

SERVES 12

PREP: 25 TO 30 MINUTES ✳ GRILL: 15 TO 20 MINUTES

TOTE NOTES

You can either tote the vegetables on a large platter covered with plastic wrap or you can tote them in a lightweight pan and transfer them to the platter when you arrive.

Bring the pesto vinaigrette in a small plastic container and don't forget a pretty serving bowl to put it in.

THE ULTIMATE DO-AHEAD SIDE DISH, IF YOU ENJOY grilling—and getting things done and checked off your list. It is bright in color, fresh in flavor, and healthy, with all sorts of vegetables. Arrange them attractively on a large white platter, and serve the pesto sauce in a small bowl alongside. These are just some of the veggies I like grilled. Suit yourself!

FOR THE VEGETABLES

2 red bell peppers, cored, seeded, and cut into quarters

2 green bell peppers, cored, seeded, and cut into quarters

2 yellow bell peppers, cored, seeded, and cut into quarters

3 medium-size zucchini, sliced diagonally ½ inch thick

6 small eggplant (see box, page 273), unpeeled, sliced lengthwise in half or thirds

3 medium-size red onions, peeled and cut into quarters

36 thick asparagus spears (about 2 pounds), tough ends removed

36 cherry tomatoes, cut in half through the stem end

1 cup olive oil, or more as needed

Kosher salt and freshly ground black pepper

FOR THE PESTO VINAIGRETTE

1 cup prepared pesto

¼ cup white wine vinegar

¼ cup olive oil

Fresh basil sprigs, for garnish

1. Prepare the vegetables: Put all of the bell peppers in a medium-size bowl. Put the zucchini, eggplant, and onions in another medium-size bowl. Put the asparagus and tomatoes in a third medium-size bowl. Drizzle olive oil over all of the vegetables, season them with salt and pepper to taste, and toss with a spoon or your hands to coat.

2. Preheat the grill to hot, then turn down the heat on a gas grill to medium-high or let the charcoal die down to a hot gray ash.

3. When ready to cook, grill the vegetables, keeping each kind together; this way you can keep a better eye on how quickly they cook. Arrange the cherry tomatoes on the grill cut side up and cook them only until their skins begin to blister, a total of 3 to 4 minutes. Cook the bell peppers, zucchini, onions, and eggplant until they are lightly charred with grill marks, 4 to 5 minutes per side for the bell peppers, zucchini, and onions, 7 to 8 minutes per side for the eggplant. Cook thick asparagus until it softens and has light grill marks, 6 to 7 minutes per side (more slender asparagus will be done in 3 to 4 minutes per side). Transfer the vegetables to a platter as soon as they are done. Season the vegetables again with salt and pepper as needed.

4. Make the pesto vinaigrette: Place the pesto in a small mixing bowl. Stir in the wine vinegar, then whisk in the 1/4 cup of olive oil a little at a time, until the vinaigrette thickens.

5. When ready to serve, spoon the vinaigrette into a small bowl and serve alongside the platter of vegetables. Garnish the vegetables with basil sprigs.

BIG BATCH: *As long as you have the grill space and help in tending the grill, you can double and triple this recipe as needed. For large groups, add a second sauce for dipping, such as a bottled sesame vinaigrette or Thai peanut dressing.*

RECIPE REMINDERS

Made for

Prep notes

Don't forget

Special touches

Bring again

Summertime Ratatouille

SERVES 6 TO 8

PREP AND COOK: 50 TO 55 MINUTES ✳ **BAKE: 45 MINUTES**

TOTE NOTES

Make the ratatouille in a pretty casserole and you can tote it in the dish. Or, transfer the ratatouille to a serving bowl. Cover the container with plastic wrap for traveling.

Bring along the garnishes in separate plastic bags.

PLAN AHEAD

Ratatouille is best made in advance—you can do this up to a day ahead and refrigerate it, covered. Let the ratatouille return to room temperature before serving.

WHEN THE WEATHER IS WARM, BELL PEPPERS AND summer squash are in season, and your palate craves light, fresh flavors, ratatouille is the best side dish around. The wonderful French vegetable dish is perfect with goat cheese or roast chicken and can hold its own garnished with black olives and served with garlic bread. Make ratatouille when you've got the time to chop all the vegetables and sauté each one individually before mixing them together and baking them. If possible, prepare it the day before, to make things easier on you and so that the flavors have time to grow and get even better.

1 large eggplant, or 2 medium-size eggplants (1½ pounds total)

Kosher salt

½ cup olive oil, or more as needed

1 cup chopped onion (1 medium-size onion)

3 medium-size cloves garlic, minced

1 pound ripe tomatoes (about 3), peeled and chopped

Table salt and freshly ground black pepper

1 pound zucchini (3 to 4 small), cut into ½-inch cubes

1 yellow or green bell pepper, cored, seeded, and cut into ⅓-inch strips

1 red bell pepper, cored, seeded, and cut into ⅓-inch strips

2 tablespoons dry red wine

¼ loosely packed cup chopped fresh basil, plus more chopped basil (optional), for garnish

¼ teaspoon dried thyme

1 tablespoon capers, for garnish

Pitted kalamata olives, for garnish

Lemon wedges (optional), for garnish

1. Cut the eggplant into strips about 2 inches long, ½ inch wide, and ¼ inch thick. Place these in a colander in the sink and sprinkle them generously with kosher salt. Let the eggplant sit for 20 to 25 minutes.

2. Place a rack in the center of the oven and preheat the oven to 350°F.

3. Meanwhile, place 2 tablespoons of the olive oil in a large skillet over medium heat. When hot, add the onion and garlic and cook, stirring, until soft, about 3 minutes. Add the tomatoes and season with table salt and black pepper to taste. Cook, stirring, until the tomatoes cook down, lose their juice, and thicken a bit, 6 to 7 minutes. Pour the tomato sauce into a 2-quart baking dish and set it aside. Wipe out the skillet.

4. Place 1 tablespoon of olive oil in the skillet and when it is hot, add the zucchini and cook, stirring, until soft, 5 to 6 minutes. Season the zucchini with table salt and black pepper to taste, then add it to the baking dish with the tomato sauce. Wipe out the skillet.

5. Add another tablespoon of olive oil to the skillet and when it is hot, add the bell peppers and cook, stirring, until they soften and take on a deep color, about 5 minutes. Add the bell peppers to the baking dish. Wipe out the skillet.

6. Pat the strips of eggplant dry with paper towels. Heat the remaining ¼ cup of olive oil in the skillet over medium heat and when the oil is hot, add the eggplant. Cook, stirring, until it softens and browns, 8 to 10 minutes. Season the eggplant with table salt and black pepper to taste, adding more oil as needed if the skillet becomes dry.

RECIPE REMINDERS

Made for

Prep notes

Don't forget

Special touches

Bring again

**NOT JUST
A SIDE**

Leftover is a word seldom used at our house because I like to think of extra food as "planned-over." So when I have "planned-over" ratatouille, I use it the next day as a sauce for grilled fish or chicken or spoon it over hot pasta or onto grilled bread. The flavors of ratatouille intensify each day, and it can be refrigerated for up to a week.

7. Add the wine to the eggplant and stir to combine. Add the eggplant mixture to the rest of the vegetables along with the basil and thyme. Gently stir to combine. Cover the baking dish with a lid or aluminum foil.

8. Bake the ratatouille for 15 minutes, then remove the lid or foil and let bake, uncovered, until the vegetables are tender and the sauce has cooked down, about 30 minutes longer. Garnish the ratatouille with the capers and olives and the lemon wedges and chopped basil, if desired, and serve it warm from the baking dish. Or, let the ratatouille cool to room temperature, then garnish and serve.

BIG BATCH: *Ratatouille can be made in larger batches, but it always turns out best if you sauté like veggies together and then combine them to bake.*

HOW TO HAVE SIDES IN NO TIME?
STOCK YOUR PANTRY

For last-minute fixings, keep your freezer stocked with ingredients you can turn into tempting side dishes. And, keep your cupboard ready to go with easy-to-doctor canned goods.

BROCCOLI: For a classic pairing, add frozen chopped broccoli to a chicken casserole or try the Broccoli Brag Casserole on page 260.

CORN: Turn frozen corn into corn puddings and soufflés or add kernels to your favorite corn bread recipe. You can substitute three cups of frozen corn kernels (I prefer white corn) for the six ears in the corn pudding recipe on page 270.

FRENCH GREEN BEANS: Gently steam frozen green beans, then toss them with melted butter, salt, and toasted almonds.

HASH BROWNS: Keep frozen hash browns on hand to make Creamy Scalloped Potatoes (page 282). You can vary the recipe by adding sliced garlic, grated lemon zest, or slices of roasted red pepper.

CHOPPED SPINACH: Cook frozen chopped spinach and stir it into sautéed onions and cream cheese, then add a little shredded Parmesan cheese.

LOAVES OF ITALIAN BREAD: Thaw frozen Italian bread and you can turn it into Cheesy Garlic Bread (page 333) in no time.

BAKED BEANS: Turn canned baked beans into an easy potluck bean bake by adding ketchup or barbecue sauce, chopped onion, and some seasonings, such as chili powder, ground cumin, or a tad of ground cayenne pepper, before popping them in the oven.

ITALIAN GREEN BEANS: Cook canned Italian green beans down with brown sugar, olive oil, and onion to make Bebe's Green Beans (page 274).

CRANBERRY SAUCE: Dress canned cranberry sauce up with grated orange zest, canned crushed pineapple, or a little port.

PINEAPPLE: With canned pineapple and some buttery crackers in the cupboard and Cheddar cheese in the fridge, you're all set to make the wonderful pineapple casserole you'll find on page 310.

Hot Curried Fruit

SERVES 8 TO 12

**PREP: 20 MINUTES ✳ BAKE: 25 TO 30 MINUTES
COOL: 15 TO 20 MINUTES**

**TOTE
NOTES**

*Tote the curried fruit by
wrapping the baking dish
well first with aluminum
foil and then in a towel.
Or, you can bake the
fruit in most any shallow
3-quart casserole—often,
ceramic casseroles are
prettier than glass ones.
No matter what, make
sure you wrap the dish
well to catch any spills.*

*When you arrive,
place the baking dish in
a 300°F oven just long
enough to heat the fruit
through before serving,
15 to 20 minutes.*

*If you like, sprinkle
on a tad of ground
cinnamon right before
serving to dress up the
top (just remember to
bring the cinnamon
with you).*

I GREW UP EATING HOT FRUIT CASSEROLES MADE WITH
curry, especially at Easter, when they were served
with a ham or for brunch along with eggs. This is
a retro recipe but one that can be resurrected with ease,
using canned fruits from the supermarket shelf, a fresh
apple, and some staples from your kitchen. The cinnamon
helps bring out the curry, there is only enough brown
sugar to just sweeten the fruit, and the butter provides
richness without being heavy. Curried fruit is delicious
the next day at room temperature—if there are leftovers.

1 medium-size apple, such as Golden Delicious
    or Gala, peeled, cored, and very thinly sliced
1 can (15¼ ounces) pineapple chunks with no sugar added
1 can (15 ounces) sliced peaches, in light syrup
1 can (15 ounces) pear halves, in light syrup
1 can (15 ounces) pitted dark sweet bing cherries,
    in heavy syrup
1 can (11 ounces) mandarin oranges, in light syrup
¾ packed cup light brown sugar
1 teaspoon curry powder
½ teaspoon ground cinnamon
3 tablespoons butter, cut into thin slices

1. Place a rack in the center of the oven and preheat the oven
to 350°F.

2. Place the apple slices on the bottom of a 13 by 9–inch glass
or ceramic baking dish. Drain the pineapple chunks and set

aside the juice; you should have about ½ cup. Scatter the pineapple over the apple. Drain the peaches, pears, cherries, and mandarin oranges and discard the liquid. Add the fruit to the baking dish.

3. Place the pineapple juice in a small bowl and stir in the brown sugar, curry powder, and cinnamon. Pour the juice mixture over the fruit and scatter the slices of butter on top.

4. Bake the fruit, uncovered, until bubbly, 25 to 30 minutes. Let the fruit cool for 15 to 20 minutes before serving.

BIG BATCH: *The ingredients in the curried fruit recipe double and triple easily, so you can make many batches—as long as you have enough baking dishes.*

Pineapple Casserole with a Cheddar Crust

SERVES 8 TO 12

ABOUT 12 MINUTES ✳ BAKE: ABOUT 25 MINUTES ✳ COOL: 10 MINUTES

TOTE NOTES

To keep the casserole warm en route, wrap it with aluminum foil and then a towel or tote it in an insulated casserole carrier.

PLAN AHEAD

You can bake the pineapple casserole a day ahead, let it cool, then cover and refrigerate it. Put the casserole back in a 350°F oven for about 15 minutes to reheat it and crisp the cracker topping just before you leave home or when you arrive.

HOW CAN SOMETHING SO SIMPLE TASTE SO GOOD? Hot savory fruit gratins, such as this one and the apricot version that follows, are recipes to keep in your emergency file—you can assemble them effortlessly. Warm and comforting, they're especially welcome in the fall and winter. A great partner for baked ham, this pineapple side is also a perfect match for roast turkey and pork loin and is perfect for brunch.

1 can (20 ounces) pineapple chunks, drained
1 can (8 ounces) crushed pineapple in juice, with its juice
1 cup sugar
2 tablespoons all-purpose flour
1½ cups (6 ounces) shredded sharp Cheddar cheese
1½ cups crushed buttery round crackers (about 36), such as Ritz
3 tablespoons butter, melted

1. Place a rack in the center of the oven and preheat the oven to 350°F.

2. Place the drained pineapple chunks and the undrained crushed pineapple in a medium-size bowl and stir to combine. Transfer the pineapple to a 2-quart glass or ceramic casserole.

3. Place the sugar and flour in a small bowl and stir to combine. Sprinkle the sugar mixture over the pineapple. Scatter the Cheddar on top, followed by the cracker crumbs, then drizzle the melted butter over the cracker topping.

4. Bake the casserole until browned and bubbly, 23 to 28 minutes. Let it cool about 10 minutes before serving.

BIG BATCH: *A double batch of the casserole baked in a deep 13 by 9–inch baking dish will take 5 to 8 minutes longer to cook.*

TOTING TIPS
FOR THANKSGIVING DINNER

I vividly remember the Thanksgiving I offered to bring a gelatin salad. Early that day, with the car loaded, my children's faces pressed against the glass, and my husband fuming in the driver's seat, I was in the garage trying to force a large ring mold into a much smaller cooler. When I offered to bring the salad to my mother-in-law's, I hadn't thought about how I would keep it cold in transit. So now I bring homemade cranberry sauce in a jar and baked rolls. No more jiggly gelatin for me!

How about you? Do you wonder what to bring when you travel for Thanksgiving?

Not the turkey, unless you roast it ahead of time, slice it, and place it on ice.

No sloppy casseroles. Sweet potatoes travel well, but mashed white potatoes do not. Creamed onions are a no. Baked apricots are a yes. If you bring a vegetable side, bake it, cover it with aluminum foil, and tote it in a shallow box or bin lined with a towel.

Say yes to salads you can assemble on site. Bring the greens, the fruit, the avocado to peel, and so on. Tote the dressing in a glass jar.

Bread and rolls? You bet. Wrap them in aluminum foil. Then they're ready to reheat when you arrive.

The best desserts—how about a sweet potato cake or a cranberry tart? Or, a pumpkin pie; loosely tent it with aluminum foil and put it in a shallow box lined with a towel or in a pie saver.

RECIPE
REMINDERS

Made for

Prep notes

Don't forget

Special touches

Bring again

Sweet and Savory Baked Apricots

SERVES 8 TO 12

PREP: 10 MINUTES ✳ **BAKE: ABOUT 50 MINUTES** ✳ **COOL: 10 MINUTES**

TOTE NOTES

This casserole is a great do-ahead and take-along because it can weather reheating. But it doesn't even need reheating because it is delicious warm or cold! Once it's baked, wrap it well in aluminum foil, then wrap it in a towel or place it in a casserole carrier if you want to keep it warm.

When you arrive, if you like, reheat the apricots, covered, in a 300°F oven for 15 to 20 minutes.

A COMPLEMENT TO ROAST TURKEY OR PORK, BAKED apricots are ideal for those fall and winter meals where you want to bring something savory but not potatoes, not a green vegetable, not a salad. They are also wonderful with the first grilled salmon of the spring or at a summertime barbecue. And you cannot beat this recipe's simplicity—just canned apricots, brown sugar, a little cinnamon, crushed crackers, and butter. A sort of "cobbler meets side," the dish is a wonderful warm addition to any meal.

4 cans (about 15 ounces each) canned apricot halves, packed in heavy syrup

¾ packed cup light brown sugar

¼ teaspoon ground cinnamon, or more to taste

1⅓ cups crushed buttery round crackers (about 32), such as Ritz

5 tablespoons butter, at room temperature

1. Place a rack in the center of the oven and preheat the oven to 375°F.

2. Drain the apricots and set aside ¼ cup of the juice. Place half of the apricots cut side up in the bottom of a 13 by 9–inch glass or ceramic baking dish. Sprinkle half of the brown sugar over the apricots followed by ⅛ teaspoon of the cinnamon. Sprinkle half of the cracker crumbs evenly over the top. Repeat with the remaining apricots, brown sugar, cinnamon, and cracker crumbs. Pour the reserved ¼ cup of apricot juice evenly over the apricots and scatter the butter by teaspoonfuls over the top.

3. Bake the apricots until they are bubbly and the top has lightly browned, about 50 minutes. Let the apricots cool about 10 minutes before serving.

BIG BATCH: *You can double this recipe and bake it in two 13 by 9–inch baking dishes. Or, you can make a smaller version by cutting the ingredients in half and baking it in a 2-quart dish. Either way, just make sure that you bake it long enough for the apricots to soften and for the top to brown.*

RECIPE REMINDERS

Made for

Prep notes

Don't forget

Special touches

Bring again

Spiced Cranberry Sauce

SERVES 8 (MAKES 4½ CUPS)

PREP: 5 MINUTES ✳ COOK: ABOUT 12 MINUTES ✳ COOL: 25 TO 30 MINUTES

**TOTE
NOTES**

*Tote the cranberry
sauce in its serving
dish, covered with
plastic wrap.*

PLAN AHEAD

*This cranberry sauce
begs to be made a day
or two ahead of time.
Store it in a glass
container, covered with
plastic wrap, in the
refrigerator.*

TRADITION USUALLY DOES NOT ALLOW YOU TO MESS with the cranberry sauce. I know this from experience, for my requests to prepare a cranberry relish, gelatin salad, or homemade sauce have been met with puzzlement. You can hear people thinking, "Why would anyone not want to serve cranberry sauce straight from the can? After all, it comes in both smooth and chunky." Well, the answer is that it's nice to cook fresh cranberries. They only come into season during the holidays, and it's fun to let your kids see them pop in the pan. This version is enlivened with cinnamon, nutmeg, and allspice. And it is to die for spooned onto a turkey sandwich.

2 cups sugar

2 cups water

2 packages (12 ounces each) fresh cranberries,
    rinsed and picked over

½ teaspoon ground cinnamon

¼ teaspoon ground nutmeg

¼ teaspoon ground allspice

Place the sugar and water in a medium-size saucepan over medium heat and stir until the sugar dissolves, 1 to 2 minutes. Add the cranberries, cinnamon, nutmeg, and allspice and cook, stirring, until the cranberries pop, 10 to 12 minutes. Remove the pan from the heat and let the cranberry sauce cool to room temperature before serving, 25 to 30 minutes.

WANT AN ORANGE AND CRANBERRY SAUCE?
Substitute orange juice for the water and add a teaspoon of grated orange zest along with the cranberries. Omit the spices.

BIG BATCH: *You can double this recipe; cook the cranberry sauce in a large saucepan.*

TEN WAYS TO FLAVOR FRESH CRANBERRIES

Fresh cranberries are delicious cooked down with sugar following the instructions on the package, but they benefit from a dash of extra flavor. Try adding any of these before you cook the cranberries.

1. Use half orange juice and half water when you add liquid.

2. Add the grated zest of an orange or lemon.

3. Add 2 tablespoons of orange marmalade.

4. Add a small can of crushed pineapple.

5. Add a teaspoon of orange liqueur, such as Cointreau or Grand Marnier.

6. Add a handful of finely chopped apple and let it cook down with the cranberries.

7. Add a pinch of cinnamon.

8. Add a couple of tablespoons of port wine.

9. Add a small handful of finely chopped dried apricots and a dash of brandy and let the cranberries cook down until the apricots soften.

10. Add a pint of fresh blueberries and let them cook down as well.

My Favorite
Turkey Dressing

SERVES 12 TO 16

PREP: 40 MINUTES ✴ BAKE: ABOUT 45 MINUTES ✴ COOL: 5 MINUTES

**TOTE
NOTES**

*You can tote the turkey
dressing in an insulated
casserole carrier or in
its baking dish, covered
with aluminum foil and
wrapped in a towel to
keep it warm.*

PLAN AHEAD

*The dressing can be baked
ahead and kept warm in a
300°F oven. Check it from
time to time, pouring a
little extra turkey or
chicken broth over the
dressing to moisten it.*

*Or, you can prepare the
dressing through Step 6,
then cover the baking dish
with plastic wrap and
refrigerate it up to a day
in advance. Tote it cold
and, once you arrive,
bake it in a 350°F oven;
it will be done in 40 to
45 minutes.*

WHO CARES ABOUT TURKEY WHEN YOU'VE GOT
this wonderful dressing that steals the show?
Seriously, I have been known to skip the
turkey and pile the dressing high on my plate instead.
It's moist, substantial, and bold, made with crumbled
corn bread, French bread, and any sandwich bread—
or hamburger buns, as my mother liked to use. For
vegetarians, just omit the sausage and add more apple
plus some dried fruits, such as diced apricots or golden
raisins. This dressing bakes outside the turkey in a
casserole, so it's the perfect dish to delegate.

5 tablespoons butter

2 cups chopped onion (2 medium-size onions)

2 cups chopped apple, such as Golden Delicious or Gala
    (2 medium-size apples)

1 cup chopped celery

1 pound bulk Italian or breakfast sausage

3 cups crumbled corn bread

3 cups crumbled French bread

3 cups crumbled sandwich bread

1½ teaspoons dried thyme

1 cup chopped fresh parsley

2 large eggs, lightly beaten

Salt and freshly ground black pepper

About 2 cups turkey or chicken broth

1. Place a rack in the center of the oven and preheat the oven to 350°F.

2. Melt 2 tablespoons of the butter in a large skillet over medium heat. Add the onion and cook, stirring, until softened, 4 to 5 minutes. Transfer the onion to a large mixing bowl and place the skillet back over the heat.

3. Add 2 more tablespoons of butter to the skillet and when it melts, add the apple and cook, stirring, until lightly colored but not mushy, 5 to 6 minutes. Transfer the apple to the mixing bowl with the onion.

4. Melt the remaining 1 tablespoon of butter in the skillet. Add the celery and cook, stirring, until it softens, 5 to 6 minutes. Transfer the celery to the mixing bowl.

5. Place the skillet back over the heat and crumble the sausage into it. Cook, stirring to break up the sausage, until it is lightly browned and has cooked through, 7 to 8 minutes. Using a slotted spoon, transfer the sausage to paper towels to drain, then add it to the mixing bowl with the other ingredients and stir to combine.

6. Add the corn bread, French bread, sandwich bread, thyme, parsley, and eggs to the bowl and stir just to combine. Season with salt and pepper to taste. Pour in enough broth to moisten the dressing but not enough to make it runny. Spoon the dressing into a 13 by 9–inch glass or ceramic baking dish.

7. Bake the dressing until it browns lightly on top and is firm to the touch, about 45 minutes. Let the dressing cool 5 minutes, then cover with aluminum foil to keep warm.

BIG BATCH: *You can easily double this and bake two casseroles, or, bake half as dressing and use the other half to stuff up to a 20-pound turkey.*

RECIPE REMINDERS

Made for

Prep notes

Don't forget

Special touches

Bring again

Potluck Baked Beans

SERVES 12

**PREP: 10 MINUTES ✴ BAKE: ABOUT 1 HOUR
PLUS 10 MINUTES RESTING TIME**

**TOTE
NOTES**

*You can tote the warm
beans in their baking
dish, covered with
aluminum foil and
wrapped in a towel.*

PLAN AHEAD

*Beans are a great do-
ahead. Bake, cover,
and refrigerate them.
Then, once you get to
the gathering, rewarm
them, covered, in a 325°F
oven until heated through,
about 20 minutes.*

NO SUMMER POTLUCK IS COMPLETE WITHOUT BAKED beans, and chances are you have been asked to bring them. This is our family recipe, one that works time and time again. You can season it as you like with cumin or hot pepper sauce. And you can even fold in a half pound of browned ground beef to turn this into what we call "cowboy beans." I prefer to buy vegetarian beans without the little pieces of pork floating in the can. And, I don't always add the bacon. But, my mother made beans topped with the bacon along with the onion. She used ketchup and would add a generous spoonful or two of brown sugar; I have found that if I add a good sweet thick barbecue sauce I don't need the sugar.

2 large cans (28 ounces each), or 4 small cans
  (15 ounces each), vegetarian baked beans or
  the baked beans of your choice

⅔ cup sweet barbecue sauce or ketchup

1 tablespoon Dijon mustard

½ teaspoon hot pepper sauce, or more to taste (optional)

Dash of ground cumin or chili powder (optional)

Dash of black pepper

1 cup thinly sliced onion (1 medium-size onion)

3 to 4 bacon slices (optional)

1. Place a rack in the center of the oven and preheat the oven to 350°F.

2. Spoon the beans into a 13 by 9–inch glass or ceramic baking dish. Stir in the barbecue sauce or ketchup, mustard, hot pepper sauce and cumin or chili powder, if desired, and the pepper. Scatter the onion slices on top of the beans and, if desired, arrange the bacon strips on top of the onions.

3. Bake the beans until they are bubbly and the onions have cooked down into them, 55 minutes to 1 hour. Let the beans rest for 10 minutes before serving.

BIG BATCH: *Bake two casseroles at a time for a crowd. Or, you can halve this recipe and bake the beans in a 2-quart pan to feed six.*

RECIPE REMINDERS

Made for

Prep notes

Don't forget

Special touches

Bring again

Braised White Beans with Rosemary

SERVES 12

PREP: ABOUT 15 MINUTES ✳ COOK: 20 MINUTES

TOTE NOTES

It's easy to tote the beans in their cooking pot; it will take 10 to 15 minutes to reheat them over low heat when you arrive.

Or, bring the beans in a 3-quart microwave-safe bowl. Lightly covered with a paper towel or some waxed paper, they'll be heated through after 2 to 3 minutes on high power.

PLAN AHEAD

These beans are delicious cooked a day or two in advance.

ONE OF MY FAVORITE *CONTORNI*—THOSE WONDERFUL Italian vegetable side dishes—is white beans. This is a quick American version of the Italian classic, using canned great northern or cannellini beans, fresh rosemary, and good canned chicken broth. Simple to cook, the beans simmer with onion and rosemary until soft. At the table you add some Parmesan cheese. Let this be part of the supporting cast for steaks on the grill, a pork roast, or grilled fish.

⅓ cup olive oil

2 cups chopped onion (2 medium-size onions)

1 cup chopped carrots

3 medium-size cloves garlic, sliced

2 bay leaves

4 cans (15 to 16 ounces each) great northern or Italian cannellini beans, drained

2 cups canned low-sodium chicken broth, or more as needed

Salt and freshly ground black pepper

1 large sprig fresh rosemary, plus 1 tablespoon fresh rosemary leaves, for garnish

¼ cup shredded Parmesan cheese, for garnish

1. Place the olive oil in a large saucepan over medium heat. Add the onion, carrots, and garlic and cook, stirring, until soft, 3 to 4 minutes.

2. Add the bay leaves, beans, and chicken broth. Season the beans with salt and pepper to taste and add the sprig of rosemary. Let the beans come to a boil, then reduce the heat to low and let them simmer, covered, until cooked down, about 15 minutes.

3. When ready to serve, add more chicken broth to the beans if needed for a spoonable consistency. Remove and discard the bay leaves and rosemary sprig. Spoon the beans onto a serving platter and garnish with the Parmesan cheese and rosemary leaves, if desired.

BIG BATCH: *This bean recipe doubles very well if you need to feed a lot of people.*

RECIPE
REMINDERS

Made for

Prep notes

Don't forget

Special touches

Bring again

Hoppin' John

SERVES 10 TO 12

PREP: 20 MINUTES ✳ SOAK: 20 MINUTES
COOK: ABOUT 1 HOUR AND 30 MINUTES

A DELIGHTFUL MIX OF BLACK-EYED PEAS AND RICE, Hoppin' John is a wonderful dish to take to others. It is the de rigueur meal of New Year's Day in the South, but my family eats it year-round because black-eyed peas and rice are always on the pantry shelf. I have streamlined and lightened up this recipe through the years, omitting bacon grease and adding olive oil. I do like a smidgen of pork for flavor, so I add a cupful of chopped country ham if I have it, or just sweet cured ham if I do not. Serve the beans with barbecued ribs, corn bread, a green salad, and deviled eggs.

2 cups (1 pound) dried black-eyed peas, picked over

2 tablespoons olive oil

1 cup chopped white onion (1 medium-size onion)

1 cup chopped ham

½ cup chopped carrots

1 chicken-flavored bouillon cube (optional)

2 bay leaves

About 8 cups of water

Salt

2 cups basmati or jasmine rice

Freshly ground black pepper and hot pepper sauce

Chopped red onion (optional), for garnish

Parsley sprigs (optional), for garnish

1. Rinse and drain the black-eyed peas in a colander under cold running water and place them in a large heatproof bowl.

2. Bring a teakettle of water to a boil. Pour enough boiling water over the black-eyed peas to cover them by 1 inch. Let the peas soak in the hot water for 20 minutes, then drain them. Set the peas aside.

3. Place the olive oil in a large pot over medium heat. Add the white onion, ham, and carrots and cook, stirring, until the onion is soft, 3 to 4 minutes. Turn off the heat and add the drained black-eyed peas, bouillon cube, if desired, bay leaves, and 4 cups of water. Bring to a boil over medium-high heat, stirring, then reduce the heat to low, cover the pot, and let the peas simmer until they are soft, 1 hour and 15 minutes to 1 hour and 30 minutes. Add more water as needed if the liquid evaporates.

4. Meanwhile, place the remaining 4 cups of water and a pinch of salt in a medium-size saucepan over medium-high heat. Let come to a boil, then stir in the rice. Reduce the heat to low, cover the pan, and let the rice simmer until it is fluffy and the water evaporates, about 20 minutes.

5. Remove and discard the bay leaves from the black-eyed peas. Spoon the cooked rice into the pot with the peas and stir to combine. Taste for seasoning, adding more salt as needed and pepper and hot sauce to taste. Spoon the peas into a large serving dish and garnish them with chopped red onion and/or parsley sprigs, if desired.

BIG BATCH: *You can double the beans and cook them in a large soup pot. Make a double batch of rice as well.*

RECIPE REMINDERS

Made for

Prep notes

Don't forget

Special touches

Bring again

Baked Rice with Mushrooms and Consommé

SERVES 8

PREP: ABOUT 15 MINUTES ✴ BAKE: ABOUT 1 HOUR AND 30 MINUTES

TOTE NOTES

You can bake the rice ahead of time, taking it out of the oven about 15 minutes early. Then, cover the baking dish securely with aluminum foil and wrap it with a kitchen towel or place it in a casserole carrier to tote.

When you arrive, keep the rice warm in a warming drawer or on a warming tray. Or, if needed, return it to the oven to reheat for 15 minutes at 350°F.

I LOVE BAKED RICE, NOT ONLY BECAUSE YOU DON'T HAVE to worry about it sticking to the pan but also because you can infuse it with all sorts of wonderful flavors. This recipe was one my mother made often, using canned beef consommé and fresh mushrooms. You can vary it, using a mix of wild and white rice or making it with brown rice and different kinds of mushrooms (if you use another kind of rice, be sure to check the package for the approximate cooking time). Add a sprig of fresh thyme or rosemary to the rice as it cooks. Or if you want, for a more subtle flavor use chicken broth instead of the beef consommé. Whether you prepare the rice to take with you or fix it for dinner guests in your home, it is a timesaver, baking away on its own while you are busy with other things.

8 tablespoons (1 stick) butter
1 cup basmati or long-grain rice
2 cups (8 ounces) sliced mushrooms
2 cans (10½ ounces each) beef consommé
¼ cup chopped fresh parsley (optional), for garnish

1. Place a rack in the center of the oven and preheat the oven to 350°F.

2. Melt 4 tablespoons of butter in a large skillet over medium-low heat. Add the rice and cook, stirring, until it begins to brown slightly, 3 to 4 minutes. Spoon the rice and butter into a 13 by 9–inch glass or ceramic baking dish.

3. Add the remaining 4 tablespoons of butter to the skillet and place it over medium heat. Add the mushrooms and cook, stirring, until they begin to lose their liquid, 3 to 4 minutes. Add the mushrooms to the baking dish with the rice.

4. Pour the beef consommé into the baking dish with the rice and mushrooms. Fill a consommé can with water and add this to the rice. Stir gently to combine and carefully place the baking dish in the oven.

5. Bake the rice, uncovered, until it tests done and the liquid has nearly evaporated, 1 hour and 20 minutes to 1 hour and 30 minutes. Stir the rice every 15 minutes to keep the top from drying out. If you are serving the rice at home, you can keep it warm for up to an hour by covering it with aluminum foil and leaving it in the oven after turning it off. Serve the rice garnished with chopped parsley, if desired.

BIG BATCH: *You can double and triple this recipe as needed; bake the rice in one of those disposable aluminum foil pans that is 3 inches deep. The deeper the pan, the longer the rice will take to cook.*

RECIPE REMINDERS

Made for

Prep notes

Don't forget

Special touches

Bring again

Cindy's Chile Cheese Grits

SERVES 16

**PREP: 15 MINUTES ✳ BAKE: ABOUT 1 HOUR
PLUS 10 MINUTES RESTING TIME**

**TOTE
NOTES**

*Tote the cheese grits in
the baking dish in a
casserole carrier or
covered with aluminum
foil and a towel to keep
the grits warm.*

PLAN AHEAD

*The grits may be made
through Step 3 up to two
days in advance, covered
with plastic wrap, and
refrigerated. When you
are ready to bake them,
uncover the casserole
and bake the grits until
golden and bubbly, about
1 hour and 15 minutes.*

ATLANTA'S CINDY COTE AND HER FAMILY HOST A
pig roast every October for one hundred people.
They set up tables in their driveway, and all
their friends bring side dishes to go with the delicious
barbecued pork. Cindy makes this cheese grits casserole,
which is a wonderful accompaniment for all types of
barbecue, be it pork ribs, whole chickens, or beef brisket.
It's bountiful and rich, proportioned here to feed sixteen,
and can be made a day or so in advance.

Vegetable oil spray, for misting the baking dish
6 cups water
1½ teaspoons salt
1½ cups quick (not instant) grits
1 cup (2 sticks) butter (see Note)
4 cups (1 pound) shredded Mexican-style cheese blend
    with jalapeño peppers
2 medium-size cloves garlic, minced
2 teaspoons Worcestershire sauce
4 large eggs, well beaten
2 cans (4 ounces each) chopped green chiles,
    undrained
Paprika

1. Place a rack in the center of the oven and preheat the oven
to 350°F. Lightly mist a 13 by 9–inch glass or ceramic baking
dish with vegetable oil spray and set the dish aside.

2. Place the water and salt in a medium-size saucepan and bring to a boil over medium-high heat. Add the grits and cook according to package directions, 5 to 7 minutes, stirring.

3. Remove the pan from the heat. Add the butter and the cheese blend and stir until melted. Add the garlic, Worcestershire sauce, eggs, and chiles and stir until well combined. Pour the grits into the prepared baking dish and sprinkle the top with paprika.

4. Bake the grits until the top is golden, the edges are bubbly, and a knife inserted in the center comes out clean, about 1 hour. Let the grits rest for 10 minutes before serving.

NOTE: You can make a less rich version of this recipe by reducing the amount of butter to a stick and a half.

BIG BATCH: *If you want to double the amount of grits you cook, use a large stockpot. Be sure to stir the grits continuously as they cook to keep them from getting lumpy. Then assemble two casseroles.*

RECIPE REMINDERS

Made for

Prep notes

Don't forget

Special touches

Bring again

Midsummer's Night Pasta

SERVES 8

**PREP: 15 TO 20 MINUTES PLUS 1 HOUR DRAINING TIME FOR THE TOMATOES
COOK: ABOUT 9 MINUTES**

**TOTE
NOTES**

*Tote the pasta in a large
shallow bowl covered
with plastic wrap.*

PLAN AHEAD

*You can keep the pasta
in a cool place at room
temperature for 3 or 4
hours; the flavors are
better when served at
room temperature.*

THIS IS PRECISELY WHAT YOU WANT TO BE EATING ON a summer's night in Italy—or in your backyard with friends. It is a casual but elegant side dish of pasta, fresh herbs, and good tomatoes you can pair with just about any grilled or roast meat, poultry, or fish. Choose penne, spirals, shells, or whatever short pasta you have on hand. Begin with the best ripe tomatoes you can find, your own if they're on the vine. And, give yourself some time to let the tomatoes drain their liquid because they will have a lot more flavor that way.

8 very ripe medium-size tomatoes, chopped
    (about 4 cups)
Kosher salt
4 cups rinsed and chopped arugula
1 tablespoon chopped fresh oregano
1 tablespoon chopped fresh basil
1 tablespoon fresh thyme leaves
2 medium-size cloves garlic, crushed in a garlic press
1 teaspoon red pepper flakes (optional)
¼ cup olive oil, or more as needed
1 pound (4 cups) penne, fusilli, or medium-size
    shell pasta
½ cup (2 ounces) shredded Parmesan cheese, for serving

1. Place the chopped tomatoes in a colander in the sink and toss them with 1 tablespoon of salt. Let the tomatoes drain until the liquid draws out of them, about 1 hour.

2. Meanwhile, place the arugula, oregano, basil, thyme, garlic, red pepper flakes, if desired, and olive oil in a large mixing bowl. Season with salt to taste. When the tomatoes have drained, stir them into the herb mixture and set aside.

3. Bring a large pot of water to a boil over high heat. Stir in the pasta and 1 teaspoon of salt, reduce the heat, and cook the pasta, uncovered, according to the package directions until just done, 8 to 9 minutes.

4. Drain the pasta well in a colander, shaking it to remove excess water. Add the pasta to the tomato mixture and stir to combine. Add more olive oil, as needed, to coat the pasta well. Serve the pasta at once, with the Parmesan on the side, or let the pasta cool to room temperature before serving.

BIG BATCH: *The pasta is easy to double for crowds—or cut the recipe in half for smaller gatherings. You can vary the fresh herb mixture, using whatever you have on hand.*

RECIPE REMINDERS

Made for

Prep notes

Don't forget

Special touches

Bring again

Baked Macaroni and Cheese

SERVES 8

PREP: 20 MINUTES ✳ BAKE: 40 TO 45 MINUTES

🛍 **TOTE NOTES**

Cover the macaroni and cheese with aluminum foil after it has baked, tote it in the baking dish, and serve it close to room temperature.

PLAN AHEAD

A great bake-ahead, this casserole reheats well, covered, in a 300°F oven for 15 to 20 minutes.

MACARONI AND CHEESE IS PRETTY SACRED STUFF. And families tend to have their own revered versions to tote to gatherings. So who am I to tell you how to make mac and cheese? I'm just passing along a keeper of a recipe that adults like and kids adore. And you can add some frozen peas to the macaroni and cheese as well—although my kids always scrunch up their noses at the mention of this. A variation that uses ham, which I love, follows.

1 tablespoon butter plus 1 teaspoon butter

8 ounces (2 cups) uncooked elbow macaroni

½ teaspoon table salt

2 cups milk

¼ cup all-purpose flour

1 teaspoon onion salt

3 cups (12 ounces) shredded cheese (see Note)

½ cup crushed buttery round crackers (about 12), such as Ritz

1. Place a rack in the center of the oven and preheat the oven to 350°F. Lightly butter a 13 by 9–inch glass or ceramic baking dish with 1 teaspoon of the butter and set it aside.

2. Bring a large pot of water to a boil over high heat. Stir in the macaroni and the table salt, reduce the heat to medium-high, and cook the macaroni, uncovered, according to the

M
E
N
U

VEGETARIAN COVERED DISH

The venue might be your office for lunch or your driveway for dinner. Have friends each bring a dish. And if you must, add a baked ham, but really the fun here is the assortment of vegetarian sides, salads, and desserts—and the conversation.

BABY BLUE SALAD
WITH SWEET AND SPICY PECANS, *page 100*
✳
TOMATO, MOZZARELLA, AND BASIL SALAD
WITH FRESH TOMATO VINAIGRETTE, *page 118*
✳
WARM POTATO SALAD
WITH ROSEMARY AND CAMEMBERT, *page 133*
✳
BLACK BEAN TORTILLA BAKE, *page 212*
✳
GREEN BEANS WITH A SPICY TOMATO SAUCE, *page 276*
✳
BAKED MACARONI AND CHEESE
✳
CARROT CAKE WITH MAPLE CREAM CHEESE FROSTING,
page 362
✳
MINDY'S POUND CAKE LOAVES, *page 452*

RECIPE REMINDERS

Made for

Prep notes

Don't forget

Special touches

Bring again

package directions until just done, 7 to 8 minutes. Drain the macaroni in a colander, shaking it to remove excess water.

3. Place the milk in a large mixing bowl and whisk in the flour and onion salt until smooth. Stir in the cheese. Add the warm macaroni to the milk mixture and stir to combine well. Spoon the macaroni mixture into the prepared baking dish,

BAKED MAC
AND HAM

If adding ham to your mac and cheese, you'll need ¼ cup—about 2 ounces. I like to use country ham, which I grind. If you are using sugar-cured ham from the deli, cube about a cup and place it in a food processor fitted with a steel blade. Pulse until finely chopped. Fold the ground ham into the macaroni mixture, or sprinkle it on top with the cracker crumbs and butter before baking.

smoothing the top. Sprinkle the cracker crumbs evenly over the casserole and dot the top with the remaining 1 tablespoon of butter cut into bits.

4. Bake the macaroni and cheese until it bubbles throughout and the topping is golden, 40 to 45 minutes. Serve the macaroni at once or cover it and keep warm until serving time.

NOTE: I like a mixture of cheeses in this casserole. I use 1 cup extra-sharp Cheddar for flavor, plus 1½ cups of the Monterey Jack and Cheddar blend because it melts nicely, and ½ cup Parmesan for its sharp, nutty flavor. This is a good mix, but feel free to use whatever bits and bobs of cheese you have in the fridge.

BIG BATCH: *The macaroni and cheese recipe doubles and triples well. You can boil all of the pasta at one time and toss it with a little olive oil. Keep the pasta at room temperature until you are ready to finish preparing the macaroni, and then spoon it into two or three baking dishes.*

Cheesy Garlic Bread

SERVES 8

PREP: 15 MINUTES ✳ BAKE: ABOUT 12 MINUTES

G ARLIC BREAD IS SUCH A GREAT SIDE DISH TO OFFER to bring. No one wants to go to the trouble to make it, and yet everyone will tear into the loaf, especially with all the goodies this recipe offers. Oregano, red pepper if you like it, and a mixture of butter and olive oil, as well as melted mozzarella on top, make this garlic bread to the max. It goes with chili, spaghetti, barbecue, brisket, and vegetarian suppers, too.

1 loaf (1 pound) Italian bread

4 tablespoons (½ stick) butter,
    at room temperature

1 to 2 tablespoons olive oil

3 medium-size cloves garlic, crushed
    in a garlic press

1 teaspoon dried oregano

1 cup (4 ounces) shredded mozzarella cheese

Red pepper flakes (optional)

Chopped fresh parsley (optional), for garnish

1. Place a rack in the center of the oven and preheat the oven to 400°F. Place a piece of aluminum foil about 2 inches longer than the loaf of bread on a baking sheet.

2. Partially cut the bread into slices 1 to 2 inches thick; do not slice all the way through the loaf. Carefully transfer the cut loaf to the baking sheet.

3. Place the butter, olive oil, garlic, and oregano in a small bowl and stir to mix. Spread some of the butter mixture evenly on

TOTE NOTES

Save the plastic bag and twist tie from the bread—the best way to tote this is to prepare it, wrap it in aluminum foil, and place the foil-wrapped loaf back in the plastic bag. Secure it with a twist tie and you're ready to travel.

When you arrive, remove the foil-wrapped loaf from the plastic bag, unwrap the top, and bake the bread in a 400°F oven on a baking sheet or right on the oven rack.

both sides of each of the slices of bread. Scatter the mozzarella cheese over the top of the loaf and sprinkle red pepper flakes over it, if desired.

4. Pull the aluminum foil up around the loaf, folding it together at each end to secure them but leaving the top of the loaf exposed. Bake the bread until the cheese melts and the loaf has browned, 10 to 12 minutes. If desired, garnish with parsley. Serve at once.

BIG BATCH: *It's easy to prepare as many loaves of garlic bread as you need. Each loaf serves eight.*

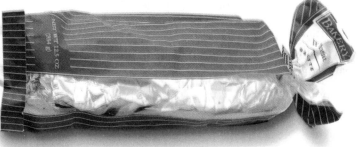

DAZZLING DESSERTS

I've got an arsenal of cake recipes at my fingertips, but when faced with the question, "What can I bring?" I can't make up my mind what to bake. When put on the spot, it's hard to pinpoint just what dessert is best for a gathering. So writing this chapter helped me identify those desserts that people gravitate to at a party—the ones I have made that received the most applause and always left an empty plate. I also chose those that work well for a group, feature the seasons' best offerings, and tote with little fuss.

In the cake category, Bundts, pound cakes, and sheet cakes are perennial potluck stars. They are sturdy, moist, and good travelers. Bundts and tube cakes look terrific on a platter with only the simplest glaze or dusting of sugar. People of all ages beg for a slice.

I recommend the Fresh Apple Cake with Caramel Glaze, Mrs. Collins's Sweet Potato Cake, and Lelia's Easy Chocolate Pound Cake. Sheet cakes, on the other hand, tend to feed a bigger crowd and are ideal for more casual affairs. You can turn them out of the pan and frost them on a long platter for a more glamorous look, but people who adore sheet cakes—such as my Carrot Cake with Maple Cream Cheese Frosting or Chocolate Buttermilk Sheet Cake—usually opt for flavor over appearance.

Layer cakes, too, are a crowd-pleasing must. They're a bit more troublesome to take with you, however, so invest in a sturdy cake carrier to make the tote less stressful. From the Sixty-Minute Caramel Cake to the classic German Chocolate Cake to the colorful Orange Marmalade Cake, layer cakes are just the right offering for birthdays, anniversaries, and going-away parties. They pay perfect tribute at graduations, christenings, bridal showers, and all the other wonderful gatherings that celebrate life's milestones.

I've included fun twists on the cake theme with Tres Leches Cakes Piled with Strawberries, a Lemon Icebox Cheesecake with a Gingersnap Crust, and a Chocolate Zuccotto Cake. The last begins with store-bought pound cake and becomes so much more. And how could I not include my Aunt Elizabeth's Banana Pudding with its meringue topping and vanilla wafer crust—always requested at our family get-togethers—or the fabulous tiramisu recipe I picked up on a recent trip to Italy?

Humble pies, cobblers, crumbles, and crisps are also always welcome at summertime picnics and fall tailgate parties. They showcase the seasons' best fruits, such as as peaches, blackberries, and pears. I especially love the Cranberry Tart and the Pear and Apple Crumble in this chapter. For pecan pie lovers I've offered two of the very best—one traditional and one made with bourbon and chocolate.

As for hardy travelers, bar cookies can't be beat. You can bake them, cut them, and pack them into storage containers that travel easily, whether by car, train, or air. Of course, I had to include recipes for Lemon Squares, Seven-Layer Bars, and the delightful and delicious Chocolate Chip Brownies with Cream Cheese "Goo." Want drop cookies? You'll also find a wonderful peanut butter cookie recipe and the best oatmeal cookies I have ever sampled.

Dessert, whether it's an elaborate cake or a simple plate of cookies, is always a welcome guest. It's equally appropriate as a gift for new neighbors and as a token of thanks for old friends. Pack it in a sturdy but decorative container, attach a card, and you've got something sweet to take to a gathering—large or small.

CAKES

When I think of toting a dessert to a gathering, I naturally turn to cake. Some of my earliest food memories involve cake on the go. Childhood picnics were not complete without one of my mother's Coca-Cola cakes. Then when carrot cake was all the rage in the seventies, that became the cake of choice. And pound cakes of all flavors have always been popular.

No matter the occasion, layer cakes, sheet cakes, and Bundt cakes are all greatly appreciated. And companies like Tupperware now make cake carriers, so transporting your dessert is a breeze. Layer cakes no longer have to be homebodies, sitting out potlucks and picnics. You can easily find cake boxes online or from your favorite bakery. Hat boxes make fun cake carriers, too.

You'll find a selection of some of my favorite cakes here. They never fail to be well received and they're always ready to hit the road.

Chocolate Buttermilk Sheet Cake

SERVES 16 TO 20 (MAKES ONE 13 BY 9-INCH CAKE)

PREP: 30 MINUTES ✳ BAKE: 30 TO 35 MINUTES
COOL: ABOUT 30 MINUTES

TOTE NOTES

Tote the chocolate sheet cake in the pan in which it was baked. When you arrive, cut the cake into squares and transfer them to a platter.

PLAN AHEAD

The sheet cake can be made the day before the party.

WHEN I LIVED IN GEORGIA, I USED THIS RECIPE often. I baked one of these sheet cakes to bring home to my mother, and she loved it so much that she quit baking her brownies and Coca-Cola cake and made this her chocolate cake of choice. She would make double batches and keep some in the freezer for unexpected guests. It is cakey and moist but rich and dense like a brownie. Bring the cake to large family gatherings, cutting and serving it right from the pan. Or, tote the cake to a summer barbecue or fall tailgate party.

FOR THE CAKE

¾ cup chopped pecans (optional)

Vegetable oil spray, for misting the pan

2 cups all-purpose flour, plus flour for dusting the baking pan

2 cups granulated sugar

1 cup (2 sticks) butter or margarine

4 heaping tablespoons unsweetened cocoa

1 cup water

1 teaspoon baking soda

⅓ cup buttermilk

2 large eggs, beaten

1 teaspoon pure vanilla extract

FOR THE CHOCOLATE ICING

8 tablespoons (1 stick) butter

4 heaping tablespoons unsweetened cocoa powder

$\frac{1}{3}$ cup milk

$3\frac{1}{2}$ to 4 cups confectioners' sugar, sifted

1. Make the cake: Place a rack in the center of the oven and preheat the oven to 350°F.

2. If you are using pecans, this is a good time to toast them. Spread the pecans out on a pie plate and toast in the oven as it preheats until they are lightly browned and fragrant, 8 to 10 minutes. Set the toasted pecans aside for topping the cake.

3. Lightly mist a 13 by 9–inch metal baking pan with vegetable oil spray and dust it with flour. Shake out the excess flour. Set the pan aside.

4. Place the flour and granulated sugar in a large heatproof mixing bowl and stir with a fork to combine.

5. Place the 1 cup of butter, 4 tablespoons of cocoa, and water in a small saucepan over medium-high heat and bring to a boil, stirring constantly, then remove from the heat and stir again. Pour the hot cocoa mixture over the dry ingredients and stir to combine. Stir the baking soda into the buttermilk and add the buttermilk mixture, eggs, and vanilla to the batter, stirring with a wooden spoon to combine well. Transfer the batter to the prepared pan, smoothing the top with a rubber spatula.

6. Bake the cake until it just begins to pull away from the sides of the pan and the center springs back when you press it lightly with a finger, 30 to 35 minutes. Place the baking pan on a wire rack and let the cake cool completely, about 30 minutes.

7. Make the chocolate icing: Melt the 8 tablespoons of butter in a 2-quart saucepan over medium-high heat. Remove the pan from the heat and stir in the 4 tablespoons of cocoa until well

DOES CAKE GO BETTER WITH COCA-COLA?

My mother made a chocolate cake using Coca-Cola. If you'd like to try one, follow the directions in the recipe for the sheet cake here and add 2 cups of miniature marshmallows to the batter before putting it in the pan to bake. Replace the milk in the icing with $\frac{1}{3}$ cup of Coca-Cola.

If you'd prefer a rocky road icing, fold $\frac{3}{4}$ cup of chopped dry-roasted peanuts and $\frac{3}{4}$ cup of miniature marshmallows into the icing before spreading it on the cake.

mixed. Add the milk and stir until combined, then whisk in enough confectioners' sugar so that the icing is smooth; start with 3½ cups, adding more as needed. Using smooth strokes, spread the icing over the cooled cake. Top the cake with the toasted pecans, if desired.

NOTE: If you refrigerate the sheet cake for 30 minutes it will be easier to slice it.

German Chocolate Cake

SERVES 16 (MAKES ONE 9-INCH ROUND LAYER CAKE)

PREP: 30 MINUTES ⁂ BAKE: ABOUT 32 MINUTES
COOL: ABOUT 40 MINUTES ⁂ ASSEMBLE: 5 MINUTES

THIS CAKE WILL INSPIRE A TRIP DOWN MEMORY lane—it's a tall German chocolate cake layered with wonderful pecan and coconut icing like your grandmother used to make. Lay a checkered cloth on the patio table, pour glasses of milk, and spend the afternoon with family and friends. Or, bring this cake to a dinner party, covered-dish supper, or bake sale and wow everyone. The recipe was super popular when it appeared in *The Chocolate Cake Mix Doctor* and good things deserve repeating.

TOTE NOTES

The easiest way to tote the German Chocolate Cake is in a cake saver. Place a paper doily under the cake and it's ready to serve. Or, bring a cake plate and slide the cake onto it using two metal pancake spatulas.

FOR THE PECAN-COCONUT ICING

$1\frac{1}{2}$ cups chopped pecans

1 package (7 ounces; $2\frac{1}{3}$ cups) sweetened flaked coconut

1 can (12 ounces) evaporated milk

$1\frac{1}{2}$ cups sugar

12 tablespoons ($1\frac{1}{2}$ sticks) unsalted butter

4 large egg yolks, slightly beaten

$1\frac{1}{2}$ teaspoons pure vanilla extract

FOR THE CAKE

Solid vegetable shortening, for greasing the cake pans

Flour, for dusting the cake pans

1 package ($18\frac{1}{4}$ ounces) plain German chocolate cake mix

1 cup buttermilk

$\frac{1}{2}$ cup vegetable oil

3 large eggs

1 teaspoon pure vanilla extract

PLAN AHEAD

The German Chocolate Cake can be baked a day or two in advance. You can store it in a cake saver, but don't tell anyone where you've put it or there will be no cake left to tote.

1. Place a rack in the center of the oven and preheat the oven to 350°F.

2. Make the icing: Spread the pecans and coconut out on a rimmed baking sheet and toast them in the oven until the pecans deepen in color and the coconut turns golden brown, about 7 minutes. Set the pecans and coconut aside.

3. Place the evaporated milk, sugar, butter, egg yolks, and 1½ teaspoons of vanilla in a large saucepan over medium heat. Cook, stirring constantly, until the mixture thickens and turns golden brown in color, 10 to 12 minutes. Remove from the heat. Stir in the toasted pecans and coconut. Let the icing cool to room temperature, about 30 minutes; it will develop a spreading consistency. (To speed the cooling process, place the pan in a bowl of ice water. Stir the icing constantly; it will cool in about 15 minutes. Or, pour the icing out into a shallow pan and stir it until cool.)

4. Meanwhile, make the cake: Grease two 9-inch round cake pans with shortening, then dust them with flour. Shake out the excess flour. Set the pans aside.

5. Place the cake mix, buttermilk, oil, eggs, and 1 teaspoon of vanilla in a large mixing bowl. Beat with an electric mixer on low speed for 1 minute. Stop the machine and scrape down the side of the bowl with a rubber spatula. Increase the mixer speed to medium and beat until well combined, about 2 minutes longer, scraping down the side of the bowl again, if needed. Divide the batter between the prepared pans, smoothing the tops with a rubber spatula. Place the pans in the oven side by side.

6. Bake the cakes until they spring back when lightly pressed with a finger, 32 to 34 minutes. Let the cakes cool on wire racks, about 10 minutes. Run a dinner knife around the edge of each cake and invert them onto a wire rack, then invert them again onto another wire rack so they are right side up. Let the layers cool completely, about 30 minutes longer.

7. Place one cake layer, right side up, on a serving platter. Spread the top with some of the icing. Place the second layer, right side up, on top of the first layer and ice the top with the remaining icing, leaving the sides bare.

Chocolate Peppermint Ice Cream Cake

SERVES 12 TO 16 (MAKES ONE 9-INCH ROUND LAYER CAKE)

PREP: 30 MINUTES ✳ BAKE: 25 TO 30 MINUTES
ASSEMBLE: 30 MINUTES ✳ CHILL: 5 HOURS TOTAL

TOTE NOTES

A plastic cake saver is great for storing the cake in the freezer and toting it to the party. If you want to transport the cake on a serving plate, be sure the plate can withstand the cold of the freezer. Cover the cake with a loose layer of heavy-duty aluminum foil.

Try to get to your destination quickly, and keep the cake wrapped in foil and on ice in a cooler until you have a chance to return it to the freezer.

MY FRIEND BETH MEADOR MADE THIS CAKE FOR her daughter's sixteenth birthday, and it was unforgettable not only because of the lethal chocolate-peppermint combo but also because of its looks. The recipe comes from Beth's cousin, Laurie Abel of Mt. Washington, Kentucky, outside of Louisville. Made from scratch, this delicious eggless cake is dense—just right for a sandwich of pink peppermint or green chocolate-mint ice cream. For the topping, you can either fold cocoa into a store-bought one or use sweetened whipped cream. Then garnish the cake with a lot of crushed peppermint candy, chopped chocolate-mint wafers, or crushed chocolate-mint sandwich cookies and sprigs of mint.

Vegetable oil spray, for misting the pans

3 cups all-purpose flour, plus flour for dusting the cake pans

2 cups sugar

½ cup unsweetened cocoa powder, plus 2 to 3 tablespoons unsweetened cocoa powder for the topping (optional)

2 teaspoons baking soda

1 teaspoon salt

2 cups water

¾ cup vegetable oil

1 tablespoon white vinegar or cider vinegar

2 teaspoons pure vanilla extract

2 cups Sweetened Whipped Cream (page 367), or
  1 container (12 ounces) frozen whipped topping,
  thawed

1 half-gallon (2 quarts) peppermint or chocolate-mint
  ice cream

1 cup crushed peppermint candies, 1 cup chopped
  chocolate-mint candies, 1 cup crushed chocolate-mint
  sandwich cookies, or chocolate shavings

Fresh mint sprigs (optional)

1. Place a rack in the center of the oven and preheat the oven to 350°F. Lightly mist two 9-inch round cake pans with vegetable oil spray and dust them with flour. Shake out the excess flour. Set the pans aside.

2. Place the flour, sugar, ½ cup of cocoa, baking soda, and salt in a large mixing bowl and stir with a fork to combine. Make a well in the center and add the water, oil, vinegar, and vanilla. Beat with an electric mixer on medium-low speed until well blended and smooth, 2 to 3 minutes. Divide the batter evenly between the 2 prepared cake pans, smoothing the tops with a rubber spatula. Place the pans in the oven side by side.

3. Bake the cakes until the tops spring back when lightly pressed with a finger, 25 to 30 minutes. Let the cakes cool on wire racks for about 10 minutes.

4. When the cakes have cooled, run a long, sharp knife around the edge of each cake and invert them onto a wire rack, then invert them again onto another wire rack so that they are right side up. Place one layer in a cake saver, cover it with waxed paper, and place the second layer on top. Place the cake in the freezer until firm, at least 1 hour, or up to 1 week.

5. Meanwhile, fold the remaining cocoa, if desired, into the whipped cream or whipped topping and refrigerate until ready to use.

PLAN AHEAD

The chocolate layers can be baked, cooled, placed in a cake saver, and stored in the freezer for up to one week.

You can assemble this cake up to two days in advance, and I recommend this because the recipe has many steps and it is less stressful when you make it ahead. Plus, the cake is easier to slice when it has been frozen.

RECIPE
REMINDERS

Made for

Prep notes

Don't forget

Special touches

Bring again

6. Remove the ice cream from the freezer and place it on a plate. Using kitchen scissors or a sharp knife, cut through the cardboard container and peel it away from the ice cream.

7. Remove the cake layers from the freezer. Using a serrated knife, slice each layer in half horizontally. Set one of the layer cake tops aside for the top of the cake. Place one of the bottom layers on the base of the cake saver. Using a knife and working quickly, cut a third of the ice cream into slices and arrange these on top of the bottom cake layer. Cut smaller slices to fill in the gaps. Place a cake layer on top of the ice cream–covered cake. Cut half of the remaining ice cream into slices, and arrange these on top of that cake layer, then repeat with another cake layer and the remaining ice cream. Top that layer of ice cream with the reserved cake top. Quickly cover the cake with the lid of the cake saver and place it in the freezer for at least 1 hour.

8. Working quickly, spread the side and top of the cake—or just the top of the cake—with the whipped cream or topping. Sprinkle the peppermint candies, chocolate-mint candies, crushed cookies, or chocolate shavings on top of the cake. Replace the cake saver lid and return the cake to the freezer for at least 3 hours. When ready to serve, remove the cake from the freezer and let it sit for about 10 minutes before serving. Garnish it with mint sprigs, if desired.

BIG BATCH: *You could make two cakes; if you do, use a different ice cream—coffee, vanilla, or butter pecan—in the second one. Be creative with the toppings, too.*

Lelia's Easy Chocolate Pound Cake

SERVES 16 (MAKES ONE 10-INCH TUBE CAKE)

PREP: 15 MINUTES ✶ BAKE: 50 TO 55 MINUTES ✶ COOL: 40 MINUTES

L ELIA BAILEY OF VIRGINIA CAME UP WITH THIS RECIPE by using a method I often enjoy—trial and error. While preparing her usual chocolate pound cake, she didn't think the batter looked chocolatey enough so she added Hershey's chocolate syrup. The result is delightful. No frosting is really needed for this pure and simple pound cake, just a dusting of confectioners' sugar, which makes the cake a dream to tote in warm weather. But if you must gild the lily, a wonderful and simple chocolate glaze recipe follows. And, if you'd rather have a plain—not chocolate—pound cake, you'll find the recipe for a delicious one on page 452.

Vegetable oil spray, for misting the tube pan

1 cup all-purpose flour, plus flour for dusting the tube pan

1 package (18¼ ounces) plain devil's food cake mix

1 cup (2 sticks) unsalted butter, at room temperature

1 cup granulated sugar

1 can (8 ounces) Hershey's chocolate syrup

6 large eggs

½ cup water

2 teaspoons confectioners' sugar, for dusting the cake

Love This Chocolate Glaze (optional; recipe follows)

1. Place a rack in the center of the oven and preheat the oven to 350°F. Lightly mist a 10–inch tube pan with vegetable oil

TOTE NOTES

Tote the chocolate pound cake in a cake saver or on a plate loosely covered with plastic wrap. Don't slice it until just before serving to prevent it from drying out.

PLAN AHEAD

You can bake the pound cake a day ahead. Or, wrap it in heavy-duty aluminum foil and freeze it for up to six months, then let the cake thaw in the refrigerator or on the kitchen counter. Dust the cake with confectioners' sugar to dress it up right before you're ready to travel.

spray and dust it with flour. Shake out the excess flour. Set the tube pan aside.

2. Place the cake mix, flour, butter, granulated sugar, chocolate syrup, 1 egg, and ½ cup of water in a large mixing bowl. Beat with an electric mixer on low speed for 30 seconds. Add the remaining eggs one at a time, beating on low speed until each is incorporated, stopping in between to scrape down the side of the bowl with a rubber spatula. When all of the eggs have been added, increase the mixer speed to medium and beat the batter 1 minute longer, scraping down the side of the bowl again if needed. The batter should look smooth and thick. Transfer the batter to the prepared tube pan, smoothing the top with a rubber spatula.

3. Bake the cake until the top springs back when lightly pressed with a finger, 50 to 55 minutes. Transfer the tube pan to a wire rack and let the cake cool for about 20 minutes.

4. Run a long, sharp knife around the edges of the cake and invert it onto a wire rack, then invert it again onto another wire rack so that the cake is right side up. Let the cake cool completely, about 20 minutes. Dust the cake with confectioners' sugar or top it with the chocolate glaze, if desired, before serving.

Love This Chocolate Glaze

MAKES 1½ TO 2 CUPS

PREP: 12 MINUTES
PLUS 30 MINUTES FOR THE GLAZE TO HARDEN

I LOVE THIS EASY GLAZE, WHETHER DRIZZLED OVER POUND cake or angel food cake, or simply spooned onto vanilla ice cream. It is similar to the pan frosting from my previous books, but the recipe makes a smaller batch. Often you want just a little glaze to cascade down the side of a cake, and this is it.

6 tablespoons (¾ stick) butter
¼ cup unsweetened cocoa powder
¼ cup milk
2 to 2½ cups sifted confectioners' sugar

Melt the butter in a small saucepan over low heat, about 2 minutes. Stir in the cocoa powder and milk. Cook the glaze, stirring, until it thickens and comes to a boil, about 2 minutes. Remove the pan from the heat and stir in 2 cups of confectioners' sugar, adding more if needed to make the mixture smooth and a little thicker than pancake syrup; don't let the glaze get too thick. Ladle the warm glaze over a room temperature cake and let sit until the glaze hardens, about 30 minutes.

HAVE FROSTING, WILL TRAVEL

We've just about all witnessed cakes sliding downhill because of a runny frosting in warm weather. If it's hot and you are toting a cake, here are toppings that will work with you, not against you.

* *Cooked frostings of caramel or chocolate. They go on warm and harden on the cake.*

* *Glazes of confectioners' sugar mixed with fruit juice or milk. Use just enough to drizzle over the top of the cake.*

* *A dusting of confectioners' sugar. When the cake has cooled, sift a small amount of powdered sugar over the top. If you're feeling fancy, you can decorate a cake by placing a stencil or doily on top before dusting it with sugar. Lift up the doily to reveal a pretty pattern.*

Mrs. Collins's Sweet Potato Cake

SERVES 12 (MAKES ONE 10-INCH BUNDT CAKE)

PREP: 40 MINUTES ✳ BAKE: ABOUT 1 HOUR AND 15 MINUTES
COOL: 20 MINUTES

TOTE NOTES

Carry the cake in a plastic cake saver or place it on a cake stand and cover it with plastic wrap.

Betty Bruce Collins, who lives in Nashville, bakes this cake for her grown children's birthdays and ships the cakes overnight as far away as California. She said she began baking sweet potato cakes after the vegetable grew with abundance in her family's backyard garden. "We called our daughter Beth the sweet potato queen," Mrs. Collins admitted, because of Beth's prowess in growing so many sweet potatoes. No doubt she tended to the tubers in hopes that her mother would bake one of these stellar cakes. I enjoyed a slice of the cake while visiting Mrs. Collins after the Christmas holidays. It seemed deliciously glazed, and Mrs. Collins revealed the secret: If the confectioners' sugar is sprinkled on while the cake is warm, it forms a simple glaze. Tote this cake to parties all year long, especially in the fall and during the holidays.

1 large or 2 medium-size sweet potatoes

Vegetable oil spray, for misting the Bundt pan

2 cups all-purpose flour, sifted, plus flour for dusting the Bundt pan

$\frac{1}{2}$ cup finely chopped pecans or walnuts, or $\frac{1}{2}$ cup currants

$1\frac{1}{2}$ teaspoons baking soda

1 teaspoon baking powder

1 teaspoon salt

1½ teaspoons ground cinnamon

1 teaspoon ground nutmeg

½ teaspoon ground cloves

¼ teaspoon ground ginger

1½ cups vegetable oil

2 cups granulated sugar

2 teaspoons pure vanilla extract

4 large eggs

1 tablespoon confectioners' sugar

1. Peel and quarter the sweet potatoes. Place them in a medium-size saucepan and add enough cold water to cover. Bring to a boil over medium-high heat, then reduce the heat to low and cover the pan. Let the sweet potatoes simmer until tender, about 20 minutes. Drain the potatoes, let them cool, and then mash them (you should have about 2 cups). Set the mashed sweet potatoes aside.

2. Preheat the oven to 325°F. Lightly mist a 12-cup Bundt pan with vegetable oil spray and dust it with flour. Shake out the excess flour. Set the pan aside.

3. Spread out the pecans or walnuts, if using, in a small baking dish and lightly toast them in the oven while it preheats, 5 to 7 minutes.

4. Meanwhile, combine the flour, baking soda, baking powder, salt, cinnamon, nutmeg, cloves, and ginger in a small mixing bowl and stir with a fork to combine.

5. If using nuts, remove them from the oven and set aside.

6. Place the oil and granulated sugar in a large mixing bowl and beat with an electric mixer on medium-low speed until they come together, 1 to 2 minutes. Add the vanilla, then the eggs, one at a time, beating well after each addition, until the mixture is thickened and smooth, about 2 minutes. Stop the mixer and add the mashed sweet potatoes and dry ingredients and beat

RECIPE REMINDERS

Made for

Prep notes

Don't forget

Special touches

Bring again

GREAT CAKES COME IN SMALLER PACKAGES

Think about the size of the household when you are planning to bring a cake as a gift. With two or more children in the clan that family might well eat an entire Bundt cake in a day or two. But for one- or two-person households, opt for smaller cakes. Bundt pans come in a 6-cup size, so you can make two from one recipe; bake them for 30 to 35 minutes. Or, bake cupcakes instead of a cake. And, make individual tarts instead of an entire pie.

on low speed until all just combined and the batter is smooth, 45 seconds to 1 minute longer. Fold in the toasted nuts or the currants. Transfer the batter to the prepared Bundt pan, smoothing the top with a rubber spatula.

7. Bake the cake until it is golden brown and the top springs back when lightly pressed with a finger, 1 hour and 15 to 20 minutes. Remove the pan from the oven. Let the cake cool in the pan for about 20 minutes.

8. Run a knife around the edge of the cake, give the pan a few good shakes to loosen it, and invert the cake onto a plate. Then, sprinkle the confectioners' sugar over it.

Orange Marmalade Cake

SERVES 12 (MAKES ONE 9-INCH ROUND LAYER CAKE)

PREP: 30 MINUTES ✳ BAKE: 25 TO 30 MINUTES ✳ COOL: 55 MINUTES

ONE OF MY NEWSLETTER READERS, LESLIE D'AGOSTINO of Oak Park, Illinois, came up with this terrific cake. It's a pretty cake that begs to be baked ahead of time because it improves in flavor after a day. Place it on a lime green plate and it will look very stylish, especially if you garnish the side of the cake with orange slices and surround the base with orange flowers just before serving.

FOR THE CAKE AND ORANGE SYRUP

Vegetable oil spray, for misting the cake pans
Flour, for dusting the cake pans
1 package (18¼ ounces) plain yellow cake mix
1 package (about 3 ounces) vanilla instant pudding mix
1⅓ cups plus ¾ cup orange juice
3 large eggs
½ cup vegetable oil
1 teaspoon pure vanilla extract
1 tablespoon grated orange zest
2 tablespoons sugar

FOR THE FILLING AND FROSTING

1 cup orange marmalade
¾ cup heavy (whipping) cream
3 tablespoons sugar
¾ cup sour cream

TOTE NOTES

Tote the cake to the party in a cake saver and slice the cake directly from it or carefully transfer the cake to a stand before serving.

PLAN AHEAD

The Orange Marmalade Cake can be made a day in advance.

1. Make the cake: Place a rack in the center of the oven and preheat the oven to 350°F. Lightly mist two 9-inch round cake pans with vegetable oil spray and dust them with flour. Shake

**PLEASE DO EAT
THE POSIES**

*Edible flowers, such as
orange blossoms, pansies,
and violets, are pretty
garnishes for cakes, but don't
use blooms from a florist.
Most commercially grown
flowers are not meant for
consumption. To be edible,
flowers must have been
grown without pesticides.
When selecting a kitchen
bouquet, look for flowering
herbs—think chives, mint,
and thyme. Cheerful
nasturtiums add a distinctive
touch of color to salads. No
matter what kind of blossom
you pick, a floral garnish
always makes an elegant
and memorable statement.*

out the excess flour. Set the pans aside. Place a large mixing
bowl and the beaters of an electric mixer in the refrigerator
to chill.

2. Place the cake mix, pudding mix, 1 1/3 cups of orange juice,
and the eggs, oil, vanilla, and orange zest in a second large
mixing bowl. Beat the cake mix mixture with an electric mixer
on low speed until the ingredients are moistened. Increase the
mixer speed to medium and beat until well combined, about
2 minutes longer. Divide the batter between the 2 prepared cake
pans, smoothing the tops with a rubber spatula. Place the cake
pans in the oven side by side and bake until the tops of the cakes
spring back when lightly pressed with a finger, 25 to 30 minutes.

3. Meanwhile, make the orange syrup: Pour the 3/4 cup of orange
juice into a small bowl and add the 2 tablespoons of sugar.
Whisk until the sugar dissolves, then set the orange syrup aside.

4. Prepare the filling and frosting: Place the orange marmalade
in a small saucepan and heat it over low heat until it is soft
enough to spread or heat it in a microwave-safe glass bowl in
the microwave oven on high power for 1 minute.

5. Remove the chilled bowl and beaters from the refrigerator.
Pour the cream into the bowl and beat it on high speed until
soft peaks form, about 2 minutes. Continue beating the cream
on high while adding the 3 tablespoons of sugar and beat until
stiff peaks form, about 1 minute longer. Fold in the sour cream
and place the frosting in the refrigerator.

6. Transfer the cake pans to a wire rack and let the layers cool
for about 5 minutes. Run a long, sharp knife around the edge
of each cake layer and invert them onto a wire rack, then again
onto another wire rack so that they are right side up. Let cool
for 20 minutes longer. Poke holes in the tops of each layer with
a bamboo skewer or a chopstick and slowly spoon the orange
syrup over the surface. Allow the layers to cool until they are
at room temperature, about 30 minutes longer.

7. To assemble, place one layer on a cake plate. Spread two thirds of the marmalade evenly on top. Place the second layer on top. Spoon the remaining marmalade in the center of the cake and then spread it toward the edge of the cake, leaving a border of cake about 1¼ inches wide. Frost the side and the cake border, leaving the marmalade exposed. Place the cake in a cake saver in the refrigerator to store.

WANT AN ORANGE MARMALADE SHEET CAKE?
Bake the batter in a 13 by 9–inch cake pan; it will take 30 to 35 minutes. Brush the top of the cake with the glaze, followed by the marmalade, spreading it thinly to cover as much of the top of the cake as possible. Last of all, smooth on the frosting.

M E N U

MOTHER'S DAY SUNDAY BRUNCH

Let's not forget about brunch, that civilized meal combining breakfast and lunch that came to be so appreciated on Sundays. It's perfect for Mother's Day or a post-christening party or a birthday gathering. Or brunch might be just the chance to reconnect.

LOU ANN'S SPINACH, PROSCIUTTO,
AND MUSHROOM MIDNIGHT STRATA, *page 196*
∗
ANN'S HOME-SMOKED SALMON
WITH OLIVES AND LEMON, *page 50*
∗
MY SWEET AND SOUR BROCCOLI SALAD, *page 124*
∗
WARM ROLLS
∗
ORANGE MARMALADE CAKE, *page 353*

RECIPE REMINDERS

Made for

Prep notes

Don't forget

Special touches

Bring again

Fresh Apple Cake with Caramel Glaze

SERVES 16 (MAKES ONE 10-INCH TUBE CAKE)

PREP: 20 MINUTES ✳ BAKE: 75 TO 80 MINUTES
COOL: 25 MINUTES

TOTE NOTES

Apple cake is a great traveler: Place it in a plastic cake saver to tote. You can slice and serve it right from the carrier or slide it onto a cake plate or stand before serving.

PLAN AHEAD

The apple cake can be baked a day in advance.

D URING THE FALL, WHEN FRESH, LOCAL APPLES ARE in season, you must bake this cake. It is one of our family favorites. Use any flavorful apples: Golden Delicious, Granny Smith, winesap—you name it. And if you've got more pears than apples, you can use firm, ripe ones instead. This is a great cake to take tailgating or to a neighborhood potluck because it won't slip and slide, and you will come home with a clean plate.

FOR THE APPLE CAKE

Vegetable oil spray, for misting the pan

3 cups all-purpose flour, plus flour for dusting the tube pan

1½ cups granulated sugar

½ packed cup light brown sugar

1½ cups vegetable oil

3 large eggs

2 teaspoons ground cinnamon

1 teaspoon baking soda

½ teaspoon ground nutmeg

½ teaspoon salt

3 large apples, peeled, cored, and cut into 1-inch chunks (3½ cups)

1 cup chopped walnuts or pecans (optional)

2 teaspoons pure vanilla extract

FOR THE CARAMEL GLAZE

3 tablespoons butter

3 tablespoons granulated sugar

3 tablespoons light brown sugar

3 tablespoons heavy (whipping) cream

½ teaspoon pure vanilla extract

1. Make the apple cake: Place a rack in the center of the oven and preheat the oven to 325°F. Lightly mist a 10-inch tube pan with vegetable oil spray and dust it with flour. Shake out the excess flour. Set the pan aside.

2. Place the 1½ cups of granulated sugar, ½ cup of brown sugar, and the oil in a large mixing bowl. Beat with an electric mixer on medium-low speed until the mixture lightens, about 2 minutes. Add the eggs, one at a time, beating well after each addition.

3. Sift together the flour, cinnamon, baking soda, nutmeg, and salt. Add the dry ingredients to the sugar mixture and, using a wooden spoon, stir to combine. Fold in the apples, walnuts or pecans, if desired, and vanilla. Transfer the batter to the prepared tube pan, smoothing the top with a rubber spatula.

4. Bake the apple cake until it begins to pull away from the sides of the pan and the top springs back when lightly pressed with a finger, 75 to 80 minutes. Transfer the tube pan to a wire rack and let the cake cool for about 25 minutes.

5. Meanwhile, make the caramel glaze: Place the butter, 3 tablespoons of granulated sugar, 3 tablespoons of brown sugar, and the cream and vanilla in a small saucepan and bring to a boil over medium-high heat. Let the caramel glaze boil for 1 minute, stirring, then remove the pan from the heat.

6. Run a long, sharp knife around the edges of the apple cake and invert it onto a wire rack, then invert it again onto another wire rack so that the cake is right side up. Using a bamboo

RECIPE REMINDERS

Made for

Prep notes

Don't forget

Special touches

Bring again

FOR APPLE CAKE LOAVES

Mist two 9 by 5–inch loaf pans with vegetable oil spray and dust them with flour. Then, divide the apple cake batter between them and bake it at 325°F for 55 to 60 minutes. After they are cool remove the loaves from the pans and glaze them.

skewer, chopstick, or fork, poke a few holes in the top of the cake. Then spoon the caramel glaze over the cake while it's still warm. Let the cake cool completely before slicing it.

BIG BATCH: *You can bake two apple cakes in the same oven. Double the batter and divide it between two tube pans. Don't forget—you'll also need to make a double batch of the caramel glaze.*

Sixty-Minute Caramel Cake

SERVES 12 (MAKES ONE 9-INCH LAYER CAKE)

PREP: 25 MINUTES ✳ BAKE: ABOUT 30 MINUTES
COOL: 15 MINUTES

A GOOD CARAMEL CAKE IS ONE OF MY ALL-TIME favorite desserts, yet to make it the traditional way often seems too time-consuming. This recipe is my shortcut. To save precious time, assemble the frosting ingredients while the cake is baking. Then, while the cake cools, you can prepare the frosting. If you add slightly less confectioners' sugar than the recipe calls for, you can work ahead, because the frosting will not be so thick and will not set up as quickly.

FOR THE CAKE
Vegetable oil spray, for misting the cake pans
Flour, for dusting the cake pans
1 package (18¼ ounces) plain yellow cake mix
1 package (about 3 ounces) vanilla instant pudding mix
1 cup milk
1 cup vegetable oil
4 large eggs
1 teaspoon pure vanilla extract

FOR THE CARAMEL ICING
8 tablespoons (1 stick) butter
½ packed cup light brown sugar
½ packed cup dark brown sugar
About ¼ cup milk
About 2 cups confectioners' sugar, sifted
1 teaspoon pure vanilla extract

TOTE NOTES

This is a great cake to tote in hot weather because the icing hardens and won't melt. The cake travels well in the car.

PLAN AHEAD

The caramel cake can be made a day in advance.

**RECIPE
REMINDERS**

Made for

Prep notes

Don't forget

Special touches

Bring again

1. Make the cake: Place a rack in the center of the oven and preheat the oven to 350°F. Lightly mist two 9-inch round cake pans with vegetable oil spray and dust them with flour. Shake out the excess flour. Set the pans aside.

2. Place the cake mix, pudding mix, 1 cup of milk, oil, eggs, and 1 teaspoon of vanilla in a large mixing bowl. Beat with an electric mixer on low speed until the ingredients are incorporated, 30 to 45 seconds. Increase the mixer speed to medium and beat until the mixture lightens and is smooth, about 1½ minutes. Divide the batter between the two prepared cake pans, smoothing the tops with a rubber spatula.

3. Place the pans in the oven side by side and bake until the cakes are golden brown and the tops spring back when lightly pressed with a finger, 28 to 32 minutes. Transfer the cake pans to a wire rack and let the layers cool for about 15 minutes. Run a long, sharp, knife around the edge of each cake layer and invert them onto a wire rack, then again onto another wire rack so that they are right side up.

4. While the layers are cooling, make the caramel icing: Place the butter and ½ cup each light and dark brown sugars in a medium-size heavy saucepan over medium heat. Cook, stirring, until the mixture comes to a boil, about 2 minutes. Add the ¼ cup of milk, stir, and let come to a boil, then remove the pan from the heat. Add about 1½ cups of the confectioners' sugar and the 1 teaspoon of vanilla. Beat with a wooden spoon or whisk until the icing is smooth. Add up to ½ cup more sugar if the icing is too thin, but not so much that it thickens and hardens.

5. While the icing is warm, place one cake layer on a cake plate or the base of a cake saver and ladle a generous spoonful of the warm icing over it. Using a long metal icing spatula, spread out the icing. Add more icing as needed and smooth it out.

6. Place the second cake layer on top of the first and ladle generous spoonfuls of warm icing over it, spreading it over the top of cake. Then ice the side. As the icing cools, it will thicken. Dip the spatula into the icing and remove just enough to easily apply to the side of the cake. Keep adding more icing, going around the cake twice. Use clean and smooth strokes. If the icing hardens before you have finished covering the cake, place the saucepan back over low heat and stir the icing until it softens. Add a little more milk if needed.

TEN TANTALIZING BIRTHDAY DESSERTS

1. *German Chocolate Cake (see page 341)*

2. *Chocolate Peppermint Ice Cream Cake (see page 344)*

3. *Mrs. Collins's Sweet Potato Cake (see page 350)*

4. *Orange Marmalade Cake (see page 353)*

5. *Sixty-Minute Caramel Cake (see page 359)*

6. *Tres Leches Cakes Piled with Strawberries (see page 365)*

7. *Lemon Icebox Cheesecake with a Gingersnap Crust (see page 370)*

8. *Chocolate Zuccotto Cake (see page 372)*

9. *My Favorite Key Lime Pie (see page 414)*

10. *Elena's Tiramisu (see page 438)*

Carrot Cake with Maple Cream Cheese Frosting

SERVES 16 TO 20 (MAKES ONE 13 BY 9-INCH SHEET CAKE)

**PREP: 45 MINUTES * BAKE: ABOUT 40 MINUTES
COOL: 10 MINUTES**

TOTE NOTES

To tote the cake while it's still in the pan, cover it with a plastic lid that fits a 13 by 9-inch pan or use plastic wrap.

If the cake is removed from the pan and frosted, it is best to tote it in a rectangular cake saver. Or, you can refrigerate the frosted cake uncovered, so the frosting sets, and then cover it loosely with aluminum foil, taking care that the foil doesn't touch the frosting.

PLAN AHEAD

Bake the carrot cake a day ahead of time, frost it in the pan, cover, and refrigerate it until serving time.

TURN ON A CAROLE KING ALBUM, PUT ON YOUR faded bell-bottom jeans, and bake a fresh carrot cake. Just like good music and favorite jeans, carrot cakes never go out of style. Whereas a carrot layer cake is perfect for birthdays and celebrations, I think a carrot cake baked in a 13 by 9–inch pan is better suited to feeding a crowd. You don't have to worry about the cream cheese frosting slipping in warm weather, and the cake can be baked a day ahead, covered, and refrigerated. What makes this cake a little different from other recipes is that it does not contain nuts. I think they dry out carrot cake and are better as a garnish on top of the frosting. The carrots here are freshly grated, not preshredded from a bag. And I use golden raisins, which seem to blend in nicely with the batter but also add that touch of sweetness.

FOR THE CAKE

Vegetable oil spray, for misting the cake pan

2 cups self-rising flour, plus flour for dusting the cake pan

1 tablespoon ground cinnamon

4 large eggs

1¼ cups vegetable oil

1 cup granulated sugar

1 cup light brown sugar

2 teaspoons pure vanilla extract

3 cups peeled and grated carrots

¾ cup golden raisins tossed in 2 teaspoons flour

½ cup coarsely chopped walnuts

FOR THE MAPLE CREAM CHEESE FROSTING

8 tablespoons (1 stick) butter, at room temperature

8 ounces reduced-fat cream cheese, at room temperature

3 cups confectioners' sugar, sifted

½ teaspoon pure vanilla extract

½ teaspoon maple flavoring

1. Make the cake: Place a rack in the center of the oven and preheat the oven to 325°F. Lightly mist a 13 by 9–inch metal cake pan with vegetable oil spray and dust it with flour. Shake out the excess flour. Set the pan aside.

2. Place the flour and cinnamon in a small bowl, stir with a fork to combine, and set aside.

3. Place the eggs, oil, granulated sugar, brown sugar, and 2 teaspoons of vanilla in a large mixing bowl. Beat with an electric mixer on medium speed for 1 minute. Add the flour mixture and beat on low until just combined, about 30 seconds. Stir in the carrots and raisins with a wooden spoon. Transfer the batter to the prepared baking dish, smoothing the top with a rubber spatula.

4. Bake the cake until a toothpick inserted in the center comes out clean, 40 to 43 minutes. Remove the cake from the oven and let it cool on a wire rack for about 10 minutes. Leave the oven on.

5. Spread out the walnuts in a pie pan and toast them in the oven for about 5 minutes, then let cool.

6. You can either leave the cake in the pan or turn it out onto a long rectangular platter. To do this, run a sharp knife around the edges of the cake to loosen it, then invert it onto the platter.

RECIPE REMINDERS

Made for

Prep notes

Don't forget

Special touches

Bring again

**FOR A BROWN
BUTTER AND
CREAM CHEESE
FROSTING**

*Instead of blending the
room temperature butter
with the cream cheese, cook
the butter over low heat
until it is lightly browned,
4 to 5 minutes. Remove the
butter from the heat and
pour it over the cream
cheese, then proceed with
the frosting recipe, omitting
the maple flavoring.*

7. Make the frosting: Place the butter and cream cheese in
a large mixing bowl and beat with an electric mixer on low
speed until combined, about 1 minute. Add the confectioners'
sugar, $\frac{1}{2}$ teaspoon of vanilla, and the maple flavoring and beat
on low to incorporate the sugar, then increase the speed to
medium-high and beat until lightened, about 1 minute.

8. If you are leaving the cake in the pan, cover the top
generously with frosting and sprinkle the toasted walnuts
over it. If you have removed the cake from the pan, spread
the frosting on the top and sides of the cake and sprinkle the
toasted walnuts over it.

Tres Leches Cakes Piled with Strawberries

SERVES 12 (MAKES ONE 9-INCH AND ONE 7-INCH CAKE)

PREP: 20 MINUTES ✳ BAKE: 35 TO 40 MINUTES
COOL: 1 HOUR ✳ CHILL: 2 HOURS ✳ ASSEMBLE: 10 MINUTES

ONE SPRING OUR MOMS' GROUP WAS GATHERING for a birthday dinner and I was asked to bring a dessert that would go with Mexican food. I immediately thought of *tres leches* cake, that wonderful confection in which the cake soaks up a rich milk syrup like a sponge. But, *tres leches* cake baked in a 13 by 9–inch pan is pretty homely looking, not the dazzling dessert I needed. So I came up with this exquisite creation, a sort of strawberry shortcake meets *tres leches*. We lit the candles, sang "Happy Birthday," and dug in.

FOR THE CAKE

Vegetable oil spray, for misting the springform pans

1 package (18¼ ounces) plain yellow cake mix

1 package (about 3 ounces) vanilla instant pudding mix

1 cup whole or low-fat milk

1 cup vegetable oil

4 large eggs

FOR THE MILK SYRUP AND TOPPINGS

1 can (14 ounces) sweetened condensed milk

1 can (12 ounces) evaporated milk

1 cup heavy (whipping) cream

1 teaspoon pure vanilla extract

2 cups Sweetened Whipped Cream (recipe follows)

2 cups sliced, lightly sweetened strawberries

TOTE NOTES

Tote the ungarnished cakes in their springform pans. Bring the strawberries and Sweetened Whipped Cream in separate plastic containers.

Unmold the cakes when you get to the party, garnish them, and they're ready to serve.

RECIPE REMINDERS

Made for

Prep notes

Don't forget

Special touches

Bring again

1. Make the cake: Place a rack in the center of the oven and preheat the oven to 350°F. Using the vegetable oil spray, lightly mist a 9-inch springform pan and a smaller 7-inch springform pan to hold the remaining batter. Each pan should be about 2½ inches deep.

2. Place the cake mix, pudding mix, milk, oil, and eggs in a large mixing bowl. Beat with an electric mixer on low speed until combined, about 1 minute. Stop the machine and scrape down the side of the bowl with a rubber spatula. Increase the mixer speed to medium and beat until well blended, about 2 minutes longer, scraping down the side of the bowl again if necessary. Transfer the batter to the prepared springform pans, filling the larger pan two thirds full first, then the smaller pan. Smooth out the top of the batter with a rubber spatula. Place the pans on a large baking sheet and place the baking sheet in the oven.

3. Bake the cakes until they are golden brown and the tops spring back when lightly pressed with a finger. The smaller cake will be done in about 28 to 30 minutes; let it cool on a wire rack. The larger cake will take from 35 to 40 minutes; let it cool on the baking sheet for about 1 hour.

4. Meanwhile, make the milk syrup: Whisk together the sweetened condensed milk, evaporated milk, cream, and vanilla in a medium-size bowl. When the cakes are cooled poke holes all over the tops with a fork, chopstick, or bamboo skewer. Keep the cakes on the baking sheet. Using a large spoon or ladle, spoon some of the milk syrup over each of the cakes. Let the syrup soak into the cake, then continue spooning the syrup on top until you have used all of it. When you have finished, not all of the syrup will be completely absorbed but that's okay. Cover the cakes loosely with plastic wrap and refrigerate them on the baking sheet until the syrup is absorbed, at least 2 hours and preferably overnight.

5. To serve, remove the outside rims of the springform pans. Place the cakes on serving plates. Spread the top and sides of the cakes with a light coating of whipped cream, then garnish the cakes with the strawberries. Or, garnish the tops first with the strawberries and then with the whipped cream.

BIG BATCH: *If you want to serve a lot of people and don't care as much about presentation, bake the cake in a single 13 by 9–inch pan for 32 to 34 minutes. The frosting and garnish amounts listed make enough for a sheet cake. It will serve twenty.*

Sweetened Whipped Cream

MAKES ABOUT 2 CUPS

PREP: ABOUT 5 MINUTES

O FTEN, ALL YOU NEED TO TOP A CAKE, PIE, OR COBBLER is a dollop of luscious sweetened whipped cream.

   1 cup heavy (whipping) cream
   ¼ cup confectioners' sugar

Place a large mixing bowl and the beaters of an electric mixer in the freezer for a few minutes while you assemble the ingredients. Pour the cream into the chilled bowl and beat with an electric mixer on high speed until the cream has thickened, about 1½ minutes. Stop the machine and add the confectioners' sugar. Beat the cream and sugar on high speed until stiff peaks form, 1 to 2 minutes more.

IT'S THE BERRIES

When berries are in season, go all out and top the tres leches *cakes with a festive mix of raspberries, blackberries, blueberries, and, of course, strawberries. They look beautiful on the whipped cream.*

 TOTE NOTES

Place the whipped cream in a plastic or stainless steel bowl with a snap-on lid. Keep it in a cooler while you are traveling, then refrigerate it when you arrive.

Pumpkin Spice Cheesecake

SERVES 12 (MAKES ONE 9-INCH CHEESECAKE)

PREP: 25 MINUTES ✴ BAKE: 55 MINUTES PLUS 2 HOURS RESTING TIME
COOL: 1 HOUR ✴ CHILL: 4 HOURS

TOTE NOTES

Tote the cheesecake in the springform pan; it will keep its shape better that way.

Once you remove the side of the pan, don't bother to take the cake off the bottom; just put the whole thing on a pretty serving plate.

Don't forget the whipped cream for serving. Put it in a plastic container with a lid and transport it in a cooler.

PLAN AHEAD

Bake the cheesecake a day ahead and refrigerate it—slicing will be easier.

IT'S NO WONDER CHEESECAKE IS SO WIDELY APPRECIATED. Although it takes some time to make, it is one of those fantastic desserts that everyone looks forward to. My advice is to plan ahead. Your only hands-on time is the twenty-five minutes of preparation. The cheesecake will do the rest of the work, spending forty-five minutes baking and two hours resting in the turned-off oven, plus another four hours chilling in the refrigerator. This autumnal version is perfect for Halloween, Thanksgiving, and holiday parties where you want something decadent and a bit different on the table.

FOR THE CRUST

1½ cups graham cracker crumbs
   (from 12 whole graham crackers)
¼ cup sugar
5 tablespoons butter, melted

FOR THE FILLING

4 packages (8 ounces each) cream cheese,
   at room temperature
1¼ cups sugar
3 tablespoons all-purpose flour
1 cup canned pumpkin
2 tablespoons pumpkin pie spice
1 teaspoon pure vanilla extract
4 large eggs

Whipped cream, for serving

1. Make the crust: Place a rack in the center of the oven and preheat the oven to 350°F.

2. Place the graham cracker crumbs, ¼ cup of sugar, and the butter in a small bowl and stir with a fork until the crumbs are thoroughly moistened. Press the graham cracker mixture into the bottom of a 9-inch springform pan. Bake the crust in the oven until it is lightly browned around the edges, about 10 minutes. Set the crust aside to cool but leave the oven on.

3. Make the filling: Place the cream cheese and 1¼ cups of sugar in a large mixing bowl and beat with an electric mixer on low speed until smooth and creamy, 1 to 2 minutes. Add the flour and beat until combined, then add the pumpkin, pumpkin pie spice, and vanilla, beating just until combined. Add the eggs, one at a time, beating only until each one is incorporated. Place the springform pan on a baking sheet and pour the filling into it, smoothing the top with a rubber spatula.

4. Reduce the oven temperature to 300°F and bake the cheesecake for 45 minutes, then turn off the oven and leave the cheesecake in it for 2 hours; do not open the oven door.

5. Remove the cheesecake from the oven and let cool for 1 hour. Cover the pan with plastic wrap and refrigerate the cheesecake until firm, at least 4 hours. Serve the cheesecake with whipped cream.

RECIPE REMINDERS

Made for

Prep notes

Don't forget

Special touches

Bring again

Lemon Icebox Cheesecake with a Gingersnap Crust

SERVES 12 TO 16 (MAKES ONE 9-INCH CHEESECAKE)

**PREP: 20 MINUTES ✳ BAKE: ABOUT 70 MINUTES
COOL: 1 HOUR ✳ CHILL: 4 HOURS**

TOTE NOTES

By all means, tote the cheesecake in its pan; you couldn't have a better way to protect it, and the high sides make covering the top with plastic wrap so easy.

Bring a pretty serving plate to slide the cheesecake onto once you've removed the side of the pan (no need to take the cake off the bottom), and don't forget the raspberries and Sweetened Whipped Cream, if you want a garnish. Bring them in separate plastic containers.

PLAN AHEAD

Bake the cheesecake a day in advance and refrigerate it.

WHAT'S NOT TO LOVE ABOUT THIS RECIPE? IT'S A cheesecake with the creamy texture of an icebox pie. It's got just the right amount of fresh lemon flavor. And the gingersnap crust is a great match for the lemon and a real palate teaser when you are expecting graham cracker. I know cheesecake baking is a bit of an art, but this recipe is simple enough for anyone to master. Just allow enough time for the cheesecake to cool to room temperature—one hour—and then another four hours to chill it enough so you can slice it. The combination of regular and reduced-fat cream cheese makes a lighter batter well-suited to the lemon flavor; the result is seasonless and goes with all types of meals.

FOR THE CRUST

2 cups (about 8 ounces) gingersnap cookie crumbs (36 small cookies; see Note)

5 tablespoons unsalted butter, melted

FOR THE FILLING

2 packages (8 ounces each) regular cream cheese

1 package (8 ounces) reduced-fat cream cheese

1 cup sugar

3 large eggs

¾ cup sour cream

1 tablespoon grated lemon zest (1 large lemon)

2 tablespoons fresh lemon juice

FOR THE GARNISH

Fresh raspberries

Sweetened Whipped Cream (optional; page 367)

1. Make the crust: Place a rack in the center of the oven and preheat the oven to 350°F.

2. Place the gingersnap crumbs in a small glass bowl, add the butter, and stir with a fork until the crumbs are thoroughly moistened. Press the gingersnap mixture into the bottom and partially up the side of a 9-inch springform pan that is at least 3 inches deep. Bake the crust until browned, 10 to 12 minutes. Set the crust aside to cool. Reduce the oven temperature to 300°F.

3. Make the filling: Place all of the cream cheese and the sugar in a large mixing bowl and beat with an electric mixer on medium speed until smooth and creamy, about 1 to 2 minutes. Reduce the speed to medium-low and add the eggs, one at a time, beating until each has been incorporated. Add the sour cream and beat until combined. Add the lemon zest and juice and beat until combined, about 20 seconds.

4. When the crust has cooled, place the springform pan on a baking sheet and pour the filling into it, smoothing the top with a rubber spatula. Transfer the pan on the baking sheet to the oven and bake the cheesecake until the outer edge (about 2 inches) has set but the center is still a little shaky, 55 to 60 minutes. Carefully remove the cheesecake to a wire rack to cool for 1 hour at room temperature. Transfer the cheesecake to the refrigerator to chill, uncovered, for at least 4 hours so it is easier to slice. Serve with fresh raspberries and Sweetened Whipped Cream, if desired.

NOTE: To make gingersnap cookie crumbs, pulse the gingersnaps in a food processor in batches.

RECIPE REMINDERS

Made for

Prep notes

Don't forget

Special touches

Bring again

Chocolate Zuccotto Cake

SERVES 12

PREP: 45 MINUTES ∗ CHILL: 4 HOURS
ASSEMBLE: 15 MINUTES PLUS 1 HOUR FOR THE GANACHE TO SET

TOTE NOTES

Bring the cake to the gathering on a serving tray or in a cake saver, but keep it in the fridge until you are ready to serve it. If the weather is warm, transport the cake in a cooler.

L ONGTIME *CAKE MIX DOCTOR* FAN BARBARA MCCARTHY passed along this wonderful and easy recipe several years ago. She included a note with this description: "One bite into it and you'll never forget it." It's a molded cake—*zuccotto* is Italian for "little pumpkin"— and one of those recipes in which you doctor up store-bought pound cake. Barbara knew I'd appreciate it. I made it for a girls' night out dinner party, and my friends flipped. We had an Italian theme for the dinner, and this dessert was the perfect finale. A great do-ahead dessert, you can assemble the cake part a day in advance and let it chill. Frost the cake with ganache on the day of the gathering.

FOR THE ZUCCOTTO CAKE

Clean piece of cheesecloth, about 18 inches square

2 tablespoons grappa or brandy

2 tablespoons Cointreau or triple sec (orange liqueur)

2 tablespoons amaretto (almond liqueur)

1 loaf (10¾ ounces) store-bought or homemade pound cake, crusts trimmed

5 ounces semisweet chocolate (see Note)

2 cups heavy (whipping) cream

¾ cup confectioners' sugar

¾ cup slivered almonds, toasted (see box, page 99) and chopped

½ cup hazelnuts, toasted (see box, page 99), husked, and chopped

FOR THE CHOCOLATE GANACHE

8 ounces semisweet chocolate (see Note), coarsely chopped

¾ cup heavy (whipping) cream

1 tablespoon grappa or brandy

FOR THE GARNISH

1 edible flower (see box, page 354) or maraschino cherries

1 tablespoon sifted confectioners' sugar

PLAN AHEAD

You can assemble the zuccotto *cake a day in advance—fill the bowl with the pound cake and whipped cream fillings, then cover and refrigerate it. Make the ganache and frost the* zuccotto *cake the following day.*

1. Make the *zuccotto* cake: Place a large mixing bowl and the beaters of an electric mixer in the freezer.

2. Dampen the piece of cheesecloth with water, then squeeze out the water. Line a 1½-quart bowl with the cheesecloth, draping the ends over the rim. Set the bowl aside.

3. Place the 2 tablespoons of grappa, the orange liqueur, and the amaretto in a small bowl and stir to combine.

4. Cut twelve ⅜-inch-thick slices from the pound cake, reserving any extra cake. Cut each slice of pound cake in half diagonally to make 2 triangles. Arrange the cake triangles in a single layer on a baking sheet and brush them with the liqueur mixture. Set aside 12 triangles for the top of the cake.

5. Line the bottom and side of the cheesecloth-lined bowl with 12 cake triangles, placing them in a sunburst pattern with the liqueur-brushed sides facing up. Fill in the gaps with smaller pieces of the extra cake. Do not overlap the triangles. Set the bowl aside.

6. Coarsely chop 2 ounces of the chocolate. Place it in a microwave-safe glass dish and heat in the microwave on high power until melted, about 1 minute, stirring after 30 seconds. Let the melted chocolate cool to room temperature.

7. Place the 2 cups of cream and ¾ cup of confectioners' sugar in the chilled bowl and beat with an electric mixer on high speed until firm peaks form, 3 to 4 minutes. Finely chop 3 ounces of the chocolate. Fold the finely chopped chocolate and the almonds and hazelnuts into the whipped cream mixture. Using a rubber spatula, spread half of the whipped cream mixture over the cake triangles, covering them completely but leaving a well in the center.

8. Fold the melted chocolate into the remaining whipped cream mixture and spoon this into the well in the center of the cake triangles. Arrange the 12 reserved cake triangles, liqueur-brushed side down, on top of the whipped cream, trimming them to fit. Pull up the cheesecloth to cover the cake or cover the top with plastic wrap. Place a round baking pan on top of the cake triangles and weigh down the pan with 2 or 3 cans of food to compact the filling. Refrigerate the cake for at least 4 hours, or as long as overnight.

9. Make the ganache: Place the 8 ounces of chocolate in a large stainless steel mixing bowl. Place the ¾ cup of cream in a small, heavy saucepan over medium heat and bring to a boil, stirring. Remove the cream from the heat and pour it over the chocolate. Stir with a wooden spoon until the chocolate has melted. Stir in the 1 tablespoon of grappa or brandy. Let the ganache stand at room temperature for about 10 minutes.

10. When you are ready to frost the cake, pull back the cheesecloth or remove the plastic wrap from the top of the bowl. Invert the cake onto a serving plate and remove the cheesecloth. Frost the cake with the ganache. The cake can be refrigerated, uncovered or in a cake saver, until the ganache sets, about 1 hour.

11. When ready to serve, garnish the cake with an edible flower or with maraschino cherries and dust it with the 1 tablespoon of sifted confectioners' sugar.

NOTE: Semisweet baking chocolate comes in bars that are scored so that they can be broken into 1 ounce segments; you can break off as much as you need for the cake and the ganache.

TEN WAYS TO DRESS UP FROZEN POUND CAKE

Let a loaf of frozen pound cake do the work for you. Thaw it, cut it into slices, and serve it with:

1. *Sweetened sliced peaches and whipped cream*

2. *Sweetened strawberry halves and sour cream*

3. *Fresh blueberries and lemon curd*

4. *Hot fudge sauce, whipped cream, and maraschino cherries*

5. *Sliced bananas, warm caramel sauce, and a splash of rum*

6. *Raspberry sorbet and fresh raspberries*

7. *Crushed pineapple sautéed in butter with brown sugar*

8. *Coffee ice cream and grated semisweet chocolate*

9. *Strawberry ice cream*

10. *Crème de menthe, hot fudge sauce, whipped cream, and a sprig of fresh mint*

WHAT CAN I BRING TO THE BAKE SALE?

There's really no limit. Bring a whole cake, a pie, or a dozen bar cookies, ready for someone's freezer. To make it easy for everyone, place the cake on a cardboard square covered with aluminum foil, the pie in a disposable foil tin, or the cookies on a paper plate or in a plastic bag. Cover the goodies with plastic wrap, and add a label to the package with the name of the recipe and a little something interesting about it—is it a family recipe, or perfect for freezing, or made from local peaches? Then, if it fits, tie a loose raffia bow around the package. Everything is more inviting when it looks like a present.

But don't stop there. To ensure an incredible bake sale success serve beverages, such as chilled lemonade, bottled water, spiced warm cider, or hot coffee. To go with the beverages, sell individual cookies, bars, even slices of cake. And you can also sell personalized recipe cards, monogrammed aprons and hand towels, or pretty baskets for toting the baked goodies home.

A DOZEN BAKE SALE FAVORITES

Here are a dozen of my bake sale "must-makes" from this chapter. But don't just take my word for it—have fun finding twelve favorites of your own!

1. Lelia's Easy Chocolate Pound Cake (see page 347)

2. Fresh Apple Cake with Caramel Glaze (see page 356)

3. Sixty-Minute Caramel Cake (see page 359)

4. The Best Chocolate Chip Cookies (see page 378)

5. Classic Peanut Butter Cookies (see page 384)

6. Barbara's Oatmeal Raisin Cookies (see page 386)

7. Lemon Squares (see page 395)

8. Easy Linzer Bars (see page 398)

9. Seven-Layer Bars (see page 400)

10. Bebe's Chess Cake (see page 402)

11. Nashville Fudge Pie (see page 412)

12. Shirley's Snickerdoodles (see page 382)

COOKIES AND BARS

Everyone eagerly devours cookies, bars, and brownies. They're the perfect dessert to tote to a gathering, easily packed into plastic bags and cardboard boxes or, in the case of bars, they can travel right in the pan in which they were baked.

Cookies are not only most children's dessert of choice, adults find them irresistible as well. No matter the season, a simple plate of cookies or bars is guaranteed to please. Peanut butter, chocolate chip, oatmeal, and snickerdoodle cookies are perennial favorites. You can't go wrong serving these by the basketful. In the spring and summer opt for the classic Lemon Squares—a sublime combination of lemon pie and shortbread cookie baked in one pan.

Or try my mom's chess cake, a light blondie that's beloved by all.

When fall rolls around, think bake sales and road trips. The best bars for packing are the seven-layer ones and, of course, my quick chocolate chip brownies with that delicious gooey, cheesecakelike topping.

What's left? The winter holidays. Turn to Butter Pecan Sugar Cookies, Thumbprint Cookies, Coconut Almond Macaroons, and Holiday Fruit Drops—all my family's favorites at Christmastime. And don't forget the Easy Linzer Bars, a dandy of a recipe that begins with a cake mix.

When you show up with a batch of cookies, bars, or brownies, everyone will think you're sweet.

The Best Chocolate Chip Cookies

MAKES ABOUT 4 DOZEN COOKIES

PREP: 15 MINUTES ✳ CHILL: 30 MINUTES ✳ BAKE: ABOUT 14 MINUTES

I HAD BEEN FRUSTRATED THAT MY CHOCOLATE CHIP cookies varied from batch to batch. Sometimes flat, sometimes domed; sometimes chewy, sometimes crisp. My family didn't complain, but I didn't think they were worthy of taking anywhere! So I began that painful but delicious task of testing to come up with this chewy, buttery, flavorful, and reliable chocolate chip cookie. To keep the cookies uniform in size it's best to let the cookie dough chill for about an hour before baking. And you want to measure the flour carefully because too much will make a dry cookie. I like walnuts or pecans in these cookies because the nuts tend to cut the sweetness and marry nicely with the chocolate. Add a handful of quick-cooking oats or a small handful of sweetened dried cranberries if you're feeling festive.

1 cup (2 sticks) butter, at room temperature
1 cup packed light brown sugar
1 cup granulated sugar
1 tablespoon pure vanilla extract
3 large eggs
3 cups all-purpose flour
1 teaspoon baking soda
¼ teaspoon salt
3 cups semisweet chocolate chips
1 cup chopped walnuts or pecans

1. Place the butter, brown sugar, and granulated sugar in a large mixing bowl and beat with an electric mixer on low speed until the mixture lightens, about 1 minute. Add the vanilla and eggs and beat on medium-low speed until smooth and the eggs are incorporated, about 2 minutes.

2. Place the flour, baking soda, and salt in a small bowl and stir with a fork to combine. Spoon the dry ingredients on top of the butter mixture and beat on low speed until it just pulls together, scraping down the side of the bowl as needed. Fold in the chocolate chips and nuts. Cover the bowl with plastic wrap and refrigerate the cookie dough for 30 minutes to 1 hour.

3. Place a rack in the center of the oven and preheat the oven to 350°F.

4. Spoon heaping tablespoons of cookie dough 2 to 3 inches apart on an ungreased baking sheet. Bake the cookies until the edges are lightly browned but the centers are still a little soft to the touch, 12 to 14 minutes. Remove the baking sheet from the oven and let the cookies cool on it until they firm up, about 3 minutes. Using a metal spatula, transfer the cookies to wire racks to cool completely. Refrigerate the remaining cookie dough as the first batch bakes. Scrape the baking sheet and let it cool, then repeat the process with the remaining cookie dough.

BIG BATCH: *You can absolutely double or triple this recipe. Make two or three batches of dough at a time, and you will be able to bake all the cookies in one afternoon. Freeze them for later in aluminum foil and resealable plastic bags or in plastic containers with snap-on lids; they'll keep for up to three months. Let them thaw on the kitchen counter—it will take about 2 hours.*

RECIPE REMINDERS

Made for

Prep notes

Don't forget

Special touches

Bring again

Butter Pecan Sugar Cookies

MAKES 4 TO 5 DOZEN COOKIES

PREP: 12 MINUTES ✳ BAKE: ABOUT 10 MINUTES

TOTE NOTES

Tote Butter Pecan Sugar Cookies arranged on a pretty platter covered with plastic wrap or in a pretty tin lined with waxed paper. What could be easier?

SUGAR COOKIES ARE GREAT ANYTIME BUT ESPECIALLY during the winter, rolled out and cut into holiday shapes, coated with cinnamon and sugar like Shirley's Snickerdoodles on page 382, or studded with toffee bits, as they are here. My cousin Joe would often tell us not to get him anything for Christmas except a box of homemade sugar cookies, and he was onto something— what a treat! These cookies will be a treat for you, too, because your kitchen smells heavenly while they bake. Take them to friends and neighbors, or to a bridal or baby shower. Or, wrap them up for your cousin Joe.

12 tablespoons (1½ sticks) butter, at room temperature

1 cup sugar

1 large egg

1 teaspoon pure vanilla extract

2 cups all-purpose flour

1½ teaspoons baking powder

¼ teaspoon baking soda

½ cup toffee bits (see Note)

½ cup finely chopped pecans (optional)

1. Place a rack in the center of the oven and preheat the oven to 350°F.

2. Place the butter and sugar in a large mixing bowl and beat with an electric mixer on medium-low speed until the sugar is incorporated, about 1 minute. Add the egg and vanilla and continue to beat on medium-low speed until the mixture is creamy and thickened, about 1 minute.

3. Place the flour, baking powder, and baking soda in a small bowl and stir with a fork to combine. Add the dry ingredients to the butter mixture and beat on low speed until well mixed, about 1 minute, scraping down the side of the bowl as needed. Using a wooden spoon, fold in the toffee bits and pecans, if desired.

4. Spoon 1-inch balls of dough 2 inches apart on an ungreased baking sheet. Bake the cookies until the edges are golden brown but the centers are still a little soft to the touch, 9 to 11 minutes. Using a metal spatula, transfer the cookies immediately from the baking sheet to wire racks to cool. Scrape the baking sheet and let it cool, then repeat the process with the remaining cookie dough.

NOTE: You can find toffee bits in the baking aisle along with chocolate chips.

WANT THE PLEASURE OF SIMPLE SUGAR COOKIES? Omit the nuts. Omit the toffee bits. Press down on the cookie dough with a glass dipped in granulated sugar just before baking. Delicious.

BIG BATCH: *You can double this recipe and freeze the dough. When you are ready to bake, let the dough come to room temperature, then spoon it onto baking sheets and proceed with the recipe.*

RECIPE REMINDERS

Made for

Prep notes

Don't forget

Special touches

Bring again

Shirley's Snickerdoodles

MAKES ABOUT 4½ DOZEN COOKIES

PREP: 15 MINUTES ✳ BAKE: ABOUT 10 MINUTES

TOTE NOTES

Tote the snickerdoodles in a tin or box and they'll arrive unbroken. Bring along an attractive platter to arrange them on.

PLAN AHEAD

You can bake the cookies days in advance. Stored in a tightly covered tin or box, snickerdoodles will stay moist for nearly a week.

SHIRLEY HUTSON OF NASHVILLE IS A WONDERFUL cook and baker—and mother to Martha Bowden who helps me test recipes. Martha raved endlessly about her mother's snickerdoodle cookies, and I finally broke down and asked her for the recipe. I'm glad I did. Who knows where the old word *snickerdoodle* comes from, but the cookies, which are rolled in cinnamon and sugar before baking, are can't-eat-only-one good.

FOR THE DOUGH
1½ cups sugar
8 tablespoons (1 stick) butter,
  at room temperature
½ cup vegetable shortening (no trans fat)
1 teaspoon pure vanilla extract
2 large eggs
2¾ cups all-purpose flour
2 teaspoons cream of tartar
1 teaspoon baking soda

FOR THE TOPPING
¼ cup plus 1 tablespoon sugar
2 teaspoons ground cinnamon

1. Place a rack in the upper third of the oven and preheat the oven to 375°F.

2. Make the cookie dough: Place the 1½ cups of sugar and the butter and shortening in a large mixing bowl and beat with an electric mixer on medium speed until creamy, about 2 minutes, scraping down the side of the bowl once. Add the vanilla and the eggs, one at a time, continuing to beat on medium speed for about 30 seconds.

3. Place the flour, cream of tartar, and baking soda in a bowl and stir with a fork to combine. Add the dry ingredients to the butter mixture and beat on low speed until incorporated, scraping down the side of the bowl as needed.

4. Make the topping: Stir together the ¼ cup plus 1 tablespoon of sugar and the cinnamon in a shallow bowl.

5. Using a teaspoon, scoop the cookie dough into balls about 1¼ inches in diameter. The dough will be soft but manageable. Roll the balls of dough in the cinnamon-sugar mixture until evenly coated. Place them on an ungreased baking sheet about 2 inches apart.

6. Bake the cookies until the edges are lightly golden but the centers are still a little soft to the touch, 8 to 10 minutes. Remove the baking sheet from the oven and let the cookies rest until they firm up, 1 to 2 minutes. Using a metal spatula, transfer the cookies to wire racks to cool completely. Scrape the baking sheet, then repeat the process with the remaining cookie dough, letting the baking sheet cool first so the dough does not spread too much.

BIG BATCH: *You can double this recipe; add a little ground nutmeg to the topping for half of them just for fun.*

RECIPE REMINDERS

Made for

Prep notes

Don't forget

Special touches

Bring again

Classic Peanut Butter Cookies

MAKES ABOUT 3 DOZEN COOKIES

PREP: 15 MINUTES * BAKE: 10 MINUTES

TOTE NOTES

Depending upon the occasion, pack the peanut butter cookies in a cute box or pile them in a pretty lined basket and tie the box or basket handle with a bow before toting.

PLAN AHEAD

The cookies will keep for a week; they don't need to be refrigerated.

P EANUT BUTTER COOKIES WERE ONE OF THE FIRST cookies I learned to bake. This recipe is so straightforward that it is perfect for beginning cooks. It's also a dream for advanced bakers, who will appreciate the genuine flavor, comfort factor, and dependability of the cookies. For a grand cookie buffet, bake these along with chocolate chip and oatmeal cookies. Bring a tinful to work or to school and you'll find they disappear quickly. You can dress up this recipe by sprinkling some chopped Reese's peanut butter cups or chopped roasted peanuts on each cookie before baking, or don't add anything—both crisp and chewy, and unadulterated, these are just the way a peanut butter cookie should be.

8 tablespoons (1 stick) unsalted butter,
    at room temperature
½ cup creamy peanut butter
½ packed cup light brown sugar
½ cup plus 2 tablespoons granulated sugar
1 large egg
½ teaspoon pure vanilla extract
1½ cups all-purpose flour
1 teaspoon baking soda
¼ teaspoon salt

1. Place a rack in the center of the oven and preheat the oven to 375°F.

2. Place the butter, peanut butter, brown sugar, and ½ cup of the granulated sugar in a large mixing bowl and beat with an electric mixer on medium speed until creamy and lighter in color, about 2 minutes, scraping down the side of the bowl once. Add the egg and vanilla and beat on medium speed until combined, about 30 seconds.

3. Place the flour, baking soda, and salt in a bowl and stir with a fork to combine. Add the dry ingredients to the peanut butter mixture and beat on low speed until just incorporated, scraping down the side of the bowl as needed.

4. Spoon heaping tablespoons of the dough 2 inches apart on an ungreased baking sheet. Place the remaining 2 tablespoons of granulated sugar in a shallow bowl. Dip a fork in the sugar and press each cookie twice with the fork to leave a dusting of sugar in a crosshatch design.

5. Bake the cookies until they are lightly browned, 8 to 10 minutes. Remove the baking sheet from the oven and let the cookies rest until they firm up, 2 to 3 minutes. Using a metal spatula, transfer the cookies to wire racks to cool completely. Scrape the baking sheet, then repeat the process with the remaining cookie dough, letting the baking sheet cool first so the dough does not spread too much.

BIG BATCH: *This recipe doubles well. You can fold a cup of miniature chocolate chips into one batch, if desired.*

Made for

Prep notes

Don't forget

Special touches

Bring again

Barbara's Oatmeal Raisin Cookies

MAKES ABOUT 6 DOZEN COOKIES

PREP: 20 MINUTES ✳ CHILL: 1 HOUR ✳ BAKE: ABOUT 8 MINUTES

TOTE NOTES

The best way to tote these cookies is to arrange them in a deep box, tin, or plastic tub in single layers separated by waxed paper. This cushions the cookies so they won't break and they won't stick together.

You can also arrange the cookies on a tray and bring it covered with plastic wrap.

PLAN AHEAD

Bake the cookies a day or two in advance and store them, covered, at room temperature. Or, you can prepare the dough a day ahead and refrigerate it, covered, then bake the cookies in the morning, before you're ready to go.

THIS RECIPE COMES FROM MY SISTER SUSAN'S mother-in-law, Barbara Anderson, who lives on Dataw Island in South Carolina. Susan kept telling me how wonderful Barbara's oatmeal cookies were, and after I begged for the recipe, she sent it my way. These wonderful oatmeal cookies are the best I have ever tasted. There are two secrets—soaking the raisins for ten minutes in warm water so they plump up and refrigerating the dough so the cookies hold their shape while baking. Better pour the milk now because these disappear quickly.

1 cup raisins

1 cup warm water

2 cups all-purpose flour

1 teaspoon baking soda

1 teaspoon salt

1 teaspoon ground cinnamon

1 cup (2 sticks) unsalted butter, at room temperature

1 cup granulated sugar

1 cup light brown sugar, not packed

2 large eggs

2 cups quick-cooking oats

1 cup chopped pecans (optional)

1. Place the raisins in a small bowl, pour the warm water over them, and let soak until plump, about 10 minutes.

2. Meanwhile, place the flour, baking soda, salt, and cinnamon in a small mixing bowl and stir with a fork to combine. Set the flour mixture aside.

3. Place the butter, granulated sugar, and brown sugar in a large mixing bowl and beat with an electric mixer on medium speed until creamy and lighter in color, about 2 minutes. Add the eggs, one at a time, beating well on medium speed after each addition, 10 to 15 seconds. Turn off the machine. Dump the flour mixture into the bowl and beat on low just until the dough comes together, about 30 seconds.

4. Drain the raisins. Stir the raisins, oats, and pecans, if desired, into the dough until just combined. Cover the bowl with plastic wrap and refrigerate the cookie dough for at least 1 hour or as long as overnight.

5. Place a rack in the center of the oven and preheat the oven to 375°F.

6. Spoon and roll the dough into 1-inch balls and place them 2 inches apart on an ungreased baking sheet. Bake the cookies until they are lightly browned but the centers are still a little soft to the touch, 7 to 9 minutes. Remove the baking sheet from the oven. Using a metal spatula, transfer the cookies to wire racks to cool. Scrape the baking sheet and let it cool, then repeat the process with the remaining cookie dough.

BIG BATCH: *You can make two batches of dough at one time. If you have two ovens, use both of them and enlist helpers to scoop out the cookie dough. This is a great way to bake ahead for teacher presents or a big party. Wrapped in aluminum foil, then placed in resealable plastic bags or plastic containers with lids, the cookies can be frozen for up to three months. Let them thaw on the kitchen counter; it will take about 3 hours.*

RECIPE REMINDERS

Made for

Prep notes

Don't forget

Special touches

Bring again

Thumbprint Cookies

MAKES 2 DOZEN COOKIES

PREP: 45 MINUTES ✳ CHILL: 1 HOUR ✳ BAKE: ABOUT 12 MINUTES

TOTE NOTES

Tote the Thumbprint Cookies in a tin or on a pretty platter covered with plastic wrap.

PLAN AHEAD

You can bake these cookies a few days in advance. They will keep for four to five days at room temperature stored between layers of waxed paper in an airtight tin.

THUMBPRINT COOKIES ARE A LOT OF FUN TO MAKE any time of the year but especially at holiday time. You press your thumb into the center of each cookie and then fill the well with your choice of jam, preserves, or lemon curd. I like to mix and match the filling with a nut coating. Try raspberry jam with finely chopped pecans, apricot jam with chopped toasted almonds, lemon curd with finely chopped walnuts, and cherry jam with flaked coconut. These cookies are gorgeous served on a silver tray or tucked into a holiday gift box.

    4 tablespoons (½ stick) butter, at room temperature
    ¼ cup solid vegetable shortening (no trans fat)
    ¼ cup packed light brown sugar
    1 large egg
    1 teaspoon pure vanilla extract
    1 cup all-purpose flour
    Dash salt
    1 cup finely chopped pecans, almonds, or walnuts,
        or 1 cup sweetened flaked coconut
    ½ cup seedless raspberry jam, apricot jam, lemon curd,
        or cherry jam, for the filling

1. Place the butter, shortening, and brown sugar in a large mixing bowl and beat with an electric mixer on medium speed until light and fluffy, about 2 minutes. Separate the egg and set the egg white aside in the refrigerator, covered. Add the egg yolk and vanilla to the butter mixture and beat for 30 seconds.

Add the flour and salt and beat on low speed just until combined, about 1 minute. Cover the bowl with plastic wrap and refrigerate the cookie dough for at least 1 hour or as long as overnight.

2. Place a rack in the center of the oven and preheat the oven to 350°F.

3. Spread the chopped nuts or coconut on waxed paper or a small plate. Place the reserved egg white in a small bowl and slightly beat it. Roll the cookie dough into 24 one-inch balls. Using a dinner fork, roll each dough ball (1 or 2 at a time) in the egg white. Immediately place the balls on top of the nuts or coconut to coat them, pressing on the balls lightly so that the nuts or coconut stick. Place the balls of dough on an ungreased baking sheet about 1 inch apart.

4. Bake the cookies for 5 minutes, then remove them from the oven. Leave the oven on. Using your thumb or index finger, quickly press an indention (a "well") into each cookie. Return the cookies to the oven and bake until golden brown, 6 to 8 minutes longer. If you are using coconut, it will turn dark brown but it will not burn, but do watch the time closely. Remove the baking sheet from the oven, and using a metal spatula, transfer the cookies to wire racks to cool.

5. Using a teaspoon, fill the indentation in each cookie with a little of the filling of your choice.

BIG BATCH: *You can easily double this recipe; use more than one filling for a variety of flavors.*

RECIPE REMINDERS

Made for

Prep notes

Don't forget

Special touches

Bring again

Coconut Almond Macaroons

MAKES ABOUT 3 DOZEN COOKIES

PREP: 25 MINUTES ∗ BAKE: ABOUT 20 MINUTES

TOTE NOTES

The macaroons should be stored in an airtight tin or box. Tote them in the container, then serve them on a pretty glass cake stand or a silver tray.

PLAN AHEAD

You can bake the macaroons a day or two ahead.

THESE MACAROONS ARE PERFECT FOR A BRIDAL shower, an anniversary celebration, a tea party, New Year's Eve—just about any celebration where you want to share a tray of sophisticated cookies. They are rich and chewy one-bite confections. If you like, go over the top and dip half of each macaroon into a melted chocolate coating.

½ cup slivered almonds
2 loosely packed cups sweetened flaked coconut
⅔ cup sugar
¼ cup all-purpose flour
¼ teaspoon salt
4 large egg whites
1 teaspoon pure almond extract
½ teaspoon pure vanilla extract
Vegetable oil spray (optional), for misting the pan

1. Place a rack in the center of the oven and preheat the oven to 325°F.

2. When the oven is hot, place the almonds on a rimmed baking sheet and toast them in the oven until golden brown, 12 to 15 minutes. Remove the baking sheet from the oven and let the almonds cool on it.

3. Meanwhile, place the coconut, sugar, flour, and salt in a large mixing bowl and stir to combine. Add the egg whites, almond extract, and vanilla, stir until blended, and set aside.

4. Place the cooled almonds in a food processor fitted with a steel blade. Process in pulses until the almonds are ground, about 10 seconds; you will have about ⅓ cup of ground almonds. Fold the ground almonds into the macaroon dough.

5. Lightly mist a baking sheet with vegetable oil spray or place a nonstick baking mat on it. Spoon teaspoons of the dough 1 inch apart on the baking sheet.

6. Bake the macaroons until they begin to turn golden brown but the centers are still a little soft to the touch, 20 to 22 minutes. Remove the baking sheet from the oven and let the macaroons cool on it for about 5 minutes. Using a metal spatula, transfer the cookies to wire racks to cool completely. Scrape the baking sheet and let it cool, then repeat the process with the remaining macaroon dough.

BIG BATCH: *You can easily double and triple the macaroon recipe. Just leave yourself plenty of time to bake all those cookies!*

RECIPE REMINDERS

Made for

Prep notes

Don't forget

Special touches

Bring again

M
E
N
U

HOLIDAY COOKIE SWAPS

How many places can you show up with one kind of cookie and come home with eight to ten more? At a cookie swap, where you bring dozens of your favorite, you carry home enough of an assortment to fill cookie trays for the entire month of December. It's the perfect way to take the stress out of the holidays. If you are organizing a cookie swap with friends, ask each to bake a different holiday cookie. This might be a childhood favorite or a hometown tradition. Ask ahead of time what cookies everyone plans on baking so there won't be any duplications. On the day of the cookie swap, everybody should arrive with enough cookies for all to take home a dozen of each type. Eight people? Bake eight dozen cookies. Offer a light lunch or hors d'oeuvres and Champagne, and place the cookies on a buffet table so they're ready to pack. You'll need to supply resealable plastic bags, pretty tins, even plastic disposable containers for toting the cookies home. Ask everyone to take a turn at the cookie bar. They'll go home with a bag full of thumbprints, cut-outs, gingerbread men—you name it!

Here are some goodies from this chapter to bake up.

BUTTER PECAN SUGAR COOKIES, *page 380*

✳

SHIRLEY'S SNICKERDOODLES, *page 382*

✳

BARBARA'S OATMEAL RAISIN COOKIES, *page 386*

✳

THUMBPRINT COOKIES, *page 388*

✳

COCONUT ALMOND MACAROONS, *page 390*

✳

HOLIDAY FRUIT DROPS, *page 393*

Holiday Fruit Drops

MAKES 7 TO 8 DOZEN COOKIES

PREP: 30 TO 35 MINUTES ✷ CHILL: 1 HOUR ✷ BAKE: ABOUT 10 MINUTES

L IKE LITTLE BITES OF FRUITCAKE, THESE SOFT COOKIES, full of candied cherries, dates, raisins, and pecans, are a taste of the holidays. Bake them in the weeks leading up to Christmas, tote them to parties, tuck them into baskets for gifts, and keep some on hand for Christmas Eve. As with fruitcake, the fruit drops stay moist and, if stored in an airtight tin, improve in flavor after a day or two.

TOTE NOTES

Store and tote the fruit drops in a resealable plastic bag or airtight tin, then arrange them on a festive tray when you arrive.

PLAN AHEAD

The fruit drops taste better made several days in advance.

1½ cups chopped pecans
1 cup red candied cherries
1 cup green candied cherries
1 cup chopped dates
1 cup golden raisins
8 tablespoons (1 stick) butter
½ cup solid vegetable shortening (no trans fat)
2 packed cups light brown sugar
2 large eggs
½ cup buttermilk
1½ teaspoons pure vanilla extract
3½ cups all-purpose flour
1 teaspoon baking soda
½ teaspoon salt

1. Place the pecans, red and green candied cherries, dates, and raisins in a large mixing bowl and stir to combine. Set aside.

2. Place the butter, shortening, and brown sugar in a large mixing bowl and beat with an electric mixer on medium speed until combined, about 2 minutes. Add the eggs, one at a time, then the buttermilk and vanilla, mixing until well blended, about 1 minute.

3. Place the flour, baking soda, and salt in a bowl and stir with a fork to combine. Slowly add the dry ingredients to the butter mixture, beating on medium speed, until just blended. Using a large wooden spoon, add the dried fruit and nuts to the dough and stir until blended. Cover the bowl with plastic wrap and refrigerate the cookie dough for at least 1 hour or as long as overnight.

4. Place a rack in the center of the oven and preheat the oven to 375°F.

5. Spoon rounded teaspoonfuls of dough about 2 inches apart on an ungreased baking sheet. Bake the cookies until they are lightly browned around the edges, but the centers are still a little soft to the touch, 8 to 10 minutes. Using a metal spatula, transfer the cookies to wire racks to cool completely. Scrape the baking sheet and let it cool, then repeat the process with the remaining cookie dough.

Lemon Squares

MAKES 2 DOZEN SQUARES

**PREP: 15 TO 20 MINUTES ✳ BAKE: 40 TO 45 MINUTES
COOL: 30 MINUTES**

M Y FRIEND JOHN WILLIAMS LIVED IN NEW YORK CITY a while ago. A Southern boy, he naturally brought something when he was invited to dine at a friend's apartment. "I carried Lemon Squares on the subway with me to dinner, and people were staring at me, wondering what I was carrying in that box," John told me when he found out I was writing this book. I can't imagine that many Lemon Squares are carried on New York subways, and I don't understand how John was able to control himself transporting such delicious contraband. It takes a lot of willpower to carry around a box of homemade Lemon Squares and not open the lid.

FOR THE CRUST
1½ cups all-purpose flour
⅔ cup confectioners' sugar
12 tablespoons (1½ sticks) butter

FOR THE FILLING AND TOPPING
3 large eggs
1½ cups granulated sugar
3 tablespoons all-purpose flour
¼ cup fresh lemon juice (from 2 large lemons)
1 tablespoon grated lemon zest
1 tablespoon confectioners' sugar

1. Prepare the crust: Place a rack in the center of the oven and preheat the oven to 350°F.

TOTE NOTES

It's easiest to tote the Lemon Squares in the baking pan; cut them before you are ready to go, but leave them in the pan. Bring a tray to arrange them on when you arrive.

If you don't want to bring the baking pan, place the Lemon Squares on a platter and loosely cover them with plastic wrap.

PLAN AHEAD

Bake the squares a day in advance. When cool, cover the pan with plastic wrap. Before serving, dust with confectioners' sugar and cut into squares.

**BAKE MINE WITH
BLUEBERRIES**

*To make Lemon Squares with
blueberries, sprinkle ¾ cup
of fresh blueberries over
the lemon filling before you
bake it. With the added
blueberries they'll need to
bake the full 25 minutes.*

2. Place the flour and ⅔ cup of confectioners' sugar in the bowl of a food processor fitted with a steel blade. Process in a few pulses to combine.

3. Cut the butter into tablespoons and place in a medium-size microwave-safe glass bowl. Heat the butter on high power in the microwave until it melts, 50 seconds to 1 minute. Transfer the hot butter to the food processor with the flour mixture and process until the dough comes together, about 10 seconds. Transfer the dough to a 13 by 9–inch metal baking pan and, using your fingers, press the dough into the bottom of the baking pan. Bake the crust until it is lightly browned around the edges, about 20 minutes.

4. While the crust is baking, make the filling: Place the eggs, granulated sugar, flour, lemon juice, and lemon zest in a large

**M
E
N
U**

BOOK CLUB LUNCH

What a wonderful way to entertain—and it's just for lunch. Grill the chicken and make the pasta salad ahead of time. Have one person bring some sliced fruit, another bring bread, and a third bring an easy dessert like Lemon Squares.

GRILLED CHICKEN FOR A CROWD, *page 228*
✳
GREEK PASTA SALAD, *page 136*
✳
FRUIT
✳
CRUSTY BREAD
✳
LEMON SQUARES, *page 395*

mixing bowl and whisk until the mixture is lemon colored
and thickened, about 2 minutes. Pour the filling over the hot
crust.

5. Bake the Lemon Squares until the filling is set and
lightly browned, 20 to 25 minutes. Let cool completely,
about 30 minutes; if you have the time put the pan in the
refrigerator for an hour, the squares will be easier to cut.

6. Dust with the 1 tablespoon of confectioners' sugar and
cut into roughly 2-inch squares.

Easy Linzer Bars

MAKES 24 TO 30 BARS

PREP: 20 MINUTES * BAKE: 35 TO 40 MINUTES
COOL: 10 TO 15 MINUTES

TOTE NOTES

To tote, leave the cut linzer bars in the pan, dust them with confectioners' sugar, and cover the pan with plastic wrap. You can remove the bars from the pan with a small spatula or knife when you arrive. Bring a platter on which to arrange them.

PLAN AHEAD

The linzer bars will keep for three to four days at room temperature.

I've HUNG ON TO THIS RECIPE FROM LAURA CUNNINGHAM, of Parsippany, New Jersey, who entered it in my online newsletter recipe contest and won. These are people-pleasing bars—moist, colorful, and full of the raspberry and almond flavors of a traditional linzer tart but with the added goodness of lemon and white chocolate. And, as with the other bars here, these are great to take places because they can be baked and toted in the same pan, especially if that pan has a handy snap-on lid.

1 package (6 ounces) slivered almonds
1 package (18¼ ounces) plain yellow cake mix
12 tablespoons (1½ sticks) unsalted butter, melted
⅓ cup evaporated milk (from a 5-ounce can)
½ teaspoon ground cinnamon
¼ teaspoon ground nutmeg
2 cups (18 ounces) raspberry jam
1 teaspoon grated lemon zest
1½ cups white chocolate chips
Confectioners' sugar, for dusting the bars

1. Preheat the oven to 350°F.

2. Finely chop ¾ cup almonds; you should have about 1 cup. Set the remaining almonds aside for the topping.

3. Place the cake mix, butter, evaporated milk, cinnamon, nutmeg, and finely chopped almonds in a large mixing bowl.

Stir with a wooden spoon until the mixture is moistened and the ingredients are well combined. Press half of the batter evenly into the bottom of a 13 by 9–inch metal baking pan. Place the pan in the oven and bake the crust until it browns around the edges, about 10 minutes. Set the remaining batter aside.

4. Meanwhile, place the raspberry jam and lemon zest in a medium-size saucepan over low heat and cook, stirring constantly, until the jam is warmed through and you are able to pour it, 2 to 3 minutes.

5. Immediately after removing the pan from the oven scatter the white chocolate chips evenly over the crust. Pour the warm raspberry jam mixture over the chocolate chips. Spoon dollops of the reserved batter on top of the raspberry jam; it will not completely cover the jam. Sprinkle the reserved slivered almonds on top and bake until the top is golden brown, 25 to 30 minutes.

6. Let the linzer bars cool for 10 to 15 minutes, then cut them. Dust the tops with confectioners' sugar, and remove the bars from the pan.

RECIPE REMINDERS

Made for

Prep notes

Don't forget

Special touches

Bring again

Seven-Layer Bars

MAKES 30 BARS

PREP: 8 TO 10 MINUTES ✳ BAKE: ABOUT 25 MINUTES
COOL: ABOUT 40 MINUTES

**TOTE
NOTES**

*Tote the Seven-Layer
Bars in a plastic storage
container and arrange
them on a tray when you
get to the gathering.*

*Or, place the bars in
decorative boxes lined
with waxed paper and
give them as festive gifts.*

PLAN AHEAD

*Seven-Layer Bars
will keep for three
to four days at room
temperature.*

I F A DESSERT COULD BE INDUCTED INTO A POTLUCK HALL
of fame, Seven-Layer Bars would be the first. I have
enjoyed these bars at picnics and parties all my life,
and if you have not baked them in a while, you should.
No other dessert bar offers so much satisfaction in one
bite: chewy layers of graham cracker crumbs, chocolate
chips, butterscotch chips, nuts, and coconut. If you're
counting, the two other layers are the melted butter that
coats the baking dish and the sweetened condensed milk
that holds everything together. My version is a little
different from the traditional recipe in that I slightly
increase the chocolate and decrease the coconut.

8 tablespoons (1 stick) unsalted butter
1½ cups graham cracker crumbs
   (from 12 whole crackers)
1⅓ cups semisweet chocolate chips
1 cup butterscotch chips
1 cup chopped walnuts or pecans
1 can (14 ounces) sweetened condensed milk
1 cup sweetened flaked coconut

1. Place a rack in the center of the oven and preheat the oven
to 350°F. Place the butter in a 13 by 9–inch glass or ceramic
baking dish and place it in the preheating oven until the butter
melts, about 10 minutes.

2. Remove the baking dish from the oven and swirl it to coat
the bottom and sides with butter. Spread the graham cracker

crumbs evenly over the bottom of the baking dish. First layer the chocolate chips, then the butterscotch chips, and then the nuts over the graham cracker crumbs. Pour the condensed milk over the nuts and top it with the coconut.

3. Bake the bars until the edges are golden brown, 25 to 28 minutes. Let the bars cool for about 40 minutes before cutting them. To get 30 bars, cut 6 on the long side and 5 on the short side of the baking dish. Transfer the bars to a plastic storage container lined with waxed paper until ready to use.

BIG BATCH: *This recipe can easily be doubled and tripled and baked in two or three baking dishes.*

PICK ME UP

There's an easy way to have perfectly cut bars. Before you fill the baking dish with batter, line it with aluminum foil so that the ends of the foil hang over the edges of the pan. After the bars have baked and cooled, remove them in one piece by taking hold of the foil edges and lifting everything up out of the baking dish. Place the whole bar on a cutting board and remove the foil. Then cut up the bars.

RECIPE REMINDERS

Made for

Prep notes

Don't forget

Special touches

Bring again

Bebe's Chess Cake

MAKES 30 BARS

PREP: 20 TO 25 MINUTES ⋆ BAKE: ABOUT 30 MINUTES
COOL: ABOUT 30 MINUTES

TOTE NOTES

These bars travel well; place them on a tray lined with paper doilies. Cover the tray with plastic wrap and you're ready to go.

PLAN AHEAD

You can bake the chess cake a day in advance and store it, covered, at room temperature. Or, bake it up to a week ahead of time, wrap it up, and freeze it.

THIS "CAKE" WAS THE BROWNIE OF MY YOUTH, and I have not a clue as to where my mother got the recipe. Probably from my grandmother, for it has a wonderfully nostalgic quality about it— delicate flavors, finely chopped pecans, a dusting of confectioners' sugar—all light and warm and loving. While the name suggests that someone thought this resembled chess pie, it doesn't really, because chess pie has cornmeal and vinegar or lemon juice in it. This version is actually a nice cakey butterscotch brownie, and my sister Susan and I make it all the time because it reminds us of our mother. Feel free to omit the pecans if you are making these for anyone who doesn't eat nuts.

> Vegetable oil spray, for misting the pan
> 2 cups all-purpose flour, plus flour for dusting the pan
> 2 packed cups light brown sugar
> ½ cup granulated sugar
> 1 cup (2 sticks) butter, melted
> 4 large eggs
> 2 teaspoons baking powder
> Pinch of salt
> 1 cup finely chopped pecans (optional)
> 1 tablespoon confectioners' sugar for dusting the cake

1. Place a rack in the center of the oven and preheat the oven to 325°F. Lightly mist a 13 by 9–inch metal baking pan with vegetable oil spray and dust it with flour. Shake out the excess flour. Set the baking pan aside.

2. Place the brown sugar and granulated sugar in a large mixing bowl and pour the melted butter over them. Beat with an electric mixer on low speed until combined, 1 to 2 minutes.

3. Separate the eggs and place the whites in a large mixing bowl and the yolks in the bowl with the sugar and butter. Beat the egg yolks and sugar mixture on medium speed until well combined, about 2 minutes.

4. Place the flour, baking powder, and salt in a small bowl and stir with a fork to combine. Add the dry ingredients to the sugar mixture and beat on low speed with the electric mixer or with a wooden spoon until just combined.

5. Using an electric mixer with clean beaters, beat the egg whites on high speed until stiff peaks form, about 3 minutes. Fold the egg whites into the batter and then fold in the pecans. Transfer the batter to the prepared baking pan, smoothing the top with a rubber spatula.

6. Bake the cake until it is well browned around the edges and still a little soft in the center, 28 to 32 minutes. Remove the pan from the oven and let the cake cool for about 30 minutes. Dust the cake with confectioners' sugar and cut it in the pan; to get 30 brownies, cut 6 on the long side and 5 on the short side of the baking dish.

BIG BATCH: *You can double this recipe, and the bars freeze well should you want to place one batch in the freezer. Remove the cooled bars from the baking pan and place them in plastic containers with tight-fitting lids before freezing them. They can be frozen for up to three months. Let them thaw on the kitchen counter; it will take about 3 hours.*

RECIPE REMINDERS

Made for

Prep notes

Don't forget

Special touches

Bring again

Chocolate Chip Brownies with Cream Cheese "Goo"

MAKES 16 BROWNIES

PREP: 15 MINUTES ∗ BAKE: ABOUT 45 MINUTES
COOL: 40 MINUTES

TOTE NOTES

Cut the brownies before you leave and place them on a pretty tray or platter. Cover them with plastic wrap and you're ready to go.

PLAN AHEAD

The brownies can be made the day before the gathering. Cover them with plastic wrap while they're still in the pan. Keep them refrigerated until you are ready to leave.

IT SEEMS UNNECESSARY TO MAKE CREAM CHEESE brownies from scratch when brownie mixes are so reliable and the most glorious part is the gooey layer of cream cheese. So when I make these, I sandwich the cheesecakelike layer between store-bought brownie batter. I like the Ghirardelli "double chocolate" brownie mix, but really any relatively simple brownie mix works in this recipe. Because these brownies are a little messy to slice, you need to let them cool for twenty minutes, then refrigerate them another twenty minutes before cutting them. For optimum slicing, freeze the brownies until they are nearly firm, then cut them into squares. Delicious.

FOR THE BROWNIE BATTER

Vegetable oil spray, for misting the pan

Flour, for dusting the pan

1 package (about 20 ounces; see Note) chocolate brownie mix

⅓ cup vegetable oil

1 large egg

⅓ cup warm water

½ cup semisweet chocolate chips

FOR THE CREAM CHEESE "GOO"

4 ounces (half an 8-ounce package) cream cheese, at room temperature

2 tablespoons (¼ stick) butter, at room temperature

¼ cup sugar

1 tablespoon all-purpose flour

1 large egg

½ teaspoon pure vanilla extract

1. Make the brownie batter: Place a rack in the center of the oven and preheat the oven to 325°F. Lightly mist a 9-inch square metal baking pan with vegetable oil spray and dust it with flour. Shake out the excess flour. Set the pan aside.

TEN TOPPERS
FOR A BOX OF BROWNIES

When making brownies from a mix, just before you place the pan of batter in the oven, why not sprinkle or spoon a handful of something yummy over the top.

1. Crushed peppermint candy

2. Chopped peppermint patties

3. Toffee bits

4. Chopped walnuts and semisweet chocolate chips

5. Dried sweetened cherries and milk chocolate chips

6. Chopped macadamia nuts and white chocolate chips

7. Minced dried apricots tossed with a dribble of almond extract

8. Miniature marshmallows and a chopped milk chocolate bar with almonds

9. Dollops of raspberry jam

10. M&M's

BROWNIES AND . . .

Ice cold milk—of course. Rich brewed coffee— naturally. But brownies also taste good with fresh lemonade, tea (both hot and iced), sparkling water with a slice of lime, fruit punch, and white or red sangria— and that's just the short list! Brownies make almost any beverage taste better.

2. Place the brownie mix, oil, 1 egg, and warm water in a large mixing bowl (or, follow the directions on the package of mix, adding what is needed). Using a wooden spoon, stir the brownie mix about 40 to 50 strokes, then fold in the chocolate chips.

3. Make the cream cheese "goo": Place the cream cheese, butter, sugar, flour, 1 egg, and the vanilla in a second large mixing bowl. Beat with an electric mixer on low speed until the batter is smooth, 1 to 2 minutes.

4. Transfer half of the brownie batter to the prepared baking pan and, using a rubber spatula, spread it out evenly to reach the corners. Spoon the cream cheese batter on top of the brownie batter, spreading it out with a clean rubber spatula to evenly reach the corners. Drop the remaining brownie batter by spoonfuls onto the cream cheese layer. Using a knife, drag the batter through the cream cheese layer to create a marbled effect.

5. Bake the brownies until the edges are set and the center is still a little soft, 45 to 48 minutes. Remove the pan from the oven and let the brownies cool for about 20 minutes. Place the pan in the refrigerator to cool for another 20 minutes before cutting the brownies into approximately 2-inch squares.

NOTE: Chocolate brownie mixes come in a range of sizes. You'll need one that is between 20 and 22 ounces for this recipe.

BIG BATCH: *To make a 13 by 9–inch pan of brownies for a larger crowd, buy two boxes of brownie mix and double the recipe for the cream cheese "goo." The larger pan will take about 10 minutes longer to bake and make 30 to 36 brownies.*

Pies and Other Sweets

Bring a pie, cobbler, or crumble to a potluck or picnic and people will smile. They're as welcome as a handshake. Pies tell a lot about you as a cook and a lot about the season in which you are baking. If it is fall, think pear, pecan, pumpkin, apple, and cranberry. When the weather warms up, bring on the fresh fruit—blackberries, blueberries, and peaches—as well as the perennial summer favorite, Key lime.

Today, baking pies couldn't be simpler, what with refrigerated pie crusts rolled out and ready to go. And then there are the handy frozen crusts. Throughout the recipes here I've sprinkled tips for making these shortcut crusts look homemade. Don't feel guilty about using them. Yes, homemade pie crust tastes better than store-bought, but it is what is in the crust that matters most. Some fantastic fillings await you. It's easy to tote your home-baked pies in special carriers with handles or in a sturdy shallow basket lined with a kitchen towel.

You won't find just pies in what follows: Try my favorite banana pudding recipe, a special tiramisu, and my friend Mindy's grilled figs. They're showstoppers, just like the pies, and easy to pack and go.

Georgia Pecan Pie

SERVES 8 (MAKES ONE 9-INCH PIE)

PREP: 10 MINUTES * BAKE: ABOUT 50 MINUTES
COOL: 1 HOUR

TOTE NOTES

Tote the pecan pie to the party in the pie pan (covered with plastic wrap) and slice it on-site.

PLAN AHEAD

You can bake the pie up to a day in advance and keep it, covered, in the refrigerator.

PECAN PIE DEVOTEES WILL TELL YOU THAT THERE IS only one right way to make pecan pie—there's the light corn syrup contingent and the dark corn syrup contingent. I love pecan pie made with either corn syrup, and yet they do produce different pies. The lighter syrup is just that—lighter. But dark corn syrup produces dreamy stuff in this authentic recipe I scribbled down years ago from the Georgia Pecan Commission. It is deep chestnut in color and both sweet and salty, gooey and crunchy. Bring this pie to an event and you will make new friends.

3 large eggs

1 cup sugar

1 cup dark corn syrup

1 teaspoon pure vanilla extract

3 tablespoons butter, melted and cooled

1½ cups coarsely chopped pecans or pecan halves

1 store-bought 9-inch piecrust, unbaked (see Note)

1. Place a rack in the center of the oven and preheat the oven to 350°F.

2. Place the eggs in a medium-size mixing bowl and whisk lightly. Add the sugar, corn syrup, vanilla, and butter and stir with a wooden spoon to combine. Stir in the pecans. Pour the filling into the unbaked pie crust.

3. Bake the pie until a toothpick inserted in the center comes out clean, 50 to 52 minutes. Place the pie on a wire rack to cool completely before slicing it, about 1 hour.

NOTE: If you are using a store-bought pie shell, you may want to slip the pie out of the foil pan and into a glass or ceramic pie pan. It will not only look nicer but also protect the pie better in transit.

Frozen piecrusts are prone to browning too quickly. You can shield the crust from overbrowning by placing pieces of aluminum foil around the edge of the pie pan to cover the crust as it bakes.

RECIPE REMINDERS

Made for

Prep notes

Don't forget

Special touches

Bring again

Bourbon Chocolate Chip Pecan Pie

SERVES 8 TO 10 (MAKES ONE 9-INCH DEEP-DISH PIE)

PREP: 20 MINUTES * BAKE: 50 TO 55 MINUTES * COOL: 10 MINUTES

TOTE NOTES

This is a gooey pie; the best way to tote it is in a pie saver, one of those round plastic containers with a lid. A pie saver is just the right size for a pie pan. Don't slice the pie until you arrive at the gathering.

PLAN AHEAD

The pecan pie can be baked the day before the gathering.

Don't think your eyes are playing tricks on you. This *is* the pie often served in May to celebrate the running of that most famous horse race, the Kentucky Derby. But I cannot call it Derby Pie because that is a trademarked name. So, bake this on Derby Day—and any other time you want a pecan and chocolate pie perfumed with bourbon. Served warm with the chocolate chips still melted, this is one of the best pies I have ever tasted. Honest.

1 store-bought frozen deep-dish 9-inch piecrust
2 large eggs
¾ cup sugar
⅔ cup light corn syrup
1 tablespoon flour
¼ cup bourbon
1 teaspoon pure vanilla extract
8 tablespoons (1 stick) butter, melted
1 heaping cup chopped pecans
1 cup semisweet chocolate chips

1. Place a rack in the center of the oven and preheat the oven to 350°F.

2. Unwrap the piecrust and allow it to thaw a little at room temperature while you prepare the filling. If you like, transfer the crust to a 9-inch glass or ceramic pie pan.

3. Place the eggs in a large mixing bowl and whisk until they are frothy, about 30 seconds. Add the sugar and corn syrup and whisk to blend for about 30 seconds. Add the flour, bourbon, vanilla, and butter. Whisk another 30 seconds. Using a wooden spoon, fold in the pecans and chocolate chips, then pour the filling into the piecrust.

4. Bake the pie until the crust and filling are golden brown, 50 to 55 minutes. Remove the pie from the oven and let it cool for about 10 minutes, then slice it and serve warm. Or, for cleaner slices, let the pie cool for about 1 hour, then slice.

RECIPE REMINDERS

Made for

Prep notes

Don't forget

Special touches

Bring again

Nashville Fudge Pie

SERVES 8 TO 10 (MAKES ONE 9-INCH PIE)

PREP: 15 MINUTES ✳ BAKE: 25 TO 30 MINUTES
COOL: AT LEAST 10 MINUTES

**TOTE
NOTES**

*Toted in a pie carrier
or just covered with
aluminum foil, the pie
should be sliced just
before serving. Don't
forget the ice cream or
the whipped cream. You
can bring the whipped
cream in a plastic
container with a lid;
transport it or the ice
cream in a cooler.*

PLAN AHEAD

*The fudge pie can be
baked the day before
the gathering. Cover it
with aluminum foil and
store at room temperature.*

WHAT DO YOU CALL A GOOEY BROWNIE BAKED IN A pie crust? Fudge pie. It's a Nashville tradition, served warm with vanilla ice cream. Variations abound with slightly less chocolate, nuts folded in, or a touch of bourbon, but this plain and simple rendition is my favorite. Take care not to overmix the filling. Let the pie bake until it puffs up and the crust browns. The center will fall as it cools, and this is just fine.

1 store-bought refrigerated 9-inch piecrust, unbaked
2 squares (1 ounce each) unsweetened chocolate
8 tablespoons (1 stick) unsalted butter,
    at room temperature
1 cup sugar
2 large eggs
¼ cup all-purpose flour
1 teaspoon pure vanilla extract
¼ teaspoon salt
¾ cup chopped pecans or walnuts (optional)
Vanilla ice cream or Sweetened Whipped Cream
    (page 367), for serving

1. Place a rack in the center of the oven and preheat the oven to 325°F.

2. Place the crust in a 9-inch glass or ceramic pie pan and crimp the edge between your index finger and thumb to create a fluted edge or press down on the edge of the crust with a fork. Set the piecrust aside.

3. Place the chocolate in a small saucepan over low heat and cook, stirring until melted, about 5 minutes. Remove the pan from the heat.

4. Place the butter and sugar in a large mixing bowl and beat with an electric mixer on medium-high speed for 2 minutes. Add the melted chocolate and beat well. Add the eggs, flour, vanilla, and salt. Beat on medium speed for about 1 minute. Fold in the nuts, if desired. Pour the filling into the piecrust.

5. Bake the pie until the filling rises above the crust and the crust is golden brown, 25 to 30 minutes. Remove the pie from the oven and let cool on a wire rack for about 1 hour or let it cool for about 10 minutes, then serve it warm with vanilla ice cream or whipped cream.

BIG BATCH: *You can easily double the filling for this recipe and pour it into two piecrusts. Bake them at the same time.*

RECIPE REMINDERS

Made for

Prep notes

Don't forget

Special touches

Bring again

My Favorite Key Lime Pie

SERVES 8 (MAKES ONE 9-INCH PIE)

PREP: 30 MINUTES * BAKE: ABOUT 36 MINUTES
CHILL: 8 HOURS

I DON'T KNOW ABOUT YOU, BUT FOR ME, IN THE HEAT OF the summer, no dessert satisfies more than Key lime pie. Our whole family craves it after a meal of grilled fish or burgers. Company loves it, too, and it is one of the best do-ahead desserts because it *must* be prepared in advance—otherwise, it will be too runny to slice! For a sophisticated dessert to tote, bake this pie and bring along the blueberry sauce. For a faster version, try my Ten-Minute Key Lime Pie (see page 417). Key lime pies are a little runny when sliced, so serve them in shallow bowls. You won't believe how much flavor you get in one fast dessert.

FOR THE PIE

$1\frac{1}{4}$ cups graham cracker crumbs
(from 10 to 12 whole graham crackers)

$\frac{1}{4}$ firmly packed cup light brown sugar

$\frac{1}{3}$ cup butter, melted

$\frac{1}{4}$ cup finely chopped pecans (optional)

2 cans (14 ounces each) sweetened condensed milk

1 cup bottled Key lime juice (see Note)

FOR THE MERINGUE AND GARNISH

3 egg whites

$\frac{1}{4}$ teaspoon cream of tartar

3 tablespoons granulated sugar

Lime slices (optional)

Fresh Blueberry Sauce (optional; recipe follows)

1. Make the pie: Place a rack in the center of the oven and preheat the oven to 350°F.

2. Place the graham cracker crumbs, brown sugar, butter, and pecans, if desired, in a large mixing bowl and stir until the crumbs are well saturated with the butter. Press the mixture into the bottom of a 9-inch pie pan. Bake the crust until lightly browned, about 10 minutes, then remove the pie pan from the heat and let the crust cool. Reduce the oven temperature to 325°F.

3. Place the sweetened condensed milk and Key lime juice in a medium-size bowl and stir to combine. Pour the filling into the crust once it has cooled to room temperature.

4. Make the meringue: Place the egg whites and cream of tartar in a large mixing bowl and beat with an electric mixer on high speed until foamy. Add the granulated sugar, 1 tablespoon at a time, beating until soft peaks form and the sugar dissolves, 2 to 4 minutes. Using a rubber spatula, spread the meringue over the pie filling, making sure that the meringue reaches to the crust.

5. Bake the pie until the meringue is golden brown, 26 to 28 minutes. Let the pie cool to room temperature and then refrigerate it, uncovered, for about 8 hours. Garnish the pie with lime slices, if desired, and serve with Fresh Blueberry Sauce, if desired.

NOTE: I use a good-quality bottled Key lime juice from my supermarket. You can certainly use fresh Key lime juice if you have access to these little limes. But do not use bottled regular lime juice.

BIG BATCH: *You can double this recipe and prepare the Key lime pie in a 13 by 9–inch glass or ceramic baking dish.*

RECIPE REMINDERS

Made for

Prep notes

Don't forget

Special touches

Bring again

Fresh Blueberry Sauce

MAKES ABOUT 1 CUP

PREP: ABOUT 20 MINUTES

THIS BLUEBERRY SAUCE IS DELICIOUS ON ANY LEMON OR lime pie. Make it ahead of time and if there is any left over, refrigerate it to serve over pancakes and waffles.

> 2 cups fresh blueberries
> ¼ cup sugar

Place the blueberries and sugar in a medium-size saucepan. Bring to a simmer over medium heat, stirring, and cook until the sugar dissolves and the sauce reduces to about 1 cup, about 15 minutes. Turn off the heat and let the sauce come to room temperature. The sauce can be refrigerated, covered, for 4 to 5 days. Let it come to room temperature before serving.

Ten-Minute Key Lime Pie

SERVES 8 (MAKES ONE 9-INCH PIE)

PREP: ABOUT 10 MINUTES ✶ CHILL: 4 TO 5 HOURS

W HILE IN MIAMI ON A BOOK TOUR, MY ESCORT Carole Trope and I found our common denominator—fast, fantastic cooking. Carole shared how she makes a Key lime pie in ten minutes or less. I had always labored over Key lime pie, but I thought, "If a Floridian says it's okay to prepare one this way, then I've got to give it a try." In an even greater hurry? Spoon the filling into goblets and garnish it with graham cracker crumbs.

½ cup bottled Key lime juice
1 can (14 ounces) sweetened condensed milk
1 container (8 ounces) frozen whipped topping, thawed
1 store-bought 9-inch graham cracker crust
1 lime, for garnish
Whipped cream, for garnish

1. Place the lime juice and sweetened condensed milk in a large mixing bowl and whisk to combine. Fold in the whipped topping, incorporating it thoroughly. Spoon the filling into the graham cracker crust and refrigerate it until firm, 4 to 5 hours.

2. To serve, thinly slice the lime. Make a cut in each lime slice to the center and twist the slice like a corkscrew. Slice the pie and garnish each slice with some whipped cream and a lime twist.

TOTE NOTES

Place the pie, uncovered, in a plastic pie carrier or basket with a lid. Bring the lime slices in a little plastic bag and the whipped cream in a plastic container with a lid. Tote the pie and the whipped cream in a cooler.

Thanksgiving Pumpkin Pie

SERVES 8 (MAKES ONE 9-INCH PIE)

PREP: ABOUT 20 MINUTES ✳ BAKE: 55 MINUTES TO 1 HOUR
COOL: UP TO 2 HOURS

TOTE NOTES

Tote the pumpkin pie in a pie carrier or a basket. Don't forget the whipped cream: Put it in a plastic container with a lid and transport it in a cooler.

When you arrive, you can leave the pie on the kitchen counter for up to an hour and serve it at room temperature. Or, reheat it in a 350°F oven, uncovered, for about 15 minutes.

PLAN AHEAD

The pumpkin pie can be baked up to two days in advance.

DON'T MESS WITH TRADITION. THANKSGIVING DINNER calls for pumpkin pie. It *needs* pumpkin pie. Go ahead and serve cheesecake, apple pie, carrot cake, and pecan pie as well, but please don't forget this traditional favorite. If you want to go to a little extra trouble, you can make your own pie crust in a food processor. If not, buy the crust at the supermarket and press it into a pie pan for a homemade look. Make real whipped cream to serve on the side and, for an extra something special, flavor it with a teaspoon or two of brandy.

9-inch unbaked piecrust (store-bought or homemade; recipe follows)
1 can (15 ounces) pumpkin (not pumpkin pie mix)
1 lightly packed cup light brown sugar
1 teaspoon ground cinnamon
½ teaspoon ground ginger
½ teaspoon salt
¼ teaspoon ground nutmeg
⅛ teaspoon ground cloves
3 large eggs, lightly beaten
1 cup heavy (whipping) cream
¼ cup milk
Sweetened Whipped Cream (page 367), for serving

1. Place a rack in the center of the oven and preheat the oven to 375°F.

2. Roll out the piecrust, if necessary, and place it in a 9-inch pie pan. Crimp the edge of the crust between your index finger and thumb to create a fluted edge or press down on the edge of the crust with a fork. Set the piecrust aside.

3. Place the pumpkin, brown sugar, cinnamon, ginger, salt, nutmeg, and cloves in a large mixing bowl and stir to combine. Add the eggs, cream, and milk and mix well with a wooden spoon until smooth. Pour the filling into the crust. Cover the edge of the crust with strips of aluminum foil.

4. Bake the pie for 30 minutes, then remove the pan from the oven and carefully remove the foil strips from the crust edge. Return the pie to the oven and bake it until a knife inserted in the center comes out clean, 25 to 30 minutes longer. Transfer the pie to a wire rack to cool for up to 2 hours. If you need to store the pie longer, cover it with plastic wrap or aluminum foil and refrigerate it. Serve the pie topped with Sweetened Whipped Cream.

Food Processor Piecrust

MAKES ONE 9-INCH PIE CRUST

PREP: ABOUT 5 MINUTES

HERE IS A DANDY OF A HOMEMADE PIECRUST RECIPE I have used for years. I love it because it comes together in the food processor in just five minutes. Make the pie dough early in the day and refrigerate it. Then the crust is ready to roll!

- 1½ cups all-purpose flour
- ½ teaspoon sugar
- ¼ teaspoon salt
- ½ cup cold vegetable shortening (no trans fat), or 8 tablespoons (1 stick) cold butter
- 2 to 3 tablespoons ice water

RECIPE
REMINDERS

Made for

Prep notes

Don't forget

Special touches

Bring again

Place the flour, sugar, and salt in the bowl of a food processor fitted with a steel blade. Pulse a few times to combine. Evenly distribute the vegetable shortening in the bowl and process until the shortening is broken into bits and the mixture looks like coarse meal, 7 or 8 pulses. Add 2 tablespoons of ice water and pulse again 7 or 8 times. The dough should be crumbly but hold together; if it is too dry, add another tablespoon of ice water. With floured hands, place the dough on a floured work surface to roll out. Wrapped in waxed paper, the dough can be refrigerated for up to 2 days; when you are ready to use it, let it soften at room temperature before you roll it out.

M E N U

THANKSGIVING DINNER

Isn't this the original potluck, the one where the phrase "What can I bring?" originated? The host roasts the turkey and everyone else contributes to the most celebrated meal of them all.

ROAST TURKEY IN THE BAG, *page 230*

✳

MY FAVORITE TURKEY DRESSING, *page 316*

✳

SWEET POTATO CASSEROLE WITH PECAN CRUNCH, *page 292*

✳

SPICED CRANBERRY SAUCE, *page 314*

✳

BEBE'S GREEN BEANS, *page 274*

✳

THANKSGIVING PUMPKIN PIE, *page 418*

✳

PUMPKIN SPICE CHEESECAKE, *page 368*

Iron Skillet Apple Tart

SERVES 8 (MAKES ONE 10-INCH TART)

**PREP: 25 TO 30 MINUTES ✶ BAKE: 35 TO 40 MINUTES
COOL: 20 MINUTES**

W HAT I LOVE ABOUT THIS APPLE PIE IS THAT IT IS full of apple flavor, it's light and crisp, and it is baked in a cast-iron skillet. The best apples to use would be ones that you don't see every day— the firm, tart, crisp apples that come into season in the early fall. Make your own piecrust or rely on a handy refrigerated crust cut into a circle to fit the skillet.

1 refrigerated 9-inch piecrust, unbaked

6 tablespoons (¾ stick) butter

½ cup sugar

6 to 7 tart apples such as McIntosh, Golden Delicious, or Rome, peeled, cored, and cut into ½-inch slices

Pinch cinnamon

Vanilla ice cream, for serving

1. Place a rack in the center of the oven and preheat the oven to 425°F.

2. Roll out the piecrust on a lightly floured work surface and invert a 9-inch pie pan on top of the dough. Using a sharp knife, trim off the dough around the pan to form a circle. Discard the crust scraps and set the dough circle aside, lightly covered with a kitchen towel.

3. Place the butter in a 10-inch cast-iron skillet over medium heat. Stir until the butter melts, then remove the skillet from the heat. Sprinkle the sugar evenly over the bottom of the skillet, then arrange some of the apple slices in a circle around

 TOTE NOTES

Once the tart has baked, wrap the skillet in a clean kitchen towel and take it with you. The tart will cool in transit and you can invert it onto a plate when you get to your destination. If necessary, you can place the skillet over very low heat to warm up the sugar. Use a spatula to loosen the edge so turning the tart out of the skillet will be less messy. If a few apples stick, that's okay; tuck them back into the tart.

Bring the ice cream in its container in a cooler.

PLAN AHEAD

You can bake the apple tart a day ahead. If you like, reheat it in a 350°F oven for 10 to 15 minutes.

Made for

Prep notes

Don't forget

Special touches

Bring again

the edge of the skillet. Place the remaining apple slices in the center of the skillet. Sprinkle a little cinnamon on top. Place the skillet back over medium heat and cook until the sugar around the edges begins to lightly brown, 4 to 5 minutes. Remove the pan from the heat.

4. Bake the tart in the skillet until the apples are soft, 18 to 20 minutes. Remove the skillet from the oven and carefully place the circle of piecrust on top of the apples. Bake the tart until the crust has lightly browned and the apples are bubbling around the edges, 17 to 20 minutes.

5. Let the tart cool in the skillet for about 20 minutes. Run a knife around the edge of the skillet, then invert the tart onto a serving platter. Drizzle the apple juices over the tart and serve it warm with ice cream.

Cranberry Tart

SERVES 8 (MAKES ONE 9-INCH TART)

PREP: 10 MINUTES ✳ BAKE: 40 TO 45 MINUTES ✳ COOL: 20 MINUTES

GREAT RECIPES ARE LIKE POLITICIANS—THEY MAKE the rounds. Sally Mabry gave me this recipe, which she got from Rita Kaplan, who got it from Ophelia Paine, who got it from Sally Lagrone. So from one Sally to another Sally, and from me to you, here is a terrific tart to serve while cranberries are in season. It is best served warm, with whipped cream, plain or flavored with Grand Marnier and grated orange zest.

12 tablespoons (1½ sticks) butter, melted, plus melted butter for brushing the pie pan

2 cups cranberries, rinsed and drained

1½ cups sugar

½ cup chopped pecans

1 cup all-purpose flour

2 large eggs, beaten

1 teaspoon pure almond extract

Sweetened Whipped Cream (page 367; see Note), for serving

Confectioners' sugar (optional), for dusting the tart

1. Place a rack in the center of the oven and preheat the oven to 350°F. Lightly brush a 9-inch glass or ceramic pie pan with melted butter.

2. Scatter the cranberries in an even layer in the bottom of the pie pan. Sprinkle ½ cup of the sugar and the pecans over them.

3. Place the butter, flour, eggs, almond extract, and the remaining 1 cup of sugar in a large mixing bowl and stir

TOTE NOTES

This is a great tart to tote because once it sets, it does not shift like other fruit pies. Feel free to carry it in the pie pan.

Or, go ahead and slice it thinly, arranging the slices attractively on a platter or tray lined with doilies.

Bring the whipped cream in a plastic container with a lid; transport it in a cooler.

PLAN AHEAD

The Cranberry Tart can be baked the day before the party. Cover with plastic wrap and store at room temperature.

with a wooden spoon to combine well. Pour the butter mixture over the cranberry mixture.

4. Bake the tart until it has risen, is lightly browned, and the center has nearly set, 40 to 45 minutes. Transfer the tart to a wire rack to cool for about 20 minutes, then slice and serve warm with the whipped cream. Or, let the tart cool completely, about 1 hour, before serving. For a final touch, dust the tart with a little confectioners' sugar, if desired.

NOTE: To bring out the cranberry flavor even more, give a touch of orange to the Sweetened Whipped Cream by adding 1 tablespoon of Grand Marnier and 1 teaspoon of orange zest.

LIKE APPLES? Make an apple and cranberry tart with 1 cup of chopped apple and half of the cranberries (1 cup).

Deep Dish Cherry Cobbler

SERVES 12 (MAKES ONE 13 BY 9-INCH COBBLER)

PREP: 20 MINUTES ✳ BAKE: 40 TO 45 MINUTES ✳ COOL: 10 MINUTES

I KNOW APPLE PIE IS THE NATIONAL DESSERT, BUT WHAT IS a more all-American ending for an Independence Day picnic than cherry cobbler? It is certainly a treat for me, and I love to serve it warm or at room temperature in bowls with vanilla ice cream. Even though fresh cherries are only in season during the summer, you can make this cheerful cobbler any time of year. In fact, it's a lot easier and just as flavorful made with frozen cherries. Add a tad of almond extract to the cherries along with the sliced almonds if you want a more pronounced almond flavor.

FOR THE PASTRY

1½ cups all-purpose flour

1 teaspoon baking powder

½ teaspoon salt

8 tablespoons (1 stick) cold unsalted butter

½ cup milk

FOR THE FILLING AND TOPPING

2 pounds thawed and drained frozen pitted dark sweet cherries, or 2 pounds pitted fresh sweet cherries (about 8 cups)

1 cup plus 2 tablespoons sugar

1 to 2 tablespoons milk

½ cup sliced almonds

Sweetened Whipped Cream (page 367) or vanilla ice cream

TOTE NOTES

Cover the baking dish with aluminum foil and the cobbler is ready to tote. If you want to serve it warm, reheat it at 350°F for 10 to 15 minutes. Bring along the Sweetened Whipped Cream in a plastic container with a lid or tote a container of vanilla ice cream in a cooler.

PLAN AHEAD

The cobbler can be baked up to a day in advance and refrigerated, covered with aluminum foil. If you make it earlier on the day of the gathering, you can let it stand at room temperature.

RECIPE
REMINDERS

Made for
_____
_____
_____
_____
_____
_____
_____

Prep notes
_____
_____
_____
_____
_____
_____

Don't forget
_____
_____
_____
_____
_____
_____

Special touches
_____
_____
_____
_____
_____
_____

Bring again
_____

1. Place a rack in the center of the oven and preheat the oven to 350°F.

2. Make the pastry: Place the flour, baking powder, and salt in a large mixing bowl and stir to combine. Add the butter and, using a pastry blender or two knives, cut it into the flour mixture until well mixed but crumbly. (You can also do this in a food processor.) Stir in the ½ cup of milk with a fork, mixing just until all the flour is moistened and a soft dough forms.

3. Make the cobbler: Transfer the pastry to a floured work surface and knead it with floured hands about 10 times. Roll the pastry out into a 12 by 13–inch rectangle. Cut the dough lengthwise into 8 strips, each about 1½ inches wide. Arrange 3 of the strips in the bottom of a 13 by 9–inch glass or ceramic baking dish. Spoon the cherries over the strips of pastry. Sprinkle the cherries with 1 cup of the sugar. Arrange the remaining 5 strips of pastry lengthwise over the cherries, leaving a little space between each. Brush the pastry strips with the 1 to 2 tablespoons of milk and sprinkle the almonds and the remaining 2 tablespoons of sugar over the top.

4. Bake the cobbler until browned and bubbly in the center, 40 to 45 minutes. Remove the baking dish from the oven and let the cobbler cool for about 10 minutes. Serve it in bowls right from the baking dish, warm or at room temperature, with Sweetened Whipped Cream or vanilla ice cream.

TEN ADULT ADD-INS
TO TRANSFORM VANILLA ICE CREAM

Kids love to stir add-ins like sprinkles and candy into ice cream. Try folding these more grown-up additions into soft vanilla ice cream. Use one tablespoon of most of these add-ins for each cup of ice cream, then refreeze it.

1. Brandy and grated German chocolate

2. Coffee granules

3. Good cinnamon—add 1 teaspoon

4. Toasted slivered almonds

5. Shredded coconut and coconut "extract"

6. Crushed chocolate wafers or Thin Mint Girl Scout cookies

7. Chopped chocolate peanut butter cups

8. Minced crystallized ginger

9. Crushed lemon candies

10. Toasted pecans and grated orange zest

DOUBLE THE DESSERT

For many of the desserts in this chapter, if you want a bigger batch you simply need to double the amount of pastry crust or batter and filling and bake them in two separate baking dishes. When you are working with a large amount of pastry, remember to keep it covered with plastic wrap in the refrigerator until you are ready to use it.

Double-Crust Blackberry Cobbler

SERVES 6 TO 8

PREP: 20 MINUTES ✳ **BAKE: 30 TO 35 MINUTES**
COOL: 10 MINUTES

TOTE NOTES

Cover the baked and cooled cobbler with aluminum foil for traveling, and when you arrive, reheat it, covered, in a 350°F oven until warmed through, about 15 minutes.

Or, in warm weather, you can bake the cobbler an hour or so ahead of time and leave it at room temperature until serving. It's fine to eat blackberry cobbler at room temperature in the summertime.

Don't forget to bring the Sweetened Whipped Cream or ice cream for serving. You can put the whipped cream in a plastic container with a lid; transport it or the ice cream in a cooler.

THIS COBBLER IS FOR ALL OF YOU WHO HOG THE crust (you know who you are!). You may think it goes unnoticed when you spoon into a cobbler and pull the crisp crust off the top, leaving only fruit behind, but we're on to you. This cobbler is your dessert dream come true. It has two layers of crust—a soft one in the center and a browned and crunchy one on top. And it also contains fresh blackberries, which are so worth trying along with the crust since they are only with us during the summer months, and will be missed as soon as they're gone.

> 1 tablespoon butter, at room temperature,
>   plus 2 tablespoons butter
> 1 quart (4 heaping cups) blackberries, rinsed and drained
> ¾ cup sugar, plus 1 tablespoon sugar, for sprinkling
>   over the top
> ⅓ cup all-purpose flour
> 1 refrigerated store-bought 9- inch piecrust, unbaked
> Sweetened Whipped Cream (page 367) or vanilla ice
>   cream, for serving

1. Place a rack in the center of the oven and preheat the oven to 425°F. Rub a 2-quart glass or ceramic baking dish with the 1 tablespoon of room temperature butter and set the baking dish aside.

2. Place the blackberries, ¾ cup of sugar, and the flour in a medium-size mixing bowl and gently stir to combine. Spoon half of the blackberry mixture into the prepared baking dish and dot it with 1 tablespoon of the butter.

3. Roll out the pie crust to flatten it, then cut it in ½-inch strips. Arrange half of the strips of crust on top of the blackberries. Cover the baking dish with a glass lid or with aluminum foil and place in the oven to bake for 15 minutes.

4. Remove the baking dish from the oven and take off the lid or foil. Place the remaining blackberry mixture on top of the crust, dot it with the remaining 1 tablespoon of butter, and arrange the remaining strips of crust in a lattice pattern on top. Sprinkle the remaining 1 tablespoon of sugar over the lattice.

5. Bake the cobbler until the top crust has lightly browned and the blackberries are bubbling in the center, 15 to 20 minutes. Remove the baking dish from the oven, let the cobbler cool for about 10 minutes, then serve warm it with Sweetened Whipped Cream or vanilla ice cream.

BIG BATCH: *You can double this recipe, using twice as much filling and twice the crust and placing it in a 3- to 4-quart baking dish. It will need to bake a little longer, until the filling bubbles in the center. Tent the crust with aluminum foil if it begins to brown too quickly.*

RECIPE REMINDERS

Made for

Prep notes

Don't forget

Special touches

Bring again

Peach and Blueberry Crisp

SERVES 10 TO 12 (MAKES ONE 13 BY 9-INCH CRISP)

PREP: 30 MINUTES ✳ BAKE: ABOUT 40 MINUTES
COOL: 30 MINUTES

 TOTE NOTES

If you want to bake the crisp and keep it warm, cover the baking dish with aluminum foil, wrap a clean kitchen towel and newspapers around it, and you are ready to go.

You can also reheat the crisp, uncovered, in a 350°F oven for 15 minutes before serving. Or, you can take the crisp unbaked and bake it when you arrive.

Bring along a container of vanilla ice cream in a cooler for serving.

PLAN AHEAD

You can make the topping for the crisp early in the day; store it at room temperature.

THE PERFECT PARTY DESSERT FOR JULY AND AUGUST, this fresh peach crisp is easily assembled in a glass casserole, baked, wrapped, and brought to a gathering. Or, just make it and serve it to guests at your house. The blueberries add just the right contrast in color and sweetness to the peaches. If you like, use fresh raspberries instead of blueberries for that wonderful peach melba combination. No matter what fruits you choose, serve the crisp warm in bowls with scoops of vanilla ice cream.

FOR THE FILLING

1 tablespoon butter, at room temperature
14 medium-size ripe peaches
1½ cups fresh blueberries, rinsed and drained
¾ cup granulated sugar

FOR THE TOPPING

¾ cup all-purpose flour
¾ cup light brown sugar
1 teaspoon ground cinnamon
4 tablespoons (½ stick) butter, cold and coarsely chopped
1 cup old-fashioned rolled oats
Vanilla ice cream, for serving

1. Make the filling: Place a rack in the center of the oven and preheat the oven to 375°F. Rub a 13 by 9–inch glass or ceramic baking dish with the 1 tablespoon of butter and set aside.

2. Rinse, peel, and pit the peaches, then cut them in ½-inch slices and place them in a large bowl. You should have 7½ to 8 cups of sliced peaches. Add the blueberries and sugar and toss together with a wooden spoon. Pour the fruit into the prepared baking dish, distributing it evenly.

3. Make the topping: Place the flour, brown sugar, and cinnamon in a medium-size bowl and stir to combine. Add the 4 tablespoons of cold butter and, using a pastry blender or two knives, cut it into the flour mixture until it is well mixed but crumbly. (You can also do this in a food processor.) Add the rolled oats and toss the mixture to combine. Spoon the topping evenly over the fruit.

4. Bake the crisp until the topping is golden brown and the filling bubbles, 37 to 43 minutes. Remove the pan from the oven and let the crisp cool for 30 minutes. Serve warm with vanilla ice cream.

Pear and Apple Crumble

SERVES 8 TO 10 (MAKES ONE 13 BY 9-INCH CRUMBLE)

PREP: 25 MINUTES ✳ BAKE: 35 TO 40 MINUTES
COOL: 30 MINUTES

 TOTE NOTES

To keep the crumble warm while you are toting it, cover the baking dish with aluminum foil and wrap it in a kitchen towel or newspapers.

Or, you can reheat the crumble, uncovered, in a 350°F oven for about 15 minutes when you arrive. To keep the fruit from drying out, you might need to dribble 2 tablespoons of milk over it before reheating.

Bring the whipped cream in a plastic container with a lid; transport it in a cooler.

CRISP, CRUMBLE, COBBLER—CONFUSED? ALL ARE FRUIT-based desserts and certainly share similarities, but a crumble is different from a crisp and from a cobbler. It has those buttery and crunchy chunks on top, made from flour, butter, and sugar, often with such add-ins as nuts or granola. A crisp, on the other hand, has a thinner crunchy topping with less butter. And a cobbler is a deep-dish pie in a baking pan, with some sort of pastry crust on top. This sophisticated crumble calls for pears and apples, perfect for fall. It is so easy to make and simple in appearance that you may wonder what all the fuss is about. But the "wow" comes when you spoon a bite into your mouth.

FOR THE FILLING

1 tablespoon butter, at room temperature
3 to 4 large ripe pears
3 to 4 large tart apples
1 to 2 tablespoons sugar
1 teaspoon lemon juice
¼ cup milk

FOR THE TOPPING

½ cup all-purpose flour
½ cup sugar
8 tablespoons (1 stick) butter, cold and coarsely chopped
½ cup granola
2 tablespoons finely chopped pecans (optional)
Sweetened Whipped Cream (page 367), for serving

1. Make the filling: Place a rack in the center of the oven and preheat the oven to 400°F. Rub a 13 by 9–inch glass or ceramic baking dish with the 1 tablespoon of room temperature butter and set the baking dish aside.

2. Rinse, peel, core, and slice the pears and apples into a large bowl. You should have 6 to 7 cups of fruit. Sprinkle 1 to 2 tablespoons of sugar and the lemon juice over the pears and apples and toss with a wooden spoon to coat. Transfer the fruit to the prepared baking dish, distributing it evenly. Pour the milk over the fruit.

3. Make the topping: Place the flour and sugar in a medium-size bowl and stir to combine. Add the 8 tablespoons of cold butter and, using a pastry blender or two knives, cut it into the flour mixture until well mixed but crumbly. (You can also do this in a food processor.) Stir in the granola and the pecans, if desired. Using your fingers, scatter the crumble topping in 1-inch clumps over the fruit.

4. Bake the crumble until it is golden brown and the filling bubbles, 35 to 40 minutes. Remove the baking dish from the oven and let the crumble cool for about 30 minutes. Serve the crumble warm with Sweetened Whipped Cream.

BIG BATCH: *You can bake two crumbles at the same time— double the topping ingredients and make one crumble with only pears (use six to eight) and one with apples (use six to eight).*

RECIPE REMINDERS

Made for

Prep notes

Don't forget

Special touches

Bring again

Aunt Elizabeth's Banana Pudding

SERVES 12 TO 16

PREP: 45 MINUTES ★ BAKE: ABOUT 15 MINUTES

TOTE NOTES

Place the warm banana pudding in a box lined with a towel and leave it uncovered for traveling so as not to disrupt the meringue.

PLAN AHEAD

Don't bake this pudding more than a couple of hours ahead of time, or you will need to refrigerate it and the bananas will darken from the cooler temperature. But if you have any pudding left over, do put it in the refrigerator.

W E USED TO BEG MY MOTHER'S SISTER, ELIZABETH Nicholls, to make this amazing pudding on holidays and for picnics, so she always knew what to bring. The pudding is best cooked in glass because metal causes a reaction with the bananas and the eggs. You want the bananas to be ripe but not too soft, and to keep the bananas from turning brown, they need to be completely covered by the custard. As Elizabeth knew, if you bring a big, beautiful banana pudding, you will be a hero.

FOR THE PUDDING
$1\frac{1}{3}$ cups sugar
$\frac{2}{3}$ cup all-purpose flour
$\frac{1}{2}$ teaspoon salt
4 cups (1 quart) whole milk
6 large egg yolks
4 tablespoons ($\frac{1}{2}$ stick) butter
1 teaspoon pure vanilla extract
58 vanilla wafers, for lining the 13 by 9–inch pan
4 medium-size bananas, sliced $\frac{1}{4}$-inch thick (about 3 cups)

FOR THE MERINGUE
6 large egg whites
$\frac{3}{4}$ cup sugar

1. Make the pudding: Place the $1\frac{1}{3}$ cups of sugar, and the flour and salt in a 3-quart saucepan and stir to combine.

Set the pan aside. Place the milk in a small saucepan over medium-low heat and stir just until the milk is scalded, about 2 minutes. Gradually stir the hot milk into the flour mixture, then place this saucepan over medium-low heat. Cook, stirring with a wooden spoon, until the mixture thickens, 7 to 8 minutes. Remove the pan from the heat.

2. Place the egg yolks in a small bowl and beat with a fork until lightly combined. Spoon a tablespoon or 2 of the hot milk mixture into the egg yolks and stir with a fork to warm the eggs. Gradually spoon the egg mixture into the milk mixture in the saucepan, stirring constantly with a wooden spoon. Place the pan over medium-low heat and cook, stirring, until the mixture is smooth and thick, about 2 minutes. Stir in the butter and vanilla and let the pudding mixture cool.

3. Line the bottom and sides of a 13 by 9–inch glass or ceramic baking dish with the vanilla wafers, flat side down. Arrange the sliced bananas in a layer on top of the cookies, covering them. Spoon the pudding mixture over the bananas and spread it out until it is smooth and all of the bananas are covered.

4. Place a rack in the center of the oven and preheat the oven to 350°F.

5. Make the meringue: Place the egg whites in a large, clean mixing bowl and beat on high speed with an electric mixer until soft peaks form, about 2 minutes. Gradually add the ¾ cup of sugar and continue beating until stiff peaks form, about 4 minutes.

6. Using a rubber spatula, spread the meringue on top of the pudding so that it covers the entire surface and touches the edges of the baking dish. Bake the pudding until the meringue is lightly browned, 12 to 15 minutes.

RECIPE REMINDERS

Made for

Prep notes

Don't forget

Special touches

Bring again

Mindy's Grilled Figs with Honey, Walnuts, and Crumbled Stilton

SERVES 6

PREP: 15 MINUTES ✳ COOK: 6 MINUTES

PLAN AHEAD

Grill the figs and toast the walnuts a day in advance, if you like.

DROP-DEAD GORGEOUS DESSERTS ARE OFTEN THE easiest of all to make—they can be assembled from an assortment of well-partnered ingredients. Such is the case with this easy yet luxurious recipe, which brings together salty, blue-veined Stilton cheese, toasted walnuts, creamy mascarpone cheese, rich honey, and sweet figs. The figs are grilled, but only briefly, and this can be done hours in advance. My friend Mindy served these figs at a summer burger party, and they were so good we were speechless. If you have a sleek white platter, it makes the presentation perfect.

6 fresh figs, rinsed, drained, and cut in half lengthwise
1 tablespoon olive oil
½ cup mascarpone cheese
¾ cup (3 ounces) crumbled Stilton or any good blue cheese
⅓ cup toasted walnut halves (see box, page 99)
¼ cup honey

1. Place the fig halves in a small bowl and gently toss them with the olive oil to coat.

2. Preheat the grill to medium-high heat.

3. Place the figs on the grill grate and cook them until they are seared a bit on the outside and soft inside, about 3 minutes per side. Transfer the figs, cut side up, to a platter and set aside at room temperature until ready to serve.

4. Dollop about 2 teaspoons of mascarpone cheese on each fig half. Sprinkle the mascarpone with a little Stilton and some walnuts. Drizzle the honey over the figs and on the platter.

BIG BATCH: *You can easily double or triple the number of figs you grill; just be sure you have a large enough platter. Increase the amount of mascarpone, Stilton, walnuts, and honey to match.*

RECIPE REMINDERS

Made for

Prep notes

Don't forget

Special touches

Bring again

Elena's Tiramisu

SERVES 8 TO 10

PREP: 30 MINUTES * CHILL: 24 HOURS

TOTE NOTES

Another great do-ahead dessert, tiramisu is ready to travel once it has been refrigerated. Tote the whipped cream in a plastic container with a lid and carry it in a cooler. Bring a serving spoon with you, and keep it chilled until time to serve, too.

ONE RECENT SUMMER WE RENTED A VILLA IN TUSCANY. To my complete surprise and delight, a wonderful cook named Elena Nasoni was available to make dinner for us. We let Elena do the cooking on two of the nights, and it was the best present a busy mom could have—knowing that someone else, and a very talented Italian cook at that, had done the grocery shopping and was in the kitchen preparing dinner. Elena fried potatoes in olive oil with fresh sage, rolled out pasta on the kitchen table, and made the most heavenly tiramisu for dessert. *Tiramisu* can be translated from the Italian as "lift me up," and the lift comes from the generous amount of espresso in it. It also includes a custard layer made from mascarpone cheese, sugar, and eggs (buy pasteurized eggs because the eggs in this recipe are not cooked). If you use American-style ladyfingers, toast them first, as the Italian ladyfingers, known as Pavesini, are crunchier. And if possible, make this twenty-four hours in advance so the ladyfingers have time to soak up the flavors.

> 5 large pasteurized eggs
> ⅔ cup sugar
> 1 pound mascarpone cheese
> ⅓ cup brewed espresso (see Notes), cooled
> 3 tablespoons vin santo or cream sherry (see Notes)
> 24 ladyfingers (see Notes)
> ¾ cup shaved milk or dark chocolate, for garnish
> Sweetened Whipped Cream (optional; page 367),
>   for garnish

1. Carefully separate the eggs, placing the yolks in one large mixing bowl and the whites in another. Set aside the egg whites. Add the sugar to the yolks and whisk until well combined and lemon colored and the graininess of the sugar disappears, 2 to 3 minutes. Add the mascarpone cheese and whisk until the mixture is smooth. Measure out 1 tablespoon of the espresso and add this tablespoon to the mascarpone cheese mixture, whisking until incorporated. Set the remaining espresso aside.

2. Beat the reserved egg whites with an electric mixer on high power until soft peaks form, about 2 minutes. Fold the beaten egg whites into the mascarpone mixture until they are incorporated. Set the mascarpone mixture aside.

3. Combine the reserved espresso and the *vin santo* or sherry. Place the ladyfingers on a baking sheet or clean work surface and, using a small pastry brush, swab them generously on both sides with the espresso and wine mixture until they are quite wet.

4. Place half of the ladyfingers in the bottom of a 3-quart glass or ceramic baking dish. The ladyfingers should not be touching; you will need to space them out. Ladle half of the mascarpone mixture on top of the ladyfingers and then top it with the remaining ladyfingers. Ladle the remaining mascarpone mixture over the ladyfingers, spreading it out with a long metal spatula to smooth the top. Scatter the shaved chocolate across the top of the tiramisu or, for a nicer presentation, spread the Sweetened Whipped Cream, if desired, over the top and then add the shaved chocolate. Cover the baking dish with plastic wrap and refrigerate the tiramisu for 24 hours before serving.

NOTES: I have made this dessert with espresso I brewed myself and with a Starbucks espresso, and I have to say the Starbucks espresso is more syrupy and really adds a lot to this recipe.

PLAN AHEAD

You can assemble the tiramisu a day or two ahead of time. Cover it with plastic wrap, and pop it in the refrigerator.

RECIPE
REMINDERS

Made for

Prep notes

Don't forget

Special touches

Bring again

Vin santo is a sweet dessert wine from Italy. You can substitute cream sherry, which is the sweetest type of sherry.

The Pavesini should be quite reasonably priced if you can buy them at an Italian market in your town, but they are costly if you buy them online. To toast American-style ladyfingers, arrange them in a single layer on a baking sheet and toast them in the broiler about 6 inches from the heat until lightly browned, about 1 minute. Remove the baking sheet from the oven and turn the ladyfingers over with a metal spatula. Toast the second side until lightly browned, about 1 minute longer. Let the ladyfingers cool before using.

BIG BATCH: *The tiramisu doubles easily—just make sure you have enough ladyfingers and two 3-quart baking dishes.*

IT'S A GIFT

This book wouldn't be complete without a chapter on taking food to others as gifts. There are so many times we are all invited to gatherings and want to bring a little something to the host but can't think of anything except a bottle of wine. Nothing is wrong with a present of wine or flowers, but this chapter offers you some other ideas. Want to expand your culinary gift cache? Read on.

When I think of fall and gifts, I think of pumpkin bread, and my recipe for Big Batch Pumpkin Bread makes three big loaves or lots of little ones, just right for that harvest party or as a little something for teachers. I think, too, of a loaf of coffee cake, and for time-stretched cooks, the Sour Cream Cinnamon Streusel Loaves are just right because they begin with a box of cake mix. In addition, Cranberry and

Apple Chutney, Zesty Marinated Olives, and Sweet and Spicy Pecans are all autumn recipes perfect to package and give to others.

With winter and the holidays it brings, the gifts become a bit fancier. Bake Mindy's Pound Cake Loaves, make Jezebel Sauce, and fill jars with Warm Fudge Sauce. For a festive touch, buy a roll of clear cellophane and wrap the jars and loaves, then tie gold ribbons around them.

In the spring, look for such seasonal produce as Vidalia onions that you can turn into Vidalia Onion Marmalade and keep on hand for gifts. Bake Easy Hot Cross Buns or One-Pan Cheese Danish for spring brunches and buffets. And make the Best Banana Bread for weekend guests and new neighbors.

Get busy when summer rolls around, for many of the gifts in this chapter make good use of warm

DRESS IT UP

Most of the time I'm pretty frugal when it comes to packaging gifts. I recycle bows, save tissue paper, and hoard boxes and jars of all sizes in hopes of using them again. And yet when I receive a catalog such as one from Williams-Sonoma, filled with holiday bags and boxes, ribbons and tags, I can't resist the urge to buy. So, my advice is to do a little of both. Use what you have and be on the lookout for cute containers and wrappings that make your food gifts look great. Here are a few suggestions.

* Save department store jewelry and accessory boxes. Cover them in holiday paper and line them with waxed paper or parchment paper. Pack bars, candies, and nuts in the boxes, then secure them with attractive bows.

* Buy small plastic organizing bins and trays. Line them with parchment paper or waxed paper and fill them with loaves of bread, cookies, or jars of preserves. Attach a bow and a tag to the side.

* Let your children decorate brown paper lunch sacks with holiday drawings. Fill them with colorful waxed paper, then add a jar of something yummy. You can even punch holes around the top of the sack, thread a colorful ribbon through them, and tie a pretty bow.

* Nothing beats those handy plastic storage containers. Decorate them with permanent markers. Tie festive raffia bows around the containers and attach homemade tags.

* Buy foil loaf pans for gifts of bread, or order greaseproof paper loaf pans from baking catalogs such as Sur La Table (check out www.surlatable.com). You can bake the breads right in the loaf pans. Then cover them with plastic wrap and tie colorful raffia ribbons around them.

* Make your own gift tags: Cut out squares of heavy white paper and punch a hole in one corner. Have your children decorate one side of each square, then write the name of the recipe and your name on the back.

* Use your computer to create adhesive labels with the names of the recipes. Or, order labels from such Web sites as www.myownlabels.com. Your chutney or loaf of banana bread will look *so* sophisticated!

weather produce. You'll find Zucchini Walnut Bread, Homemade Pesto, Refrigerator Peach Preserves, and Oven-Roasted Tomatoes Soaked in Basil and Oil. Keep the bread in your freezer and the pesto, preserves, and tomatoes in the refrigerator, and you'll always have delicious gifts at the ready.

Sure, it's very easy to pick up a loaf of bakery bread and a jar of preserves from the gourmet shop, but bread you bake yourself will be appreciated far more. The tomatoes you roast in your oven, the peaches you turn into preserves on your stove, the chutney you make with the first of the season's cranberries, and the pound cake loaves you wrap lovingly in foil make precious homemade gifts all year long.

Best Banana Bread

MAKES ONE 9 BY 5-INCH LOAF

**PREP: 15 MINUTES ✳ BAKE: 1 HOUR AND 15 TO 20 MINUTES
COOL: ABOUT 1 HOUR AND 15 MINUTES**

**TOTE
NOTES**

*Wrap the banana bread
in plastic wrap and you
can slice it when you
arrive. Or, you can slice it
and arrange the slices on
an attractive plate before
you leave. Covered with
plastic wrap, it's ready
for traveling.*

**FOR GIFT
GIVING**

*Wrap the bread first
in plastic wrap then
overwrap it with colorful
cellophane and tie it
with a bow. Or, for a
more rustic look, wrap
the loaf in parchment
paper and tie a raffia
bow around it.*

THIS IS ABSOLUTELY THE BEST BANANA BREAD RECIPE around. I grew up on banana bread made with butter, but I believe this version made with oil is better. And banana bread is perfect for using up those bananas that are too ripe to eat. So, don't discard them! And, for when you don't have fresh buttermilk in the fridge, keep a container of buttermilk powder on hand; use one tablespoon of powder and three tablespoons of water in place of three tablespoons of fresh buttermilk.

> Vegetable oil spray, for misting the loaf pan
> 1½ cups all-purpose flour, plus flour for dusting
>   the loaf pan
> ¾ teaspoon baking soda
> ½ teaspoon salt
> 1 cup sugar
> ¾ cup vegetable oil
> 3 tablespoons buttermilk
> 2 large eggs, lightly beaten
> 1 cup mashed bananas (from 2 large or 3 small bananas)

1. Place a rack in the center of the oven and preheat the oven to 325°F. Lightly mist a 9 by 5–inch loaf pan with vegetable oil spray and dust it with flour. Shake out the excess flour. Set the pan aside.

2. Place the flour, baking soda, and salt in a large mixing bowl and stir with a fork to combine. Add the sugar and stir to combine. Add the oil, buttermilk, eggs, and mashed banana and stir until the mixture is smooth but just blended, 50 to 60 strokes. Pour the batter into the prepared loaf pan.

3. Bake the bread until it is golden brown and the top springs back when gently pressed with a finger, 1 hour and 15 to 20 minutes. Transfer the loaf pan to a wire rack and let the bread cool for about 15 minutes. Run a knife around the edges of the bread and give the pan a few good shakes to loosen the bread. Invert the bread onto a wire rack, then invert it again onto another wire rack, so that it cools right side up. Let the loaf continue to cool for about 1 hour.

WANT SOME MUFFIN MAGIC? Turn this recipe into a dozen muffins by dividing the batter into twelve muffin cups that have been lined with paper liners or lightly greased and floured. Bake the muffins at 350°F until they are lightly browned around the edges and spring back when you gently press on one, 20 to 25 minutes.

BIG BATCH: *The banana bread recipe doubles well to make two loaves. You can freeze one; it will keep for up to three months.*

M E N U

THE KNITTING GROUP COMES FOR COFFEE

Ask a friend or two to help provide the baked goods. Then, put on the coffee, boil water for tea, and place a big bowl of strawberries or grapes on the table.

BEST BANANA BREAD
✳
ONE-PAN CHEESE DANISH, *page 454*
✳
FRESH STRAWBERRIES OR GRAPES
✳
COFFEE AND HOT TEA

RECIPE REMINDERS

Made for

Prep notes

Don't forget

Special touches

Bring again

Big Batch Pumpkin Bread

MAKES THREE 9 BY 5-INCH LOAVES

PREP: ABOUT 12 MINUTES ✳ BAKE: ABOUT 65 MINUTES ✳ COOL: 55 MINUTES

 TOTE NOTES

When taking the pumpkin bread to a party, go ahead and slice the loaf and arrange the slices on a pretty platter. Cover the platter with plastic wrap and you're ready to go.

FOR GIFT GIVING

Wrap loaves of pumpkin bread in parchment paper or cellophane to give as presents.

PLAN AHEAD

You can bake the pumpkin bread ahead of time and freeze the loaves; they'll keep for up to three months. When you are ready to use one, let it thaw on the kitchen counter for 4 hours or overnight.

ONCE THE LEAVES BEGIN TO CHANGE COLOR IN THE fall and canned pumpkin is on the supermarket shelves, I think of pumpkin bread. It's the best recipe for bake sales or just toting to a friend. This recipe makes three big loaves or many smaller ones. It calls for a large can of pumpkin pie mix, but if you can't find the pie mix in your store, just use plain pumpkin.

Vegetable oil spray, for misting the loaf pans

5½ cups all-purpose flour, plus flour for dusting the loaf pans

1 tablespoon baking soda

2 teaspoons ground cinnamon

1½ teaspoons salt

1½ teaspoons ground nutmeg

4½ cups sugar

1½ cups vegetable oil

6 large eggs

3 cups canned pumpkin pie mix (see Note)

1 cup warm water

1. Place a rack in the center of the oven and preheat the oven to 350°F. Lightly mist three 9 by 5–inch loaf pans with vegetable oil spray and dust them with flour. Shake out the excess flour. Set the pans aside.

2. Place the flour, baking soda, cinnamon, salt, and nutmeg in a medium-size mixing bowl and stir with a fork to combine. Set the dry ingredients aside.

3. Place the sugar and oil in a very large mixing bowl and beat with an electric mixer on medium-low speed until combined, about 1 minute. Add the eggs one at a time and beat until the mixture thickens and lightens in color, about 2 minutes. Add the dry ingredients followed by the pumpkin pie mix and warm water and stir with a wooden spoon until the mixture is smooth, 60 to 70 strokes. Divide the batter evenly among the 3 prepared loaf pans, filling them two-thirds full.

4. Bake the bread until the top springs back when lightly pressed with a finger, 60 to 67 minutes. Transfer the loaf pans to wire racks and let the loaves cool for about 15 minutes. Run a knife around the edges of each loaf and give the pans a few good shakes to loosen the loaves. Invert a loaf onto a wire rack, then invert it again onto another wire rack so that it cools right side up. Repeat with the remaining loaves. Let the loaves continue to cool for about 40 minutes. Slice the pumpkin bread before serving.

NOTE: Pumpkin pie mix is a little different from ordinary canned pumpkin because it has already been seasoned. You will often find it in 30-ounce cans around the holidays. Buy several to keep in your pantry. You will need nearly an entire can for this recipe.

DON'T WANT TO LOAF AROUND? Bake the pumpkin bread any size you like. If you don't have three 9 by 5–inch loaf pans, you can also use this recipe to make:
* Five to six loaves that are about 7½ by 3½ inches
* Ten loaves that are about 5¾ by 3 inches

Baking the smaller loaves of pumpkin bread until they test done will take 40 to 50 minutes.

RECIPE REMINDERS

Made for

Prep notes

Don't forget

Special touches

Bring again

Zucchini Walnut Bread

MAKES ONE 9 BY 5-INCH LOAF

PREP: 15 MINUTES ✶ BAKE: 60 TO 65 MINUTES ✶ COOL: 1 HOUR

TOTE NOTES

You can wrap the zucchini bread in plastic wrap for traveling or slice the loaf and arrange it on a pretty platter. Cover the platter with plastic wrap to tote it.

FOR GIFT GIVING

For the holidays or special occasions, tie a raffia ribbon around the loaf, or bake the loaf in a decorative disposable loaf pan and tie it with a pretty ribbon.

PLAN AHEAD

The zucchini bread will keep for three to four days at room temperature. Or wrapped in heavy-duty aluminum foil, it can be frozen for up to three months. Let it thaw on the kitchen counter for 4 hours or overnight.

IN THE RAIN-SHOWERY SUMMERTIME WHEN THE ZUCCHINI in the garden seems to grow a foot a day, it's nice to have recipes like this one that uses zucchini when it has grown past the young and tender stage. Shred a medium-size to large zucchini and you will have two cups, just the right amount to fold into this quick cinnamon breakfast bread. It makes a nice gift, in the heat of summer or during the winter holidays.

> Vegetable oil spray, for misting the pan
> 1¾ cups all-purpose flour, plus flour for dusting the loaf pan
> 1 cup sugar
> 2 teaspoons cinnamon
> 1½ teaspoons baking powder
> 1 teaspoon salt
> ½ teaspoon ground nutmeg
> 3 large eggs, lightly beaten
> ¾ cup vegetable oil
> 1 medium-size zucchini, shredded (2 cups)
> 1 teaspoon pure vanilla extract
> ⅓ cup finely chopped walnuts

1. Place a rack in the center of the oven and preheat the oven to 325°F. Lightly mist a 9 by 5–inch loaf pan with vegetable oil spray and dust it with flour. Shake out the excess flour. Set the pan aside.

2. Place the flour, sugar, cinnamon, baking powder, salt, and nutmeg in a large mixing bowl and stir with a fork to combine.

Add the eggs, oil, zucchini, and vanilla and stir until the mixture is smooth, 1 to 2 minutes. Pour the batter into the prepared loaf pan and sprinkle the chopped walnuts over the top of the loaf.

3. Bake the bread until it is lightly browned and the top springs back when lightly pressed with a finger, 60 to 65 minutes. Transfer the loaf pan to a rack and let the bread cool for about 20 minutes. Run a sharp knife around the edges of the bread and give the pan a few good shakes to loosen the loaf. Invert the bread onto a wire rack, then invert it again onto another wire rack so that it cools right side up. Let the zucchini bread cool completely before serving, about 40 minutes.

BIG BATCH: *You can double this recipe easily and bake two zucchini walnut loaves.*

MAKING MUFFINS
FROM A LOAF OF BREAD

Isn't it so often true—the recipe is for a loaf of bread but you want to bake muffins? I have discovered that any quick bread recipe that makes one large loaf (9 by 5 inches) will make twelve 2½-inch muffins. Line the muffin tins with paper liners, spoon in enough batter to fill them about three quarters full, then bake the muffins at 375°F until the tops spring back when lightly pressed, somewhere between 20 and 25 minutes.

Sour Cream Cinnamon Streusel Loaves

MAKES TWO 9 BY 5-INCH LOAVES

PREP: 10 MINUTES ✶ BAKE: ABOUT 50 MINUTES ✶ COOL: AT LEAST 35 MINUTES

TOTE NOTES

Place the streusel loaves on a pretty serving tray, and slice a few slices from each end, leaving the rest of the loaf intact. Cover the tray with plastic wrap and you will be ready to go.
Or, place the loaves in a basket lined with a pretty napkin and wrap it loosely with aluminum foil for traveling.

FOR GIFT GIVING

Wrap the cooled loaves in plastic wrap or parchment paper.

PLAN AHEAD

The streusel loaves will keep for three to four days at room temperature.

IF YOU'VE GOT A YELLOW CAKE MIX IN YOUR PANTRY and a few staple ingredients, you're on your way to making two gorgeous loaves of coffee cake in no time. They're perfect for slicing and serving at your book club meeting, taking to a friend just home from the hospital, or wrapping as gifts for teachers. Adding nuts to the streusel makes for a nice crunch—try using finely chopped pecans, walnuts, or almonds.

Vegetable oil spray, for misting the loaf pans
¼ cup all-purpose flour, plus flour for dusting the loaf pans
1 package (18¼ ounces) plain yellow cake mix
½ packed cup light brown sugar
½ cup finely chopped nuts of your choice (pecans, walnuts, or almonds; optional)
2 teaspoons ground cinnamon
1 cup sour cream
4 large eggs
2 teaspoons pure vanilla extract
½ cup vegetable oil
½ cup warm water

1. Place a rack in the center of the oven and preheat the oven to 350°F. Lightly mist two 9 by 5–inch loaf pans with vegetable oil spray and dust them with flour. Shake out the excess flour. Set the pans aside.

2. Stir together the flour and cake mix in a large mixing bowl, then measure out 3 tablespoons and transfer this to a smaller bowl to make the streusel mixture. Add the brown sugar, nuts, if desired, and the cinnamon to the smaller bowl and stir to combine. Set the streusel mixture aside.

3. Place the sour cream, eggs, vanilla, oil, and warm water in the large bowl with the remaining cake mix and flour. Beat with an electric mixer on low speed until just combined, about 30 seconds, then stop the machine and scrape down the side of the bowl. Increase the mixer speed to medium and beat until the mixture is smooth, about 1 minute longer. Spoon about a quarter of the batter into the bottom of each prepared loaf pan and spread it out with a small rubber spatula. Spoon a quarter of the streusel evenly over the batter in each pan, then top this with the remaining batter, dividing it evenly between the 2 pans. Carefully spread the batter out with the spatula and sprinkle the remaining streusel over the tops, dividing it evenly.

4. Bake the loaves until they are golden brown and the tops spring back when lightly pressed with a finger, 48 to 52 minutes. Transfer the loaf pans to a rack and let the loaves cool for about 15 minutes. Run a sharp knife around the edges of each loaf and give the pans a few good shakes to loosen the loaves. Invert a loaf onto a wire rack, then invert it again onto another wire rack so that it cools right side up. Repeat with the remaining loaf. If you want to serve the streusel loaves warm, let them cool for 15 to 20 minutes longer. For easiest slicing, let the loaves cool completely, 30 to 40 minutes longer.

RECIPE REMINDERS

Made for

Prep notes

Don't forget

Special touches

Bring again

Mindy's Pound Cake Loaves

MAKES TWO 9 BY 5-INCH LOAVES

PREP: 15 TO 20 MINUTES ✳ BAKE: ABOUT 1 HOUR ✳ COOL: 50 TO 60 MINUTES

MY FRIEND MINDY MAKES THE BEST POUND CAKE imaginable. She always brings me a big fat almond-scented cake each December, and often it comes just in time for my husband's birthday. We enjoy thick slices with fudge sauce and vanilla ice cream, or toasted and served with fresh fruit. Any precious leftover pound cake gets sent to the freezer until January, when we appreciate it all over again. And, that's when it dawned on me that it might be best to bake this fabulous rich cake in two loaves. You can use one and freeze the other or give it away—you decide.

Vegetable oil spray, for misting the loaf pans

3 cups all-purpose flour (see Note), plus flour for dusting the pans

1½ cups (3 sticks) unsalted butter, at room temperature

2¾ cups sugar

6 large eggs

2 teaspoons pure vanilla extract

½ teaspoon pure almond extract

½ teaspoon salt

½ teaspoon baking powder

1 cup reduced-fat or regular sour cream

1. Place a rack in the center of the oven and preheat the oven to 350°F. Lightly mist two 9 by 5–inch loaf pans with vegetable oil spray and dust them with flour. Shake out the excess flour. Set the pans aside.

2. Place the butter and sugar in a large mixing bowl and beat with an electric mixer on low speed until the mixture comes together in a mass and is fluffy, 2 to 3 minutes. Add the eggs, one at a time, followed by the vanilla and almond extract and beat until the mixture is creamy and lemon colored, about 2 minutes in all. Scrape down the side of the bowl as needed.

3. Place the flour in another bowl and stir in the salt and baking powder. With the electric mixer on low speed, add the flour mixture to the butter and egg mixture alternately with the sour cream. Beat the batter until it is well blended and light, about 1 minute longer. Divide the batter evenly between the 2 prepared loaf pans.

4. Bake the pound cakes until they are well browned and the tops spring back when lightly pressed with a finger, 58 to 62 minutes. Transfer the loaf pans to a wire rack and let the pound cakes cool for at least 20 minutes; don't rush this. Run a sharp knife around the edges of the pound cakes and give the pans a few good shakes to loosen the cakes. Invert a loaf onto a wire rack, then invert it again onto another wire rack so that it cools right side up. Repeat with the remaining pound cake. Let the pound cakes cool completely, 30 to 40 minutes. Slice the pound cakes before serving.

NOTE: Measure the flour by gently spooning it into the measuring cup.

RECIPE REMINDERS

Made for

Prep notes

Don't forget

Special touches

Bring again

One-Pan Cheese Danish

MAKES ONE 13 BY 9-INCH CHEESE DANISH

PREP: 30 MINUTES ✳ BAKE: 30 TO 35 MINUTES ✳ COOL: 15 MINUTES

TOTE NOTES

If you have a 13 by 9-inch baking pan that comes with a fitted plastic cover, you are ready to travel. This is the perfect recipe for this type of pan. If not, just cover the pan with the kind of plastic wrap that seals when you press it onto the sides of the pan.

FOR GIFT GIVING

Cut the Danish into squares and place them on a pretty china plate, then cover it with plastic wrap. The host gets to eat the Danish—and keep the plate, as well.

PLAN AHEAD

The Danish can be covered and kept for up to one day.

THIS RECIPE WAS PASSED ALONG TO ME YEARS AGO, but I never tried it until I began testing recipes for this book. What a treasure it turned out to be, making a gooey cheese Danish that bakes in a single pan. It's a perfect party recipe; the Danish is just right for taking places because it can be toted in the pan, then cut into pieces and arranged on a platter once you've arrived. Or, if the gathering is at your house, make and chill one or two of these ahead of time and reheat them right in the pan just before serving.

> Vegetable oil spray, for misting the baking pan
> 2 packages (8 ounces each) refrigerated crescent rolls
> 2 packages (8 ounces each) cream cheese, at room temperature
> 1½ cups sugar
> 1 large egg
> 1 teaspoon vanilla extract
> Flour, for dusting the work surface
> 6 tablespoons (¾ stick) butter, melted
> ¼ teaspoon ground cinnamon
> 1 cup chopped pecans

1. Place a rack in the center of the oven and preheat the oven to 350°F. Lightly mist a 13 by 9-inch metal baking pan with vegetable oil spray.

2. Open one can of crescent rolls and spread them out flat in the bottom of the prepared baking pan, using your fingers to press the seams together and press the dough about ¾ inch up the sides of the pan. The dough will be thin. Set the pan aside.

3. Place the cream cheese, 1 cup of the sugar, and the egg and vanilla in a large mixing bowl. Beat with an electric mixer on medium speed until smooth and creamy, about 1 minute. Spread the cream cheese mixture evenly over the dough but do not allow it to touch the sides of the pan. Open the second can of rolls. Spread them out on a lightly floured work surface and press the seams together. Shape the dough into a 13 by 9–inch rectangle. Gently lift the rectangle of dough off the work surface and place it on top of the cream cheese mixture. Using a dinner knife, carefully pull the bottom layer of dough away from the sides of the pan, just enough to allow you to pinch the 2 layers of dough together.

4. Brush the melted butter over the top layer of dough. Combine the remaining ½ cup sugar and the cinnamon and pecans in a small bowl. Sprinkle the sugar mixture evenly over the buttered dough.

5. Bake the Danish until puffed and golden brown, 30 to 35 minutes. Transfer the pan to a wire rack and let the Danish cool for about 15 minutes. Slice the Danish and serve it at room temperature.

RECIPE REMINDERS

Made for

Prep notes

Don't forget

Special touches

Bring again

Easy Hot Cross Buns

MAKES 16 BUNS

PREP: 30 MINUTES ✳ BAKE: 12 TO 15 MINUTES ✳ COOL: ABOUT 10 MINUTES

 TOTE NOTES

You can tote the buns in an airtight container or in a 13 by 9–inch baking dish with a cover.

When you arrive, reheat the buns in a baking dish or on a baking sheet covered with aluminum foil. They will be warmed through after 8 to 10 minutes in a 350°F oven.

FOR GIFT GIVING

Arrange the buns in an attractive flat basket lined with a cloth napkin.

PLAN AHEAD

The hot cross buns can be baked the day before and stored in an airtight container at room temperature.

MARTHA BOWDEN MAKES THESE CUTE LITTLE buns each Easter, and they are a lot easier to prepare than hot cross buns that begin with a yeast dough. This recipe is based on dressed-up refrigerated biscuits, to which you add cinnamon and raisins. Somehow in the process they are wonderfully transformed and taste like so much more. Have your kids make the buns and tote them to an Easter brunch. They'll love this hands-on recipe.

> Vegetable oil spray, for misting the baking sheets
> 1 large egg white
> ¼ cup plus 2 teaspoons sugar
> 1 teaspoon ground cinnamon
> 2 cans (about 16 ounces each) large butter-flavored refrigerated biscuits
> ½ cup raisins
> 1 tube (4¼ ounces) store-bought white icing

1. Place a rack in the center of the oven and preheat the oven to 375°F. Lightly mist 2 baking sheets with vegetable oil spray.

2. Place the egg white in a small bowl and lightly beat it. Add 2 teaspoons of the sugar and stir until combined, then set the egg mixture aside.

3. Place the remaining ¼ cup of sugar and the cinnamon in a separate small bowl and stir to combine. Set the sugar and cinnamon mixture aside.

4. Open the cans of biscuits. Place a piece of parchment paper or waxed paper on a work surface. Working with one biscuit at a time, flatten each biscuit into a 4½-inch circle. Sprinkle each biscuit with about ⅓ teaspoon of the cinnamon and sugar mixture. Press 8 to 10 raisins in the center of each biscuit.

5. Pull up the edges of a biscuit so it resembles a taco, then pinch the edges together to seal the dough closed. Press down on the seam to flatten the biscuit into a bun. Repeat with the remaining biscuits. Arrange the biscuits, seam side down, on the baking sheets about 2 inches apart. Brush the top and side of each bun with the egg white and sugar mixture.

6. Bake the buns until they are golden brown, 12 to 15 minutes. Using a metal spatula, transfer the buns to a serving plate and let cool until slightly warm, about 10 minutes. Following the directions on the icing tube, squeeze two lines on top of each bun to form a cross.

BIG BATCH: *You can easily double and triple this recipe, using as many refrigerated biscuits as needed.*

RECIPE REMINDERS

Made for

Prep notes

Don't forget

Special touches

Bring again

Mother's Homemade Bread

MAKES TWO 9 BY 5-INCH LOAVES

PREP: 20 MINUTES PLUS ABOUT 2 HOURS RISING TIME
BAKE: 35 TO 40 MINUTES ✳ COOL: ABOUT 35 MINUTES

TOTE NOTES

It's best to tote these loaves unsliced so that they stay moist. Wrap the loaves in aluminum foil after they've had a chance to cool. Place them in a pretty basket and take along some butter and a serrated bread knife for slicing.

FOR GIFT GIVING

Keep the wrapping simple because these loaves are gorgeous on their own. Clear plastic wrap works well. Tie a raffia ribbon around the loaves.

I HAVE REALLY FOND MEMORIES OF SMELLING THIS YUMMY yeast bread baking when I was a child. And, you know, you don't have to be a child to appreciate the smell of bread baking because adults, too, are starved for this sort of sensory treat. So much of our bread comes from bakeries that we seldom get to appreciate how wonderful it is to experience it freshly made in our own home. Don't save this recipe for a special occasion, just bake it on a rainy day, pass the softened butter, and wait for the smiles.

2½ cups whole milk
5 tablespoons butter
3 tablespoons sugar
1 teaspoon salt
½ cup warm water
2 packages (½ ounce total) active dry yeast
2 large eggs
About 7 cups all-purpose flour
Vegetable oil spray, for misting the loaf pans

1. Place the milk, 4 tablespoons of the butter, and the sugar and salt in a medium-size saucepan over medium-low heat. Cook, stirring, until the butter melts and the milk scalds, 2 to 3 minutes. Remove the pan from the heat and let the milk mixture cool to lukewarm.

2. Meanwhile, pour the warm water into a small bowl, add the yeast, and stir until the yeast dissolves. When the milk mixture is lukewarm, stir in the yeast and water mixture. Crack the eggs into the bowl that held the yeast and beat them lightly with a fork. Add the eggs to the yeast mixture and stir until incorporated. Pour the yeast mixture into a very large mixing bowl.

3. Using a wooden spoon, stir enough flour into the yeast mixture for it to come together in a mass; the dough should be stiff enough to form a ball but still soft and sticky to the touch. Transfer the dough to a large, clean mixing bowl, cover it with a kitchen towel, and place it in a warm spot to rise until doubled in size, about 1½ hours.

4. When the dough has risen, punch it down with your fist. Lightly mist two 9 by 5–inch loaf pans with vegetable oil spray. Using floured hands, divide the dough in half and shape each half into an oval, placing one in each prepared pan. Place the pans in a warm spot so the dough can rise until doubled in size, 30 to 35 minutes.

5. Place a rack in the center of the oven and preheat the oven to 350°F.

6. When the dough has risen, bake it until the loaves rise high above the sides of the pans and are golden brown, 35 to 40 minutes. Remove the pans from the oven and spread the remaining 1 tablespoon of butter over the top of the hot loaves so that it melts and forms a glaze. Let the loaves cool in the pans for 15 minutes, then turn them out onto a wire rack to finish cooling, about 20 minutes, before slicing.

RECIPE REMINDERS

Made for

Prep notes

Don't forget

Special touches

Bring again

Whole Wheat Refrigerator Rolls

MAKES ABOUT 6 DOZEN ROLLS

PREP: 20 MINUTES PLUS 9 HOURS RISING TIME ✳ BAKE: 12 TO 15 MINUTES

TOTE NOTES

If you bake the rolls early in the day, you can return them to the pie pans after they're cool. Cover the pans with aluminum foil and you're ready to travel. Or, arrange two dozen rolls in aluminum foil and transport them that way.

When you arrive, reheat the rolls in a 350°F oven until warmed through, 8 to 10 minutes.

FOR GIFT GIVING

If you bake the rolls in disposable pie pans, place a pan of rolls in a plastic bag and tie it with ribbon. If you've baked them on a baking sheet, break off a dozen rolls and wrap them in plastic wrap or parchment paper, secured with tape.

MY MOTHER-IN-LAW, FLOWERREE OAKES, PASSED a terrific roll recipe along to me many years ago. It was similar to the recipe that follows here but contained only white flour. My kids inhaled those rolls. Still, I had been yearning for a whole wheat roll recipe, so I tinkered a bit with Flowerree's recipe and came up with this version. In spite of the whole wheat flour in the rolls, my kids inhaled these, too. The beauty of this recipe is that the dough rises slowly in the fridge overnight, making this a real hands-off recipe. Plus you end up with a bunch—around six dozen rolls. Divide the rolls into packages of two dozen and take one package to a friend, another to a dinner party, and the rest to the freezer to pair with vegetable soup later on.

¾ cup vegetable oil

¾ cup sugar

2¼ cups boiling water

2 packages (½ ounce total) active dry yeast

1 teaspoon salt

2 large eggs, beaten

About 3 cups whole wheat flour

About 2½ cups all-purpose white flour

6 tablespoons (¾ stick) butter, melted, plus butter for greasing the baking sheet

1. Place the vegetable oil and sugar in a large heatproof mixing bowl and pour the boiling water over them. Stir until the sugar dissolves. Let the oil and sugar mixture cool until lukewarm, about 5 minutes. Add the yeast, stirring until it dissolves. Stir in the salt and eggs.

2. Stir in enough whole wheat and white flour for the mixture to come together in a mass; it will still be slightly sticky. Start with 2½ cups of whole wheat flour and 2 cups of white flour. Then add ¼ cup of whole wheat flour followed by ¼ cup of white flour. If necessary add another ¼ cup each of whole wheat and white flour. Cover the bowl with plastic wrap and place it in the refrigerator for at least 8 hours, or overnight, so that the dough rises until doubled in size.

3. When the dough has risen, punch it down with your fist and turn it out onto a floured work surface. Roll out the dough until it is about ⅓ inch thick. Using a floured biscuit cutter or the rim of a glass dipped in flour, cut the dough into 2-inch rounds. Dip the rounds of dough into the melted butter, fold them in half, and place them in tight rows on a large, lightly buttered baking sheet or in lightly buttered small, round, disposable aluminum foil pie pans (you will need about 6 pie pans). Cover the rolls with a light kitchen towel and put them in a warm place to rise until doubled in size, about 1 hour.

4. Preheat the oven to 400°F.

5. Bake the rolls until they are lightly browned, 12 to 15 minutes. Remove the rolls from the oven and immediately turn them out onto wire racks. Serve at once or let cool and wrap them for freezing or storing.

PLAN AHEAD

The rolls will keep for two days at room temperature. Or, freeze them for up to three months. Let them thaw on a kitchen counter for 3 to 4 hours, then warm them through in a 300°F oven for 10 to 15 minutes.

RECIPE REMINDERS

Made for

Prep notes

Don't forget

Special touches

Bring again

Mexican Corn Bread

MAKES ONE 13 BY 9–INCH CORN BREAD

PREP: 10 MINUTES ✳ BAKE: ABOUT 40 MINUTES ✳ COOL: 10 MINUTES

ONE OF MY FAVORITE RECIPES WHEN I WORKED AT *The Atlanta Journal-Constitution* years ago was a corn bread recipe from Joe McTyre, a photographer. This recipe makes a slightly larger variation of Joe's, a deliciously heavy and dense corn bread seasoned with hot and sweet peppers. It is perfect for toting to a Super Bowl party to serve with chili. It's great at summer barbecues in the backyard. And, I am sure you will find ways to turn this into your own recipe, adding a little minced garlic, a little sugar, or perhaps a handful of chopped scallions.

Vegetable oil spray, for misting the pan
3 cups self-rising cornmeal (see Note)
2 cups buttermilk
1 can (14¾ ounces) cream-style corn
4 large eggs
1 cup finely chopped green or red bell pepper
¼ cup finely chopped hot pepper, jalapeño or serrano, with or without seeds and veins
1 teaspoon salt
½ teaspoon ground cumin
2 cups (8 ounces) shredded sharp Cheddar cheese

1. Place a rack in the center of the oven and preheat the oven to 375°F. Lightly mist a 13 by 9–inch glass or ceramic baking dish with vegetable oil spray and place it in the oven to warm.

2. Place the cornmeal, buttermilk, corn, eggs, bell pepper, hot pepper, salt, cumin, and 1½ cups of the cheese in a large mixing bowl. Stir until well blended, about 2 minutes. Remove the baking dish from the oven and pour the batter into it. Scatter the remaining ½ cup of cheese over the top.

3. Bake the corn bread until it is lightly browned around the edges and set in the middle, 38 to 42 minutes. Let the corn bread cool for about 10 minutes, then slice it into squares.

NOTE: I use white self-rising cornmeal. If you cannot find this, use 3 cups of white or yellow cornmeal plus 1 tablespoon of baking powder and ¾ teaspoon of salt (in addition to the 1 teaspoon of salt already called for in the recipe).

BIG BATCH: *You can make two and three batches of the corn bread, baking each batch in a 13 by 9–inch pan. You can also halve this recipe, baking it in a 9-inch square pan for 30 to 35 minutes.*

WRAP IT UP

After a loaf of bread has cooled completely, you can wrap it up to give or store. Cut a piece of plastic wrap or parchment paper that is large enough to cover both of the long sides of the loaf, with enough extending out on each short end to fold over as you would when wrapping a gift. If needed, secure the ends with a little tape. Tie a bow of ribbon, raffia, or kitchen string around the middle of the loaf.

If you want to freeze the loaf, omit the ribbon, wrap the loaf again in heavy-duty aluminum foil, and label it. You can freeze most breads for up to three months. Let them thaw on the kitchen counter overnight.

PLAN AHEAD

The corn bread can be kept at room temperature for up to one day.

RECIPE REMINDERS

Made for

Prep notes

Don't forget

Special touches

Bring again

Zesty Marinated Olives

MAKES 2 CUPS

PREP: 15 MINUTES ✳ MARINATE: 4 HOURS

TOTE NOTES

Tote the olives in a pretty glass bowl covered with plastic wrap.

FOR GIFT GIVING

Place the olives in a clean decorative glass jar with a lid. Tie a raffia ribbon around it and attach a label suggesting ways to use the olives.

HAVING A JAR OF THESE MARINATED OLIVES IN YOUR refrigerator means you always have an appetizer ready when friends come to visit. These are delicious with the main course, too, accompanying grilled steaks, pizzas, pastas, and salads. Vary the type of olives as you like, for supermarkets now carry such gorgeous olives in the deli department. And play with the marinade ingredients, substituting orange zest for the lemon and a tablespoon of fennel seeds for the oregano.

1 cup kalamata or brine-cured black olives
1 cup large green cracked brine-cured olives (see Note)
¾ cup olive oil
3 tablespoons fresh lemon juice
3 medium-size cloves garlic, sliced
2 tablespoons chopped fresh oregano or parsley
1 teaspoon grated lemon zest
Dash of crushed red pepper

Place all of the olives in a glass bowl. Pour in the olive oil and lemon juice and stir to coat. Stir in the garlic, oregano or parsley, lemon zest, and crushed red pepper. Cover the bowl with plastic wrap and place it in the refrigerator to marinate for at least 4 hours, preferably overnight. Let the olives come to room temperature before serving.

NOTE: Large green olives are sold either cracked or uncracked. If your olives are uncracked, you can crack them by crushing them on a cutting board using the flat side of a large knife.

WANT A QUICK HORS D'OEUVRE? Bring about 8 ounces of cubed feta cheese and some pita bread along with the olives. Scatter the feta cubes and olives on a pretty tray and drizzle some of the olive marinade on top. Cut the pita into triangles and place these on the side of the tray with a couple of small spreaders. Don't forget to put an empty small bowl on the tray for the olive pits.

BIG BATCH: *This recipe is a cinch to double, triple, and quadruple using a large glass bowl. What an easy way to make holiday gifts!*

RECIPE REMINDERS

Made for

Prep notes

Don't forget

Special touches

Bring again

My Favorite Pimiento Cheese

MAKES 3 TO 4 CUPS

PREP: 20 MINUTES

I GUESS PIMIENTO CHEESE IS JUST A SOUTHERN FOOD because I don't see it much on my book tour stops through Portland, Chicago, or New York. And in the new Southern kitchen you don't see it as much as you used to, gone the way of homemade ice cream and home-baked bread and your own jams and jellies. But pimiento cheese is a whole lot easier to make compared to bread or jam or ice cream. Yes, you must shred the cheese freshly because it mixes up so much nicer than preshredded cheese from a bag. You *should* use homemade mayo, but since almost no one makes it from scratch anymore, I suggest using either Hellmann's or Duke's mayonnaise.

The fun comes when you add ingredients that appeal to you—such as chopped parsley or a hint of hot pepper sauce, some minced onion or diced tomatoes. You can jazz the cheese up. Take this to friends and they will happily slather it on sandwiches, warm and cold. You have not lived until you have eaten a grilled pimiento cheese sandwich on sourdough bread!

4 cups (1 pound) shredded sharp Cheddar cheese
2 jars (4 ounces each) diced pimientos, drained
⅓ cup mayonnaise, or more as needed
¼ cup chopped fresh parsley
Dash of hot pepper sauce or Worcestershire sauce
Salt and freshly ground black pepper

1. Place the cheese and pimientos in a large mixing bowl and stir to combine. Add enough mayonnaise to pull the mixture together. Fold in the parsley and hot pepper or Worcestershire sauce, then season the cheese with salt and pepper to taste.

2. Spoon the pimiento cheese into a crock or glass jar and refrigerate it until time to serve. (You can smear the cheese on sandwiches and crackers.)

BIG BATCH: *You can double and triple this recipe. Use the shredding attachment of the food processor to speed things along.*

RECIPE REMINDERS

Made for

Prep notes

Don't forget

Special touches

Bring again

Oven-Roasted Tomatoes Soaked in Basil and Oil

MAKES ABOUT 4 CUPS

PREP: 10 MINUTES ✳ BAKE: 60 TO 65 MINUTES
COOL: ABOUT 1 HOUR

TOTE NOTES

Carry these tomatoes in a pretty glass jar or a plastic container with a tight-fitting lid. They can go straight from the refrigerator to the table, but for best flavor, allow about 30 minutes for them to come to room temperature before serving.

FOR GIFT GIVING

Place the tomatoes in clean decorative jars with lids or corks. Tie a ribbon around the rim of the jar and add a label.

PLAN AHEAD

The tomatoes can be refrigerated for up to three weeks.

As I TYPE THIS RECIPE, I AM EATING A GLORIOUS piece of toasted sourdough bread smeared with goat cheese and topped with an oven-roasted tomato doused with some basil and olive oil. Some of the best food flavors around are dried or oven-roasted foods because the taste intensifies as the moisture is removed. The tomatoes you can make at home in the oven are more delicious than any dried tomato you can buy. They don't have the shelf life of commercial dried tomatoes, but they will keep for up to three weeks in the refrigerator. And that is plenty of time to give a jar to a friend or to place a few on pizza, goat cheese sandwiches, and grilled chicken. Prepare these when plum tomatoes are in season.

> 4 pounds (24) plum tomatoes
> 1 tablespoon kosher salt, or more as needed
> ¼ cup olive oil, plus more olive oil to pack in the jars
> 1 packed cup fresh basil leaves

1. Place a rack in the center of the oven and preheat the oven to 350°F.

2. Rinse the tomatoes under cold running water and pat them dry with paper towels. Cover a large baking sheet with parchment paper. Cut the tomatoes in half lengthwise and arrange them on the baking sheet, cut side up, so that they are nearly touching. Sprinkle the salt over the tomatoes and drizzle ¼ cup of olive oil on top.

3. Roast the tomatoes until they shrink in size but are still tender and the juices have evaporated, 60 to 65 minutes. Let the tomatoes cool completely, about 1 hour.

4. Place the cooled tomatoes in a large bowl and toss with the basil. Transfer the tomatoes to a large (2-quart) glass jar or divide them between two 1-quart jars. Pour in enough olive oil to completely cover the tomatoes. Secure the lid(s) on the jars and refrigerate the tomatoes.

BIG BATCH: *You can double and triple this recipe by roasting several pans of tomatoes at once.*

Homemade Pesto

MAKES ABOUT 1 CUP (ENOUGH FOR 1 POUND OF PASTA)

PREP: 4 TO 5 MINUTES

**TOTE
NOTES**

*Pack the pesto into a
reusable glass dish with
a snap-on lid or a clean
jar to tote. If you want to
serve it with pasta, bring
the pasta along to cook
fresh when you arrive.*

**FOR GIFT
GIVING**

*Put the pesto in a glass
jar and tie a ribbon
around it. Or, you can
dress up the top of a
glass container with a
snap-on lid by covering
it with a circle of fabric
secured with a ribbon
tied around the rim.*

PLAN AHEAD

*The pesto can be
prepared up to a
day in advance and
refrigerated.*

PUTTING A PESTO RECIPE DOWN ON PAPER IS TOUGH because you really don't need a recipe to make it. You just need clean hands, a ready supply of fresh basil from the garden, a food processor, and pine nuts, Parmesan, garlic, and olive oil. Having this pesto on hand makes summer and fall meals a snap to prepare, and it is the perfect gift for a new neighbor or the cook who has everything. I keep the pesto bright and green by preparing it just before the meal. But I have learned that, when I need to make pesto ahead of time, using half basil and half parsley will keep it vibrant.

> 1 large clove garlic, peeled
> 3 packed cups fresh basil leaves
> ⅓ cup pine nuts
> ⅓ cup shredded Parmesan cheese, or more to taste
> Dash of salt
> ½ cup extra-virgin olive oil

With the motor running, drop the clove of garlic through the feed tube of a food processor fitted with a steel blade and process until minced. Turn off the machine. Add the basil, pine nuts, Parmesan, and salt and process in on and off pulses until the mixture is crumbly, about 10 seconds. With the motor running, pour the olive oil through the feed tube slowly in dribbles at first and then a little faster so that the sauce thickens gradually. Turn off the machine and toss the pesto at once with hot pasta. Or, spoon it into a glass or ceramic storage container, cover it with plastic wrap, and refrigerate.

TEN GRAB-AND-GO GIFTS
FROM THE GROCERY

No time for homemade? The supermarket has some nice food gifts.

1. Look in the seafood department for a package of smoked salmon or trout. Include a box of good crackers or a loaf of cocktail rye bread, as well.

2. Wander down the natural foods aisle to the bulk bins and you'll find one of my favorite candies—chocolate-covered almonds.

3. While you're there, look for dried cherries or an exotic dried fruit. These make a suitable gift for a bread baker.

4. Walk over to the dairy case for refrigerated chocolate chip cookie dough. Follow the package directions, pressing a pecan half in the top of each cookie before baking.

5. Yum—toasted walnuts or pecans: Bring the nut halves home, toss them with a little salt and melted butter, and toast them in the oven at 350°F until they take on color, seven to eight minutes. Pile the nuts into a bag and tie it with a ribbon.

6. Or, choose whole nuts. You'll find them in the produce department during the fall and winter. Arrange an assortment of nuts in a pretty bowl and include a nutcracker.

7. For kids, pile the makings for s'mores—graham crackers, marshmallows, and chocolate bars—in a colorful basket or beach bucket.

8. Select a variety of citrus fruit—clementines, grapefruit, tangelos—and bring these in a pretty sack.

9. Pick up a nice bottle of extra-virgin olive oil and a loaf of crusty bread.

10. Buy fresh flowers. You can't miss.

Made for

Prep notes

Don't forget

Special touches

Bring again

Vidalia Onion Marmalade

MAKES 4 JARS (8 OUNCES EACH)

PREP: 25 TO 30 MINUTES ⋆ COOK: ABOUT 5 MINUTES

WHEN THOSE SWEET VIDALIA ONIONS FLOOD INTO the market in May, or when sweet onions of another variety come your way, save some for this easy marmalade. It is delicious served with grilled sausages and pork chops, and it is stunningly beautiful poured over cream cheese as an appetizer. I am partial to the big flat Vidalia onions, partly because of the time I spent in Georgia and because they store so well in the bottom drawer of my refrigerator.

2 cups finely chopped sweet onion, such as Vidalia (1 extra-large onion or 2 medium-size onions)
1 cup finely chopped green bell pepper
1 cup finely chopped red bell pepper
1 tablespoon grated fresh orange zest
1 dried hot pepper, crumbled, or 1 pinch hot pepper flakes
$\frac{1}{2}$ cup orange juice
$\frac{1}{2}$ cup white wine vinegar or distilled white vinegar
1 package ($1\frac{3}{4}$ ounces) powdered fruit pectin
2 cups sugar

1. Place the onion, green and red bell peppers, orange zest, and hot pepper in a large saucepan. Stir in the orange juice and vinegar, followed by the pectin. Place the pan over medium-high heat and bring to a boil, stirring. When the onion mixture is boiling, add the sugar and stir to combine.

Once the mixture comes back to a boil, begin timing. Cook the marmalade, stirring, at a boil until the sugar dissolves and the marmalade thickens slightly, about 1 minute, then remove the pan from the heat.

2. Ladle the marmalade into 4 sterilized 8-ounce jars (see Note), leaving a ¼-inch space at the top of each jar. Wipe off the jar rims with a damp paper towel. Seal the jar lids and let the marmalade cool completely before refrigerating.

NOTE: To easily sterilize the jars and their lids, run them through the dishwasher.

BIG BATCH: *So that it can thicken properly, you need to make no more than one batch of marmalade at a time.*

RECIPE REMINDERS

Made for

Prep notes

Don't forget

Special touches

Bring again

Cranberry and Apple Chutney

MAKES 5 JARS (8 OUNCES EACH)

PREP: 35 MINUTES ✳ COOK: 20 MINUTES

THIS CHUTNEY ORIGINALLY CAME FROM MARY FERGUSON of Chattanooga, and I have made the recipe countless times, changing it each time depending on whether I had apples or pears in the fruit bowl. And I might add golden raisins—maybe currants, maybe dates. The seasoning has pretty much stayed the same. For a couple of years I gave jars of the chutney as my Christmas gift, keeping plenty of it ready in the garage refrigerator. Right before the holidays, I tied burgundy satin bows on those jars. They were gorgeous. These days I make a big batch of chutney to get us through Thanksgiving—it is just as delicious on turkey sandwiches as it is slathered over a soft goat cheese to serve with crackers.

$1\frac{1}{2}$ cups granulated sugar

$\frac{3}{4}$ cup finely chopped onion (1 small onion)

$\frac{1}{2}$ cup apple cider vinegar

1 tablespoon minced garlic

2 teaspoons ground cinnamon

$\frac{1}{2}$ teaspoon ground cloves

$\frac{1}{2}$ teaspoon salt

$\frac{1}{4}$ teaspoon cayenne pepper

$1\frac{1}{2}$ cups water

$1\frac{1}{2}$ cups (about a 12-ounce bag) fresh cranberries, rinsed and picked over

$1\frac{1}{2}$ cups finely chopped apple (2 medium-size or 1 extra-large apple)

1 cup golden raisins

½ packed cup light brown sugar

½ teaspoon ground ginger

1. Place the granulated sugar, onion, cider vinegar, garlic, cinnamon, cloves, salt, cayenne pepper, and water in a 2-quart saucepan over medium-high heat. Let come to a boil, stirring. Reduce the heat to low and let simmer, uncovered, until the flavors blend, about 5 minutes.

2. Stir the cranberries, apple, raisins, brown sugar, and ginger into the onion mixture. Let simmer until the cranberries pop and the apple has softened, about 15 minutes.

3. Spoon the chutney into 5 sterilized, pretty 8-ounce glass jars (see Note), leaving a ¼-inch space at the top of each jar. Wipe off the jar rims with a damp paper towel. Seal the jar lids. Let the chutney cool completely, then tighten the lids before refrigerating the chutney. Or, spoon the chutney into a glass dish and let it cool about 15 minutes, then cover and refrigerate it.

NOTE: To easily sterilize the jars and their lids, run them through the dishwasher.

BIG BATCH: *I have doubled this recipe and made it in a large soup pot. Take care when you add the cranberries to stir them well so that they cook evenly.*

RECIPE REMINDERS

Made for

Prep notes

Don't forget

Special touches

Bring again

Refrigerator Peach Preserves

MAKES 4 TO 5 JARS (8 OUNCES EACH)

PREP: 20 TO 25 MINUTES PLUS 30 MINUTES STANDING TIME
COOK: 35 TO 40 MINUTES

 TOTE NOTES

Homemade peach preserves are gorgeous, with a peachy-golden color that is often rosy, depending on the variety of the peach. Pack the preserves into fancy French canning jars or simple canning jars from the grocery store and they're ready to travel.

FOR GIFT GIVING

Tie ribbons around the lids and place labels on the jars of preserves. Present them in small baskets.

PLAN AHEAD

The peach preserves can be refrigerated for up to one year.

OFTEN SUMMER SLIPS BY AND I HAVE NOT MADE A batch of peach preserves. We don't notice until the dead of winter, on those dark school mornings when my kids aren't happy about getting out of a warm bed and are not pleased with any breakfast I put on the table. And then I'm sorry: The sight of peach preserves spread on toast is a ray of summer sunshine for my kids and me. It provides hope that the weather will turn warm, school will end, and the pool will open. To brighten someone's day, make this with good peaches in the summer and store it in the refrigerator for the rest of the year (hence its name).

> 6 cups peeled, pitted, and sliced peaches
> (6 to 7 large, firm, ripe peaches)
> 4 cups sugar
> 2 tablespoons fresh lemon juice

1. Place the peach slices, sugar, and lemon juice in a 4-quart or larger stainless steel or enamel-coated cast-iron (not aluminum) saucepan. Stir to combine and let the mixture stand for 30 minutes so that the juice is released from the peaches and the sugar dissolves.

2. Place the saucepan over medium heat and bring the peach mixture to a boil, stirring. Reduce the heat to medium-low and let simmer, stirring, until the peach slices are clear and the syrup thickens, 35 to 40 minutes. As the peaches cook, use a ladle to skim the foam off the top. Remove the saucepan from the heat.

3. Ladle the preserves into 4 or 5 warm sterilized 8-ounce glass jars (see Note), leaving a ¼-inch space at the top of each jar. Wipe off the jar rims with a damp paper towel. Seal the jar lids and let the preserves cool completely, then tighten the lids before refrigerating the preserves.

NOTE: To easily sterilize the jars and their lids, run them through the dishwasher. If you run the dishwasher right before you make the preserves, the jars will be warm when you are ready to fill them.

BIG BATCH: *Successful preserves and jellies are made in small batches, so don't try to double batch this recipe. Make one recipe today, another tomorrow, and so on . . .*

RECIPE REMINDERS

Made for

Prep notes

Don't forget

Special touches

Bring again

Jezebel Sauce

MAKES 4 JARS (8 OUNCES EACH)

PREP: ABOUT 10 MINUTES

TOTE NOTES

It's easy to carry Jezebel Sauce in glass jars. Turn the sauce into a quick appetizer by bringing along some goat cheese or cream cheese and crackers, too.

FOR GIFT GIVING

Place a circle of burlap or other material of your choice around the top of the jar, then tie a ribbon around it to create a pretty jar topper.

PLAN AHEAD

The Jezebel Sauce can be refrigerated for two to three weeks.

My AUNT LOUISE GAVE ME THIS FUN RECIPE YEARS ago. No one knows the sauce's origin, but we do know how delicious it is poured over goat cheese or cream cheese and served with crackers. It also makes a terrific quick glaze for pork tenderloin or salmon. Pack this peach-colored sauce in four eight-ounce jars; they're perfect for gift giving.

2 cups apricot preserves

2 cups apple jelly

$\frac{2}{3}$ cup prepared horseradish sauce

2 tablespoons dry mustard

1 teaspoon freshly ground black pepper

Place the apricot preserves, apple jelly, horseradish sauce, mustard, and pepper in a blender or food processor fitted with a steel blade. Blend or pulse until the ingredients are well combined, about 30 seconds. Spoon the sauce into 4 sterilized 8-ounce jars (see Note), leaving a $\frac{1}{4}$-inch space at the top of each jar. Wipe off the jar rims with a damp paper towel. Seal the jar lids. Label the jars and store them in the refrigerator.

NOTE: To easily sterilize the jars and their lids, run them through the dishwasher.

BIG BATCH: *You can easily make multiple jars of this sauce for gifts—blend one batch at a time in the blender or food processor.*

Warm Fudge Sauce

MAKES 3 CUPS

PREP: 5 MINUTES ✳ COOK: ABOUT 15 MINUTES

I F YOU MAKE ONLY ONE RECIPE FROM MY COOKBOOK, this is the one. You'll thank me. This sauce is to die for over vanilla or coffee ice cream. My kids used to beg for the ice cream with chocolate sauce at Carraba's restaurants; this is our version of that sinful sauce. It's up to you whether you make the sauce and keep it all for yourself or take a jar to a friend.

 TOTE NOTES

Pour the fudge sauce into a clean glass jar and it's ready to go. Add a container of ice cream (packed in a cooler) and you've got dessert.

8 tablespoons (1 stick) unsalted butter, cut into tablespoons

4 squares (4 ounces) unsweetened chocolate

1¾ cups sugar

Pinch salt

1 can (12 ounces) evaporated milk

2 teaspoons pure vanilla extract

Place the butter and chocolate in a heavy saucepan over low heat and cook, stirring, until they melt, 3 to 4 minutes. Turn off the heat. Using a wooden spoon, stir in the sugar and salt. Then, stir in the evaporated milk. Increase the heat to medium and cook at a gentle simmer, stirring constantly, until the sauce thickens enough to coat the spoon, 12 to 15 minutes. Turn off the heat and stir in the vanilla. The sauce should be refrigerated and it may be reheated on top of the stove or in the microwave on high power so that you can serve it warm, at its best.

FOR GIFT GIVING

Think about including a new ice cream scoop or a pretty ladle when you give a friend a jar of fudge sauce.

PLAN AHEAD

The fudge sauce can be refrigerated, covered, for up to a week.

BIG BATCH: *I have successfully doubled this recipe, making it in one large pan. This makes a lot of sauce, enough for twenty of your favorite friends.*

Susan's Orange-Glazed Nuts

MAKES 4 TO 5 CUPS

PREP: 10 MINUTES ✳ BAKE: ABOUT 45 MINUTES ✳ COOL: 1 HOUR

TOTE NOTES

Place the cooled nuts in a large resealable plastic bag or an airtight tin for traveling.

FOR GIFT GIVING

For gifts, package the nuts in small plastic bags or cellophane candy sacks and tie them with ribbons.

PLAN AHEAD

The glazed nuts can be kept in an airtight container at room temperature for up to a week or frozen for up to a month. Let them thaw overnight on a kitchen counter.

MY SISTER SUSAN BRINGS THESE NUTS TO OUR house to garnish a big green salad she likes to prepare. They go well with the sweetened dried cranberries and crumbled blue cheese she adds. You could also add a handful of fresh fruit or canned mandarin oranges, but it's the nuts that make the salad special.

$\frac{1}{3}$ cup sugar
4 tablespoons ($\frac{1}{2}$ stick) unsalted butter
$\frac{1}{4}$ cup orange juice
$1\frac{1}{2}$ teaspoons salt
$1\frac{1}{4}$ teaspoons cayenne pepper
$\frac{1}{4}$ teaspoon ground nutmeg
1 to $1\frac{1}{2}$ pounds pecan or walnut halves

1. Place a rack in the center of the oven and preheat the oven to 250°F. Line a rimmed baking sheet with aluminum foil and set it aside.

2. Place the sugar, butter, orange juice, salt, cayenne, and nutmeg in a large, heavy skillet over low heat. Cook, stirring, until the butter melts and the sugar dissolves, 2 to 3 minutes. Stir in 1 to $1\frac{1}{2}$ pounds of pecans, adding just enough so that the nuts are all evenly coated with the glaze. Remove the skillet from the heat.

3. Transfer the pecan mixture to the aluminum foil–lined baking sheet, spreading the nuts out in a single layer. Bake the pecans until they are deeply browned and glazed, about 45 minutes, stirring them every 15 minutes.

4. Transfer the nuts to a clean piece of aluminum foil and separate them with a fork. Let the nuts cool for about 1 hour, then store them in an airtight container.

FIFTEEN QUICK GIFTS
FOR THE HOST OR HOSTESS

Want to pick up a little something for the guy or gal who opens up a home, cleans off the kitchen counters, empties out the coat closet—and does who knows what all else before you come over? Here are some ideas:

1. A nice bottle of wine

2. A wine topper tied onto some pretty paper napkins

3. Attractive soaps for the powder room

4. A food that is hard to prepare, such as toffee or cheese straws

5. Candles

6. Personalized towels

7. A fun jar of mixer for drinks with a recipe card for your signature drink attached

8. A jar of homemade jam or jelly

9. A jar of homemade salsa

10. A basket of fruit of the season, such as fragrant peaches

11. A basket of baking ingredients—a bar of chocolate, a pound of pecans, or the like, plus a favorite recipe in which to use them

12. A box of fancy chocolates

13. A bagful of ripe tomatoes from your garden

14. Good olives

15. A framed photo of the host or hostess

RECIPE REMINDERS

Made for

Prep notes

Don't forget

Special touches

Bring again

Sweet and Spicy Pecans

MAKES 2 CUPS

PREP: 25 TO 28 MINUTES ✳ BAKE: 10 MINUTES

**TOTE
NOTES**

*Once the pecans have
cooled, put them in a
large resealable plastic
bag or in an airtight tin
for traveling.*

**FOR GIFT
GIVING**

*Place the nuts in small
cellophane bags and tie
them with pretty ribbons.
Or buy a selection of
fancy Chinese carry-
out containers sold
nowadays—they're
perfect for nuts.*

PLAN AHEAD

*The pecans can be stored
in a resealable plastic
bag for up to two weeks.*

TOSS THESE DEVILISHLY GOOD PECANS ON THE
"Baby Blue" salad (see page 100) or your favorite
one that features mixed greens. You'll want to
make extra pecans for snacking and gift giving.

Vegetable oil spray, for misting the baking sheet
¾ cup sugar
2 cups warm water
2 cups pecan halves
1 teaspoon ground cinnamon
½ teaspoon ground red pepper, or more to taste

1. Preheat the oven to 350°F. Lightly mist a rimmed baking
sheet with vegetable oil spray.

2. Place ½ cup of the sugar and the warm water in a medium-
size saucepan over medium-low heat and stir until the sugar
dissolves. Turn off the heat, add the pecans, and stir to coat
well with the syrup. Let the pecans soak for 10 minutes, then
drain them.

3. Place the remaining ¼ cup of sugar and the cinnamon
and red pepper in a large plastic resealable bag and shake to
combine. Add the drained pecans and shake to coat well.
Transfer the pecans to the prepared baking sheet and spread
them out in a single layer.

4. Bake the pecans until they are golden, about 10 minutes.
Let the pecans cool on the baking sheet before using.

BIG BATCH: *It's tempting to double or triple this recipe,
but you'll get the best results if you bake one batch at a time.*

CONVERSION TABLES

APPROXIMATE EQUIVALENTS

1 stick butter = 8 tbs = 4 oz = $\frac{1}{2}$ cup

1 cup all-purpose presifted flour or dried bread crumbs = 5 oz

1 cup granulated sugar = 8 oz

1 packed cup brown sugar = 6 oz

1 cup confectioners' sugar = $4\frac{1}{2}$ oz

1 cup honey or syrup = 12 oz

1 cup grated cheese = 4 oz

1 cup dried beans = 6 oz

1 large egg = about 2 oz or about 3 tbs

1 egg yolk = about 1 tbs

1 egg white = about 2 tbs

Please note that all conversions are approximate but close enough to be useful when converting from one system to another.

WEIGHT CONVERSIONS

U.S.	METRIC	U.S.	METRIC
$\frac{1}{2}$ oz	15 g	7 oz	200 g
1 oz	30 g	8 oz	250 g
$1\frac{1}{2}$ oz	45 g	9 oz	275 g
2 oz	60 g	10 oz	300 g
$2\frac{1}{2}$ oz	75 g	11 oz	325 g
3 oz	90 g	12 oz	350 g
$3\frac{1}{2}$ oz	100 g	13 oz	375 g
4 oz	125 g	14 oz	400 g
5 oz	150 g	15 oz	450 g
6 oz	175 g	1 lb	500 g

LIQUID CONVERSIONS

U.S.	IMPERIAL	METRIC
2 tbs	1 fl oz	30 ml
3 tbs	$1\frac{1}{2}$ fl oz	45 ml
$\frac{1}{4}$ cup	2 fl oz	60 ml
$\frac{1}{3}$ cup	$2\frac{1}{2}$ fl oz	75 ml
$\frac{1}{3}$ cup + 1 tbs	3 fl oz	90 ml
$\frac{1}{3}$ cup + 2 tbs	$3\frac{1}{2}$ fl oz	100 ml
$\frac{1}{2}$ cup	4 fl oz	125 ml
$\frac{2}{3}$ cup	5 fl oz	150 ml
$\frac{3}{4}$ cup	6 fl oz	175 ml
$\frac{3}{4}$ cup + 2 tbs	7 fl oz	200 ml
1 cup	8 fl oz	250 ml
1 cup + 2 tbs	9 fl oz	275 ml
$1\frac{1}{4}$ cups	10 fl oz	300 ml
$1\frac{1}{3}$ cups	11 fl oz	325 ml
$1\frac{1}{2}$ cups	12 fl oz	350 ml
$1\frac{2}{3}$ cups	13 fl oz	375 ml
$1\frac{3}{4}$ cups	14 fl oz	400 ml
$1\frac{3}{4}$ cups + 2 tbs	15 fl oz	450 ml
2 cups (1 pint)	16 fl oz	500 ml
$2\frac{1}{2}$ cups	20 fl oz (1 pint)	600 ml
$3\frac{3}{4}$ cups	$1\frac{1}{2}$ pints	900 ml
4 cups	$1\frac{3}{4}$ pints	1 liter

OVEN TEMPERATURES

°F	GAS MARK	°C	°F	GAS MARK	°C
250	$\frac{1}{2}$	120	400	6	200
275	1	140	425	7	220
300	2	150	450	8	230
325	3	160	475	9	240
350	4	180	500	10	260
375	5	190			

Note: Reduce the temperature by 20°C (68°F) for fan-assisted ovens.

BIBLIOGRAPHY

Thanks to the following authors and books for ideas that were helpful in planning, developing, and writing recipes for the *What Can I Bring?* cookbook.

Anderson, Jean. *The American Century Cookbook: The Most Popular Recipes of the Twentieth Century.* New York: Clarkson Potter, 1997.

Byrn, Anne. *Food Gifts for All Seasons.* Atlanta: Peachtree Publishers, 1996.

Cunningham, Marion. *Lost Recipes: Meals to Share with Friends and Family.* New York: Alfred A. Knopf, 2003.

Exum, Helen McDonald. *Chattanooga Cook Book.* Chattanooga: The Chattanooga News Free Press, 1970.

Foster, Sara. *The Foster's Market Cookbook.* New York: Random House, 2002.

Garten, Ina. *The Barefoot Contessa Cookbook.* New York: Clarkson Potter, 1999.

Junior League of Austin. *Necessities and Temptations.* Austin: Junior League of Austin Publications, 1987.

Junior League of Chattanooga. *Dinner on the Diner.* Chattanooga: Junior League of Chattanooga, 1983.

Junior League of Nashville. *Nashville Seasons.* Nashville: Junior League of Nashville, 1964.

Martha White Foods, Inc. *Southern Traditions: One Hundred Years of Recipes from the Martha White Kitchens.* Minnetonka, Minn.: Creative Publishing International, 1999.

Villas, James, with Martha Pearl Villas. *My Mother's Southern Desserts.* New York: Macmillan, 1998.

Villas, James, with Martha Pearl Villas. *My Mother's Southern Kitchen: Recipes and Reminiscences.* New York: William Morrow and Co., 1994.

Ward, Jessica Bemis *Food to Die For: A Book of Funeral Food, Tips, and Tales from the Old City Cemetery, Lynchburg, Virginia.* Lynchburg: Southern Memorial Association, 2004.

Twelve "Mini Indexes"

Often it's not so much a specific dish you are longing to take to a gathering, it's a type of recipe your host requests or that you instinctively feel would be a hit. To help you locate specific recipes in this book that fall into time-tested categories, here are a dozen "mini indexes." Browse through them when you are looking for inspiration.

THE EASIEST RECIPES

Suzanne's Guacamole, page 8
Marie's White Bean and Basil Spread, page 18
Hummus in a Hurry, page 22
The Best Caesar Salad, page 92
Sliced Tomato Salad with Basil and Buttermilk Dressing, page 116
My Sweet and Sour Broccoli Salad, page 124
Quick Tabbouleh, page 134
Slow-Cooker Chicken and Dressing, page 172
Barb's Taco Ring, page 187
Ham and Cheese Overnight Soufflé, page 194
Baked Penne with Mozzarella and Basil, page 208
Black Bean Tortilla Bake, page 212
Easy Barbecued Ribs, page 238
Eggplant Parmesan with Fresh Basil, page 272
Bebe's Green Beans, page 274
Roast Potatoes for a Crowd, page 278
Sautéed Zucchini with Garlic Slivers, page 298
Braised White Beans with Rosemary, page 320

Cheesy Garlic Bread, page 333
Orange Marmalade Cake, page 353
Sixty-Minute Caramel Cake, page 359
Easy Linzer Bars, page 398
Seven-Layer Bars, page 400
My Favorite Key Lime Pie, page 414
Mindy's Grilled Figs with Honey, Walnuts, and Crumbled Stilton, page 436
Sour Cream Cinnamon Streusel Loaves, page 450
One-Pan Cheese Danish, page 454
Zesty Marinated Olives, page 464
Homemade Pesto, page 470
Jezebel Sauce, page 478

SOMETHING GREEN

Veggies with Green Goddess Dipping Sauce, page 4
Ricotta-Filled Bresaola with Arugula and Parmesan Shavings, page 46
Asian Chicken Lettuce Wraps, page 48
The Best Caesar Salad, page 92
Big Green Salad with Orange, Avocado, and Red Wine Vinaigrette, page 94
Baby Blue Salad with Sweet and Spicy Pecans, page 100
Spinach Salad with Mahogany Roasted Mushrooms and Onions, page 103
Roasted Asparagus with Olive Oil and Salt, page 256
Steamed Asparagus with a Light Ginger and Sesame Sauce, page 258
Green Beans with a Spicy Tomato Sauce, page 276
Sautéed Zucchini with Garlic Slivers, page 298

Grilled Vegetable Platter with Pesto
Vinaigrette, page 302

WHEN YOU WANT SOMETHING LIGHT

Herbed Goat Cheese Pyramid, page 32
Smoked Fish Pâté, page 52
Summertime Gazpacho, page 69
Spinach Salad with Curried Apple and
Cashew Dressing, page 106
Arugula Salad with Grape Tomatoes and
Parmesan Shavings, page 110
Orzo and Spinach Salad with Lemon
Cranberry Vinaigrette, page 138
Lemon Garlic Shrimp with an Avocado
Salsa, page 216
Eighteen-Minute Salmon with a Fresh
Ginger Glaze, page 218
Roasted Asparagus with Olive Oil and Salt,
page 256
Summertime Ratatouille, page 304
Baked Rice with Mushrooms and
Consommé, page 324
Midsummer's Night Pasta, page 328
Coconut Almond Macaroons, page 390
Iron Skillet Apple Tart, page 421
Mindy's Grilled Figs with Honey, Walnuts,
and Crumbled Stilton, page 436

TO FEED A CROWD

Twelve-Layer Taco Dip, page 16
Cowboy Caviar, page 20
Deborah's Hot Spinach Dip, page 26
Blue Cheese Pecan Wafers, page 40
Big Green Salad with Orange and Avocado,
page 94
Antipasto Pasta Salad, page 140
Old-Fashioned Macaroni Salad, page 142
Watermelon Boat with Summer Fruits,
page 160
Currey's King Ranch Chicken, page 180

Lowcountry Shrimp Boil, page 215
Turkey Burgers on the Grill with Pesto
Mayonnaise, page 232
Broccoli Corn Bread, page 262
Roast Potatoes for a Crowd, page 278
Creamy Scalloped Potatoes, page 282
Hot Curried Fruit, page 308
Hoppin' John, page 322
Cheesy Garlic Bread, page 333
Carrot Cake with Maple Cream Cheese
Frosting, page 362
The Best Chocolate Chip Cookies, page 378
Peach and Blueberry Crisp, page 430
Deep Dish Cherry Cobbler, page 425
Aunt Elizabeth's Banana Pudding, page 434
Big Batch Pumpkin Bread, page 446

SOMETHING KIDS LIKE

Hot Chile, Cheese, and Corn Dip, page 14
Little Crisp Crab Cakes, page 56
R. B.'s Grilled Pizza, page 63
House Favorite Vegetable Soup, page 74
Jackie's Potato Soup, page 76
Old-Fashioned Macaroni Salad, page 142
Watermelon Boat with Summer Fruits,
page 160
Waldorf Salad, page 163
Parmesan Chicken Rolls, page 170
Susan's Chicken Potpie, page 174
Mexican "Lasagna" Stack, page 204
Home-Fried Chicken Tenders with Blue
Cheese Sauce, page 226
Turkey Burgers on the Grill with Pesto
Mayonnaise, page 232
Bereavement Corn, page 266
Twice-Baked Potatoes, page 280
My Favorite Turkey Dressing, page 316
Potluck Baked Beans, page 318
Baked Macaroni and Cheese, page 330
Cheesy Garlic Bread, page 333

Chocolate Buttermilk Sheet Cake, page 338
Fresh Apple Cake with Caramel Glaze,
    page 356
Shirley's Snickerdoodles, page 382
Classic Peanut Butter Cookies, page 384
Barbara's Oatmeal Raisin Cookies, page 386
Iron Skillet Apple Tart, page 421
Aunt Elizabeth's Banana Pudding, page 434
Best Banana Bread, page 444
Mother's Homemade Bread, page 458
Warm Fudge Sauce, page 479

SOMETHING PRETTY

Curried Cheese Ball Showered in Coconut,
    Chutney, and Cashews, page 38
Ann's Home-Smoked Salmon with Olives
    and Lemon, page 50
Jan's Bruschetta, page 61
Papaya and Arugula Salad, page 108
Tomato, Mozzarella, and Basil Salad with
    Fresh Tomato Vinaigrette, page 118
Tina's Corn and Black Bean Salad, page 148
Margaret's Black Cherry Salad, page 164
Mushroom and Gruyère Cheesecake,
    page 198
Lemon Garlic Shrimp with an Avocado
    Salsa, page 216
Eighteen-Minute Salmon with a Fresh
    Ginger Glaze, page 218
John's Grilled Beef Tenderloin, page 240
Grilled Leg of Lamb with Greek Chimichurri
    Sauce, page 248
David's Grilled Artichokes with Roasted
    Tomato Vinaigrette, page 253
Braised Red Cabbage with Apples and
    Wine, page 264
Fresh Corn Pudding, page 270
Spinach and Feta Pie, page 286
Butternut Squash and Tomato Gratin,
    page 290

Grilled Vegetable Platter with Pesto
    Vinaigrette, page 302
Orange Marmalade Cake, page 353
Tres Leches Cakes Piled with Strawberries,
    page 365
Chocolate Zuccotto Cake, page 372
Cranberry Tart, page 423
Cranberry and Apple Chutney, page 474
Refrigerator Peach Preserves, page 476

COOL DISHES FOR WARM WEATHER

Cowboy Caviar, page 20
Goat Cheese with Cilantro Pesto, page 34
Julia's Chilled Zucchini Soup, page 72
Cucumber and Tomato Salad with Sweet
    Dill Vinaigrette, page 112
Fresh Green Bean Salad with Crumbled Feta
    Vinaigrette, page 120
Jess's Broccolini Salad, page 122
John's Homemade Coleslaw, page 126
Parmesan Chicken Rolls, page 170
Eighteen-Minute Salmon with a Fresh
    Ginger Glaze, page 218
Cuban Chicken Legs, page 223
Roasted Asparagus with Olive Oil and Salt,
    page 256
Braised Red Cabbage with Apples and
    Wine, page 264
Sautéed Zucchini with Garlic Slivers,
    page 298
Summertime Ratatouille, page 304
Spiced Cranberry Sauce, page 314
Chocolate Peppermint Ice Cream Cake,
    page 344
Tres Leches Cakes Piled with Strawberries,
    page 365
My Favorite Key Lime Pie, page 414
Elena's Tiramisu, page 438
My Favorite Pimiento Cheese, page 466

SOMETHING SPICY

Andy's Stolen Salsa, page 12
Twelve-Layer Taco Dip, page 16
Mighty Fine Texas Chili, page 86
Asian Slaw with Peanut Dressing,
    page 128
Chicken Taco Salad with Cilantro-Lime
    Vinaigrette, page 150
Creole Chicken Spaghetti, page 176
Tex-Mex Chicken Spaghetti, page 182
Curried Corn and Bell Peppers, page 268
Green Beans with a Spicy Tomato Sauce,
    page 276
Cindy's Chile Cheese Grits, page 326
Mexican Corn Bread, page 462
Susan's Orange Glazed Nuts, page 480
Sweet and Spicy Pecans, page 482

SOMETHING SPECIAL

Layered Crabmeat Stack, page 54
BLT Canapés, page 59
Tea Sandwiches for Friends, page 65
Roasted Beet Salad with Walnuts and
    Blue Cheese Dressing, page 96
Theresa's Romaine and Apricot Salad,
    page 98
Warm Potato Salad with Rosemary and
    Camembert, page 133
Chilled Shrimp Rémoulade Salad,
    page 156
Ladies' Lunch Tomato Aspic, page 166
Turkey Tetrazzini, page 185
January Lamb Stew, page 192
Lou Ann's Spinach, Prosciutto, and
    Mushroom Midnight Strata, page 196
Braised Pork Loin with Prunes and
    Almonds, page 236
Grilled Dry-Rub Flank Steaks, page 244
Grilled Leg of Lamb with Greek Chimichurri
    Sauce, page 248
Boursin Potato Gratin, page 284

Mike's Sweet Potato "Soufflé," page 294
Fresh Tomato Pie, page 296
Mrs. Collins's Sweet Potato Cake, page 350
Holiday Fruit Drops, page 393
Cranberry Tart, page 423
Double-Crust Blackberry Cobbler, page 428
Zucchini Walnut Bread, page 448
Easy Hot Cross Buns, page 456

COZY AND COMFORTING

Can't Eat Just One Spinach Balls, page 24
Fleurie's Caramelized Onion Spread,
    page 30
Perfect Deviled Eggs, page 43
Tuscan White Bean Soup, page 78
Missy's Chicken Tortellini Soup, page 82
Southern Potato Salad, page 131
Tarragon Chicken Salad with Celery
    Shavings, page 152
Waldorf Salad, page 163
Judy's Mom's Meat Loaf, page 190
White Bean and Spinach Lasagna, page 201
Beth's Manicotti, page 210
Anita's Oven-Baked Pork Tenderloins,
    page 234
Oven-Barbecued Beef Brisket, page 246
Broccoli Corn Bread, page 262
Braised Red Cabbage with Apples and
    Wine, page 264
Bereavement Corn, page 266
Creamy Scalloped Potatoes, page 282
Sweet and Savory Baked Apricots,
    page 312
Braised White Beans with Rosemary,
    page 320
Baked Macaroni and Cheese, page 330
Carrot Cake with Maple Cream Cheese
    Frosting, page 362
Georgia Pecan Pie, page 408
Mindy's Pound Cake Loaves, page 452
Warm Fudge Sauce, page 479

SOMETHING SWEET

Pineapple Casserole with a Cheddar Crust, page 310

Sweet and Savory Baked Apricots, page 312

Orange Marmalade Cake, page 353

Pumpkin Spice Cheesecake, page 368

Lemon Icebox Cheesecake with a Gingersnap Crust, page 370

Coconut Almond Macaroons, page 390

Lemon Squares, page 395

Bebe's Chess Cake, page 402

Georgia Pecan Pie, page 408

Double-Crust Blackberry Cobbler, page 428

Elena's Tiramisu, page 438

SOMETHING CHOCOLATE

Chocolate Buttermilk Sheet Cake, page 338

German Chocolate Cake, page 341

Chocolate Peppermint Ice Cream Cake, page 344

Lelia's Easy Chocolate Pound Cake, page 347

Chocolate Zuccotto Cake, page 372

The Best Chocolate Chip Cookies, page 378

Chocolate Chip Brownies with Cream Cheese "Goo," page 404

Bourbon Chocolate Chip Pecan Pie, page 410

Nashville Fudge Pie, page 412

Warm Fudge Sauce, page 479

INDEX

A

Abel, Laurie, 344
Almond(s):
  braised pork loin with
    prunes and, 236–37
  coconut macaroons, 390–91
  linzer bars, easy, 398–99
  slices and slivers, toasting,
    99
Anderson, Barbara, 386
Anderson, Susan, 20
Antipasto pasta salad, 140–41
Anytime Surprise Party (menu),
  15
Appetizers, 1–67
  BLT canapés, 59–60
  blue cheese pecan wafers,
    40–41
  Boursin, baked, in roasted
    red pepper sauce, Mary's,
    28–29
  bruschetta, Jan's, 61–62
  cheese board for rookies, 37
  chicken lettuce wraps, Asian,
    48–49
  crab cakes, little crisp, 56–58
  crabmeat stack, layered,
    54–55
  crostini, a dozen, without a
    recipe, 60
  deviled eggs, 43–45
  fish pâté, smoked, 52–53
  olive cheese puffs, 42
  olives, feta, and pita bread,
    465
  pizza, grilled, R. B.'s, 63–64
  ricotta-filled *bresaola* with
    arugula and Parmesan
    shavings, 46–47
  salmon, home-smoked, with
    olives and lemon, Ann's,
    50–52
  spinach balls, can't eat just
    one, 24–25
  tea sandwiches for friends,
    65–67
  ten grab and gos, 7
  veggies with green goddess
    dipping sauce, 4–6
  see also Dips; Spreads
Apple(s):
  and cashew dressing,
    curried, spinach salad
    with, 106–7
  and cranberry chutney,
    474–75
  and cranberry cider, hot
    spiced, 11
  fresh, cake with caramel
    glaze, 356–58
  jelly, in Jezebel sauce,
    478
  and pear crumble, 432–33
  tart, iron skillet, 421–22
  Waldorf salad, 163
Apricot(s):
  preserves, in Jezebel sauce,
    478
  and romaine salad,
    Theresa's, 98–99
  sweet and savory baked,
    312–13
Artichoke(s):
  grilled, with roasted tomato
    vinaigrette, David's,
    253–55
  hearts, in Deborah's hot
    spinach dip, 26–27
  and rice salad, curried,
    144–45
Arugula, 102
  and papaya salad, 108
  salad with grape tomatoes
    and Parmesan shavings,
    110–11
Asian flavors:
  chicken lettuce wraps, 48–49
  slaw with peanut dressing,
    128–29
Asparagus:
  grilled vegetable platter with
    pesto vinaigrette, 302–3
  roasted, with olive oil and
    salt, 256–57
  roasted spring vegetables,
    300–301
  steamed, with light ginger
    and sesame sauce,
    258–59
Aspic, tomato, ladies' lunch,
  166–68
Avocado(s):
  big green salad with orange,
    red wine vinaigrette and,
    94–95
  cowboy caviar, 20–21
  guacamole, Suzanne's, 8–9
  salsa, 216–17
  twelve-layer taco dip, 16–17

B

Baby, It's Cold Outside (menu),
  193
Baby blue salad with sweet and
  spicy pecans, 100–101
Bacon, in BLT canapés, 59–60
Bailey, Lelia, 347

Bailey, Sally, 218
Bake sales, 376
Baking dishes, dressing up, 184
Balsamic vinaigrette, 100–101
Banana:
    bread, best, 444–45
    pudding, Aunt Elizabeth's, 434–35
Barbecued:
    oven-, beef brisket, 246–47
    ribs, easy, 238–39
Barefoot Contessa Cookbook, The, 218
Barger, Anita, 234
Bars and squares, 336, 377, 395–406
    blueberry lemon squares, 396
    chess cake, Bebe's, 402–3
    chocolate chip brownies with cream cheese "goo," 404–6
    cutting perfectly, 401
    lemon squares, 395–97
    linzer bars, easy, 398–99
    seven-layer bars, 400–401
Basil:
    baked penne with mozzarella and, 208–9
    and buttermilk dressing, 116–17
    grilled pizza, R. B.'s, 63–64
    pesto, homemade, 470
    salad of tomato, mozzarella and, with fresh tomato vinaigrette, 118–19
    and white bean spread, Marie's, 16–17
Basmati rice and chicken salad, 154–55
Bean(s):
    baked, canned, 307
    baked, potluck, 318–19

black-eyed peas, in hoppin' John, 322–23
chickpeas, in hummus in a hurry, 22–24
mighty fine Texas chili, 86–88
refried, in twelve-layer taco dip, 16–17
see also Black bean(s); Green bean(s); White bean(s)
Beef:
    bresaola, ricotta-filled, with arugula and Parmesan shavings, 46–47
    brisket, oven-barbecued, 246–47
    flank steaks, easy marinade for, 245
    flank steaks, grilled dry-rub, 244–45
    ground, freezing, 191
    ground, in Barb's taco ring, 187–89
    ground, in Judy's mom's meat loaf, 190–91
    ground, in Mexican "lasagna" stack, 204–5
    house favorite vegetable soup, 74–75
    and macaroni casserole, creamy, 206–7
    mighty fine Texas chili, 86–88
    tenderloin, grilled, John's, 240–42
    tenderloin, leftover, uses for, 242
Beet, roasted, salad with walnuts and blue cheese dressing, 96–97
Belgian endive, 102
Benson, Amy, 106
Bereavement corn, 266–67
Best Friend Bridal Shower (menu), 167

Beverages. *See* Drinks
Bibb lettuce, 102
Big batch pumpkin bread, 446–47
Big green salad with orange, avocado, and red wine vinaigrette, 94–95
Birthday desserts, ten tantalizing, 361
Black bean(s):
    and corn salad, Tina's, 148–49
    cowboy caviar, 20–21
    soup, weekend, 80–81
    tortilla bake, 212–13
Blackberry cobbler, double-crust, 428–29
Black cherry salad, Margaret's, 164–65
Black-eyed peas:
    cowboy caviar, 20–21
    hoppin' John, 322–23
BLT canapés, 59–60
Blueberry(ies):
    baby blue salad with sweet and spicy pecans, 100–101
    fresh, sauce, 416
    lemon squares, 395–97
    and peach crisp, 430–31
Blue cheese:
    baby blue salad with sweet and spicy pecans, 100–101
    dressing, 96–97
    Gorgonzola cheese ball, 36
    pecan wafers, 40–41
    sauce, 226–27
    Stilton, crumbled, grilled figs with honey, walnuts and, Mindy's, 436–37
Book Club Lunch (menu), 396
Boston lettuce, 102
Bourbon chocolate chip pecan pie, 410–11

Boursin:
  baked, in roasted red pepper
    sauce, Mary's, 28–29
  potato gratin, 284–85
Bowden, Martha, 456
Boyd, Margaret, 164
Bradbury, Sylvia, 284
Bradshaw, Nancy, 266
Bread(s):
  banana, best, 444–45
  broccoli corn, 262–63
  bruschetta, Jan's, 61–62
  cheesy garlic, 333–34
  corn, Mexican, 462–63
  crostini, a dozen, without a
    recipe, 60
  croutons, 92–93, 105
  French, toasted slices of, 19
  gift loaves, 441–49
  Italian, frozen, 307
  making muffins from loaf
    of, 449
  mother's homemade, 458–59
  pita triangles, 22–23
  pumpkin, big batch, 446–47
  spinach, prosciutto, and
    mushroom midnight
    strata, Lou Ann's, 196–97
  turkey dressing, my favorite,
    316–17
  whole wheat refrigerator
    rolls, 460–61
  wrapping, 463
  zucchini walnut, 448–49
Bresaola, ricotta-filled, with
    arugula and Parmesan
    shavings, 46–47
Bridal shower, menu for, 167
Brisket, oven-barbecued beef,
    246–47
Broccoli, 307
  brag casserole, 260–61
  corn bread, 262–63
  salad, my sweet and sour,
    124–25

Broccolini salad, Jess's, 122–23
Brown, Lou Ann, 196
Brown butter cream cheese
    frosting, 364
Brownies:
  chocolate chip, with cream
    cheese "goo," 404–6
  ten toppers for box of, 405
Brunch:
  asparagus, steamed, with
    light ginger and sesame
    sauce, 258–59
  cheese Danish, one-pan,
    454–55
  ham and cheese overnight
    soufflé, 194–95
  hot cross buns, easy, 456–57
  sour cream cinnamon
    streusel loaves, 450–51
Bruschetta, Jan's, 61–62
Bulgur wheat, in quick
    tabbouleh, 134–35
Bundt cakes, 101
Buns, hot cross, easy, 456–57
Burgers, turkey, on the grill with
    pesto mayonnaise, 232–33
Burgers in the Backyard
    (menu), 162
Burgess, Wyeth, 72
Buttermilk:
  and basil dressing, 116–17
  chocolate sheet cake, 338–40
Butternut squash and tomato
    gratin, 290–91
Butter pecan sugar cookies,
    380–81
Butterscotch:
  chess cake, Bebe's, 402–3
  chips, in seven-layer bars,
    400–401

C

Cabbage:
  Asian slaw with peanut
    dressing, 128–29

braised red, with apples and
    wine, 264–65
  coleslaw, John's homemade,
    126–27
Caesar salad, best, 92–93
Cake carriers, xviii
Cakes, 335–75
  apple, fresh, with caramel
    glaze, 356–58
  bundt, 101
  caramel, sixty-minute,
    359–61
  carrot, with maple cream
    cheese frosting, 362–64
  chocolate buttermilk sheet,
    338–40
  chocolate peppermint ice
    cream, 344–46
  chocolate pound, Lelia's
    easy, 347–48
  chocolate *zuccotto,*
    372–75
  Coca-Cola, 340
  German chocolate, 341–43
  gift, size of, 362
  lemon icebox cheesecake
    with gingersnap crust,
    370–71
  orange marmalade, 353–55
  pound, frozen, ten ways to
    dress up, 375
  pound, loaves, Mindy's,
    452–53
  pumpkin spice cheesecake,
    368–69
  rocky road, 340
  sour cream cinnamon
    streusel loaves, 450–51
  sweet potato, Mrs. Collins's,
    350–52
  tres leches, piled with
    strawberries, 365–67
Camembert, warm potato salad
    with rosemary and,
    133–34

Can't eat just one spinach balls, 24–25

Caramel:
cake, sixty-minute, 359–61
glaze, 356–57
icing, 359–61

Carrot:
cake with maple cream cheese frosting, 362–64
and raisin salad, 130

Cashew and apple dressing, curried, spinach salad with, 106–7

Catfish fry with homemade tartar sauce, 220–22

Chattanooga Junior League, 260

Checklist for potluck host, xix

Cheddar:
crust, pineapple casserole with, 310–11
Mexican corn bread, 462–63
olive cheese puffs, 42
pimiento cheese, my favorite, 466–67
squash casserole with sweet onions and, 288–89
twice-baked potatoes, 280–81

Cheese(y):
ball, curried, showered in coconut, chutney, and cashews, 38–39
board for rookies, 37
Boursin, baked, in roasted red pepper sauce, Mary's, 28–29
Boursin potato gratin, 284–85
Camembert, warm potato salad with rosemary and, 133–34
chile, and corn dip, hot, 14–15
chile grits, Cindy's, 326–27
Danish, one-pan, 454–55

garlic bread, 333–34
Gruyère and mushroom cheesecake, 198–200
ham and, overnight soufflé, 194–95
macaroni and, baked, 330–32
manicotti, Beth's, 210–11
pimiento, 7
pimiento, my favorite, 466–67
puffs, olive, 42
twelve-layer taco dip, 16–17
see also Blue cheese; Cheddar; Cream cheese; Feta; Goat cheese; Mozzarella; Parmesan; Ricotta

Cheesecakes:
lemon icebox, with gingersnap crust, 370–71
mushroom and Gruyère, 198–200
pumpkin spice, 368–69

Cherry:
black, salad, Margaret's, 164–65
cobbler, deep dish, 425–27

Chess cake, Bebe's, 402–3

Chicken, 170–84, 223–29
and basmati rice salad, 154–55
and dressing, slow-cooker, 172–73
enchiladas, 178–79
grilled, for a crowd, 228–29
King Ranch, Currey's, 180–81
legs, Cuban, 223–24
lettuce wraps, Asian, 48–49
Parmesan, rolls, 170–71
Parmesan pronto, 225
potpie, Susan's, 174–75
spaghetti, Creole, 176–77
spaghetti, Tex-Mex, 182–84

taco salad with cilantro-lime vinaigrette, 150–51
taco soup, 84–85
tarragon, salad with celery shavings, 152–53
tea sandwiches for friends, 65–67
tenders, home-fried, with blue cheese sauce, 226–27
tortellini soup, Missy's, 82–83
wings, deli hot, 7

Chickpeas, in hummus in a hurry, 22–24

Chicory, 102

Childs, Rick, 50

Chile:
cheese, and corn dip, hot, 14–15
cheese grits, Cindy's, 326–27

Chili, mighty fine Texas, 86–88

Chili sauce, 58

Chilled shrimp rémoulade salad, 156–58

Chilled zucchini soup, Julia's, 72–73

Chimichurri sauce, Greek, 250

Chipotle sauce, 58

Chocolate:
buttermilk sheet cake, 338–40
chip bourbon pecan pie, 410–11
chip brownies with cream cheese "goo," 404–6
chip cookies, the best, 378–79
chips, in seven-layer bars, 400–401
fudge pie, Nashville, 412–13
fudge sauce, warm, 479
ganache frosting, 373–75
German, cake, 341–43
glaze, love this, 349
icing, 339–40

peppermint ice cream cake, 344–46
pound cake, Lelia's easy, 347–48
tiramisu, Elena's, 438–40
white, in easy linzer bars, 398–99
zuccotto cake, 372–75
Chutney, cranberry and apple, 474–75
Cider, hot spiced apple and cranberry, 11
Cilantro:
lime vinaigrette, 150–51
pesto, goat cheese with, 34–35
Cinnamon:
snickerdoodles, Shirley's, 382–83
streusel sour cream loaves, 450–51
Cleaning platters and serving dishes, xix
Cobblers, 336, 407
blackberry, double-crust, 428–29
cherry, deep dish, 425–27
Coca-Cola cake, 340
Coconut:
almond macaroons, 390–91
pecan icing, 341–42
seven-layer bars, 400–401
Coffee cakes and pastries:
cheese Danish, one-pan, 454–55
hot cross buns, easy, 456–57
sour cream cinnamon streusel loaves, 450–51
Coleslaw, John's homemade, 126–27
Collins, Betty Bruce, 350
Comforting foods (mini index), 488
Comforting Meal for Friends, A (menu), 267

Condiments:
cranberry and apple chutney, 474–75
peach preserves, refrigerator, 476–77
tomatoes, oven-roasted, soaked in basil and oil, 468–69
Vidalia onion marmalade, 472–73
Confectioners' sugar, dusting cakes with, 349
Consommé, baked rice with mushrooms and, 324–25
Containers, xvi, xvii
host's organization of, xix–xx
Conversion tables, 483
Cookies, 336, 377–94
butter pecan sugar, 380–81
chocolate chip, the best, 378–79
coconut almond macaroons, 390–91
holiday fruit drops, 393–94
oatmeal raisin, Barbara's, 386–87
peanut butter, classic, 384–85
snickerdoodles, Shirley's, 382–83
thumbprint, 388–89
see also Bars and squares
Cookie swaps, 392
Cool Dishes for Warm Weather (mini index), 487
Corn, 307
and bell peppers, curried, 268–69
bereavement, 266–67
and black bean salad, Tina's, 148–49
bread, broccoli, 262–63
bread, Mexican, 462–63
chile, and cheese dip, hot, 14–15
cowboy caviar, 20–21

pudding, fresh, 270–71
white, salad with fresh herb vinaigrette, 146–47
Cote, Cindy, 326
Cowboy caviar, 20–21
Cozy and Comforting (mini index), 488
Crab(meat):
cakes, little crisp, 56–58
stack, layered, 54–55
Cranberry(ies):
and apple chutney, 474–75
and apple cider, hot spiced, 11
fresh, ten ways to flavor, 315
juice, in easy pink punch, 10–11
lemon vinaigrette, 138–39
sauce, canned, 307
sauce, spiced, 314–15
tart, 423–24
Cream cheese:
brown butter frosting, 364
"goo," chocolate chip brownies with, 404–6
herbed, cucumber slices with, 7
maple frosting, 362–64
one-pan cheese Danish, 454–55
ten speedy toppers for, 35
Creole chicken spaghetti, 176–77
Crescent rolls, refrigerated:
one-pan cheese Danish, 454–55
taco ring, Barb's, 187–89
Crisps, 336
peach and blueberry, 430–31
Crossman, Nancy, 56
Crostini, a dozen, without a recipe, 60
Croutons, 92–93, 105
Crowds, recipes for (mini index), 486

Crudité platters, 7
    artistic displays with, 5
    veggies with green goddess
        dipping sauce, 4–6
Crumbles, 336, 407
    pear and apple, 432–33
Crusts:
    gingersnap, 370–71
    graham cracker crumb,
        368–69
    pie, food processor, 419–20
Cuban chicken legs, 223–24
Cucumber(s):
    slices with herbed cream
        cheese, 7
    summertime gazpacho,
        69–70
    tea sandwiches for friends,
        65–67
    and tomato salad with sweet
        dill vinaigrette, 112–14
Cunningham, Laura, 398
Curly endive, 102
Curried:
    apple and cashew dressing,
        spinach salad with,
        106–7
    cheese ball showered in
        coconut, chutney, and
        cashews, 38–39
    corn and bell peppers,
        268–69
    fruit, hot, 308–9
    rice and artichoke salad,
        144–45

D

D'Agostino, Leslie, 353
Danish, one-pan cheese, 454–55
Deep dish cherry cobbler,
    425–27
Del Frisco's, Dallas, 12
Desserts, 335–440
    apple tart, iron skillet,
        421–22

banana pudding, Aunt
    Elizabeth's, 434–35
blackberry cobbler, double-
    crust, 428–29
cherry cobbler, deep dish,
    425–27
cranberry tart, 423–24
figs, grilled, with honey,
    walnuts, and crumbled
    Stilton, Mindy's, 436–37
peach and blueberry crisp,
    430–31
pear and apple crumble,
    432–33
tiramisu, Elena's, 438–40
toting, xviii
see also Bars and squares;
    Cakes; Cookies; Pies,
    sweet
Deviled egg(s):
    of the month club, 45
    perfect, 43–44
Dill vinaigrette, sweet, 112–13
Dinner on the Diner
    (Chattanooga Junior
    League), 260
Dips:
    cowboy caviar, 20–21
    green goddess dipping
        sauce, 5–6
    guacamole, Suzanne's, 8–9
    hot chile, cheese, and corn,
        14–15
    hummus in a hurry, 22–24
    salsa, Andy's stolen, 12–13
    spinach, hot, Deborah's, 26–27
    taco, twelve-layer, 16–17
    see also Spreads
Double-crust blackberry
    cobbler, 428–29
Drake, Jackie, 76
Dressings:
    slow-cooker chicken and,
        172–73
    turkey, my favorite, 316–17

Dressings, salad. See Salad
    dressings; Vinaigrettes
Drinks, 10–11
    hot spiced apple and
        cranberry cider, 11
    ice ring for, 11
    pink punch, easy, 10–11
    Southern fruit tea, 11

E

Easiest Recipes (mini index),
    485
Egg(s):
    deviled, of the month club,
        45
    deviled, perfect, 43–44
    ham and cheese overnight
        soufflé, 194–95
    spinach, prosciutto, and
        mushroom midnight
        strata, Lou Ann's, 196–97
Eggplant:
    grilled vegetable platter with
        pesto vinaigrette, 302–3
    Parmesan with fresh basil,
        272–73
    summertime ratatouille,
        304–6
Enchiladas, chicken, 178–79
Endive, curly, 102
Escarole, 102
Espresso, in Elena's tiramisu,
    438–40
Etiquette, xviii–xx

F

Fall Football Tailgate Party
    (menu), 79
Fennel, in roasted spring
    vegetables, 300–301
Ferguson, Mary, 474
Feta:
    crumbled, vinaigrette,
        120–21
    Greek pasta salad, 136–37

olive, and pita bread, 465
orzo and spinach salad with
    lemon-cranberry
    vinaigrette, 138–39
and spinach pie, 286–87
Figs, grilled, with honey,
    walnuts, and crumbled
    Stilton, Mindy's, 436–37
Fish:
    catfish fry with homemade
        tartar sauce, 220–22
    pâté, smoked, 52–53
    see also Crab(meat);
        Salmon; Shrimp
Flank steaks:
    easy marinade for, 245
    grilled dry-rub, 244–45
Food processor pie crust,
    419–20
Four Hearty Recipes for Room
    in the Inn (menu), 173
Freezing casseroles, 291
French bread slices, toasted, 19
Fried:
    catfish with homemade
        tartar sauce, 220–22
    home-, chicken tenders with
        blue cheese sauce, 226–27
Frostings:
    brown butter cream cheese,
        364
    for cakes that travel in warm
        weather, 349
    chocolate ganache, 373–75
    maple cream cheese, 362–64
    orange marmalade, 353–54
    see also Icings
Fruit(s):
    drops, holiday, 393–94
    hot curried, 308–9
    summer, watermelon boat
        with, 160–62
    tea, Southern, 11
    see also specific fruits
Frying outdoors, 222

Fudge:
    pie, Nashville, 412–13
    sauce, warm, 479

G

Ganache frosting, chocolate,
    373–75
Garlic bread, cheesy, 333–34
Gazpacho, summertime, 69–70
Gelatin:
    black cherry salad,
        Margaret's, 164–65
    tomato aspic, ladies' lunch,
        166–68
Georgia pecan pie, 408–9
German chocolate cake, 341–43
Gifts, 441–82
    banana bread, best, 444–45
    bread, mother's homemade,
        458–59
    cake size and, 362
    cheese Danish, one-pan,
        454–55
    corn bread, Mexican, 462–63
    cranberry and apple
        chutney, 474–75
    fifteen quick, for host or
        hostess, 481
    fudge sauce, warm, 479
    grab-and-go, from grocery,
        471
    hot cross buns, easy, 456–57
    Jezebel sauce, 478
    nuts, orange-glazed, Susan's,
        480–81
    olives, zesty marinated,
        464–65
    packaging and decorating,
        442
    peach preserves, refrigerator,
        476–77
    pecans, sweet and spicy, 482
    pesto, homemade, 470
    pimiento cheese, my
        favorite, 466–67

pound cake loaves, Mindy's,
    452–53
pumpkin bread, big batch,
    446–47
sour cream cinnamon
    streusel loaves, 450–51
tomatoes, oven-roasted,
    soaked in basil and oil,
    468–69
Vidalia onion marmalade,
    472–73
whole wheat refrigerator
    rolls, 460–61
zucchini walnut bread,
    448–49
Gill, Barbara, 187
Gingersnap crust, 370–71
Glazes:
    caramel, 356–57
    chocolate, love this, 349
Goat cheese, 7
    with cilantro pesto, 34–35
    pyramid, herbed, 32–33
    ten speedy toppers for, 35
Gorgonzola cheese ball, 36
Graduation Lunch (menu),
    158
Graham cracker crumb(s):
    crust, 368–69
    seven-layer bars, 400–401
Grapes, in Waldorf salad,
    163
Greek flavors:
    chimichurri sauce, 250
    pasta salad, 136–37
    spinach and feta pie,
        286–87
Green bean(s), 307
    Bebe's, 274–75
    fresh, salad with crumbled
        feta vinaigrette, 120–21
    with spicy tomato sauce,
        276–77
Green goddess dipping sauce,
    5–6

Greens, salad:
glossary of, 102
rinsing and storing, 109
Green salad, big, with orange,
avocado, and red wine
vinaigrette, 94–95
Green vegetables, recipes for
(mini index), 485–86
Grilled:
artichokes with roasted
tomato vinaigrette,
David's, 253–55
beef tenderloin, John's,
240–42
Burgers in the Backyard
(menu), 162
chicken for a crowd, 28–29
figs with honey, walnuts,
and crumbled Stilton,
Mindy's, 436–37
flank steaks, dry-rub, 244–45
leg of lamb with Greek
chimichurri sauce,
248–50
pizza, R. B.'s, 63–64
pork tenderloins, 235
turkey burgers with pesto
mayonnaise, 232–33
vegetable platter with pesto
vinaigrette, 302–3
Grilling in cold weather, 239
Grissim, Mary, 28, 133
Grits, chile cheese, Cindy's,
326–27
Gruyère and mushroom
cheesecake, 198–200
Guacamole:
ready-made, 9
Suzanne's, 8–9
Guests:
protocol for, xviii–xix
toting tips for, xvii–xviii.
See also Toting fod
"What Can I Do?" list for,
xxi

H

Halloween parties, witches'
brew for, 11
Ham(s), 243
and cheese overnight
soufflé, 194–95
cured, from supermarket, 243
spiral-sliced, 243
Hash browns, frozen, 307
Henry, Melissa, 278
Herb(ed)(s):
fresh, vinaigrette, 146–47
goat cheese pyramid, 32–33
see also specific herbs
Hill, Jess, 122, 218
Hill, Moe, 122
Holiday Cookie Swaps (menu),
392
Holiday fruit drops, 393–94
Hoppin' John, 322–23
Horseradish:
Jezebel sauce, 478
sour cream sauce, 240–41
Hosts and hostesses:
checklist for, xix
fifteen quick gifts for, 481
organizational
considerations for, xix–xx
"What Can I Do?" list for, xxi
Hot chile, cheese, and corn dip,
14–15
Hot cross buns, easy, 456–57
Hot curried fruit, 308–9
Hot spiced apple and cranberry
cider, 11
Hot spinach dip, Deborah's,
26–27
Hummus in a hurry, 22–24
Hutson, Shirley, 382

I

Iceberg, 102, 109
Ice cream:
peppermint, chocolate cake,
344–46

vanilla, ten adult add-ins to
transform, 426
Ice ring, 11
Icings:
caramel, 359–61
chocolate, 339–40
pecan-coconut, 341–42
see also Frostings
Iron skillet apple tart, 421–22
Italian flavors:
arugula salad with grape
tomatoes and Parmesan
shavings, 110–11
braised white beans with
rosemary, 320–21
bruschetta, Jan's, 61–62
crostini, a dozen, without a
recipe, 60
An Italian Night with the
Girls (menu), 62
ricotta-filled *bresaola* with
arugula and Parmesan
shavings, 46–47
tiramisu, Elena's, 438–40
tomato, mozzarella, and basil
salad with fresh tomato
vinaigrette, 118–19
Tuscan white bean soup,
78–79

J

January lamb stew, 192–93
Jezebel sauce, 478
July Fourth Celebration (menu),
127

K

Kaplan, Rita, 423
Key lime pie:
my favorite, 414–16
ten-minute, 417
Kids:
beverages for, 10
recipes suitable for (mini
index), 486–87

King Ranch chicken, Currey's, 180–81
Knitting Group Comes for Coffee, The (menu), 445

L

Laackman, Allyson, 56
Ladies' lunch tomato aspic, 166–68
Ladyfingers, in Elena's tiramisu, 438–40
Lagrone, Sally, 423
Lamb:
    grilled leg of, with Greek chimichurri sauce, 248–50
    stew, January, 192–93
Lamb's leaf lettuce, 102
Lasagna, white bean and spinach, 201–3
"Lasagna" stack, Mexican, 204–5
Last-Minute Wine Tasting, A (menu), 31
Layered crabmeat stack, 54–55
Leaf lettuce, 102
Lemon:
    cranberry vinaigrette, 138–39
    garlic shrimp with avocado salsa, 216–17
    icebox cheesecake with gingersnap crust, 370–71
    squares, 395–97
Lemonade, in easy pink punch, 10–11
Lettuce:
    BLT canapés, 59–60
    chicken wraps, Asian, 48–49
    glossary of, 102
    rinsing and storing, 109
Light foods (mini index), 486
Lima beans, in Tina's corn and black bean salad, 148–49

Lime:
    cilantro vinaigrette, 150–51
    Key, pie, my favorite, 414–16
    Key, pie, ten-minute, 417
Linzer bars, easy, 398–99
Lowcountry shrimp boil, 215
Lukins, Sheila, 61
Luncheons:
    Best Friend Bridal Shower (menu), 167
    Book Club Lunch (menu), 396
    Graduation Lunch (menu), 158
    ladies' lunch tomato aspic, 166–68

M

Mabry, Sally, 423
Macaroni:
    and beef casserole, creamy, 206–7
    and cheese, baked, 330–32
    salad, old-fashioned, 142–43
Macaroons, coconut almond, 390–91
Mâche, 102
Maddux, Julia, 72
Main dishes, 169–250
    beef brisket, oven-barbecued, 246–47
    beef tenderloin, grilled, John's, 240–42
    black bean tortilla bake, 212–13
    catfish fry with homemade tartar sauce, 220–22
    chicken, Currey's King Ranch, 180–81
    chicken, grilled, for a crowd, 228–29
    chicken, tarragon, salad with celery shavings, 152–53
    chicken and basmati rice salad, 154–55

chicken and dressing, slow-cooker, 172–73
chicken enchiladas, 178–79
chicken legs, Cuban, 223–24
chicken Parmesan pronto, 225
chicken potpie, Susan's, 174–75
chicken spaghetti, Creole, 176–77
chicken spaghetti, Tex-Mex, 182–84
chicken taco salad with cilantro-lime vinaigrette, 150–51
chicken tenders, home-fried, with blue cheese sauce, 226–27
flank steaks, grilled dry-rub, 244–45
ham, supermarket, 243
ham and cheese overnight soufflé, 194–95
lamb, grilled leg of, with Greek chimichurri sauce, 248–50
lamb stew, January, 192–93
"lasagna" stack, Mexican, 204–5
macaroni and beef casserole, creamy, 206–7
manicotti, Beth's, 210–11
matching sides to, 252
meat loaf, Judy's mom's, 190–91
mushroom and Gruyère cheesecake, 198–200
Parmesan chicken rolls, 170–71
penne with mozzarella and basil, baked, 208–9
pork loin, braised, with prunes and almonds, 236–37

pork tenderloins, Anita's oven-baked, 234–35
ribs, easy barbecued, 238–39
salmon, eighteen-minute, with fresh ginger glaze, 218–19
salmon, quick poached, 225
shrimp, lemon garlic, with avocado salsa, 216–17
shrimp and veggie platter, 225
shrimp boil, lowcountry, 215
shrimp rémoulade salad, chilled, 156–58
spinach, prosciutto, and mushroom midnight *strata*, Lou Ann's, 196–97
taco ring, Barb's, 187–89
turkey, roast, in the bag, 230–31
turkey burgers on the grill with pesto mayonnaise, 232–33
turkey tetrazzini, 185–86
white bean and spinach lasagna, 201–3
see also Soups
Mandel, Jenny, 292
Manicotti, Beth's, 210–11
Maple cream cheese frosting, 362–64
Marinade for flank steaks, easy, 245
Marmalade:
  orange, cake, 353–55
  Vidalia onion, 472–73
Martinez, Matt, 12
Mascarpone, in Elena's tiramisu, 438–40
Masterson, Marie, 16
Mayonnaise:
  jazzed-up, 65–66
  pesto, 232–33
  rémoulade, 156–57

McCarthy, Barbara, 372
McKenzie, Mary Eleanor, 284
McTyre, Joe, 462
Meador, Beth, 210, 236, 344
Meador, Bill, 236
Meat loaf, Judy's mom's, 190–91
Mediterranean flavors:
  fresh green bean salad with crumbled feta vinaigrette, 120–21
  Spring Mediterranean Supper (menu), 121
Meet the Neighbors (menu), 275
Menus:
  Anytime Surprise Party, 15
  Baby, It's Cold Outside, 193
  Best Friend Bridal Shower, 167
  Book Club Lunch, 396
  Burgers in the Backyard, 162
  A Comforting Meal for Friends, 267
  Fall Football Tailgate Party, 79
  Four Hearty Recipes for Room in the Inn, 173
  Graduation Lunch, 158
  Holiday Cookie Swaps, 392
  An Italian Night with the Girls, 62
  July Fourth Celebration, 127
  The Knitting Group Comes for Coffee, 445
  A Last-Minute Wine Tasting, 31
  Meet the Neighbors, 275
  Mother's Day Sunday Brunch, 355
  Spring Mediterranean Supper, 121
  Summer Picnic with Friends, 113
  Super Bowl with the Neighbors, 87

  Sweet Sixteen Birthday Bash, 188
  Thanksgiving Dinner, 420
  Twenty-Fifth Anniversary Party, 255
  Vegetarian Covered Dish, 331
Meringue:
  banana pudding, Aunt Elizabeth's, 434–35
  Key lime pie, my favorite, 414–16
Mexican and Tex-Mex flavors:
  Anytime Surprise Party (menu), 15
  black bean tortilla bake, 212–13
  chicken enchiladas, 178–79
  chicken spaghetti, 182–84
  chicken taco soup, 84–85
  corn and black bean salad, Tina's, 148–49
  corn bread, 462–63
  cowboy caviar, 20–21
  guacamole, Suzanne's, 8–9
  hot chile, cheese, and corn dip, 14–15
  King Ranch chicken, Currey's, 180–81
  "lasagna" stack, 204–5
  mighty fine Texas chili, 86–88
  tres leches cakes piled with strawberries, 365–67
Middle Eastern flavors:
  hummus in a hurry, 22–24
  tabbouleh, quick, 134–35
Midsummer's night pasta, 328–29
Milk syrup, 365–66
Mills, Ann, xv, 50
Morgan, Jep, 146
Mother's Day Sunday Brunch (menu), 355

Mother's homemade bread,
    458–59
Mozzarella:
    baked penne with basil and,
        208–9
    cheesy garlic bread, 333–34
    grilled pizza, R. B.'s, 63–64
    manicotti, Beth's, 210–11
    tomato, and basil salad with
        fresh tomato vinaigrette,
        118–19
Muffins, 449
Mushroom(s):
    baked rice with consommé
        and, 324–25
    and Gruyère cheesecake,
        198–200
    spinach, and prosciutto
        midnight strata, Lou
        Ann's, 196–97
Myers, Missy, 82

N

Nashville fudge pie, 412–13
Nasoni, Elena, 438
New Basics Cookbook, The
    (Rosso and Lukins), 61
Nicholls, Elizabeth, 434
Nichols, Carol, 234
Nuts:
    orange-glazed, Susan's,
        480–81
    toasting, 99
    see also specific nuts

O

Oakes, Flowerree, 460
Oatmeal raisin cookies,
    Barbara's, 386–87
Old-fashioned macaroni salad,
    142–43
Olive(s), 7
    cheese puffs, 42
    feta, and pita bread, 465
    zesty marinated, 464–65

One-pan cheese Danish, 454–55
Onion(s):
    caramelized, spread,
        Fleurie's, 30–31
    sweet, squash casserole with
        Cheddar and, 288–89
    Vidalia, marmalade, 472–73
Orange(s):
    avocado salsa, 216–17
    big green salad with
        avocado, red wine
        vinaigrette and, 94–95
    and cranberry sauce, 315
    -glazed nuts, Susan's, 480–81
    marmalade cake, 353–55
    sections, making, 95
Orzo and spinach salad with
    lemon-cranberry
    vinaigrette, 138–39
Oschman, Tina, 148
Oxmoor House, 172

P

Paine, Ophelia, 423
Papaya and arugula salad, 108
Parmesan:
    can't eat just one spinach
        balls, 24–25
    chicken, pronto, 225
    chicken rolls, 170–71
    eggplant, with fresh basil,
        272–73
    shaving, 111
Parsley, in Quick Tabbouleh,
    134–35
Pasta:
    baked penne with
        mozzarella and basil,
        208–9
    chicken tortellini soup,
        Missy's, 82–83
    Creole chicken spaghetti,
        176–77
    manicotti, Beth's, 210–11
    midsummer's night, 328–29

orzo and spinach salad with
    lemon-cranberry
    vinaigrette, 138–39
    pesto for, homemade, 470
    salad, antipasto, 140–41
    salad, Greek, 136–37
    Tex-Mex chicken spaghetti,
        182–84
    turkey tetrazzini, 185–86
    white bean and spinach
        lasagna, 201–3
    see also Macaroni
Pâté, 7
    smoked fish, 52–53
Patten, Mike, 294
Patterson, David, 253
Peach:
    and blueberry crisp, 430–31
    preserves, refrigerator,
        476–77
Peanut butter cookies, classic,
    384–85
Peanut dressing, Asian slaw
    with, 128–29
Pear and apple crumble,
    432–33
Pecan(s):
    blue cheese wafers, 40–41
    bourbon chocolate chip pie,
        410–11
    butter, sugar cookies, 380–81
    coconut icing, 341–42
    crunch topping, 292–93
    halves, toasting, 99
    one-pan cheese Danish,
        454–55
    orange-glazed nuts, Susan's,
        480–81
    pie, Georgia, 408–9
    seven-layer bars, 400–401
    sweet and spicy, 482
Penne with mozzarella and
    basil, baked, 208–9
Pepper(s) (bell):
    curried corn and, 268–69

grilled vegetable platter with pesto vinaigrette, 302–3
roasted red, sauce, baked Boursin in, Mary's, 28–29
summertime gazpacho, 69–70
summertime ratatouille, 304–6
Peppermint ice cream chocolate cake, 344–46
Pesto:
  cilantro, goat cheese with, 34–35
  homemade, 470
  mayonnaise, 232–33
  vinaigrette, 302–3
Phyllo dough, in spinach and feta pie, 286–87
Piecrust, food processor, 419–20
Pies, savory:
  chicken potpie, Susan's, 174–75
  spinach and feta, 286–87
  tomato, fresh, 296–97
Pies, sweet, 336, 352, 407–20
  bourbon chocolate chip pecan, 410–11
  fudge, Nashville, 412–13
  Key lime, my favorite, 414–16
  Key lime, ten-minute, 417
  pecan, Georgia, 408–9
  pumpkin, Thanksgiving, 418–20
Pimiento cheese, 7
  my favorite, 466–67
Pineapple, 307
  black cherry salad, Margaret's, 164–65
  casserole with Cheddar crust, 310–11
Pine nuts, toasting, 287
Pink punch, easy, 10–11
Pita triangles, 22–23

Pizza:
  fast, 7
  grilled, R. B.'s, 63–64
Planning potlucks, xv–xvii
Platters:
  toting food on, xvii–xviii
  washing, for guests to take home, xix
Pork, 234–39
  loin, braised, with prunes and almonds, 236–37
  ribs, easy barbecued, 238–39
  tenderloins, Anita's oven-baked, 234–35
  see also Ham(s)
Potato(es):
  creamy scalloped, 282–83
  gratin, Boursin, 284–85
  hash browns, frozen, 307
  new, in roasted spring vegetables, 300–301
  roast, for a crowd, 278–79
  roasted, ten ways to season, 283
  salad, Southern, 131–32
  salad, warm, with rosemary and Camembert, 133–34
  salad variations, 132
  soup, Jackie's, 76–77
  twice-baked, 280–81
Potluck baked beans, 318–19
Potlucks, xiii–xxxii
  arranging food in, xxii
  checklist for host of, xix
  etiquette for, xviii–xx
  picking right recipe for, xiii–xv
  planning, xv–xvii
  salad, 159
  in small space, xx
  toting tips for, xvii–xviii. See also Toting food
Potpie, chicken, Susan's, 174–75
Pound cake(s):
  chocolate, Lelia's easy, 347–48

chocolate *zuccotto* cake, 372–75
frozen, ten ways to dress up, 375
loaves, Mindy's, 452–53
Preserves, peach, refrigerator, 476–77
Pretty foods (mini index), 487
Prosciutto, spinach, and mushroom midnight *strata,* Lou Ann's, 196–97
Prunes, braised pork loin with almonds and, 236–37
Puckett, Susan, ix–x
Pudding, banana, Aunt Elizabeth's, 434–35
Puffs, olive cheese, 42
Pumpkin:
  bread, big batch, 446–47
  pie, Thanksgiving, 418–20
  spice cheesecake, 368–69

Q
Quinn, R. B., 63

R
Radicchio, 102
Rafer, Suzanne, 8
Ramsey, Jan, 61
Rancho Martinez, Dallas, 12
Raspberry(ies):
  baby blue salad with sweet and spicy pecans, 100–101
  jam, in easy Linzer bars, 398–99
Ratatouille, summertime, 304–6
Recipe selection, xiii–xv
  matching side to main, 252
Red cabbage, braised, with apples and wine, 264–65
Red wine vinaigrette, 94–95
Refrigerator peach preserves, 476–77
Rémoulade, 58, 156–57

Ribs, easy barbecued, 238–39
Rice:
    and artichoke salad, curried,
        144–45
    baked, with mushrooms and
        consommé, 324–25
    basmati, and chicken salad,
        154–55
    hoppin' John, 322–23
Rice-A-Roni, in curried rice and
    artichoke salad, 144–45
Ricotta:
    filled *bresaola* with arugula
        and Parmesan shavings,
        46–47
    manicotti, Beth's, 210–11
Rocky road cake, 340
Rolls, whole wheat refrigerator,
    460–61
Romaine, 102
    and apricot salad, Theresa's,
        98–99
    Caesar salad, best, 92–93
Room in the Inn, 173
Rosso, Julee, 61

S

Salad dressings:
    basil and buttermilk, 116–17
    blue cheese, 96–97
    Caesar, 92–93
    curried, 106–7
    see also Vinaigrettes
Salad potlucks, 159
Salads, 89–168, 150–58
    antipasto pasta, 140–41
    arugula, with grape
        tomatoes and Parmesan
        shavings, 110–11
    baby blue, with sweet and
        spicy pecans, 100–101
    bagged, disguising, 101
    beet, roasted, with walnuts
        and blue cheese dressing,
        96–97

big green, with orange,
    avocado, and red wine
    vinaigrette, 94–95
black cherry, Margaret's,
    164–65
bresaola with arugula and
    Parmesan shavings, 47
broccoli, my sweet and sour,
    124–25
broccolini, Jess's, 122–23
Caesar, best, 92–93
carrot and raisin, 130
chicken, tarragon, with
    celery shavings, 152–53
chicken and basmati rice,
    154–55
chicken taco, with cilantro-
    lime vinaigrette, 150–51
coleslaw, John's homemade,
    126–27
corn and black bean, Tina's,
    148–49
croutons for, 92–93, 105
cucumber and tomato, with
    sweet dill vinaigrette,
    112–14
curried rice and artichoke,
    144–45
glossary of greens for, 102
green bean, fresh, with
    crumbled feta
    vinaigrette, 120–21
macaroni, old-fashioned,
    142–43
orange-glazed nuts for,
    Susan's, 480–81
orzo and spinach, with
    lemon-cranberry
    vinaigrette, 138–39
papaya and arugula, 108
pasta, Greek, 136–37
potato, Southern, 131–32
potato, variations, 132
potato, warm, with rosemary
    and Camembert, 133–34

rinsing and storing greens
    for, 109
romaine and apricot,
    Theresa's, 98–99
serving in bowl or on plate,
    141
shrimp rémoulade, chilled,
    156–58
slaw, Asian, with peanut
    dressing, 128–29
spinach, with curried apple
    and cashew dressing,
    106–7
spinach, with mahogany
    roasted mushrooms and
    onions, 103–4
sweet and spicy pecans for,
    482
tabbouleh, quick, 134–35
timetable for, 91
tomato, mozzarella, and
    basil, with fresh tomato
    vinaigrette, 118–19
tomato, sliced, with basil
    and buttermilk dressing,
    116–17
topper ideas for, 159
Waldorf, 163
watermelon boat with
    summer fruits, 160–62
white corn, with fresh herb
    vinaigrette, 146–47
Salami, hard, 7
Salmon:
    eighteen-minute, with fresh
        ginger glaze, 218–19
    home-smoked, with
        olives and lemon, Ann's,
        50–52
    quick poached, 225
Salsas:
    Andy's stolen, 12–13
    avocado, 216–17
Sandwiches:
    keeping fresh, 67

mini, with deli dinner rolls, 7
tea, for friends, 65–67
Sauces:
  blueberry, fresh, 416
  blue cheese, 226–27
  chili, 58
  chimichurri, Greek, 250
  chipotle, 58
  fudge, warm, 479
  green goddess dipping, 5–6
  Jezebel, 478
  mayonnaise, jazzed-up, 65–66
  pesto, homemade, 470
  pesto mayonnaise, 232–33
  rémoulade, 58, 156–57
  sour cream horseradish, 240–41
  tarragon tartar, 58
  tartar, 58, 220–21
Sesame seeds, toasting, 99
Seven-layer bars, 400–401
Shellfish. See Crab(meat); Shrimp
Shrimp:
  boil, lowcountry, 215
  lemon garlic, with avocado salsa, 216–17
  rémoulade salad, chilled, 156–58
  and veggie platter, 225
Sides, 251–334
  apricots, sweet and savory baked, 312–13
  artichokes, grilled, with roasted tomato vinaigrette, David's, 253–55
  asparagus, roasted, with olive oil and salt, 256–57
  asparagus, steamed, with light ginger and sesame sauce, 258–59

  avocado salsa, 216–17
  beans, potluck baked, 318–19
  broccoli brag casserole, 260–61
  broccoli corn bread, 262–63
  butternut squash and tomato gratin, 290–91
  cheesy garlic bread, 333–34
  corn, bereavement, 266–67
  corn and bell peppers, curried, 268–69
  corn pudding, fresh, 270–71
  cranberry sauce, spiced, 314–15
  dressing, turkey, my favorite, 316–17
  eggplant Parmesan with fresh basil, 272–73
  freezer and pantry fixings for, 307
  fruit, hot curried, 308–9
  green beans, Bebe's, 274–75
  green beans with spicy tomato sauce, 276–77
  grilled vegetable platter with pesto vinaigrette, 302–3
  grits, chile cheese, Cindy's, 326–27
  hoppin' John, 322–23
  macaroni and cheese, baked, 330–32
  matching to main dish, 252
  pasta, midsummer's night, 328–29
  pineapple casserole with Cheddar crust, 310–11
  potatoes, creamy scalloped, 282–83
  potatoes, roast, for a crowd, 278–79
  potatoes, twice-baked, 280–81
  potato gratin, Boursin, 284–85

  ratatouille, summertime, 304–6
  red cabbage, braised, with apples and wine, 264–65
  rice, baked, with mushrooms and consommé, 324–25
  spinach and feta pie, 286–87
  spring vegetables, roasted, 300–301
  squash casserole with sweet onions and Cheddar, 288–89
  sweet potato casserole with pecan crunch, 292–93
  sweet potato "soufflé," Mike's, 294–95
  tomato pie, fresh, 296–97
  white beans, braised, with rosemary, 320–21
  zucchini, sautéed, with garlic slivers, 298–99
  see also Salads
Simcoe, Kathy, 20
Slaws:
  Asian, with peanut dressing, 128–29
  coleslaw, John's homemade, 126–27
Slow-cooker chicken and dressing, 172–73
Small spaces, potlucks in, xx
Smoked:
  fish pâté, 52–53
  home-, salmon with olives and lemon, Ann's, 50–52
Smokers, electric, 51
Snickerdoodles, Shirley's, 382–83
Something Chocolate (mini index), 489
Something Green (mini index), 485–86
Something Kids Like (mini index), 486–87

Something Pretty (mini index), 487
Something Special (mini index), 488
Something Spicy (mini index), 488
Something Sweet (mini index), 489
Sommers, Fleurie, 30
Soufflé, ham and cheese overnight, 194–95
"Soufflé," sweet potato, Mike's, 294–95
Soups, 2, 68–88
    black bean, weekend, 80–81
    chicken taco, 84–85
    chicken tortellini, Missy's, 82–83
    freezing, 83
    gazpacho, summertime, 69–70
    potato, Jackie's, 76–77
    serving, 77
    toting, 71
    vegetable, house favorite, 74–75
    white bean, Tuscan, 78–79
    zucchini, chilled, Julia's, 72–73
Sour cream:
    cinnamon streusel loaves, 450–51
    horseradish sauce, 240–41
Southern dishes:
    fruit tea, 11
    Georgia pecan pie, 408–9
    hoppin' John, 322–23
    lowcountry shrimp boil, 215
    Nashville fudge pie, 412–13
    pimiento cheese, my favorite, 466–67
    potato salad, 131–32
    squash casserole with sweet onions and Cheddar, 288–89

sweet potato casserole with pecan crunch, 292–93
Southern Living, 54, 172
Southwestern Caesar, 93
Spaghetti:
    Creole chicken, 176–77
    Tex-Mex chicken, 182–84
    turkey tetrazzini, 185–86
Special recipes (mini index), 488
Spice(d):
    cranberry sauce, 314–15
    pumpkin, cheesecake, 368–69
Spicy foods (mini index), 488
Spinach, 102, 307
    balls, can't eat just one, 24–25
    dip, hot, Deborah's, 26–27
    and feta pie, 286–87
    and orzo salad with lemon-cranberry vinaigrette, 138–39
    prosciutto, and mushroom midnight strata, Lou Ann's, 196–97
    salad with curried apple and cashew dressing, 106–7
    salad with mahogany roasted mushrooms and onions, 103–4
    and white bean lasagna, 201–3
Spreads:
    crabmeat stack, layered, 54–55
    curried cheese ball showered in coconut, chutney, and cashews, 38–39
    goat cheese pyramid, herbed, 32–33
    goat cheese with cilantro pesto, 34–35
    Gorgonzola cheese ball, 36

mayonnaise, jazzed-up, 65–66
    onion, caramelized, Fleurie's, 30–31
    white bean and basil, Marie's, 16–17
    see also Dips
Spring Mediterranean Supper (menu), 121
Spring vegetables, roasted, 300–301
Squares. See Bars and squares
Squash:
    butternut, and tomato gratin, 290–91
    casserole with sweet onions and Cheddar, 288–89
    see also Pumpkin; Zucchini
Starters. See Appetizers; Soups
Stews:
    chili, mighty fine Texas, 86–88
    lamb, January, 192–93
Stilton, crumbled, grilled figs with honey, walnuts and, Mindy's, 436–37
Strata, spinach, prosciutto, and mushroom midnight, Lou Ann's, 196–97
Strawberries:
    baby blue salad with sweet and spicy pecans, 100–101
    tres leches cakes piled with, 365–67
Streusel, cinnamon, sour cream loaves, 450–51
Succotash salad, 149
Sugar cookies:
    butter pecan, 380–81
    snickerdoodles, Shirley's, 382–83
Sugar snap peas, in roasted spring vegetables, 300–301

Summer Picnic with Friends (menu), 113
Summertime gazpacho, 69–70
Summertime ratatouille, 304–6
Super Bowl with the Neighbors (menu), 87
Sweet and savory baked apricots, 312–13
Sweet and sour broccoli salad, my, 124–25
Sweet and spicy pecans, 482
Sweet dill vinaigrette, 112–13
Sweet foods:
    mini index of, 489
    see also Bars and squares; Cakes; Cookies; Desserts; Pies, sweet
Sweet potato:
    cake, Mrs. Collins's, 350–52
    casserole with pecan crunch, 292–93
    "soufflé," Mike's, 294–95
Sweet Sixteen Birthday Bash (menu), 188
Syrups:
    milk, 365–66
    orange, 353–54

T
Tabbouleh, quick, 134–35
Table toppers, quick, 257
Taco:
    chicken, salad with cilantro-lime vinaigrette, 150–51
    chicken, soup, 84–85
    dip, twelve-layer, 16–17
    ring, Barb's, 187–89
Tarragon:
    chicken salad with celery shavings, 152–53
    tartar sauce, 58
Tartar sauce, 58, 220–21
Tarts, 352
    apple, iron skillet, 421–22
    cranberry, 423–24

Tea, Southern fruit, 11
Tea sandwiches for friends, 65–67
Teren, Kren, 128
Tetrazzini, turkey, 185–86
Tex-Mex. See Mexican and Tex-Mex flavors
Thanksgiving dinner:
    menu for, 420
    toting tips for, 311
Thanksgiving pumpkin pie, 418–20
Thompson, Joan, 234
Thornton, Currey, 26, 180
Thumbprint cookies, 388–89
Tiramisu, Elena's, 438–40
Toasting:
    nuts and seeds, 99
    pine nuts, 287
To Feed a Crowd (mini index), 486
Tomato(es):
    aspic, ladies' lunch, 166–68
    BLT canapés, 59–60
    and butternut squash gratin, 290–91
    cherry, in grilled vegetable platter with pesto vinaigrette, 302–3
    and cucumber salad with sweet dill vinaigrette, 112–14
    fresh, vinaigrette, 118–19
    grape, arugula salad with Parmesan shavings, 110–11
    grilled pizza, R. B.'s, 63–64
    midsummer's night pasta, 328–29
    mozzarella, and basil salad with fresh tomato vinaigrette, 118–19
    oven-roasted, soaked in basil and oil, 468–69
    pie, fresh, 296–97

roasted, vinaigrette, 253–54
salsa, Andy's stolen, 12–13
sauce, spicy, green beans with, 276–77
sliced, salad with basil and buttermilk dressing, 116–17
summertime gazpacho, 69–70
summertime ratatouille, 304–6
tea sandwiches for friends, 65–67
Tortellini chicken soup, Missy's, 82–83
Tortilla(s):
    black bean bake, 212–13
    chicken enchiladas, 178–79
    King Ranch chicken, Currey's, 180–81
    Mexican "lasagna" stack, 204–5
Toting food, xvii–xviii
    containers for, xvi, xvii
    desserts, xviii
    soups, 71
    Thanksgiving dinner, 311
Tres leches cakes piled with strawberries, 365–67
Trope, Carole, 417
Turkey:
    burgers on the grill with pesto mayonnaise, 232–33
    dressing, my favorite, 316–17
    ground, in Barb's taco ring, 187–89
    ground, in Mexican "lasagna" stack, 204–5
    roast, in the bag, 230–31
    tetrazzini, 185–86
Tuscan white bean soup, 78–79
Twelve-layer taco dip, 16–17

Twenty-Fifth Anniversary Party
   (menu), 255
Twice-baked potatoes, 280–81

V

Vanilla ice cream, ten adult add-
   ins to transform, 426
Vegetable(s):
   green, recipes for (mini
      index), 485–86
   grilled, platter with pesto
      vinaigrette, 302–3
   soup, house favorite, 74–75
   spring, roasted, 300–301
   veggies with green goddess
      dipping sauce, 4–6
   see also Sides; specific
      vegetables
Vegetarian Covered Dish
   (menu), 331
Vegetarian entrées:
   black bean tortilla bake,
      212–13
   mushroom and Gruyère
      cheesecake, 198–200
Veggies with green goddess
   dipping sauce, 4–6
Veneto, Linda, 34
Vidalia onion marmalade,
   472–73
Vinaigrettes:
   apricot, 98–99
   balsamic, 100–101
   cilantro-lime, 150–51
   dill, sweet, 112–13
   feta, crumbled, 120–21
   herb, fresh, 146–47
   lemon-cranberry, 138–39
   pesto, 302–3
   red wine, 94–95

   ten variations, 115
   tomato, fresh, 118–19
   tomato, roasted, 253–54

W

Wafers, blue cheese pecan,
   40–41
Waldorf salad, 163
Walnut(s):
   orange-glazed nuts, Susan's,
      480–81
   seven-layer bars, 400–401
   toasting, 99
   Waldorf salad, 163
   zucchini bread, 448–49
Warm fudge sauce, 479
Warm potato salad with
   rosemary and
   Camembert, 133–34
Warm weather:
   cool dishes for (mini index),
      487
   frostings for cakes that
      travel in, 349
Watercress, 102
Watermelon boat with summer
   fruits, 160–62
Weekend black bean soup,
   80–81
Westcott, Holly, 262
"What Can I Do?" lists, xxi
When You Want Something
   Light (mini index), 486
Whipped cream, sweetened,
   367
White bean(s):
   and basil spread, Marie's,
      16–17
   braised, with rosemary,
      320–21

   soup, Tuscan, 78–79
   and spinach lasagna,
      201–3
White chocolate, in easy linzer
   bars, 398–99
White corn salad with fresh
   herb vinaigrette, 146–47
Whole wheat refrigerator rolls,
   460–61
Wieners, mini, 7
Williams, John, 395
Wine:
   red, vinaigrette, 94–95
   seasonal choices for, 6
   tasting, menu for, 31
Witches' brew, 11
Woodland Elementary School,
   Atlanta, 20
Workman, Katie, 208
Wraps, Asian chicken lettuce,
   48–49
Wright, Judy, 190, 198

Y

Young, Andy, 12

Z

Zesty marinated olives,
   464–65
Zucchini:
   grilled vegetable platter with
      pesto vinaigrette, 302–3
   sautéed, with garlic slivers,
      298–99
   soup, chilled, Julia's, 72–73
   summertime ratatouille,
      304–6
   walnut bread, 448–49
Zuccotto cake, chocolate,
   372–75